Boy Princess

Vol. 3

Seyoung Kim

Boy Princess Vol. 3

Story and Art by Seyoung Kim

English translation rights in USA, Canada, UK, NZ, Australia arranged by
Ecomix Media Company
395-21 Seogyo-dong, Mapo-gu, Seoul, Korea 121-840 info@ecomixmedia.com

- Produced by **Ecomix Media Company**
- Translator **Jeanne**
- Editors **Zhanna Veyts, Philip Daay**
- Managing Editor **Soyoung Jung**
- Graphic Design **Soohyun Park, Yeongsook Yi**
- President & Publisher **Heewoon Chung**

P.O.Box 16484, Jersey City, NJ 07306
info@netcomics.com
www.NETCOMICS.com

ISBN: 1-60009-032-X

First printing: June 2006
10 9 8 7 6 5 4 3 2 1
Printed in Korea

Boy Princess

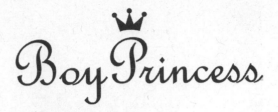

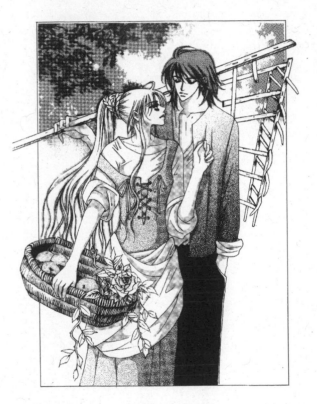

Vol. 3

Seyoung Kim

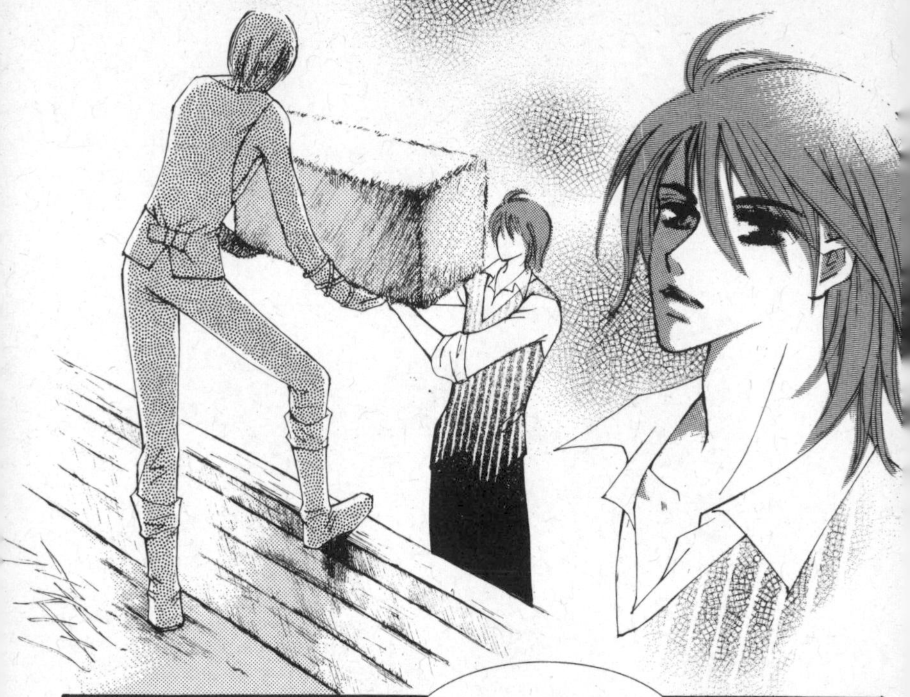

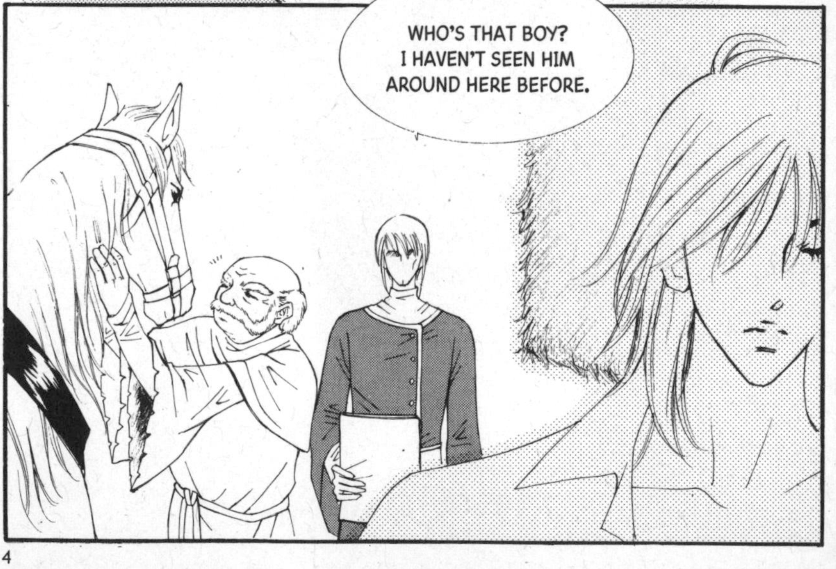
WHO'S THAT BOY?
I HAVEN'T SEEN HIM
AROUND HERE BEFORE.

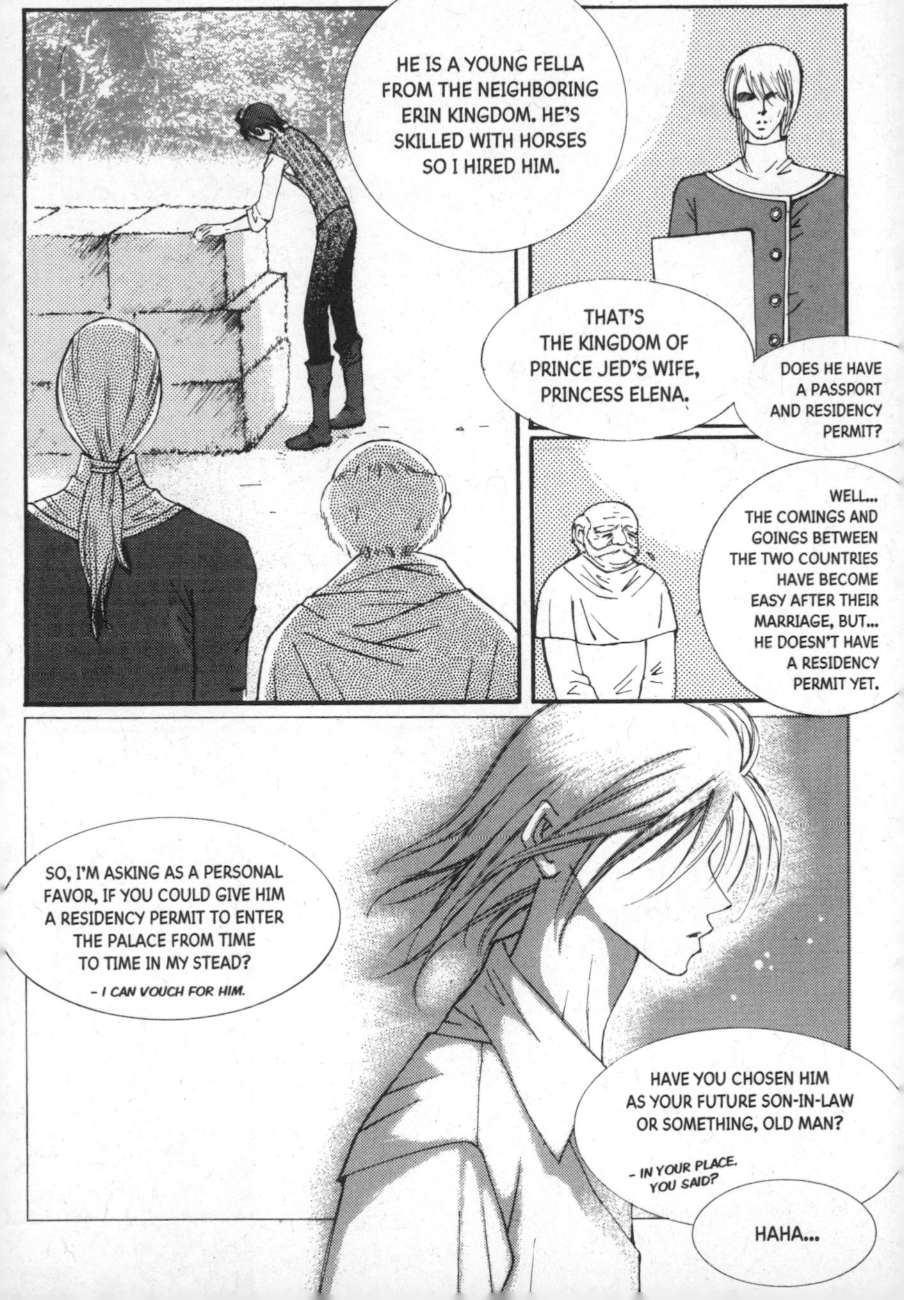
HE IS A YOUNG FELLA FROM THE NEIGHBORING ERIN KINGDOM. HE'S SKILLED WITH HORSES SO I HIRED HIM.
THAT'S THE KINGDOM OF PRINCE JED'S WIFE, PRINCESS ELENA.
DOES HE HAVE A PASSPORT AND RESIDENCY PERMIT?
WELL... THE COMINGS AND GOINGS BETWEEN THE TWO COUNTRIES HAVE BECOME EASY AFTER THEIR MARRIAGE, BUT... HE DOESN'T HAVE A RESIDENCY PERMIT YET.
SO, I'M ASKING AS A PERSONAL FAVOR, IF YOU COULD GIVE HIM A RESIDENCY PERMIT TO ENTER THE PALACE FROM TIME TO TIME IN MY STEAD?
- I CAN VOUCH FOR HIM.
HAVE YOU CHOSEN HIM AS YOUR FUTURE SON-IN-LAW OR SOMETHING, OLD MAN?
- IN YOUR PLACE, YOU SAID?
HAHA...

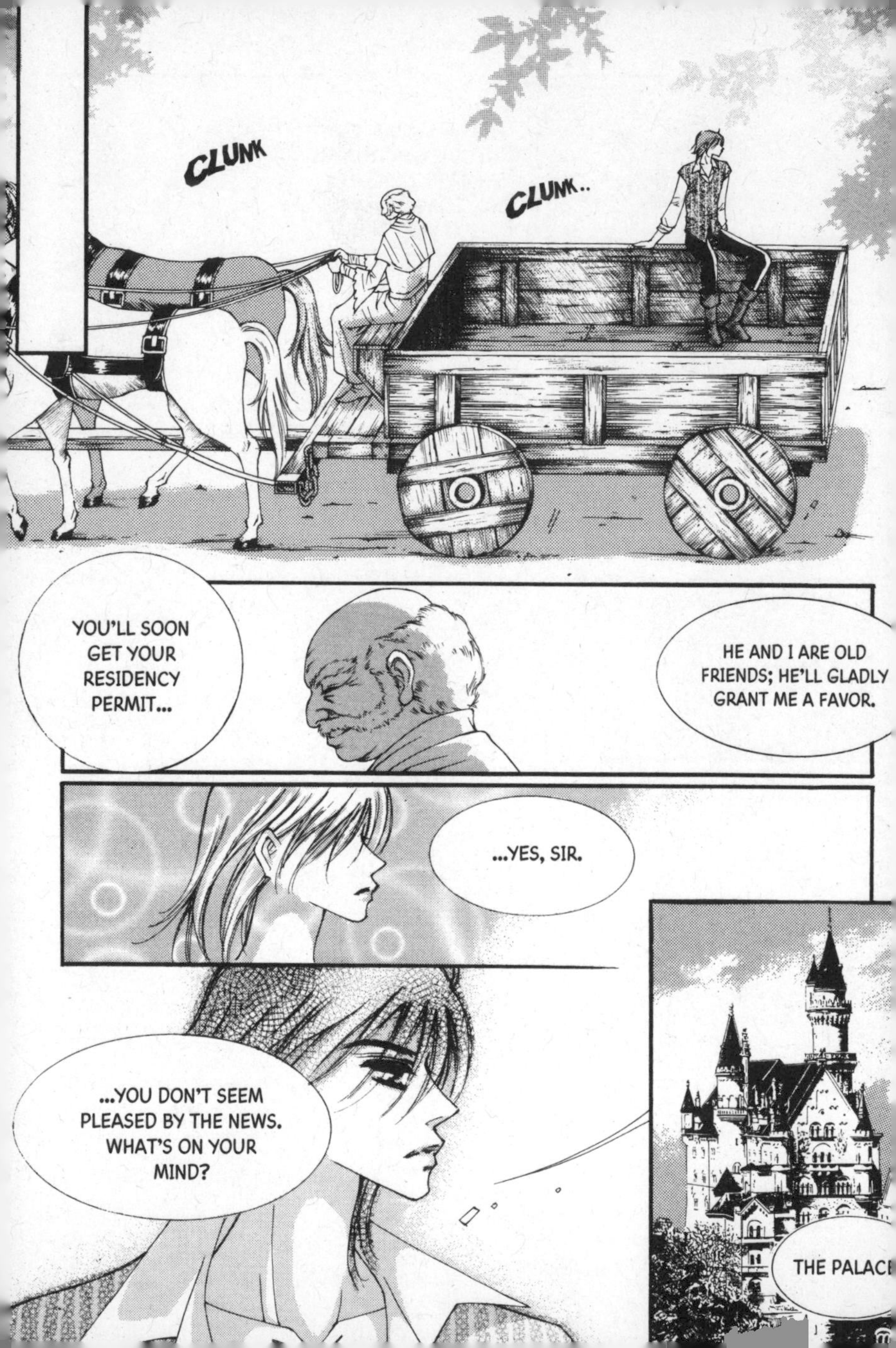
CLUNK
CLUNK..
YOU'LL SOON GET YOUR RESIDENCY PERMIT...
HE AND I ARE OLD FRIENDS; HE'LL GLADLY GRANT ME A FAVOR.
...YES, SIR.
...YOU DON'T SEEM PLEASED BY THE NEWS. WHAT'S ON YOUR MIND?
THE PALACE

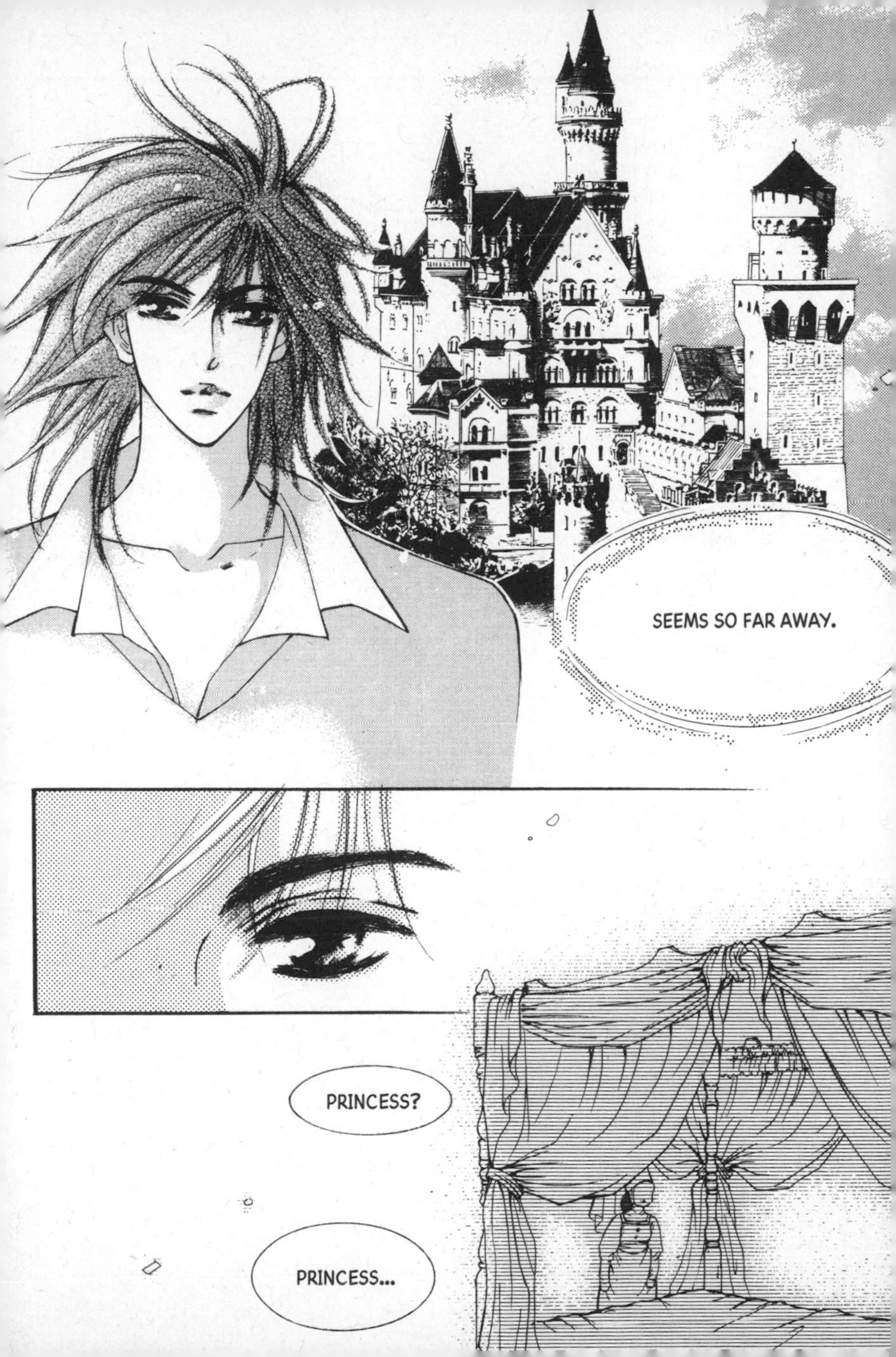
SEEMS SO FAR AWAY.
PRINCESS?
PRINCESS...

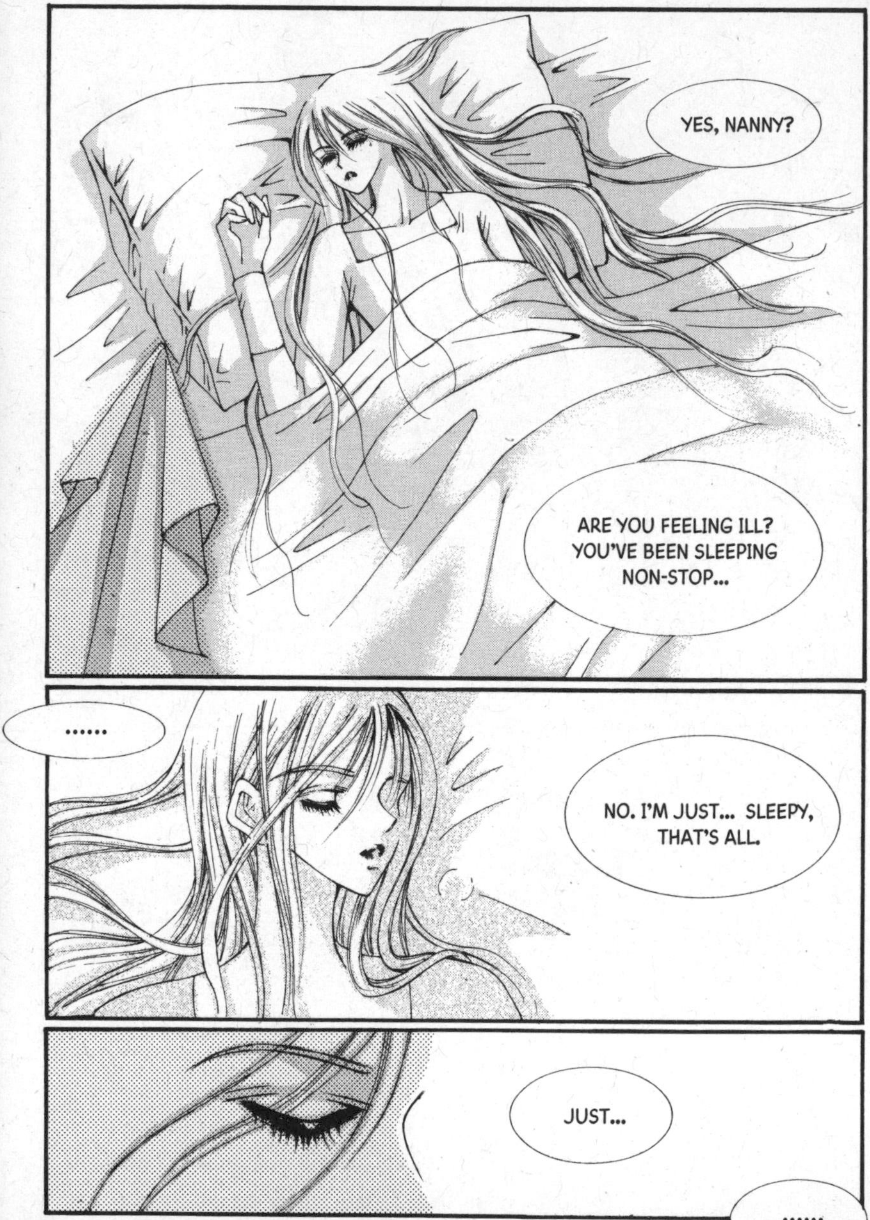
YES, NANNY?
ARE YOU FEELING ILL? YOU'VE BEEN SLEEPING NON-STOP...
......
NO. I'M JUST... SLEEPY, THAT'S ALL.
JUST...
......

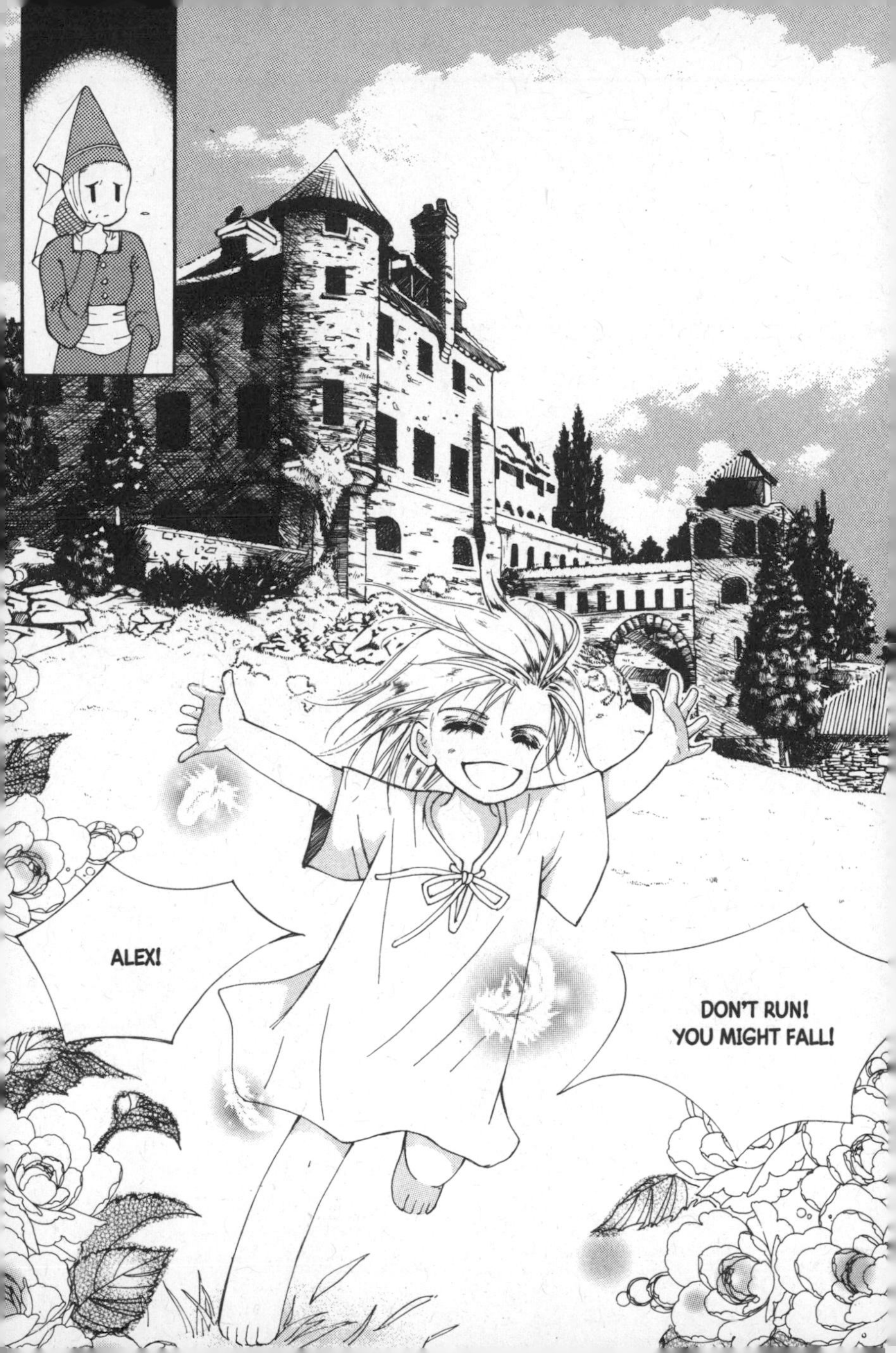

DON'T RUN! YOU MIGHT FALL!
ALEX!

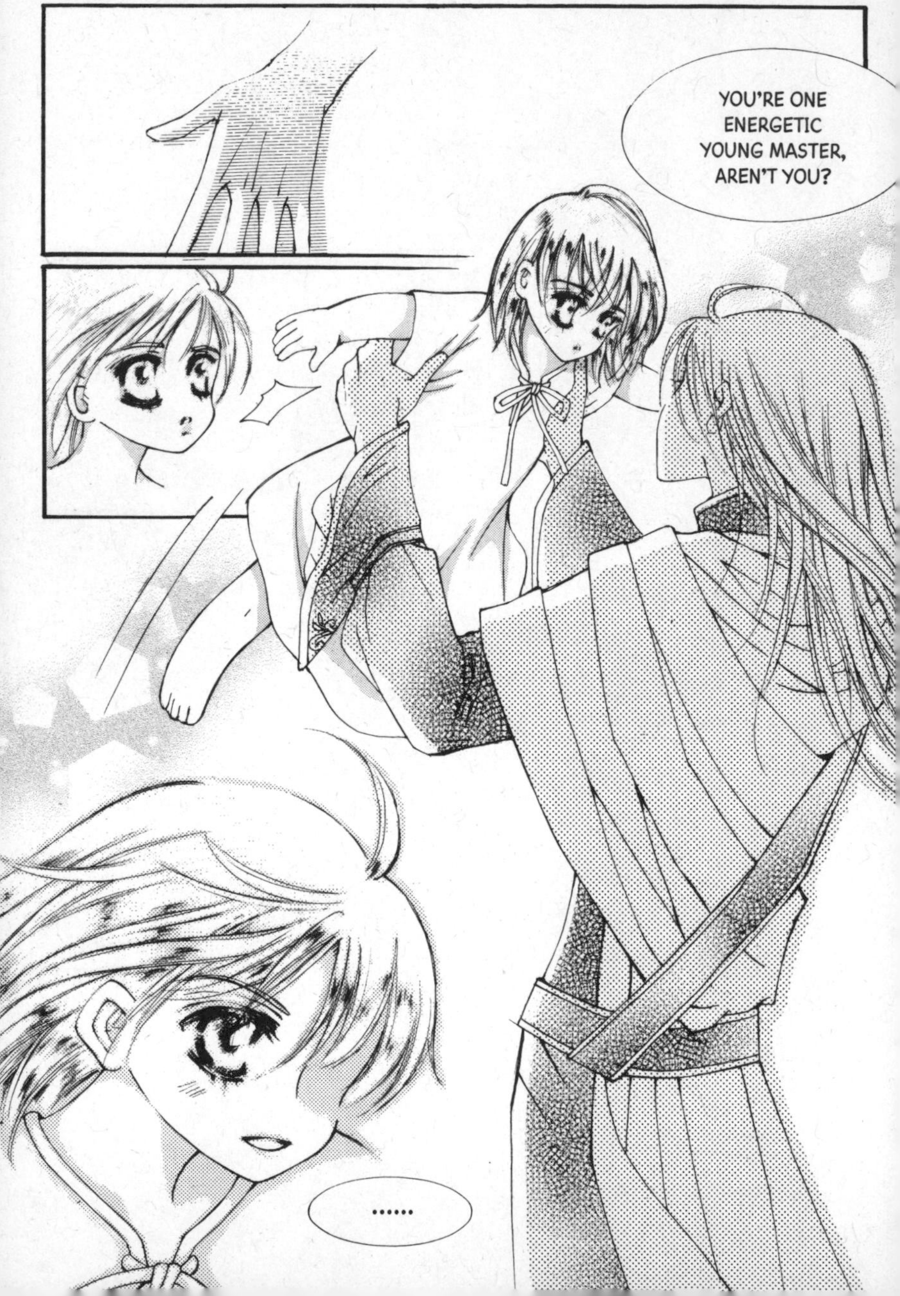
YOU'RE ONE ENERGETIC YOUNG MASTER, AREN'T YOU?
......

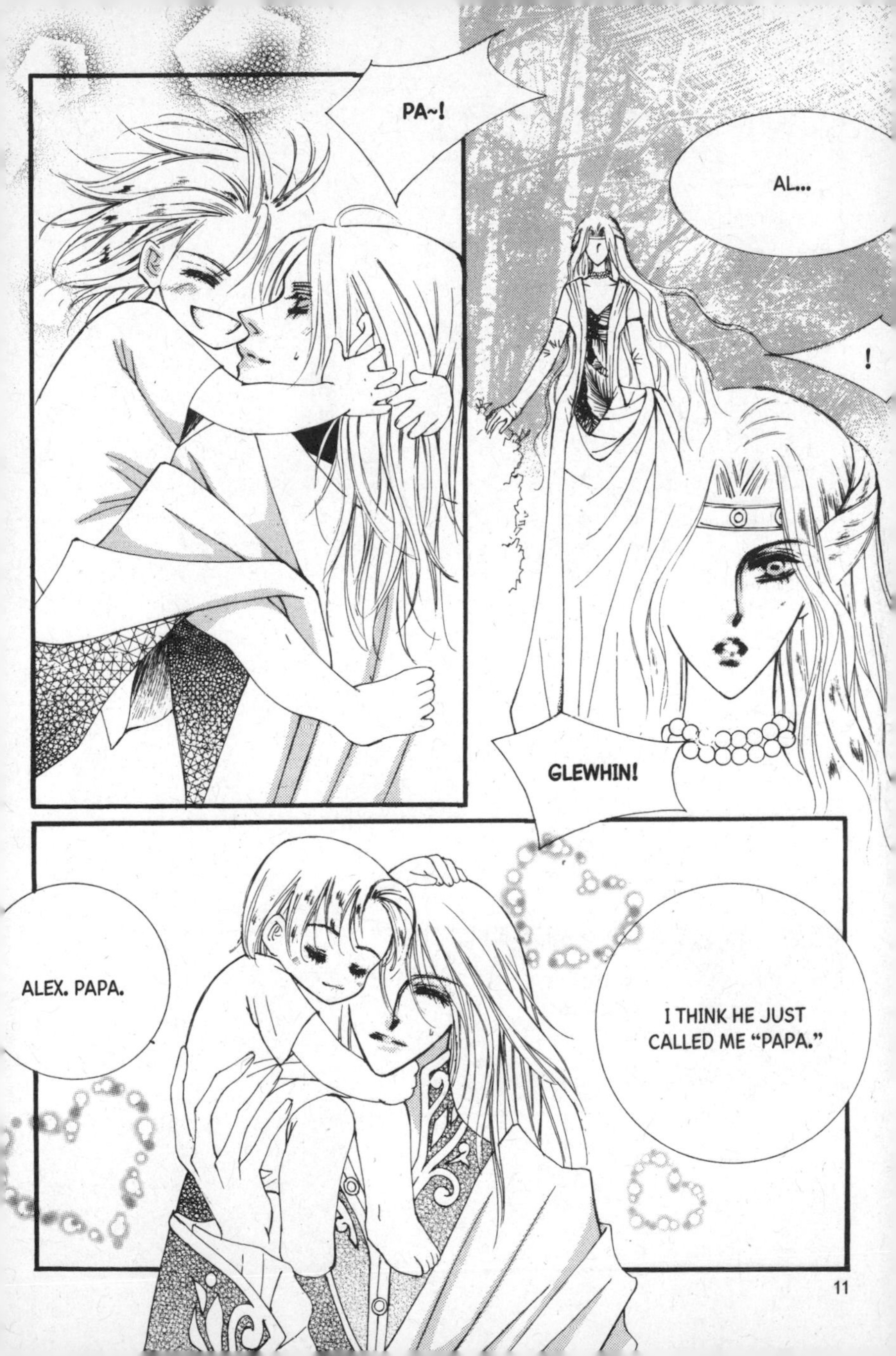
PA~!
AL...
!
GLEWHIN!
ALEX. PAPA.
I THINK HE JUST CALLED ME "PAPA."

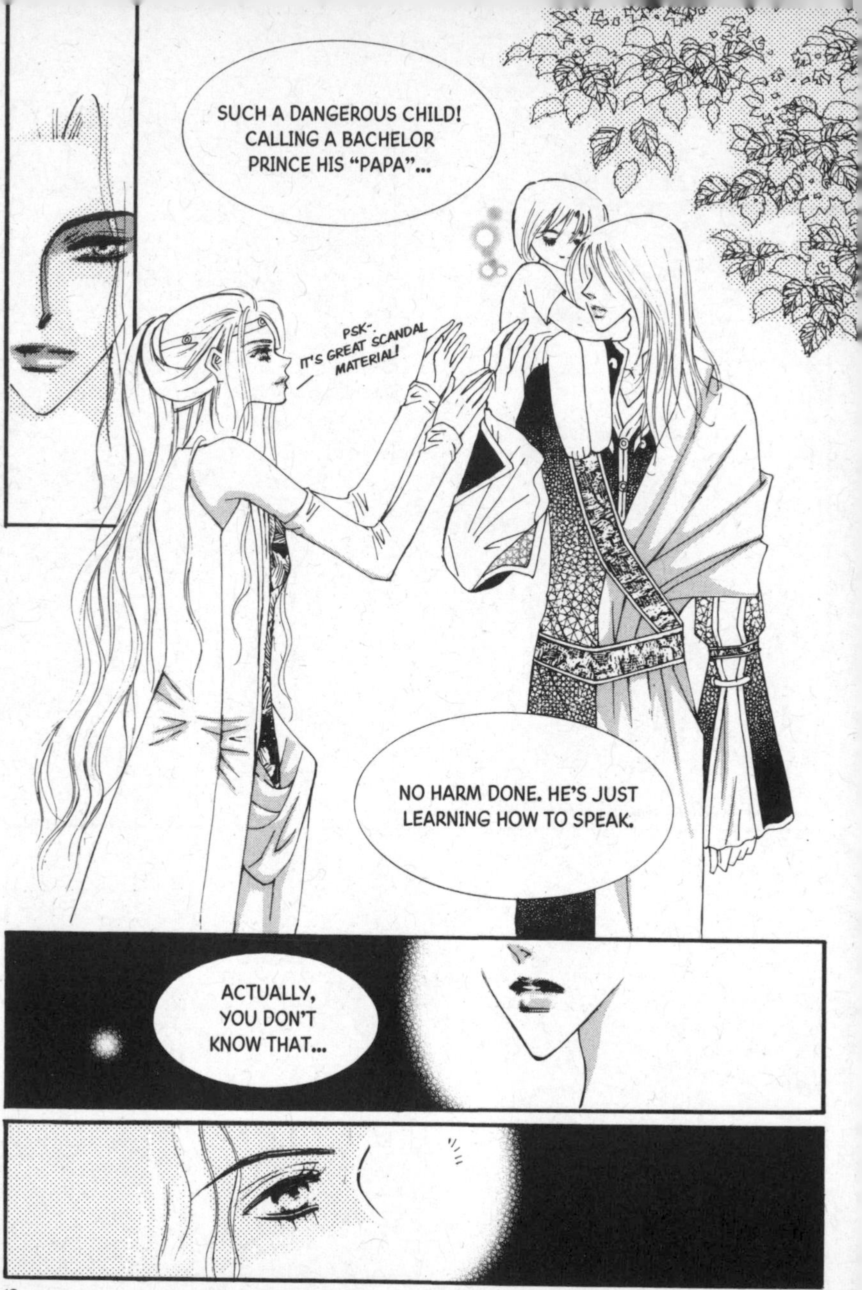
SUCH A DANGEROUS CHILD! CALLING A BACHELOR PRINCE HIS "PAPA"...
PSK-. IT'S GREAT SCANDAL MATERIAL!
NO HARM DONE. HE'S JUST LEARNING HOW TO SPEAK.
ACTUALLY, YOU DON'T KNOW THAT...

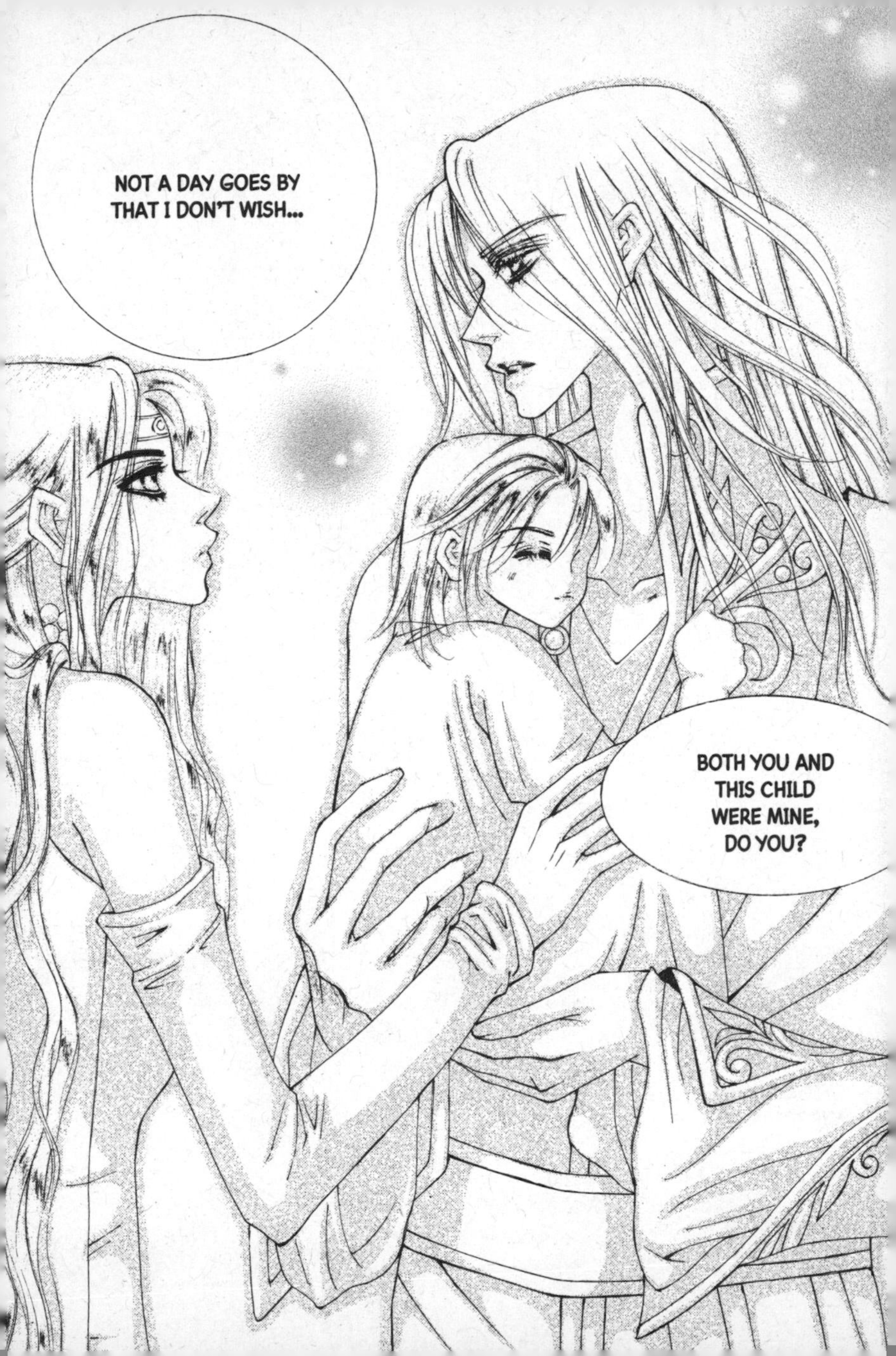
NOT A DAY GOES BY THAT I DON'T WISH...
BOTH YOU AND THIS CHILD WERE MINE, DO YOU?

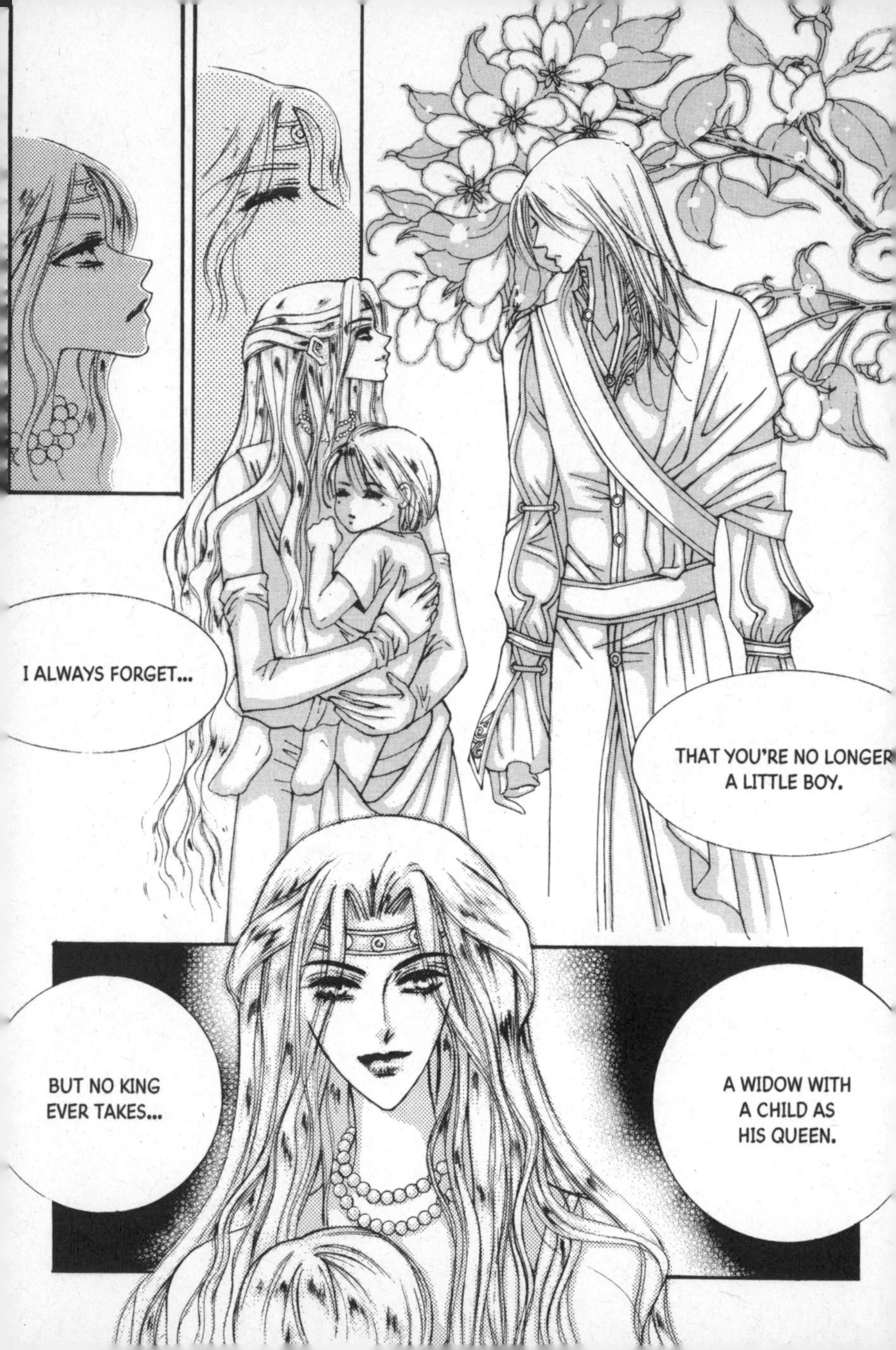
I ALWAYS FORGET...
THAT YOU'RE NO LONGER A LITTLE BOY.
BUT NO KING EVER TAKES...
A WIDOW WITH A CHILD AS HIS QUEEN.

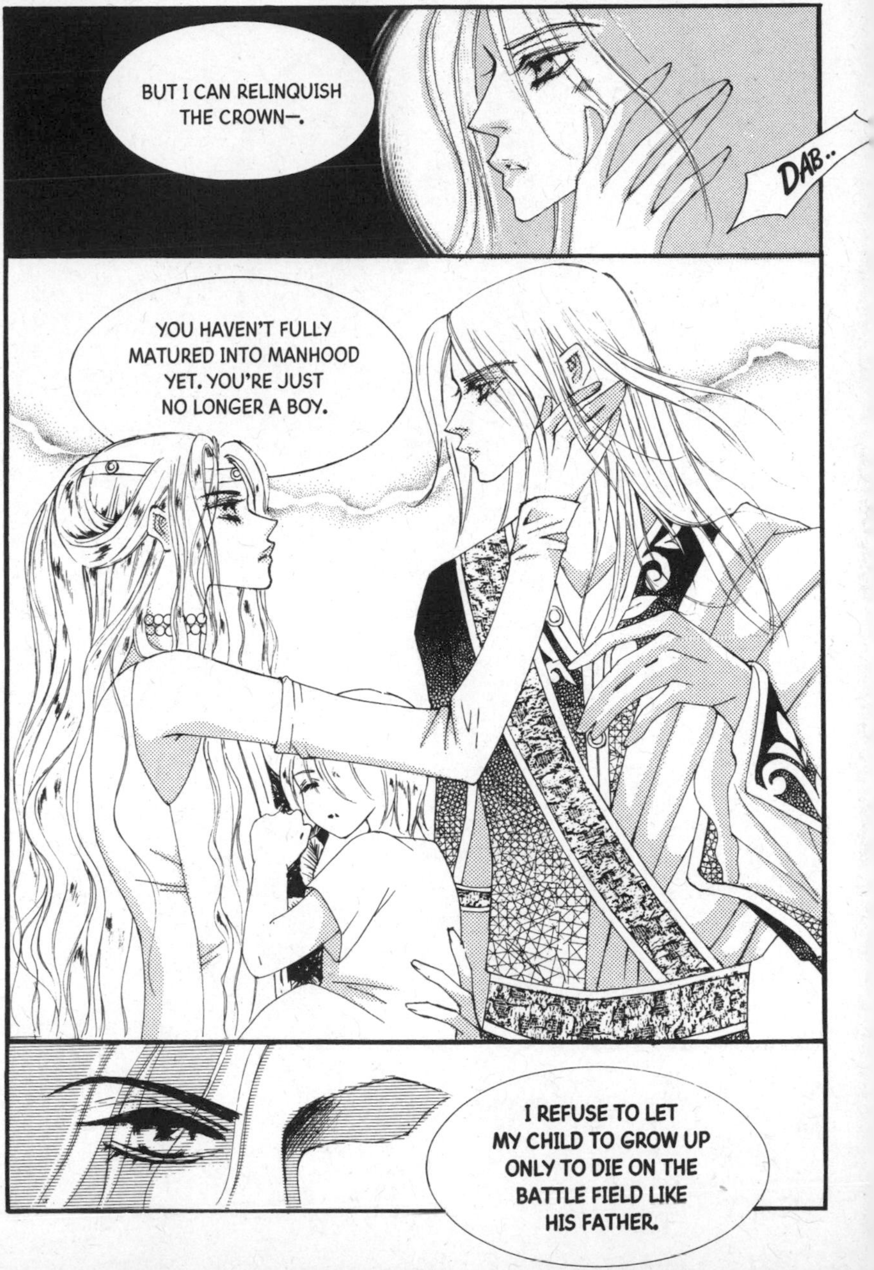
BUT I CAN RELINQUISH THE CROWN—.
DAB..
YOU HAVEN'T FULLY MATURED INTO MANHOOD YET. YOU'RE JUST NO LONGER A BOY.
I REFUSE TO LET MY CHILD TO GROW UP ONLY TO DIE ON THE BATTLE FIELD LIKE HIS FATHER.

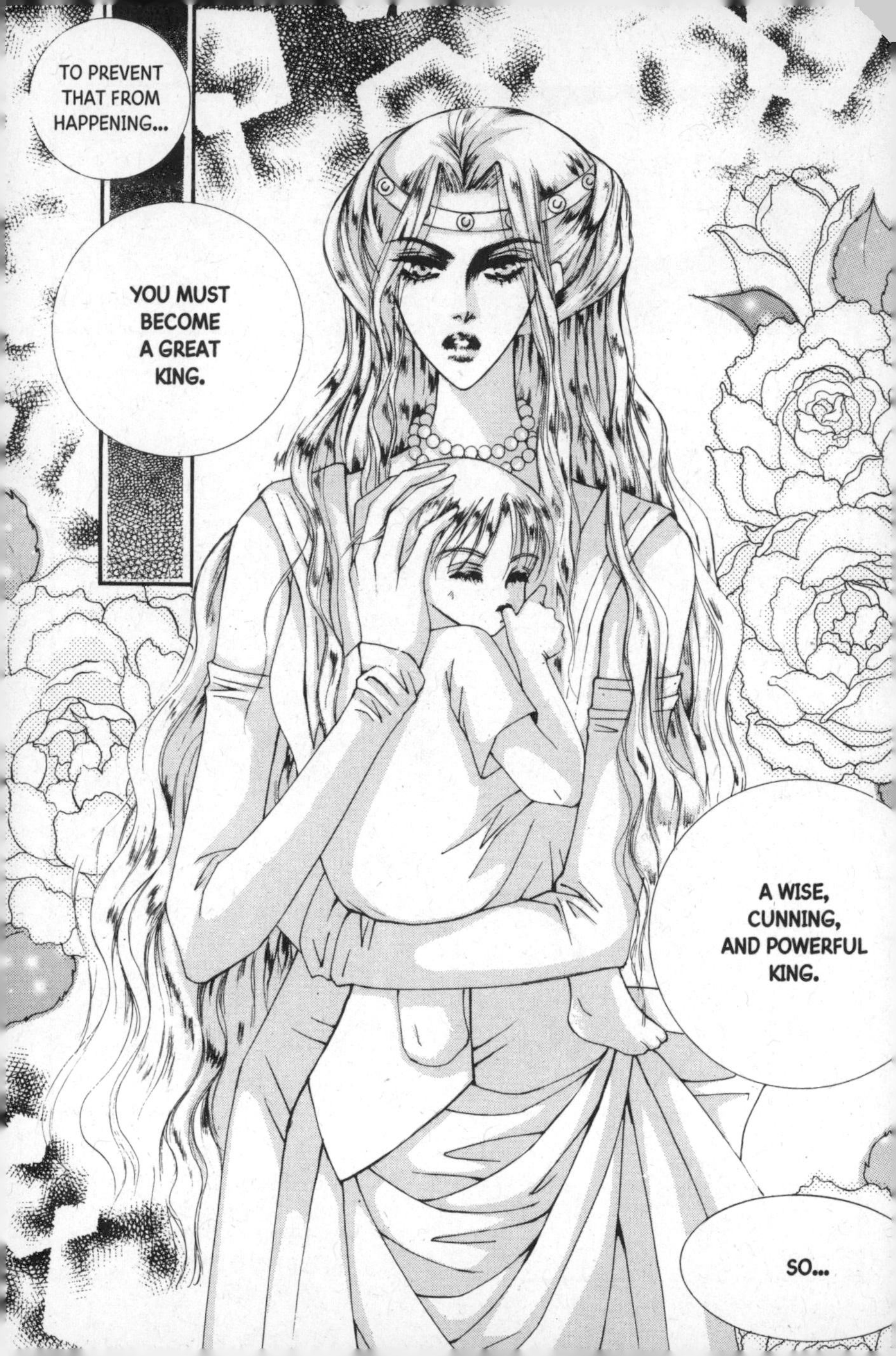
TO PREVENT THAT FROM HAPPENING...
YOU MUST BECOME A GREAT KING.
A WISE, CUNNING, AND POWERFUL KING.
SO...

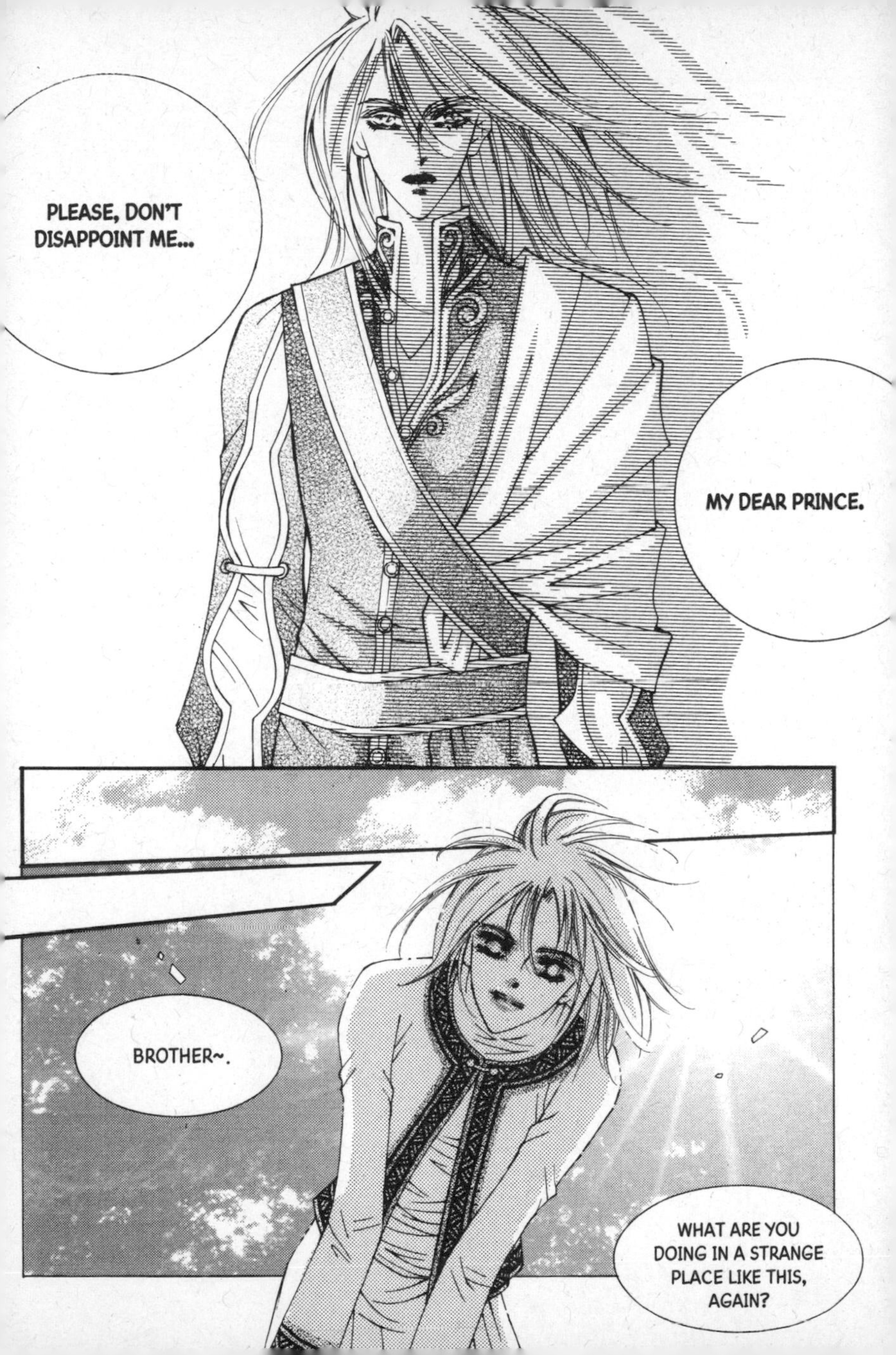
PLEASE, DON'T DISAPPOINT ME...
MY DEAR PRINCE.
BROTHER~.
WHAT ARE YOU DOING IN A STRANGE PLACE LIKE THIS, AGAIN?

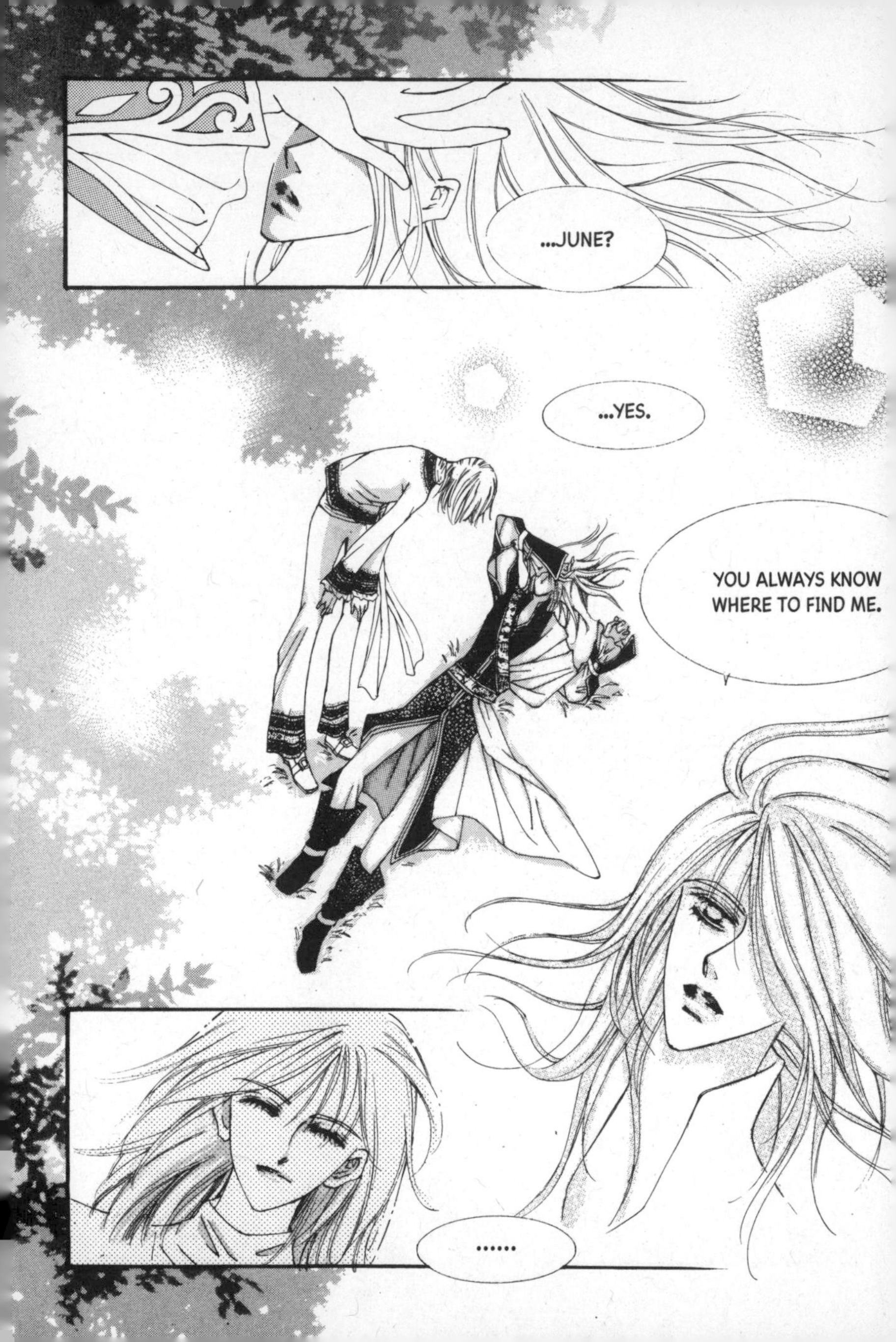
...JUNE?
...YES.
YOU ALWAYS KNOW WHERE TO FIND ME.
......

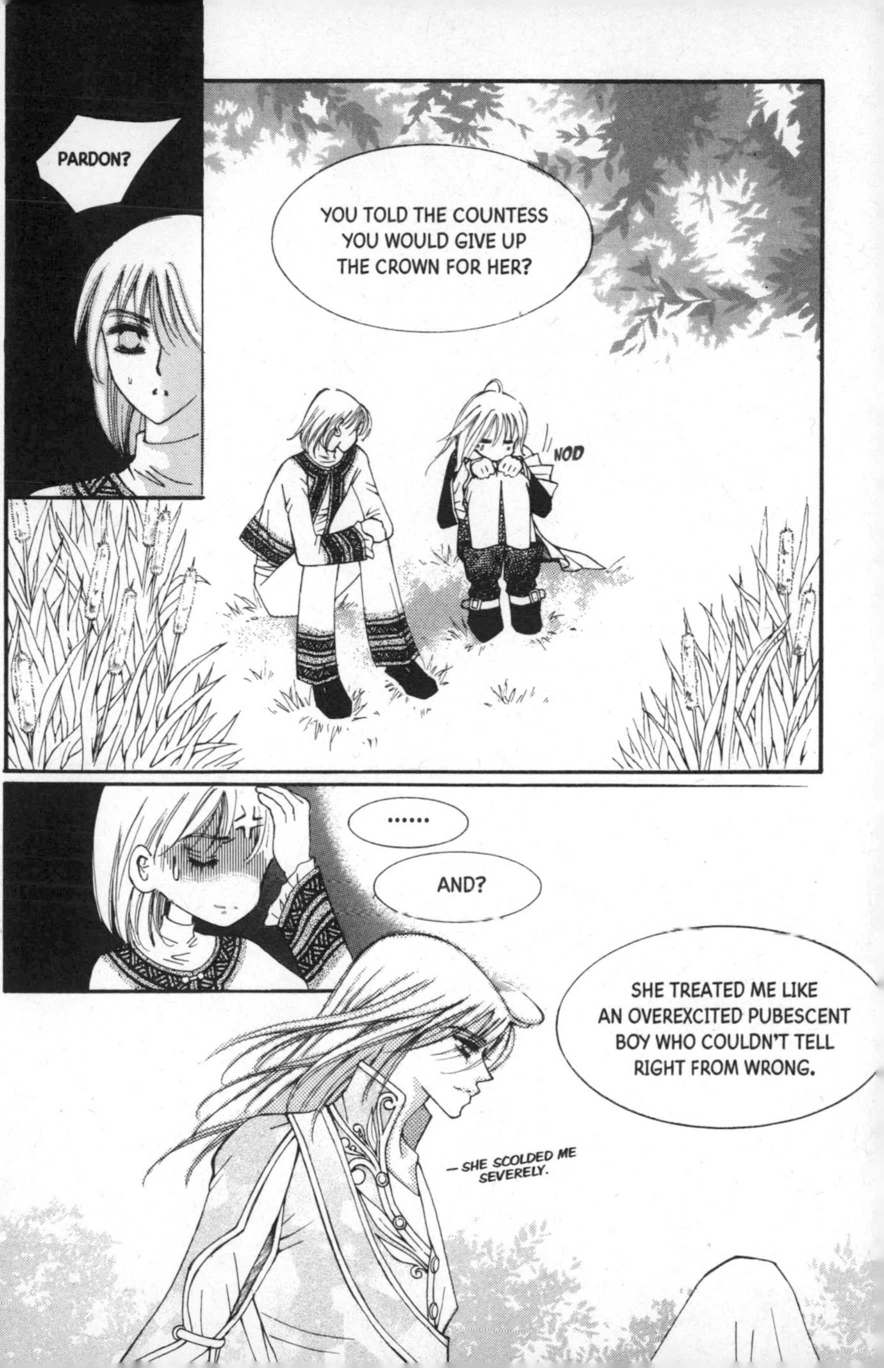
PARDON?
YOU TOLD THE COUNTESS YOU WOULD GIVE UP THE CROWN FOR HER?
NOD
......
AND?
SHE TREATED ME LIKE AN OVEREXCITED PUBESCENT BOY WHO COULDN'T TELL RIGHT FROM WRONG.
—SHE SCOLDED ME SEVERELY.

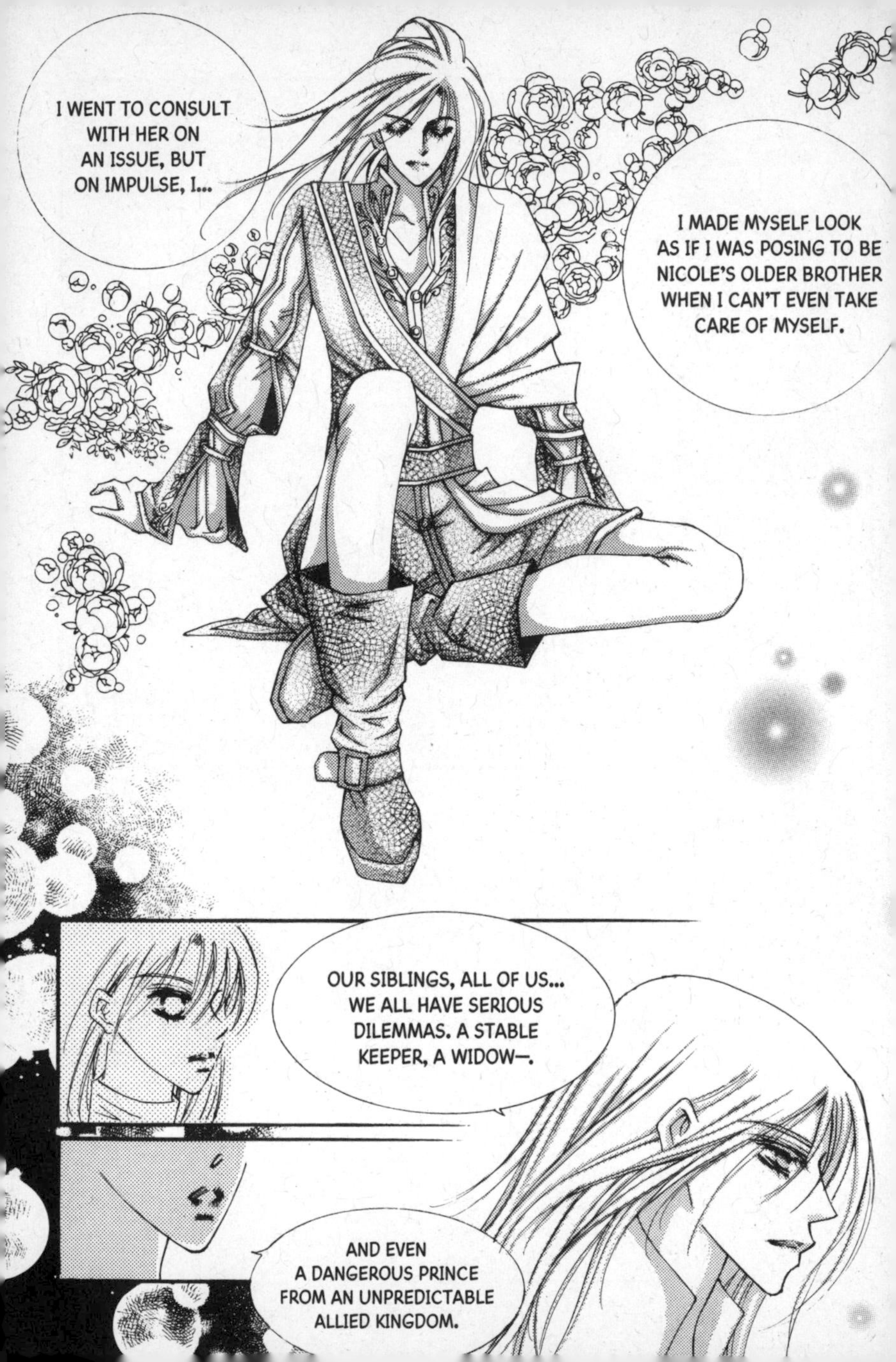
I WENT TO CONSULT WITH HER ON AN ISSUE, BUT ON IMPULSE, I...
I MADE MYSELF LOOK AS IF I WAS POSING TO BE NICOLE'S OLDER BROTHER WHEN I CAN'T EVEN TAKE CARE OF MYSELF.
OUR SIBLINGS, ALL OF US... WE ALL HAVE SERIOUS DILEMMAS. A STABLE KEEPER, A WIDOW—.
AND EVEN A DANGEROUS PRINCE FROM AN UNPREDICTABLE ALLIED KINGDOM.

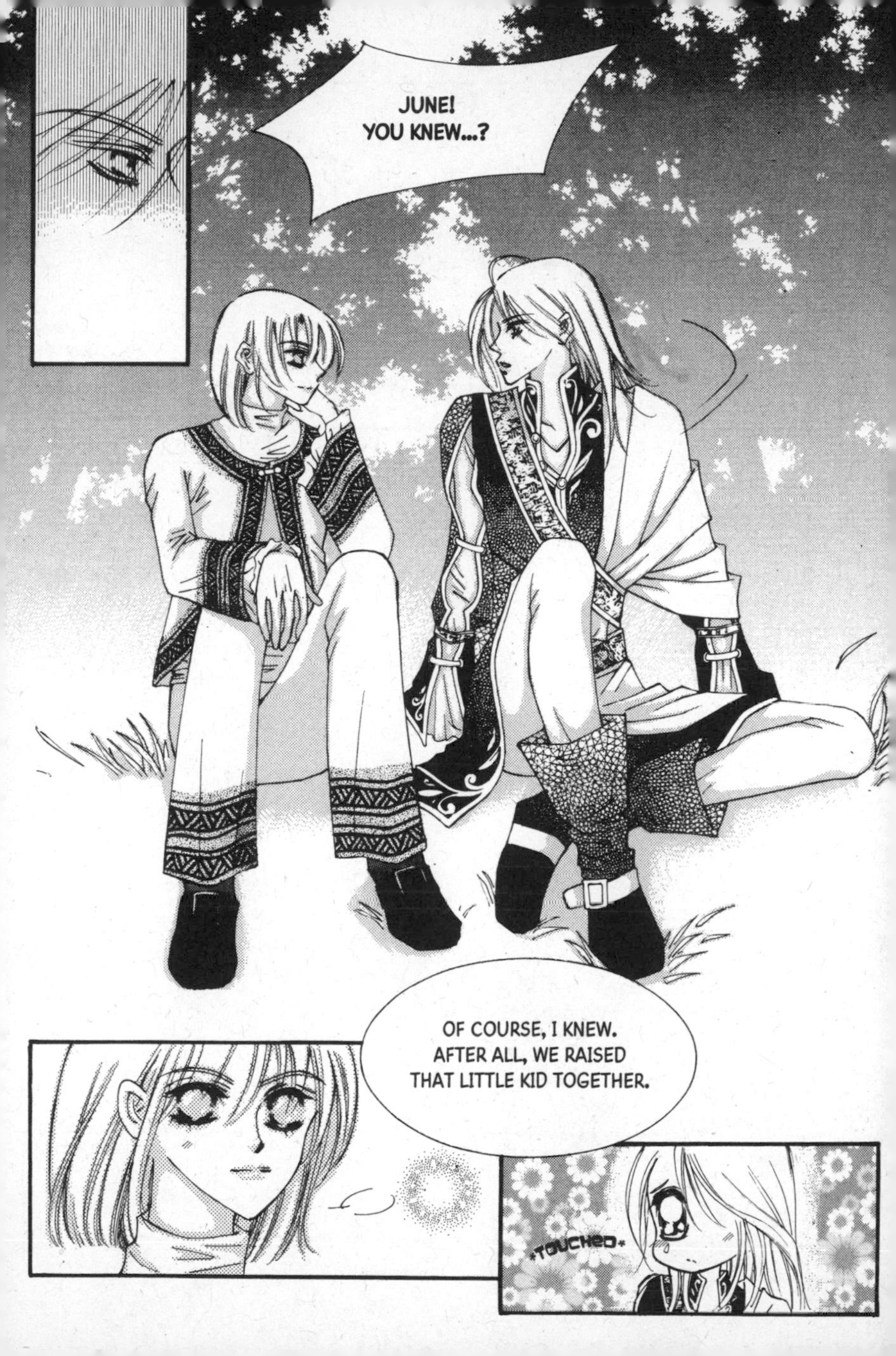
JUNE!
YOU KNEW...?
OF COURSE, I KNEW.
AFTER ALL, WE RAISED
THAT LITTLE KID TOGETHER.
TOUCHED

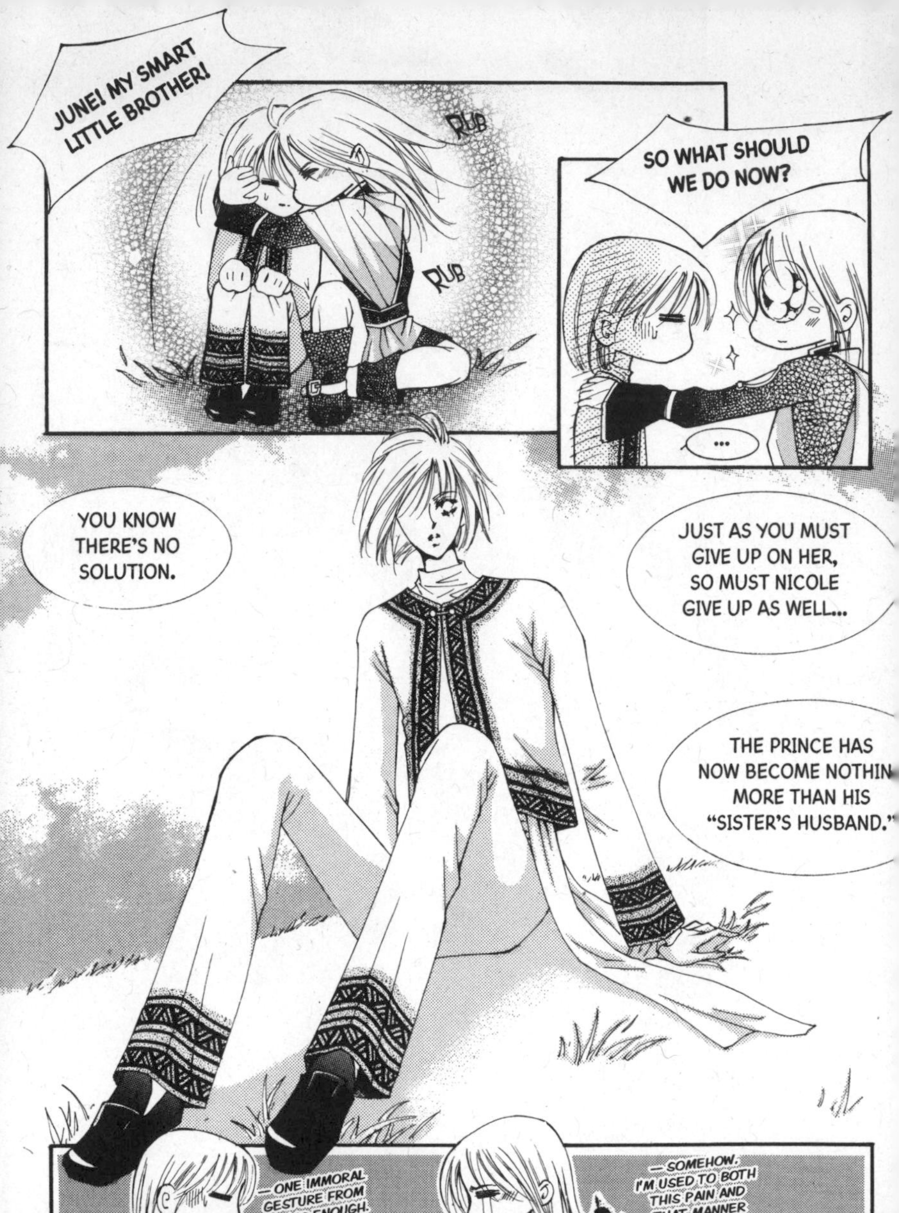
JUNE! MY SMART LITTLE BROTHER!
RUB
RUB
SO WHAT SHOULD WE DO NOW?
...
YOU KNOW THERE'S NO SOLUTION.
JUST AS YOU MUST GIVE UP ON HER, SO MUST NICOLE GIVE UP AS WELL...
THE PRINCE HAS NOW BECOME NOTHIN MORE THAN HIS "SISTER'S HUSBAND."
—ONE IMMORAL GESTURE FROM YOU IS ENOUGH.
—SOMEHOW, I'M USED TO BOTH THIS PAIN AND THAT MANNER OF SPEECH.
STAB
......

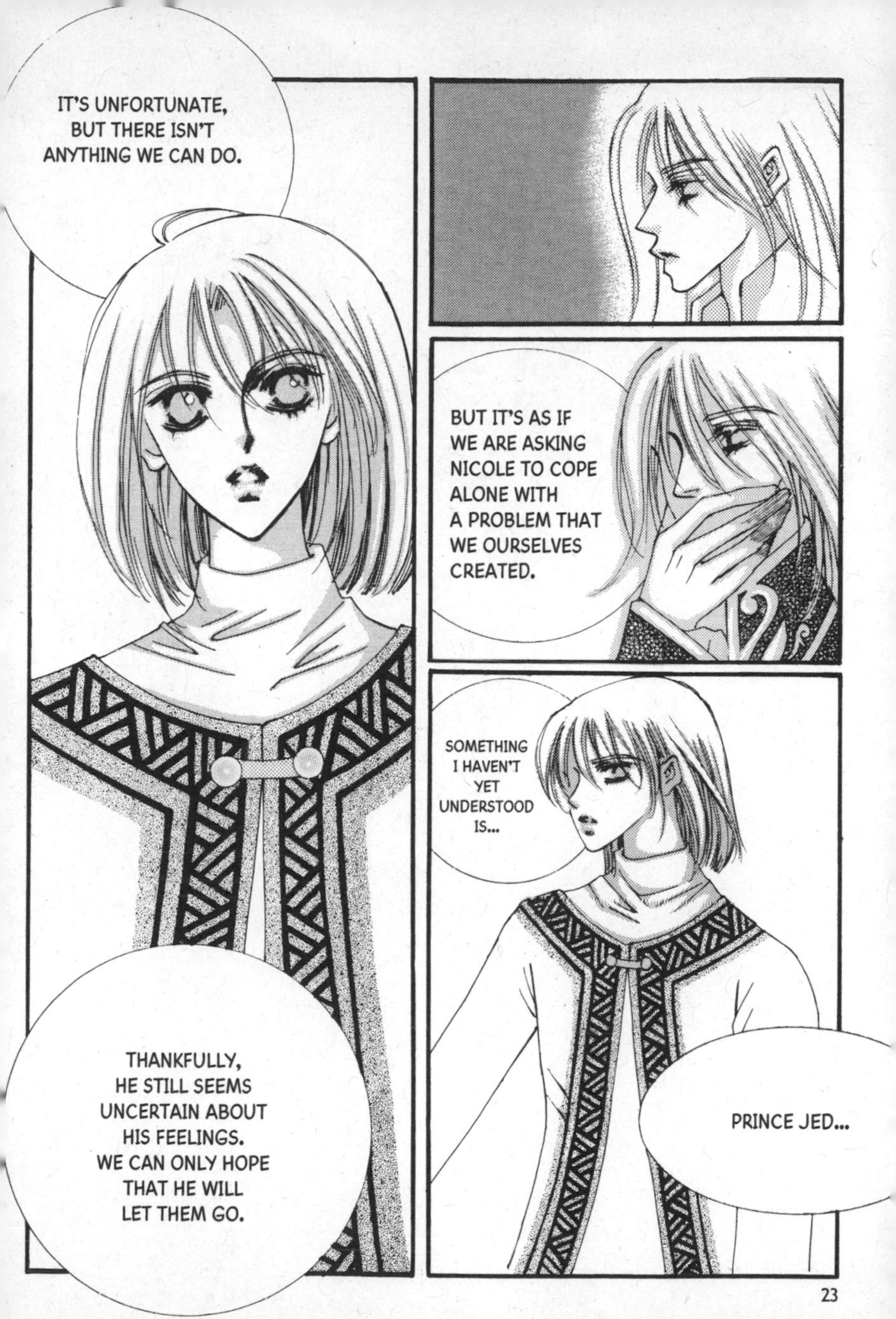
IT'S UNFORTUNATE, BUT THERE ISN'T ANYTHING WE CAN DO.
THANKFULLY, HE STILL SEEMS UNCERTAIN ABOUT HIS FEELINGS. WE CAN ONLY HOPE THAT HE WILL LET THEM GO.
BUT IT'S AS IF WE ARE ASKING NICOLE TO COPE ALONE WITH A PROBLEM THAT WE OURSELVES CREATED.
SOMETHING I HAVEN'T YET UNDERSTOOD IS...
PRINCE JED...

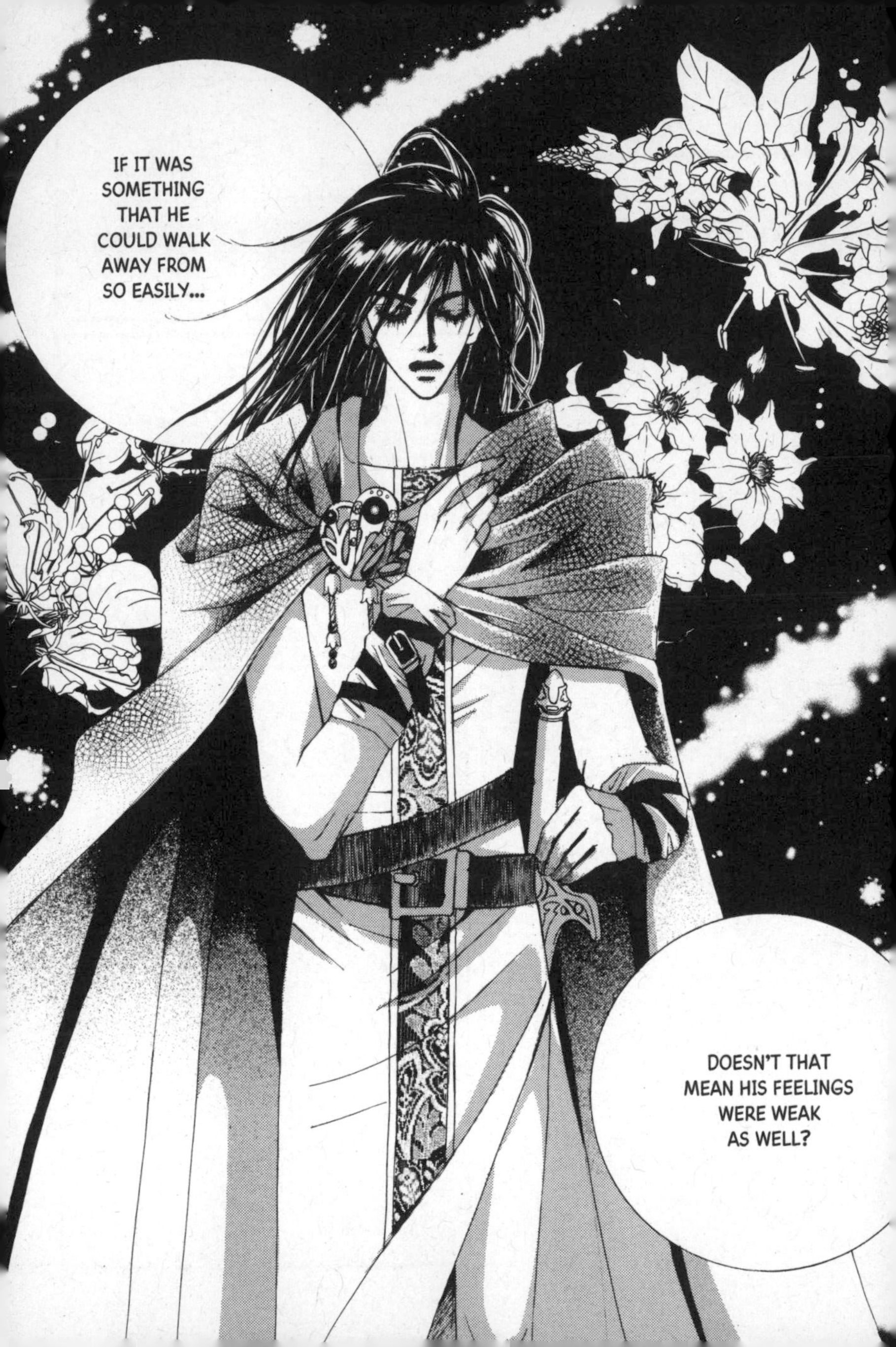
IF IT WAS SOMETHING THAT HE COULD WALK AWAY FROM SO EASILY...
DOESN'T THAT MEAN HIS FEELINGS WERE WEAK AS WELL?

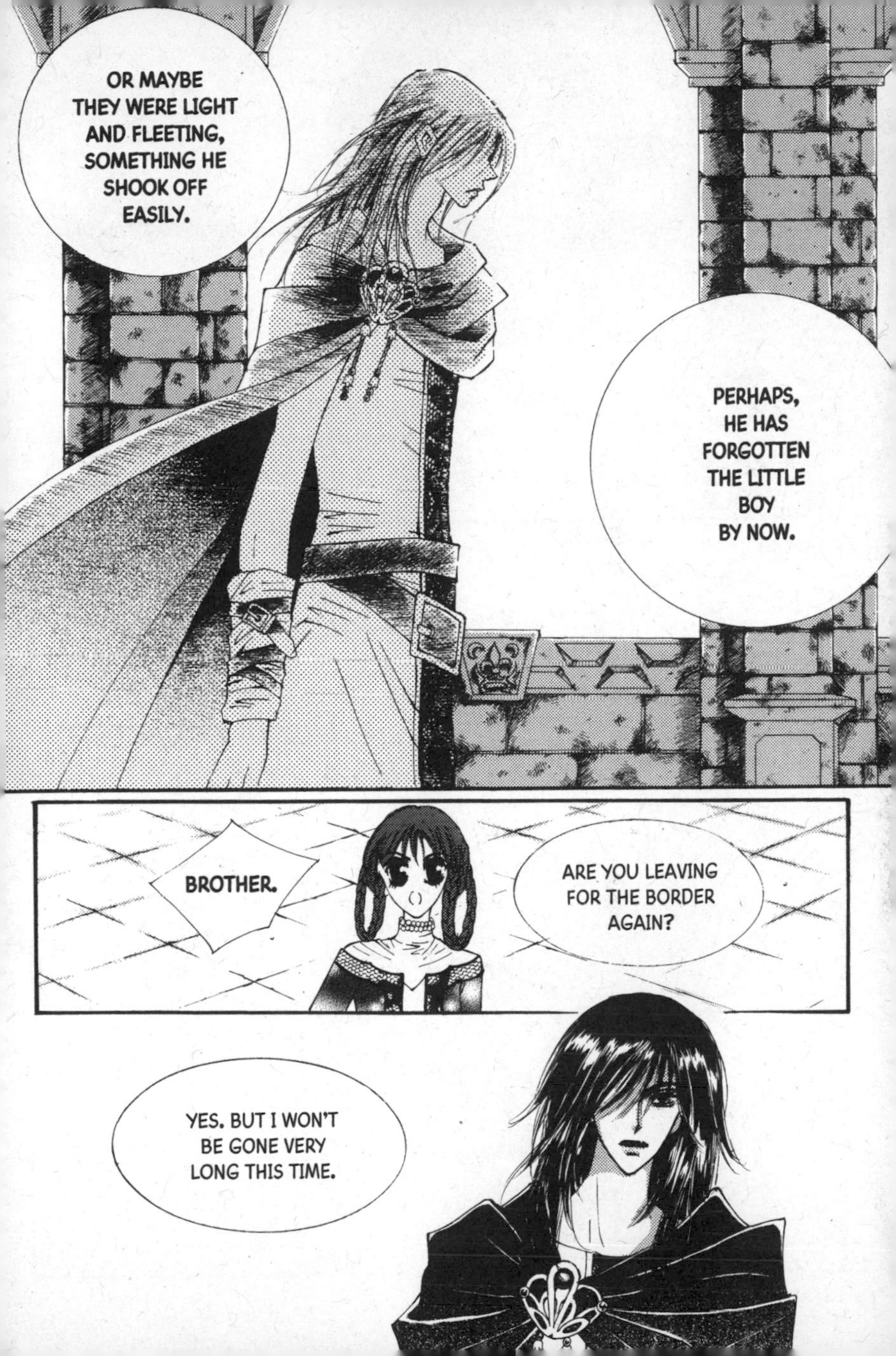
OR MAYBE THEY WERE LIGHT AND FLEETING, SOMETHING HE SHOOK OFF EASILY.
PERHAPS, HE HAS FORGOTTEN THE LITTLE BOY BY NOW.
BROTHER.
ARE YOU LEAVING FOR THE BORDER AGAIN?
YES. BUT I WON'T BE GONE VERY LONG THIS TIME.

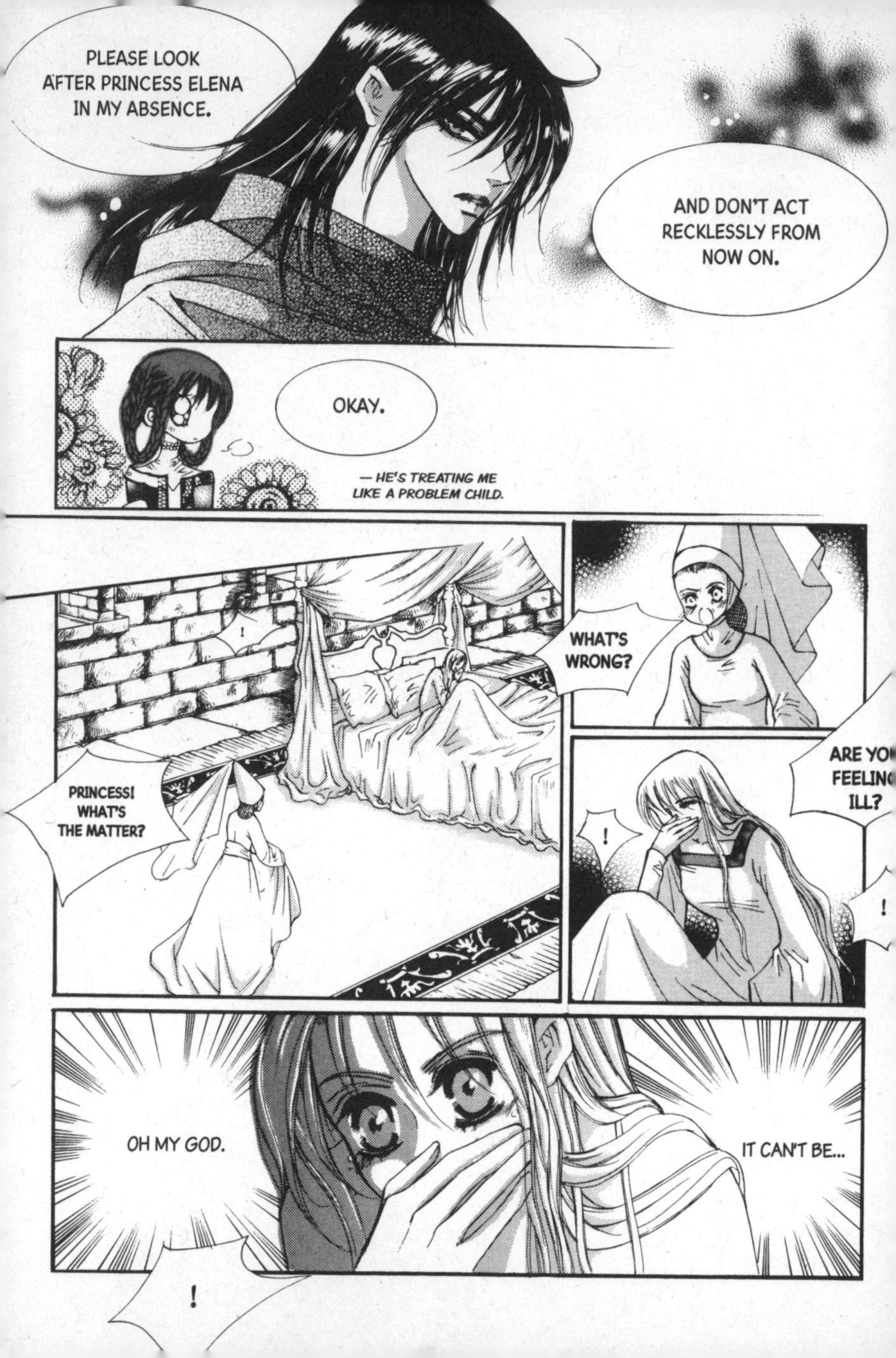
PLEASE LOOK AFTER PRINCESS ELENA IN MY ABSENCE.
AND DON'T ACT RECKLESSLY FROM NOW ON.
OKAY.
— HE'S TREATING ME LIKE A PROBLEM CHILD.
!
PRINCESS! WHAT'S THE MATTER?
WHAT'S WRONG?
ARE YO FEELIN ILL?
!
!
OH MY GOD.
IT CAN'T BE...
!

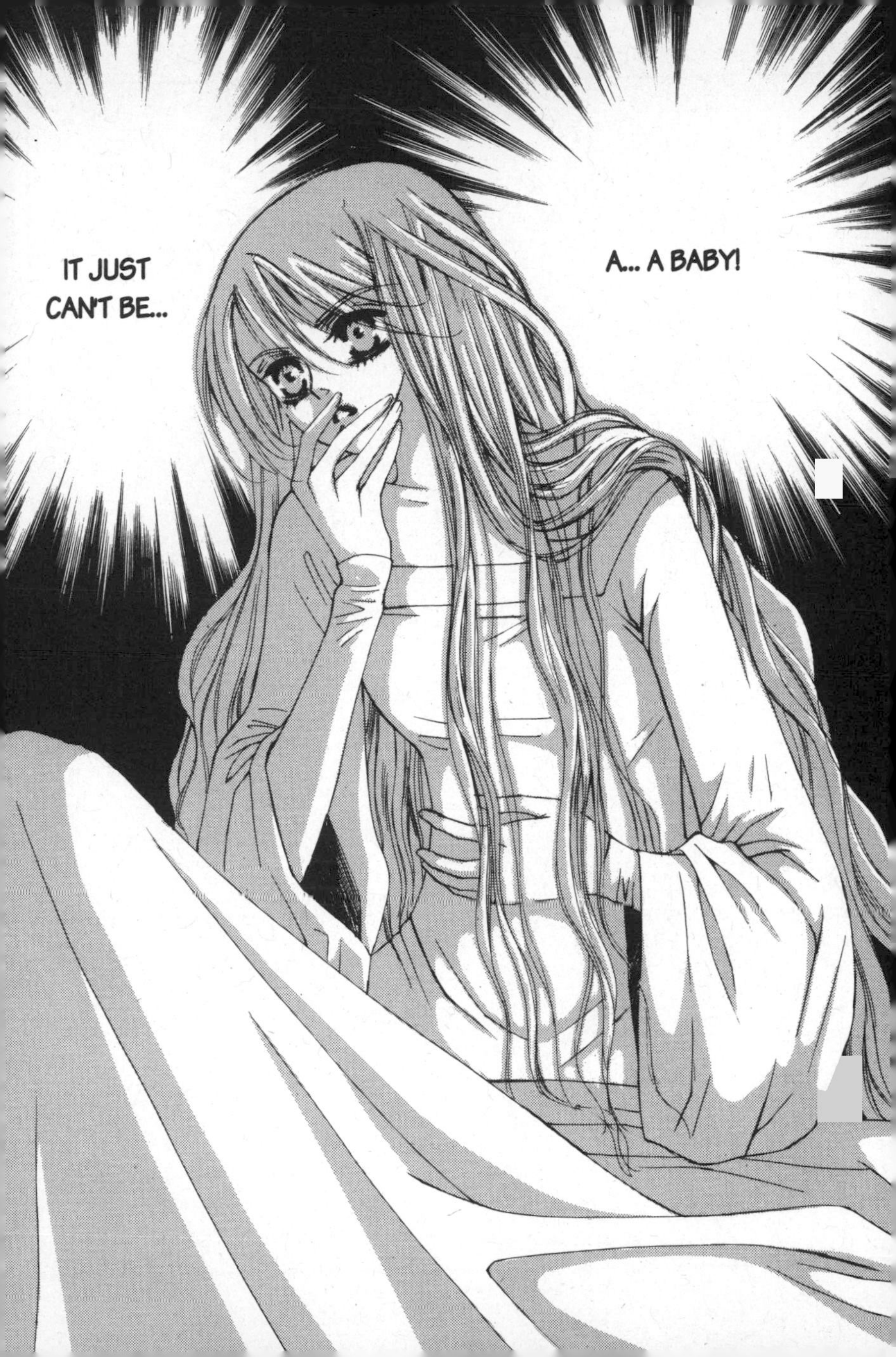
A... A BABY!
IT JUST CAN'T BE...

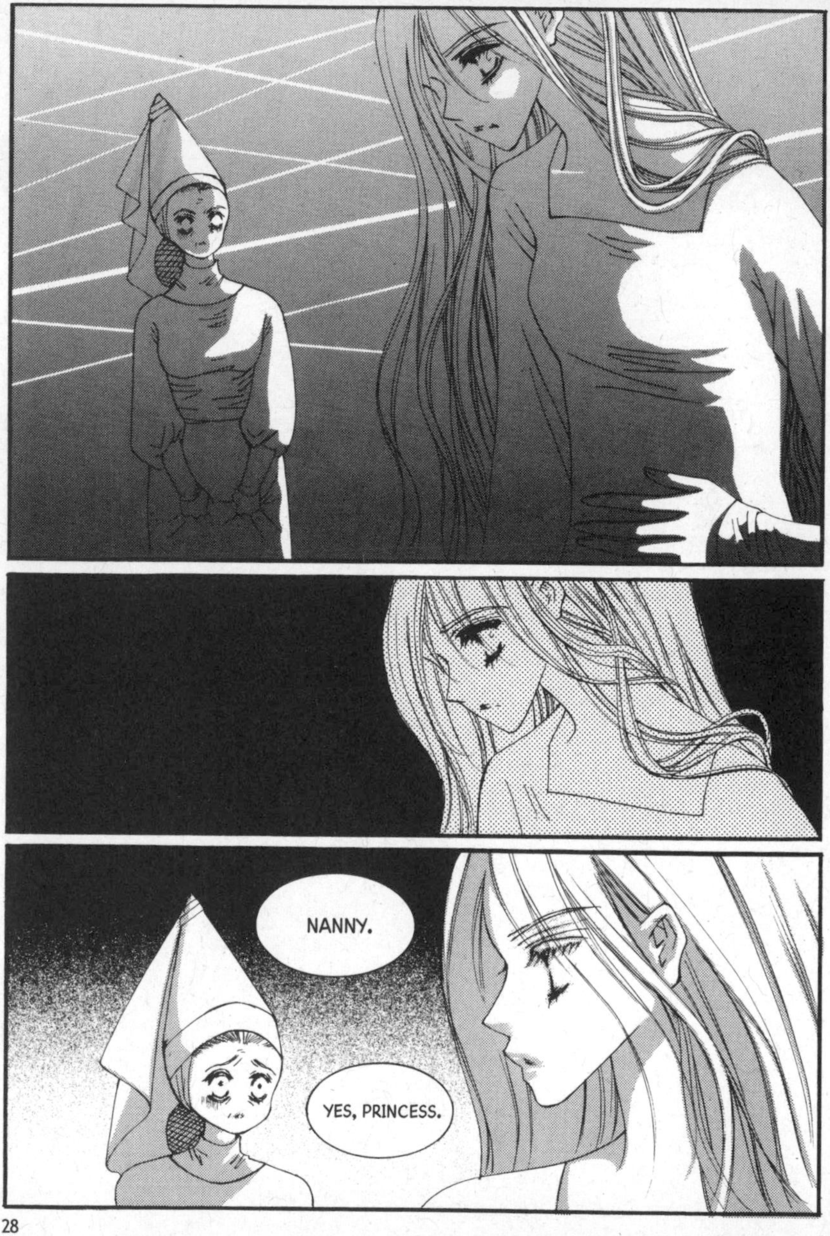
NANNY.
YES, PRINCESS.

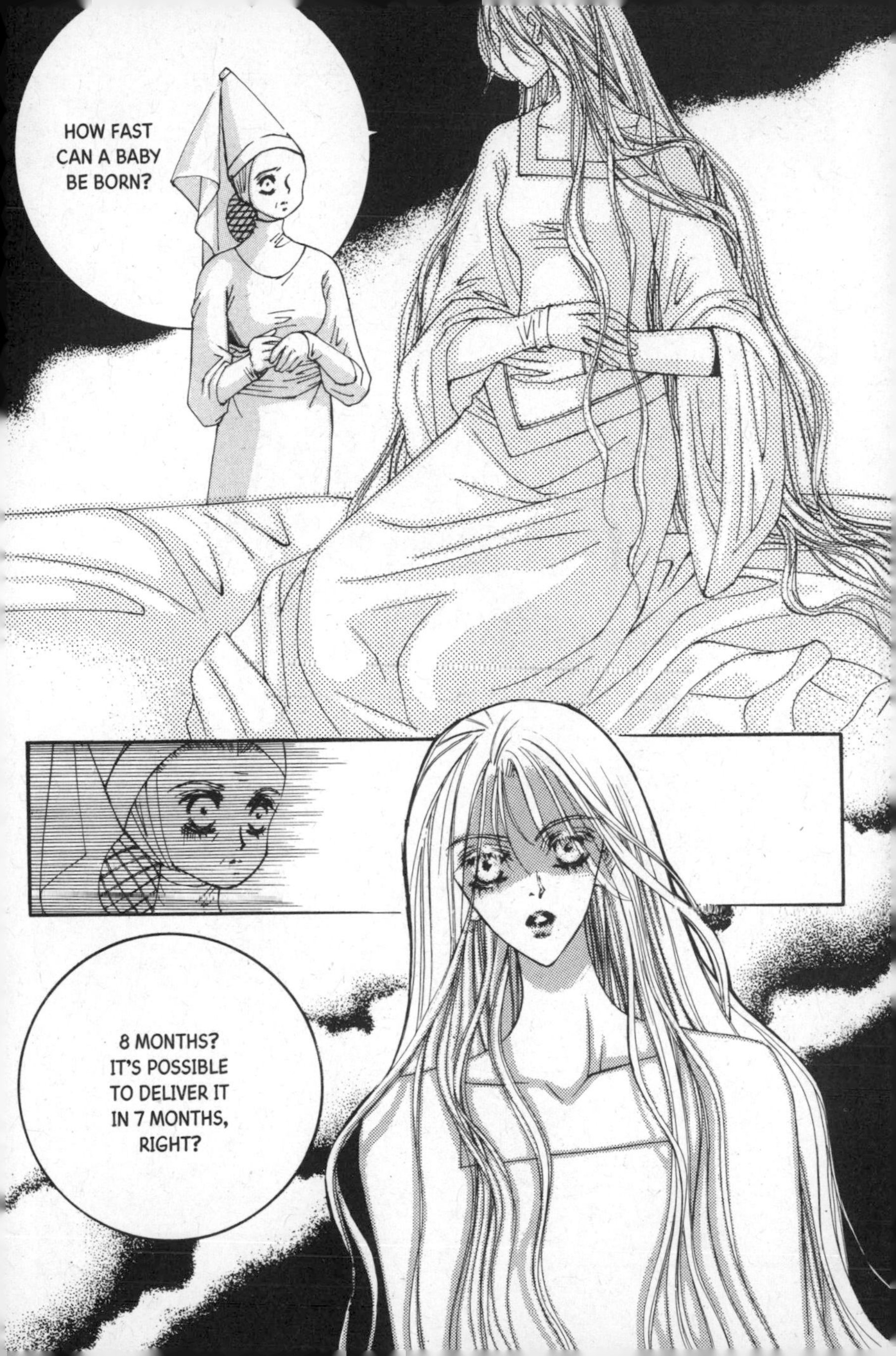
HOW FAST CAN A BABY BE BORN?
8 MONTHS? IT'S POSSIBLE TO DELIVER IT IN 7 MONTHS, RIGHT?

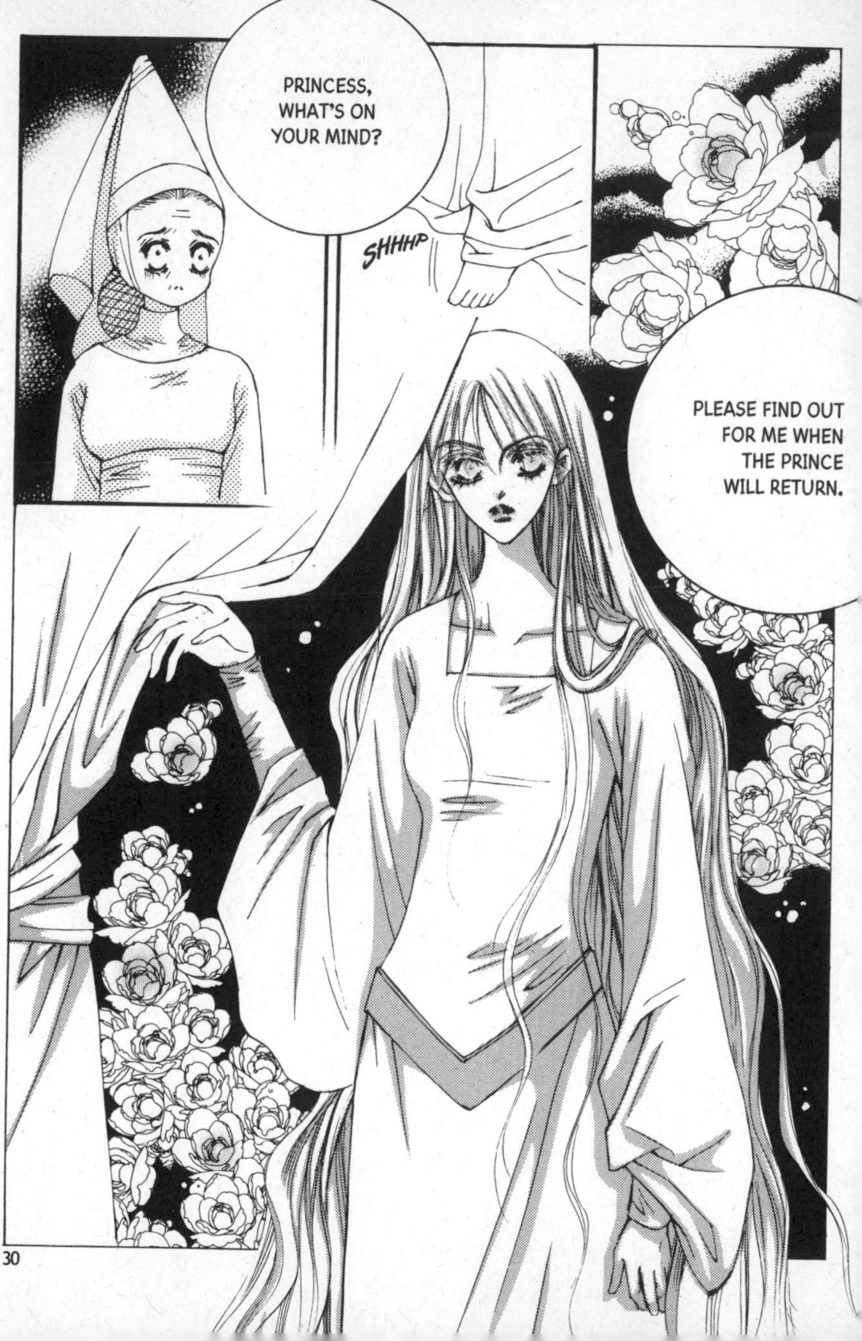

PRINCESS, WHAT'S ON YOUR MIND?
SHHHP
PLEASE FIND OUT FOR ME WHEN THE PRINCE WILL RETURN.

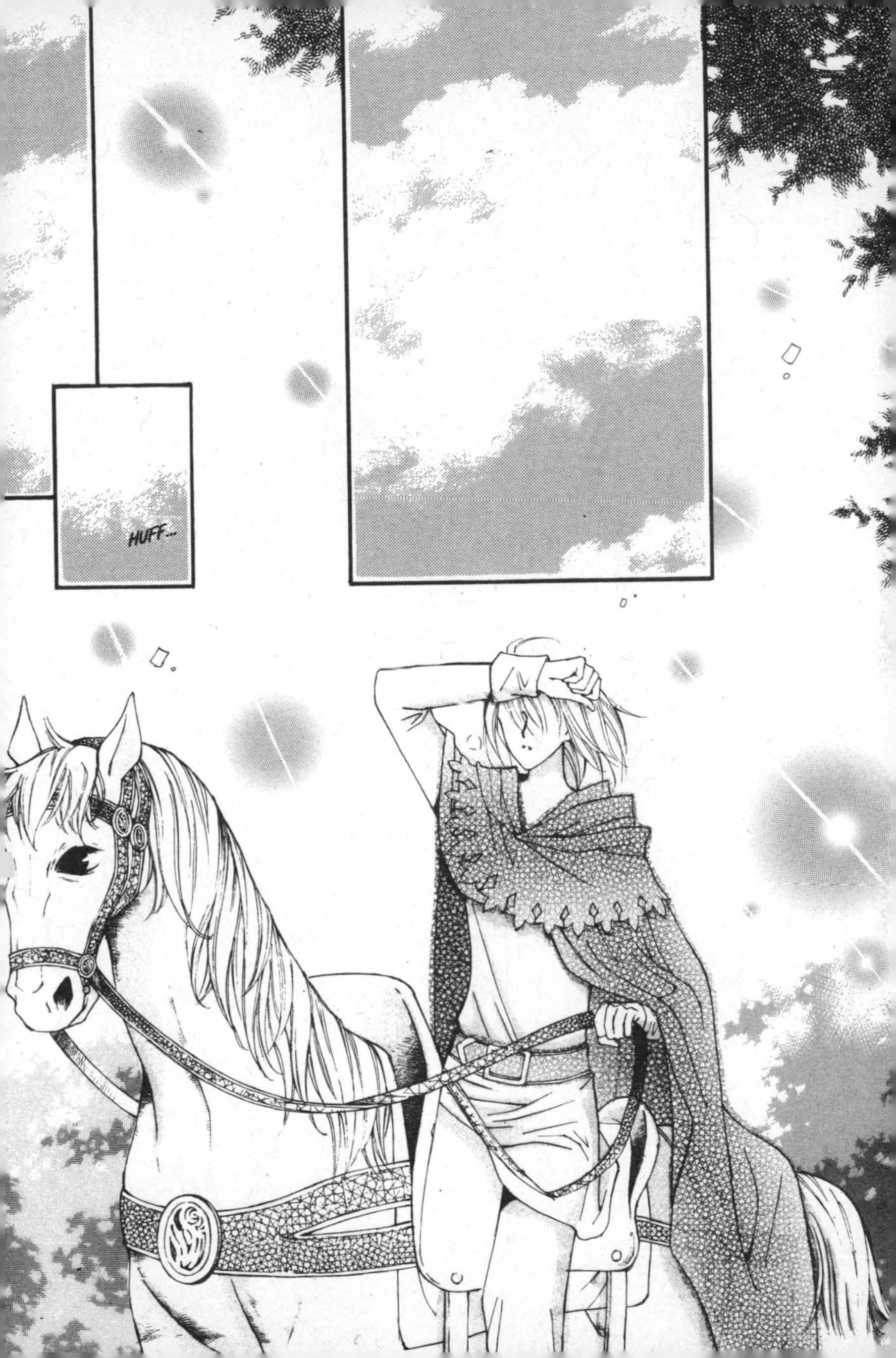
HUFF...

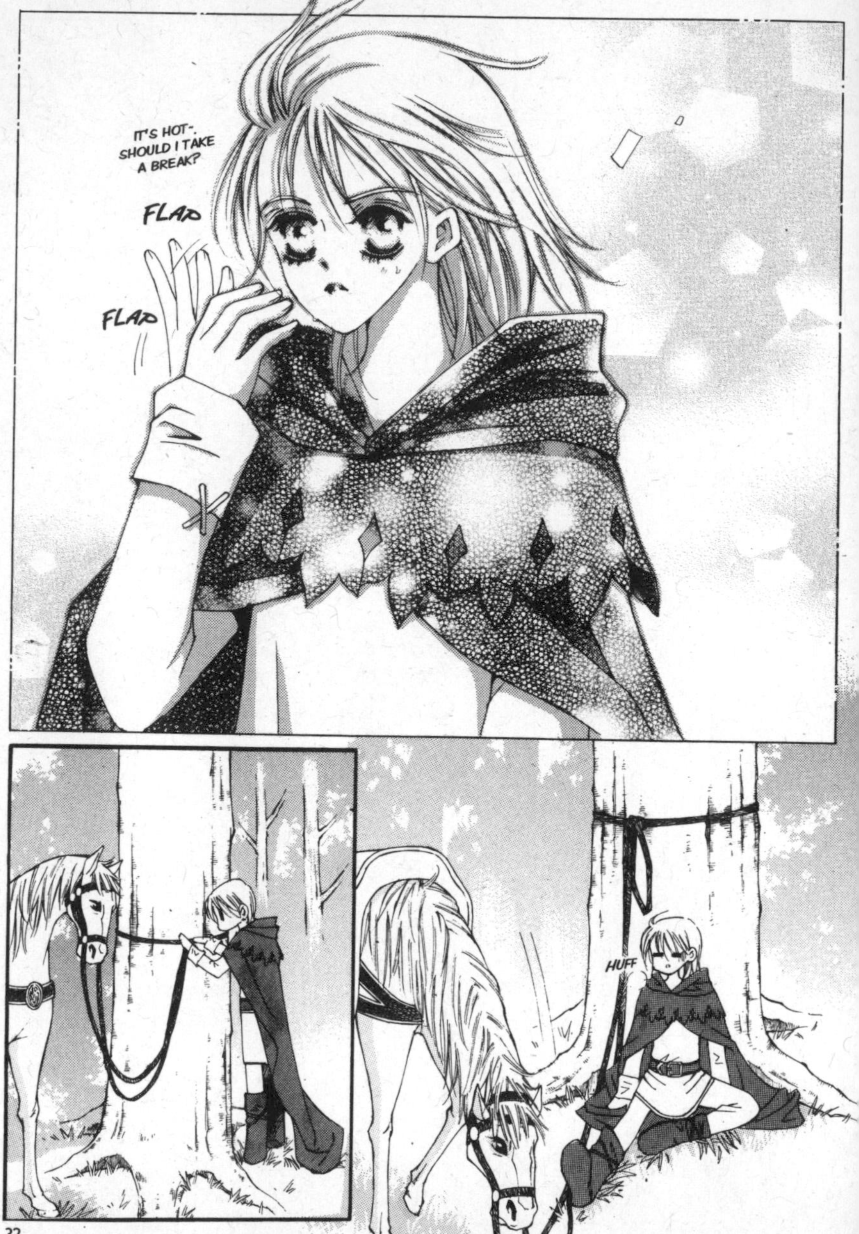
IT'S HOT-. SHOULD I TAKE A BREAK?
FLAP
FLAP
HUFF

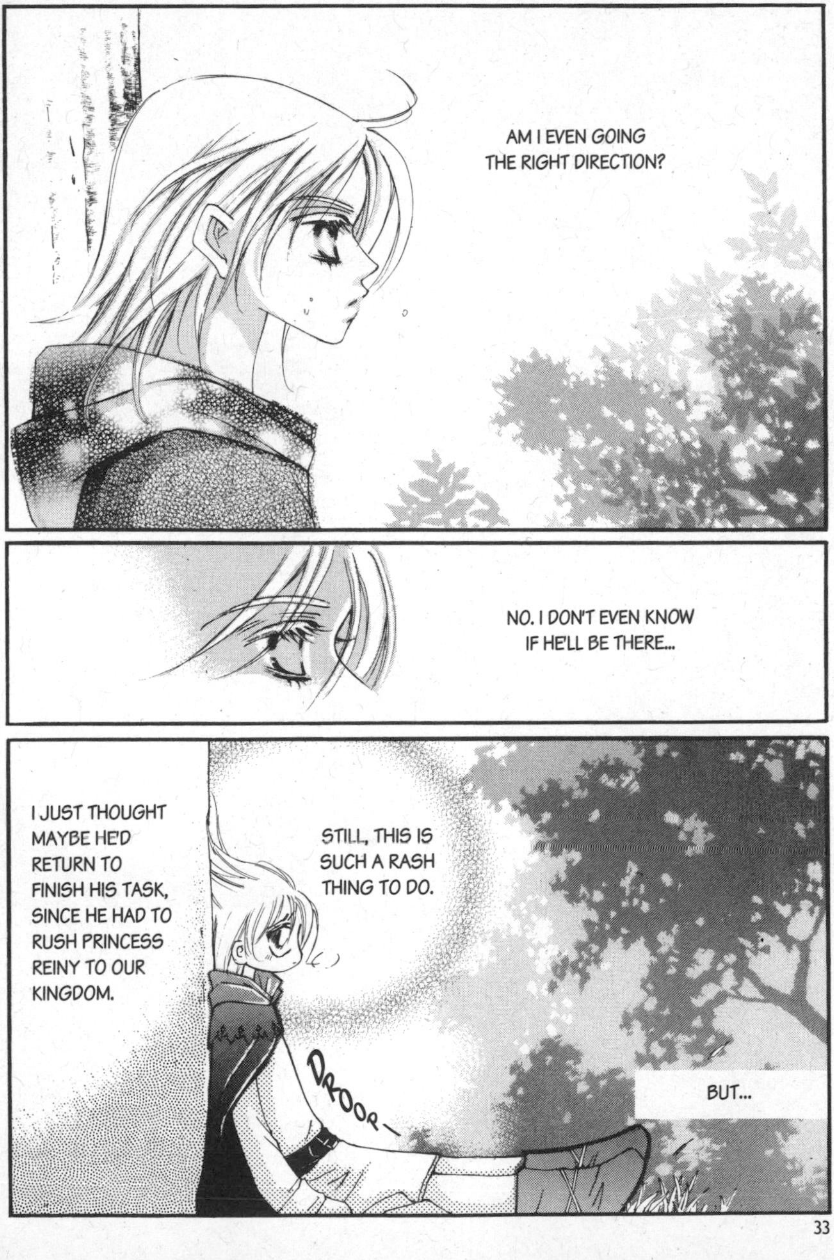
AM I EVEN GOING THE RIGHT DIRECTION?
NO. I DON'T EVEN KNOW IF HE'LL BE THERE...
STILL, THIS IS SUCH A RASH THING TO DO.
I JUST THOUGHT MAYBE HE'D RETURN TO FINISH HIS TASK, SINCE HE HAD TO RUSH PRINCESS REINY TO OUR KINGDOM.
BUT...
DROOP—

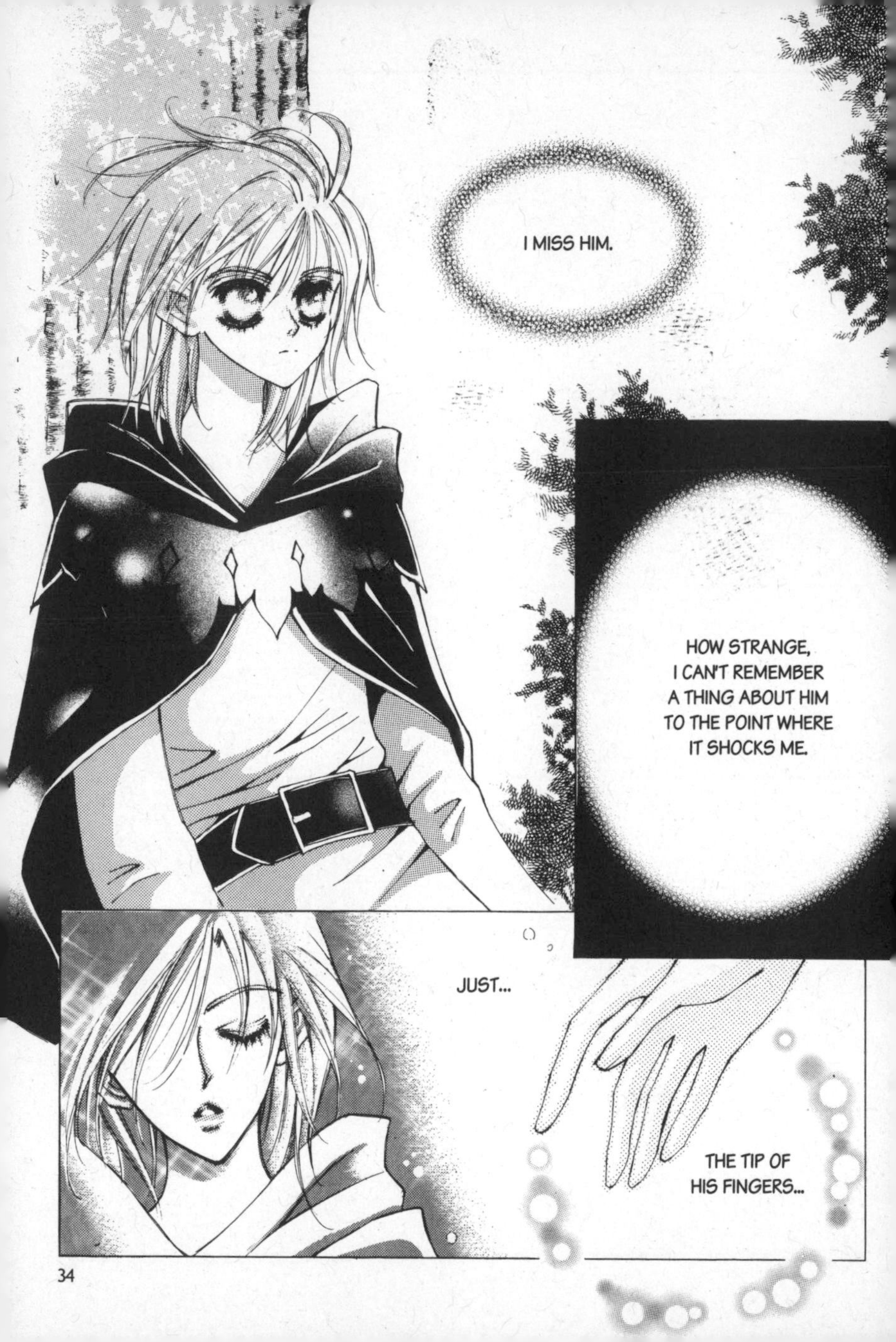
I MISS HIM.
HOW STRANGE, I CAN'T REMEMBER A THING ABOUT HIM TO THE POINT WHERE IT SHOCKS ME.
JUST...
THE TIP OF HIS FINGERS...

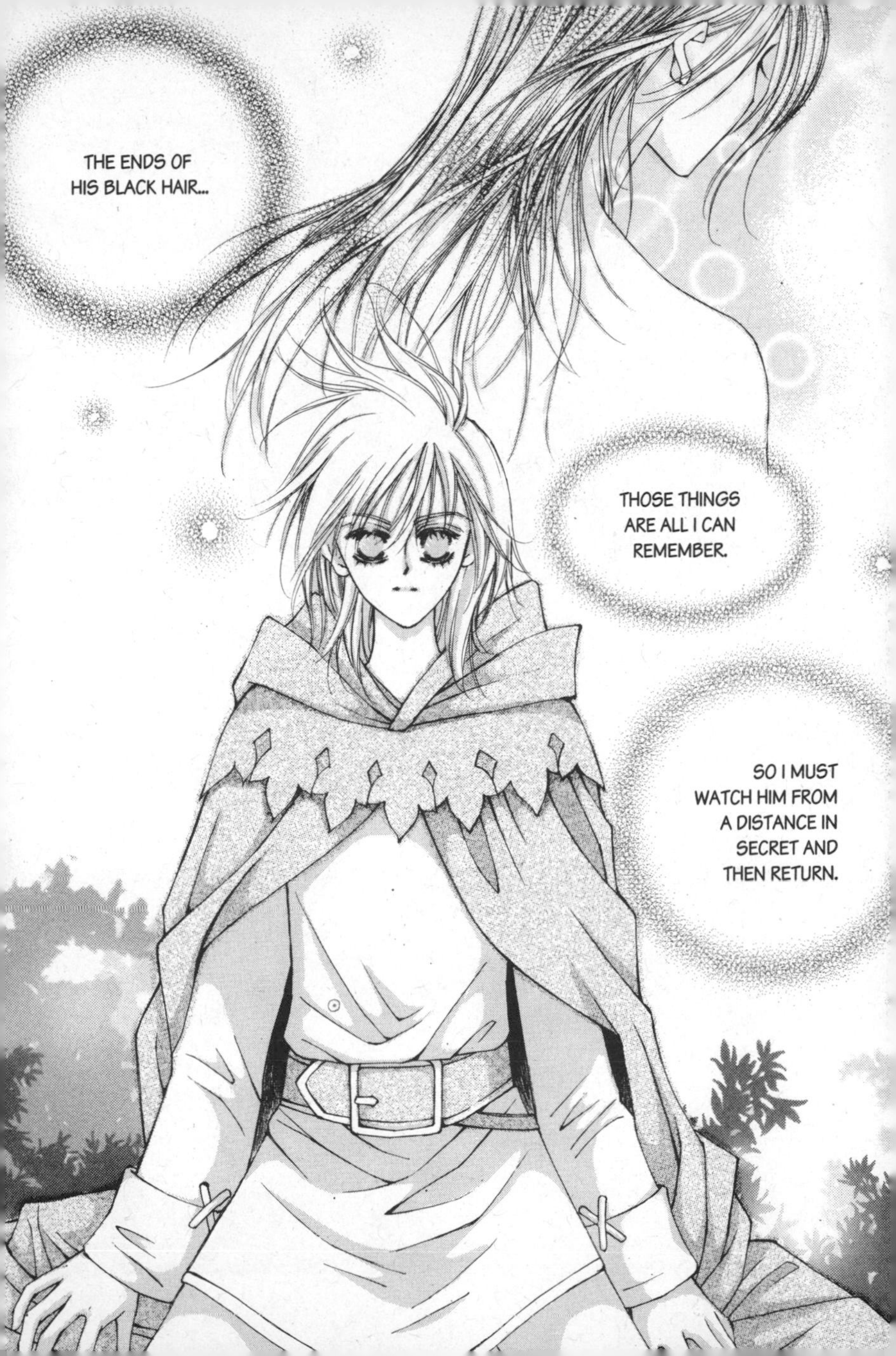
THE ENDS OF HIS BLACK HAIR...
THOSE THINGS ARE ALL I CAN REMEMBER.
SO I MUST WATCH HIM FROM A DISTANCE IN SECRET AND THEN RETURN.

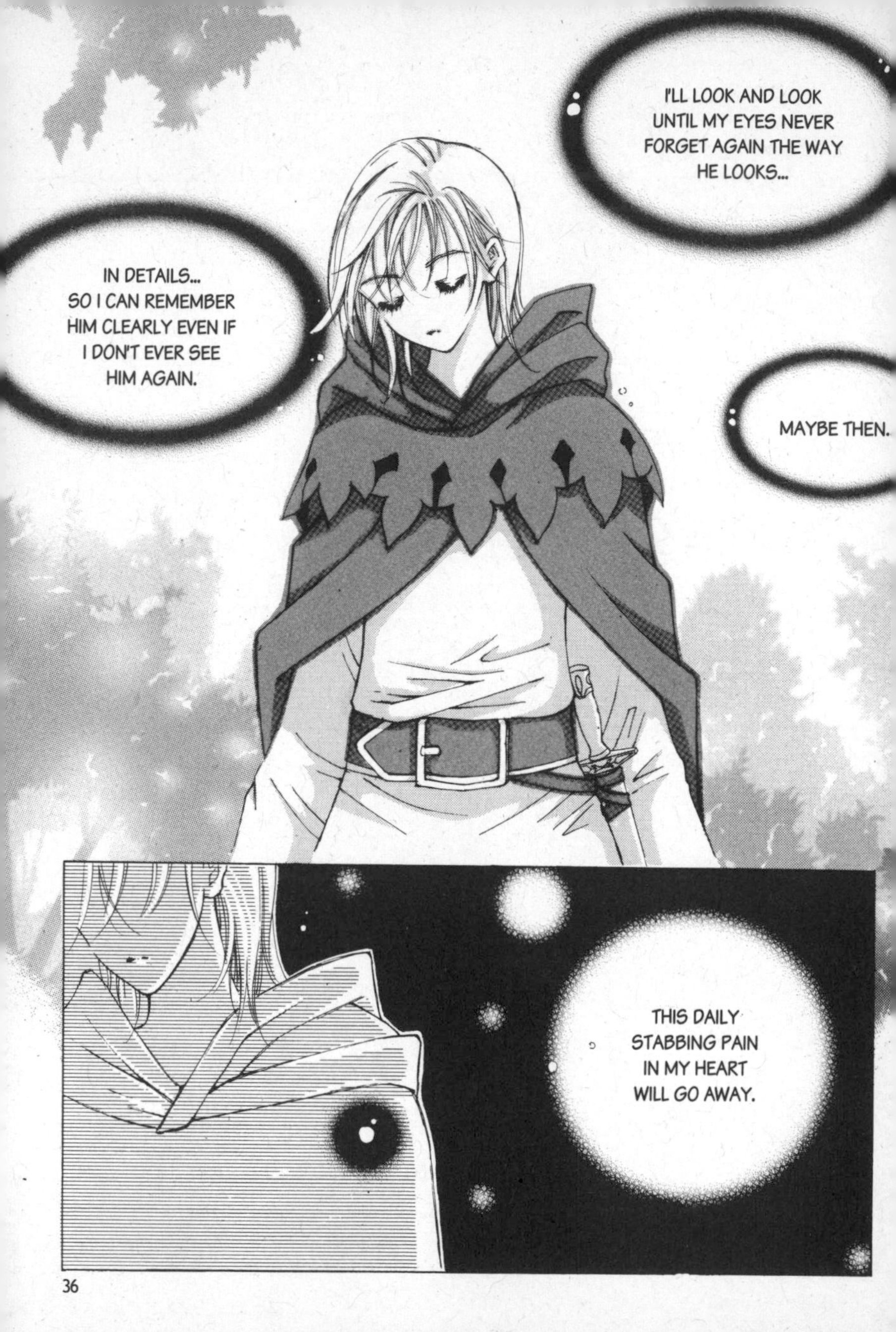
I'LL LOOK AND LOOK UNTIL MY EYES NEVER FORGET AGAIN THE WAY HE LOOKS...
IN DETAILS... SO I CAN REMEMBER HIM CLEARLY EVEN IF I DON'T EVER SEE HIM AGAIN.
MAYBE THEN.
THIS DAILY STABBING PAIN IN MY HEART WILL GO AWAY.

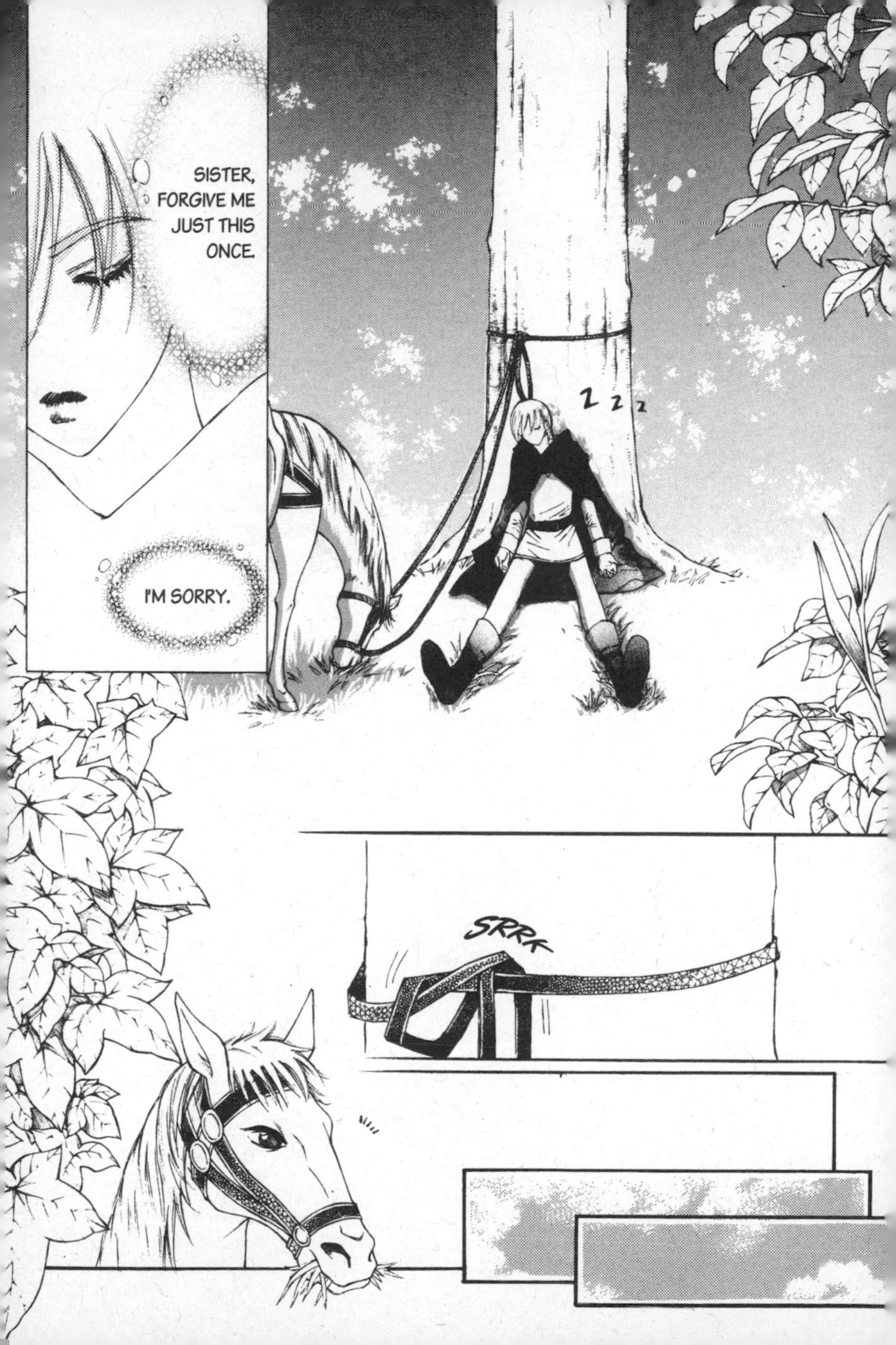
SISTER, FORGIVE ME JUST THIS ONCE.
I'M SORRY.
Z Z Z
SRRK

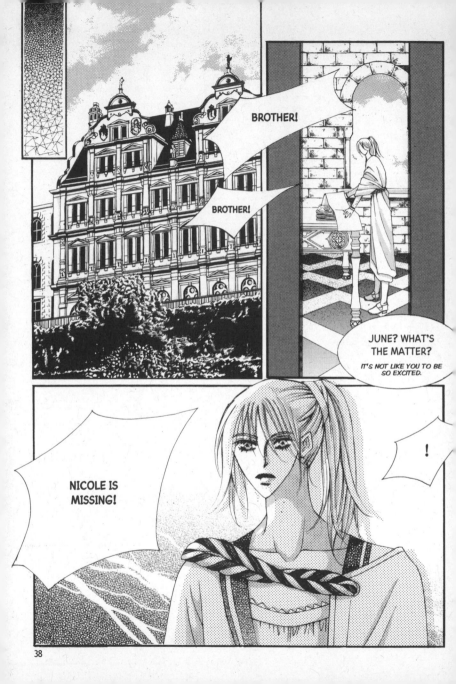

BROTHER!

BROTHER!

JUNE? WHAT'S THE MATTER?

IT'S NOT LIKE YOU TO BE SO EXCITED.

!

NICOLE IS MISSING!

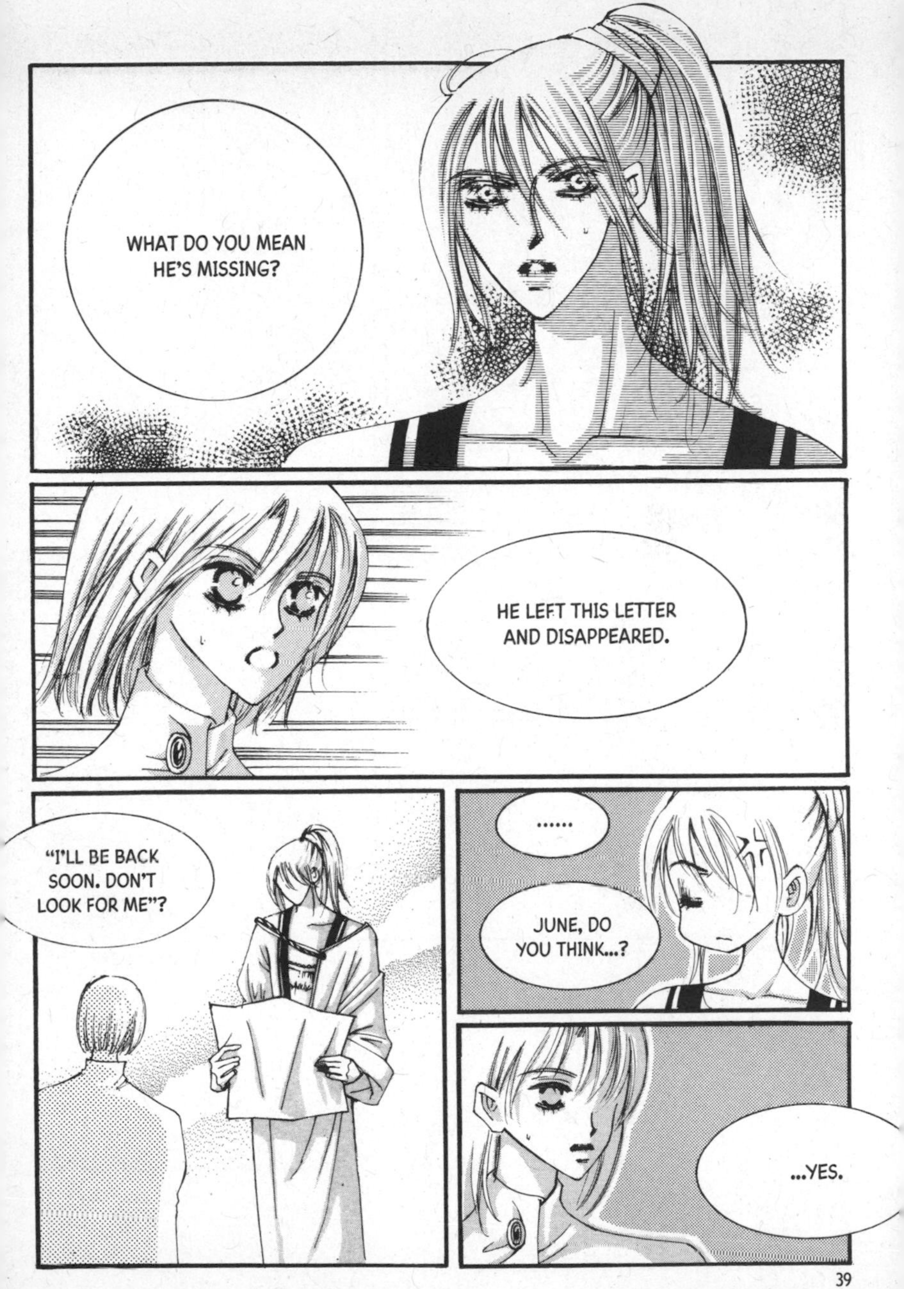
WHAT DO YOU MEAN HE'S MISSING?
HE LEFT THIS LETTER AND DISAPPEARED.
"I'LL BE BACK SOON. DON'T LOOK FOR ME"?
......
JUNE, DO YOU THINK...?
...YES.

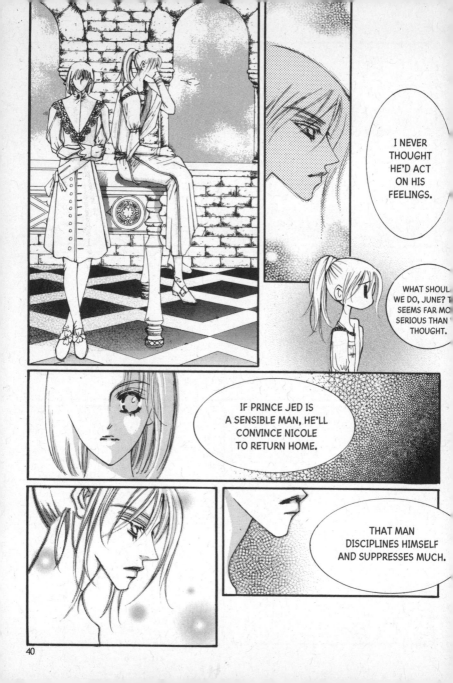

I NEVER THOUGHT HE'D ACT ON HIS FEELINGS.

WHAT SHOUL WE DO, JUNE? T SEEMS FAR MC SERIOUS THAN THOUGHT.

IF PRINCE JED IS A SENSIBLE MAN, HE'LL CONVINCE NICOLE TO RETURN HOME.

THAT MAN DISCIPLINES HIMSELF AND SUPPRESSES MUCH.

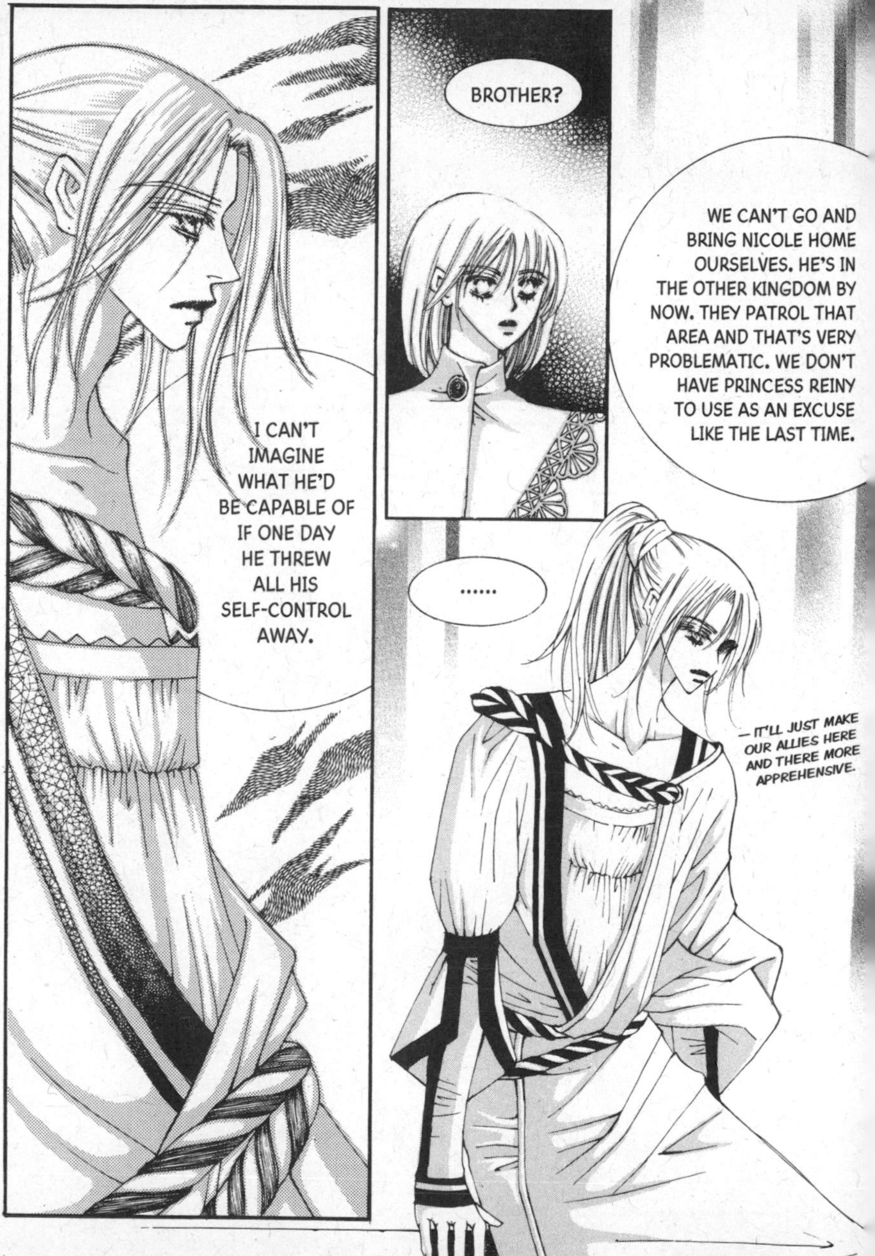
I CAN'T IMAGINE WHAT HE'D BE CAPABLE OF IF ONE DAY HE THREW ALL HIS SELF-CONTROL AWAY.
BROTHER?
WE CAN'T GO AND BRING NICOLE HOME OURSELVES. HE'S IN THE OTHER KINGDOM BY NOW. THEY PATROL THAT AREA AND THAT'S VERY PROBLEMATIC. WE DON'T HAVE PRINCESS REINY TO USE AS AN EXCUSE LIKE THE LAST TIME.
......
—IT'LL JUST MAKE OUR ALLIES HERE AND THERE MORE APPREHENSIVE.

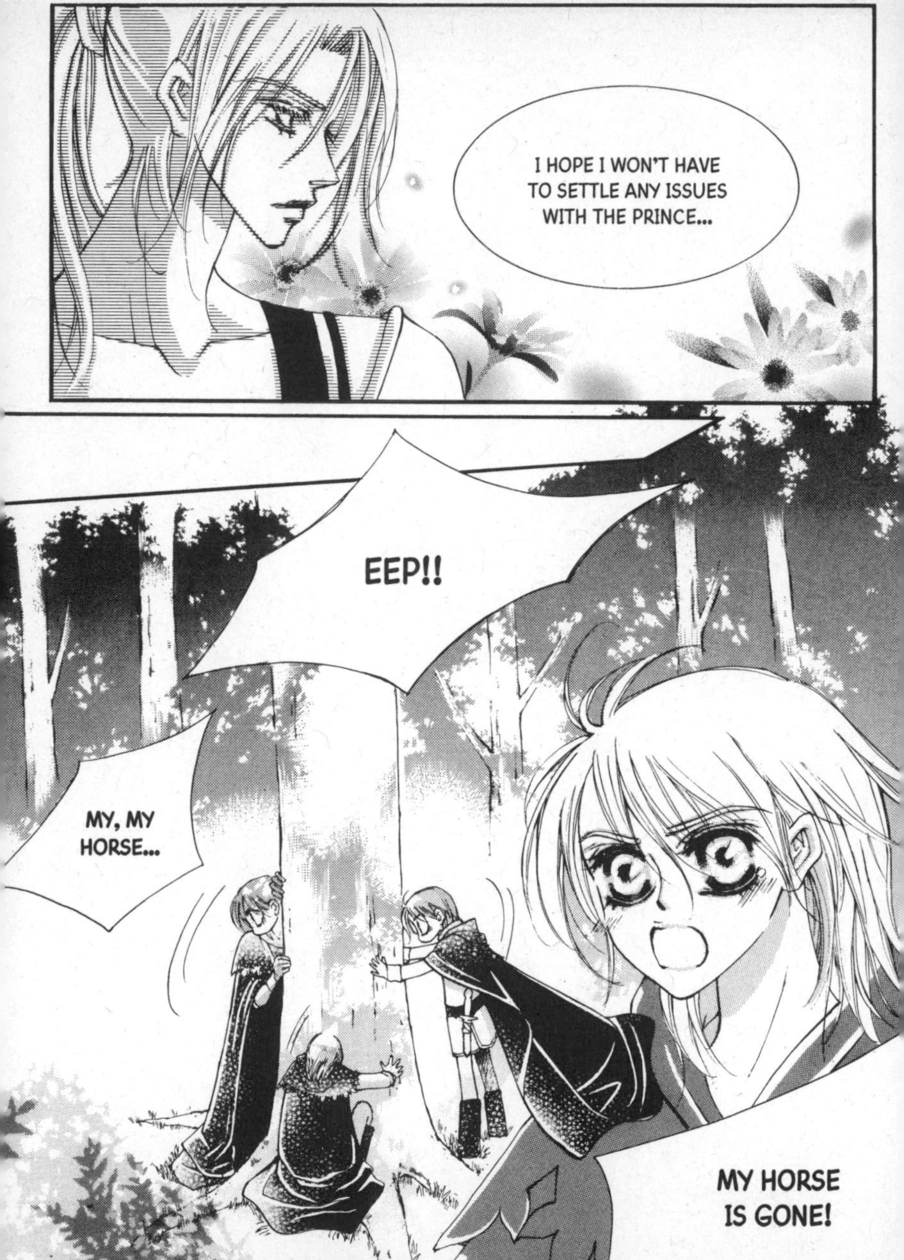
I HOPE I WON'T HAVE TO SETTLE ANY ISSUES WITH THE PRINCE...
EEP!!
MY, MY HORSE...
MY HORSE IS GONE!

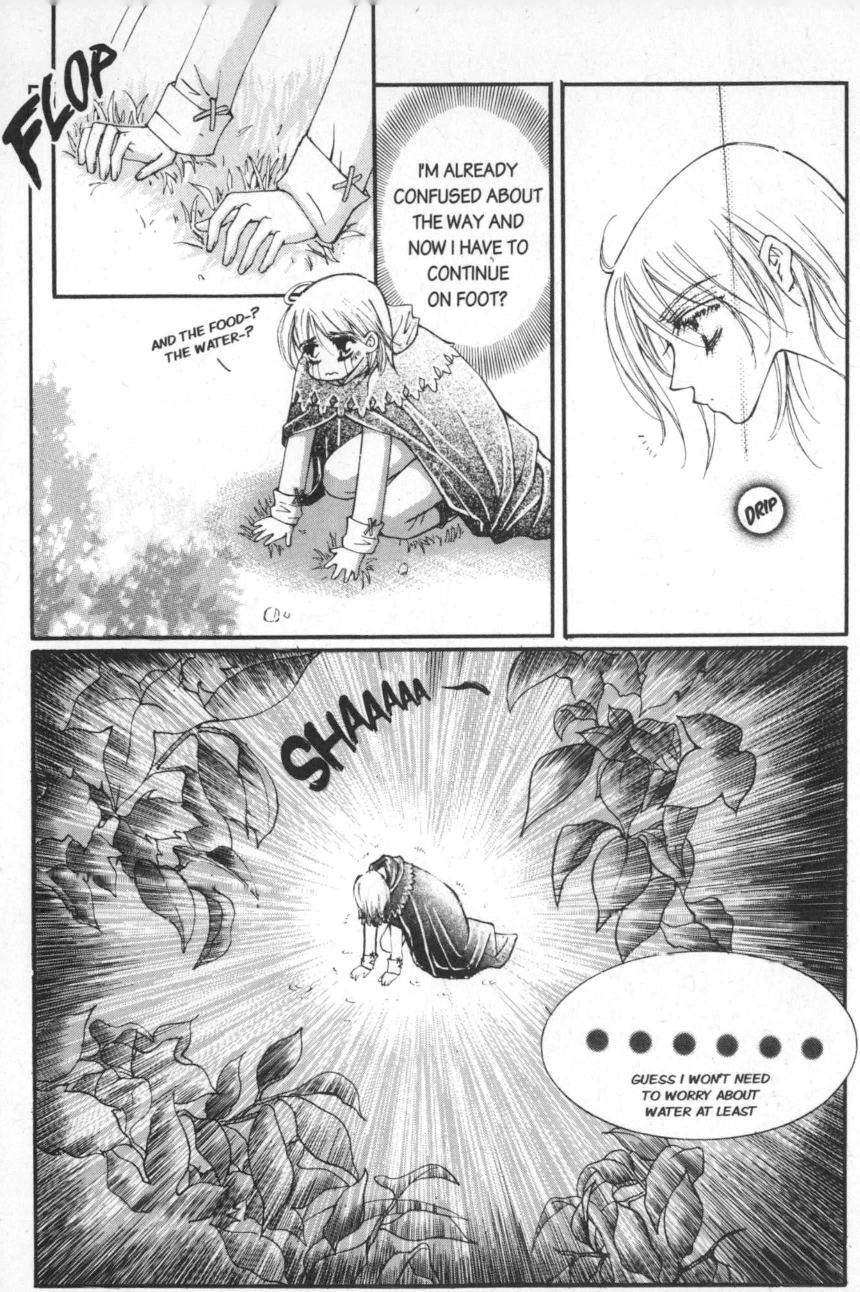
FLOP
I'M ALREADY CONFUSED ABOUT THE WAY AND NOW I HAVE TO CONTINUE ON FOOT?
AND THE FOOD-? THE WATER-?
DRIP
SHAAAAA
● ● ● ● ● ●
GUESS I WON'T NEED TO WORRY ABOUT WATER AT LEAST

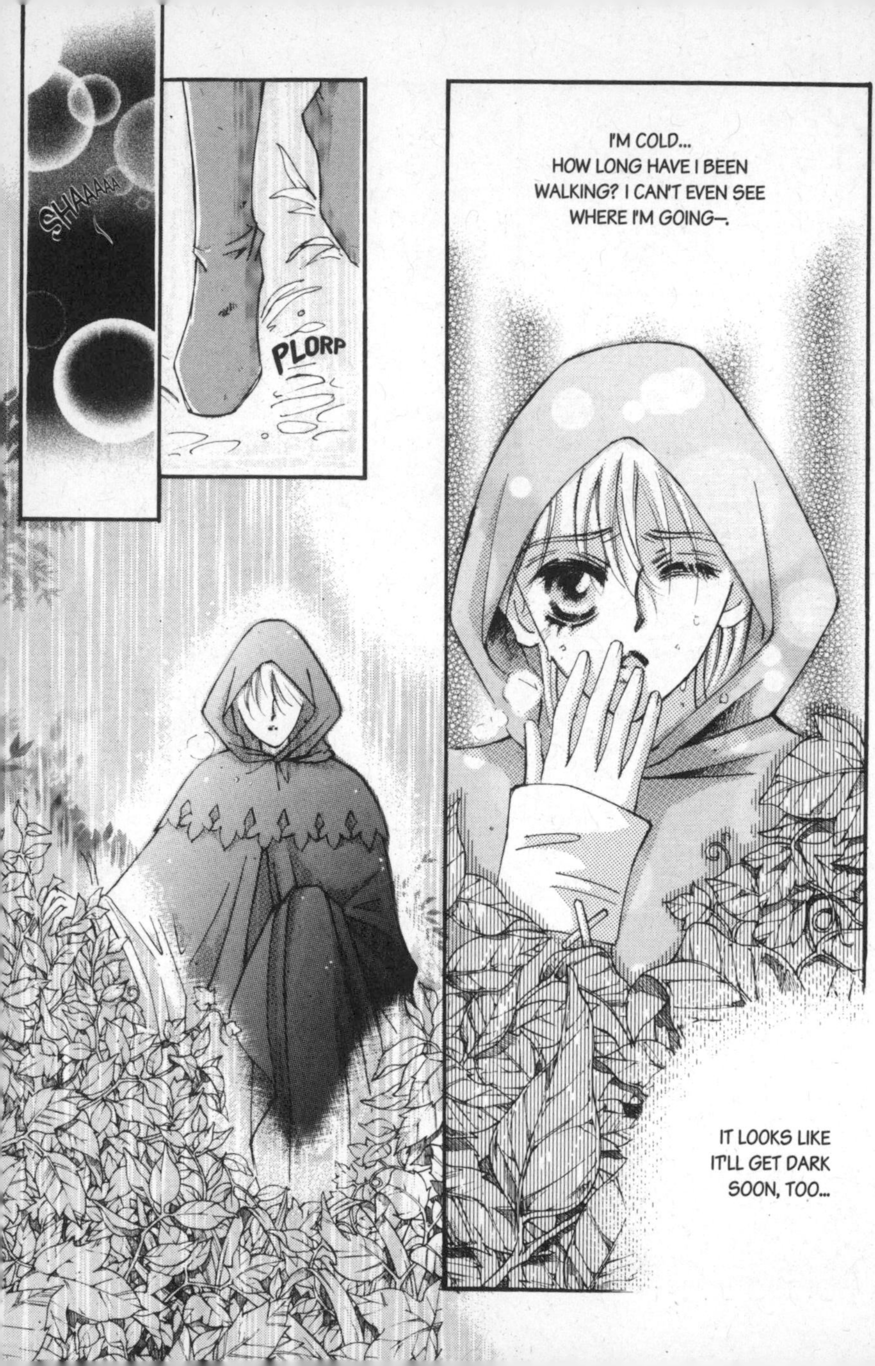
SHAAAAA
PLORP
I'M COLD... HOW LONG HAVE I BEEN WALKING? I CAN'T EVEN SEE WHERE I'M GOING—.
IT LOOKS LIKE IT'LL GET DARK SOON, TOO...

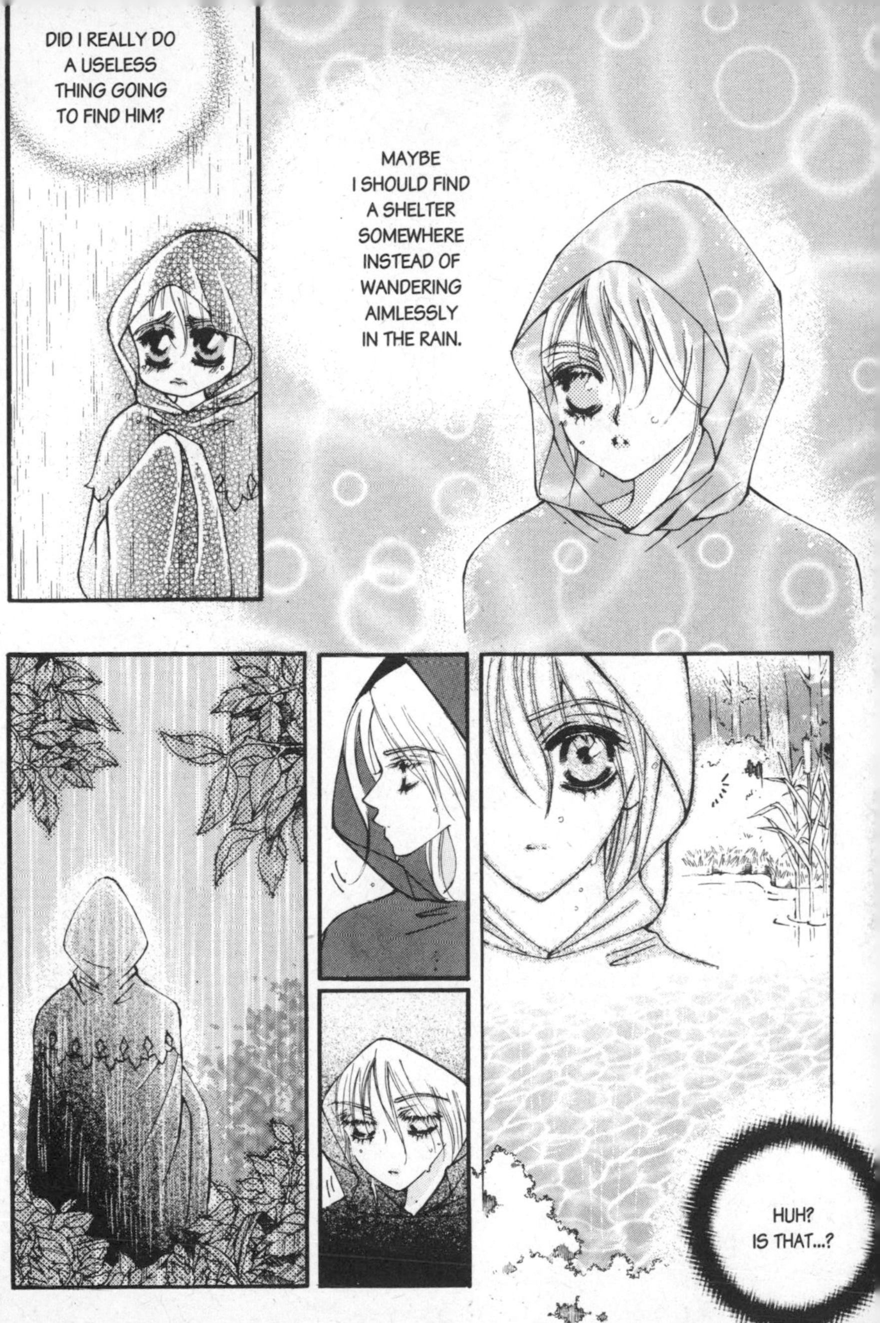
DID I REALLY DO A USELESS THING GOING TO FIND HIM?
MAYBE I SHOULD FIND A SHELTER SOMEWHERE INSTEAD OF WANDERING AIMLESSLY IN THE RAIN.
HUH? IS THAT...?

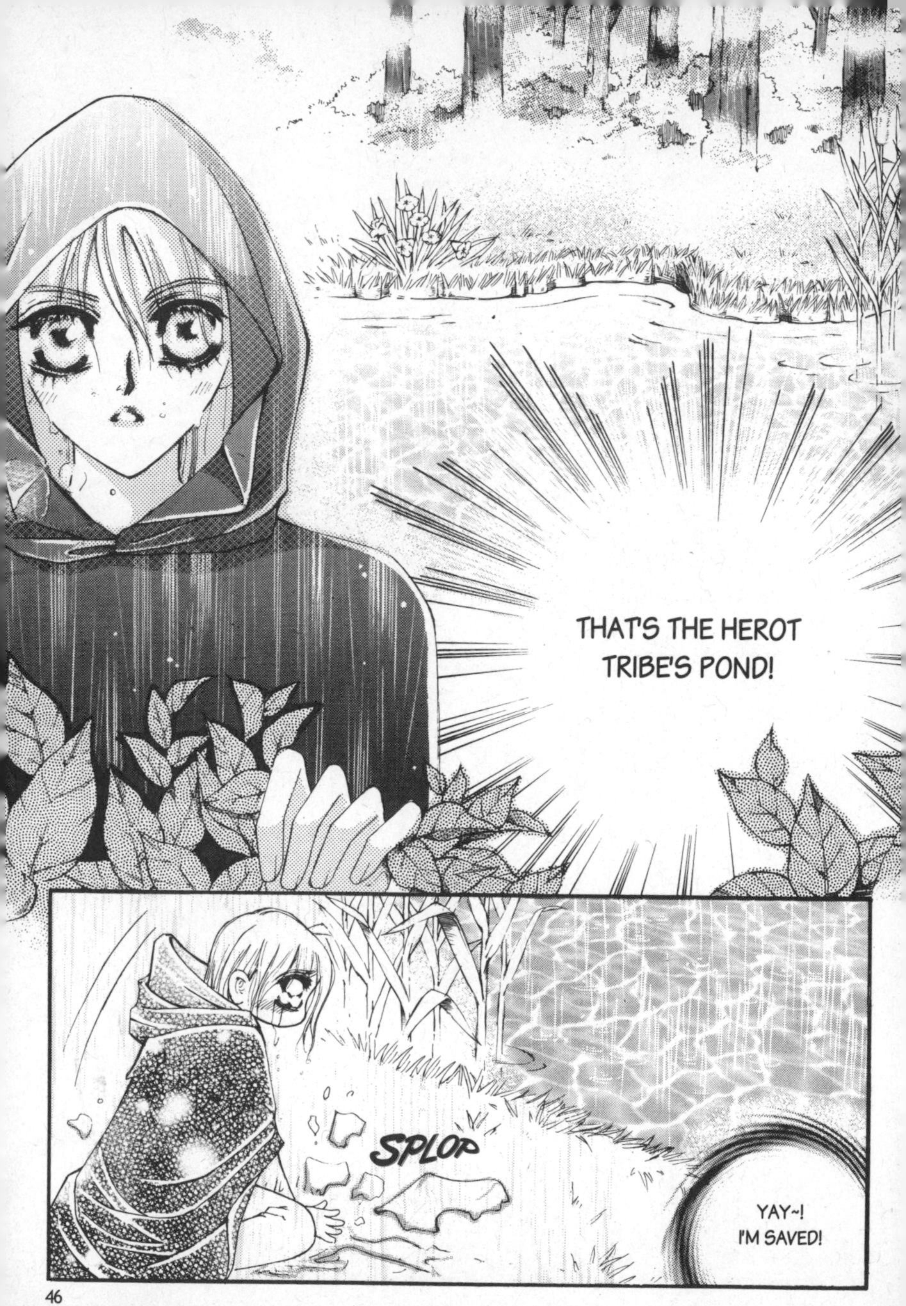
THAT'S THE HEROT
TRIBE'S POND!
SPLOP
YAY~!
I'M SAVED!

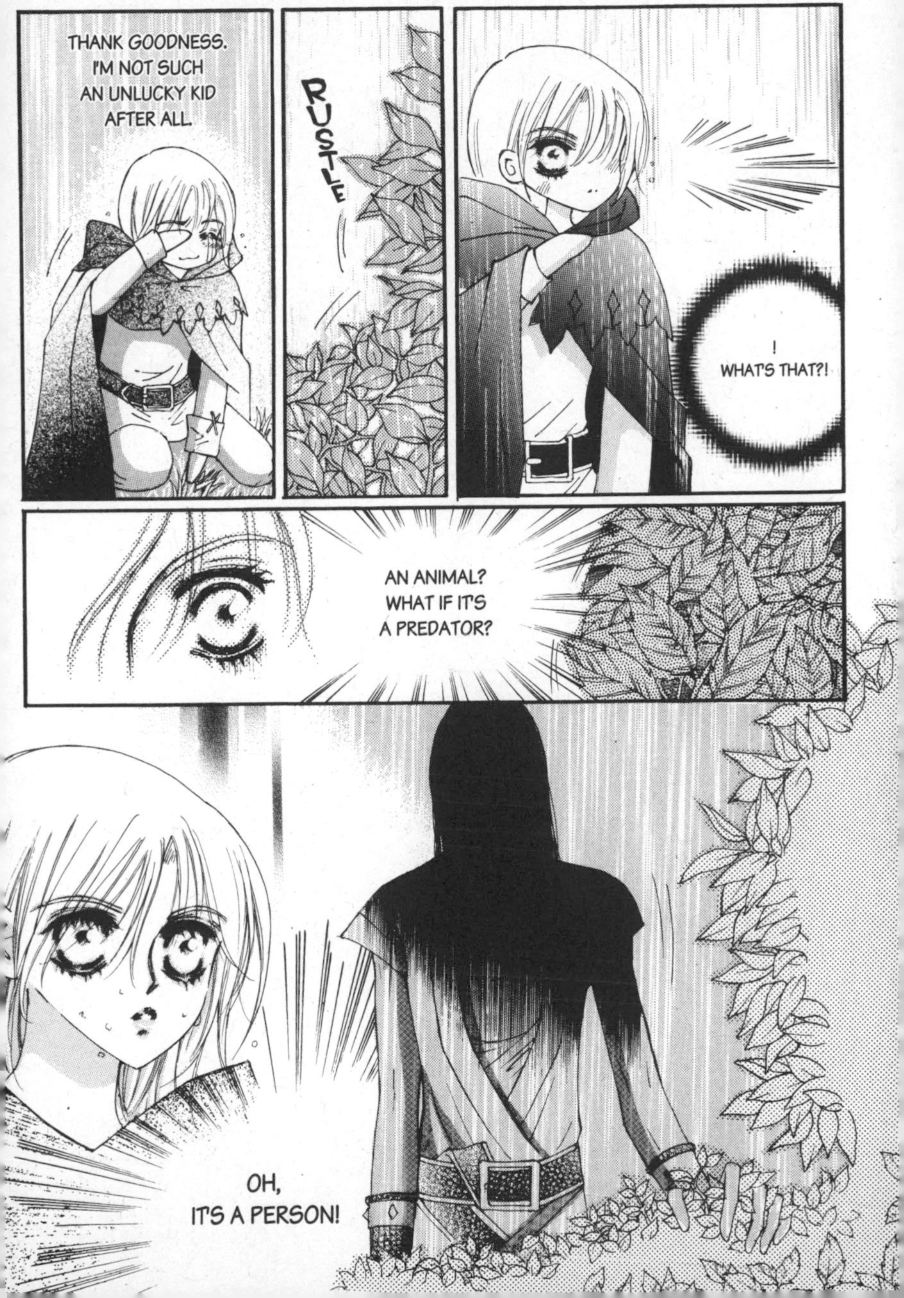
THANK GOODNESS. I'M NOT SUCH AN UNLUCKY KID AFTER ALL.
RUSTLE
!
WHAT'S THAT?!
AN ANIMAL? WHAT IF IT'S A PREDATOR?
OH, IT'S A PERSON!

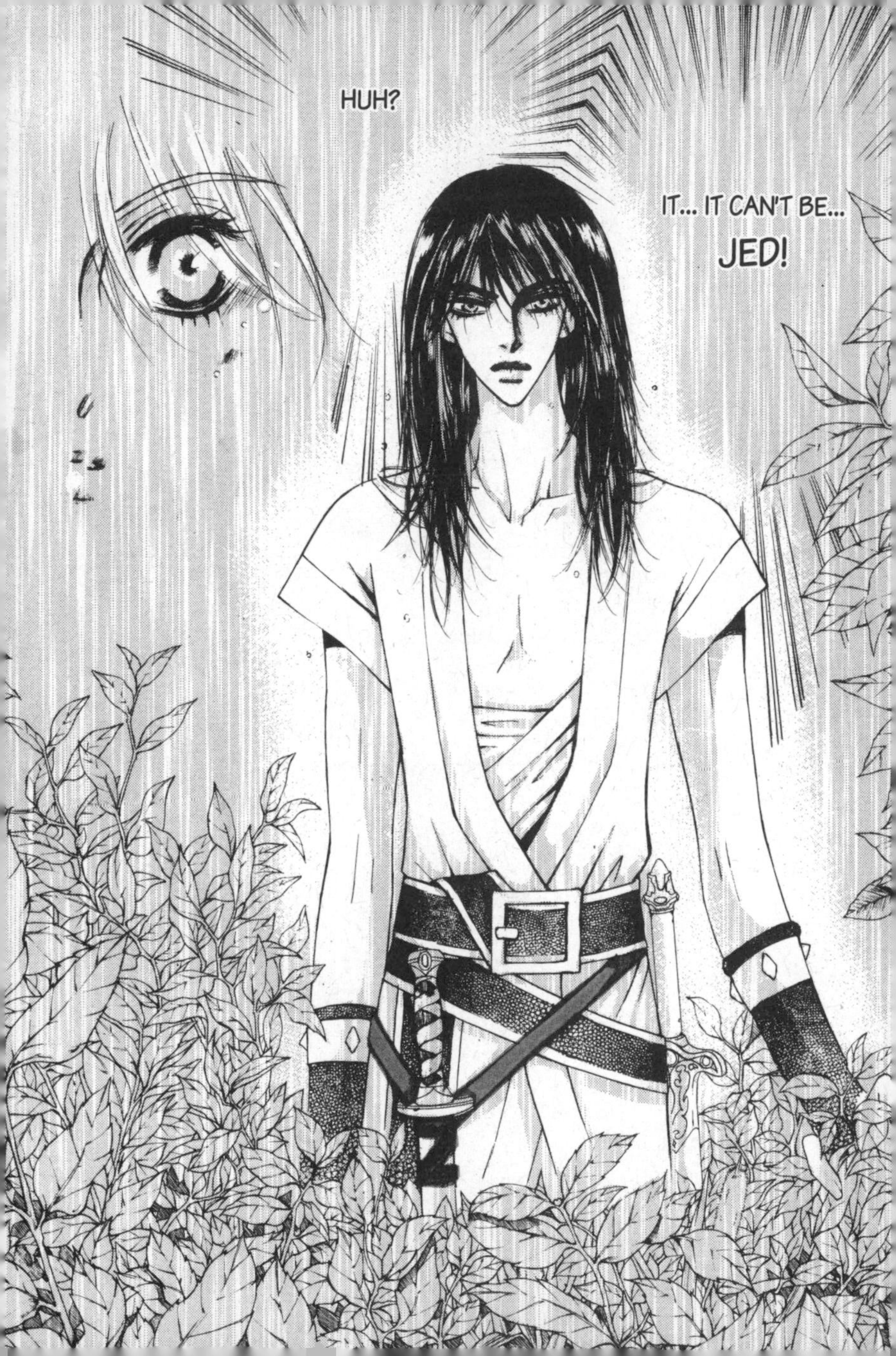
HUH?
IT... IT CAN'T BE...
JED!

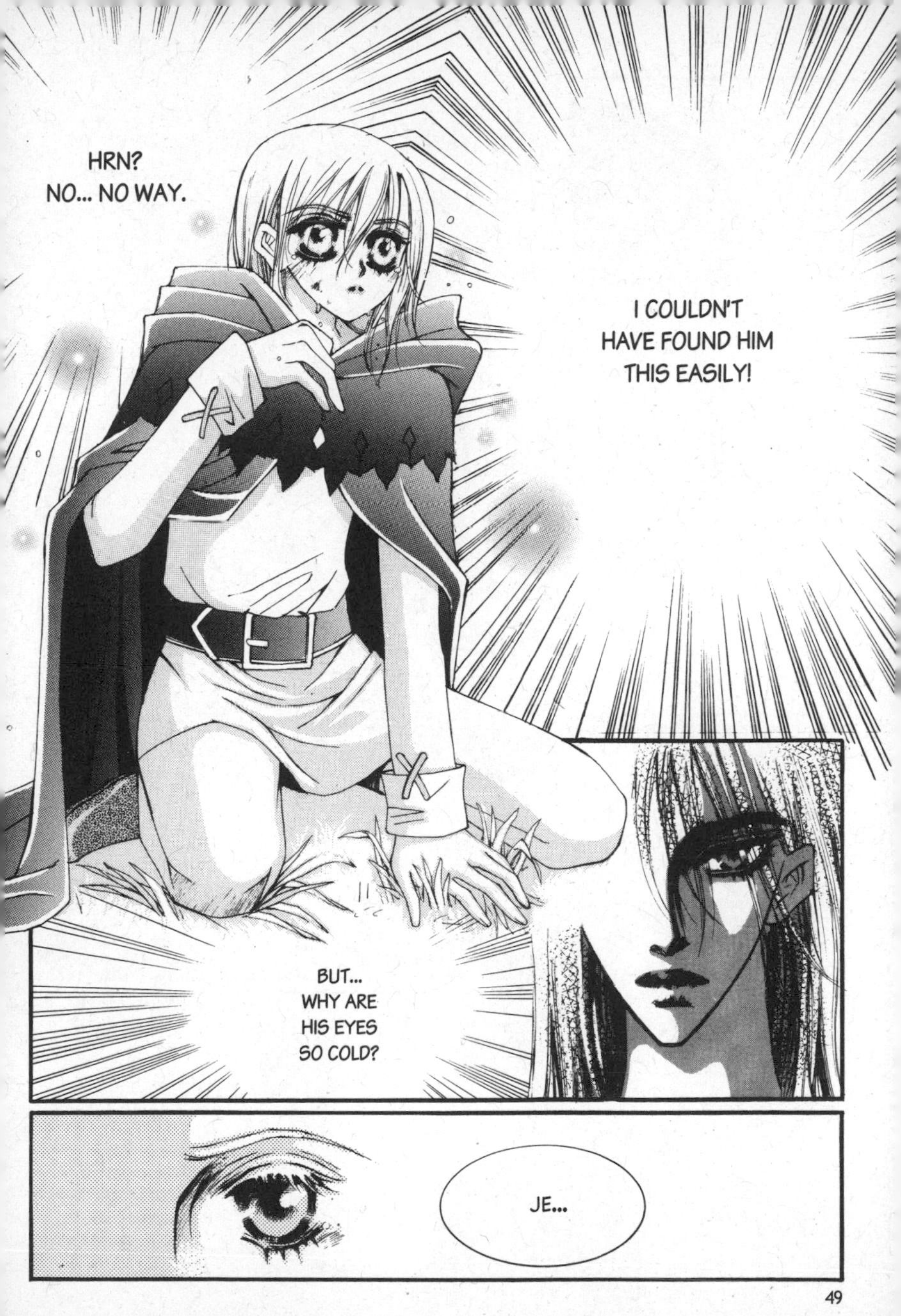
HRN?
NO... NO WAY.
I COULDN'T HAVE FOUND HIM THIS EASILY!
BUT... WHY ARE HIS EYES SO COLD?
JE...

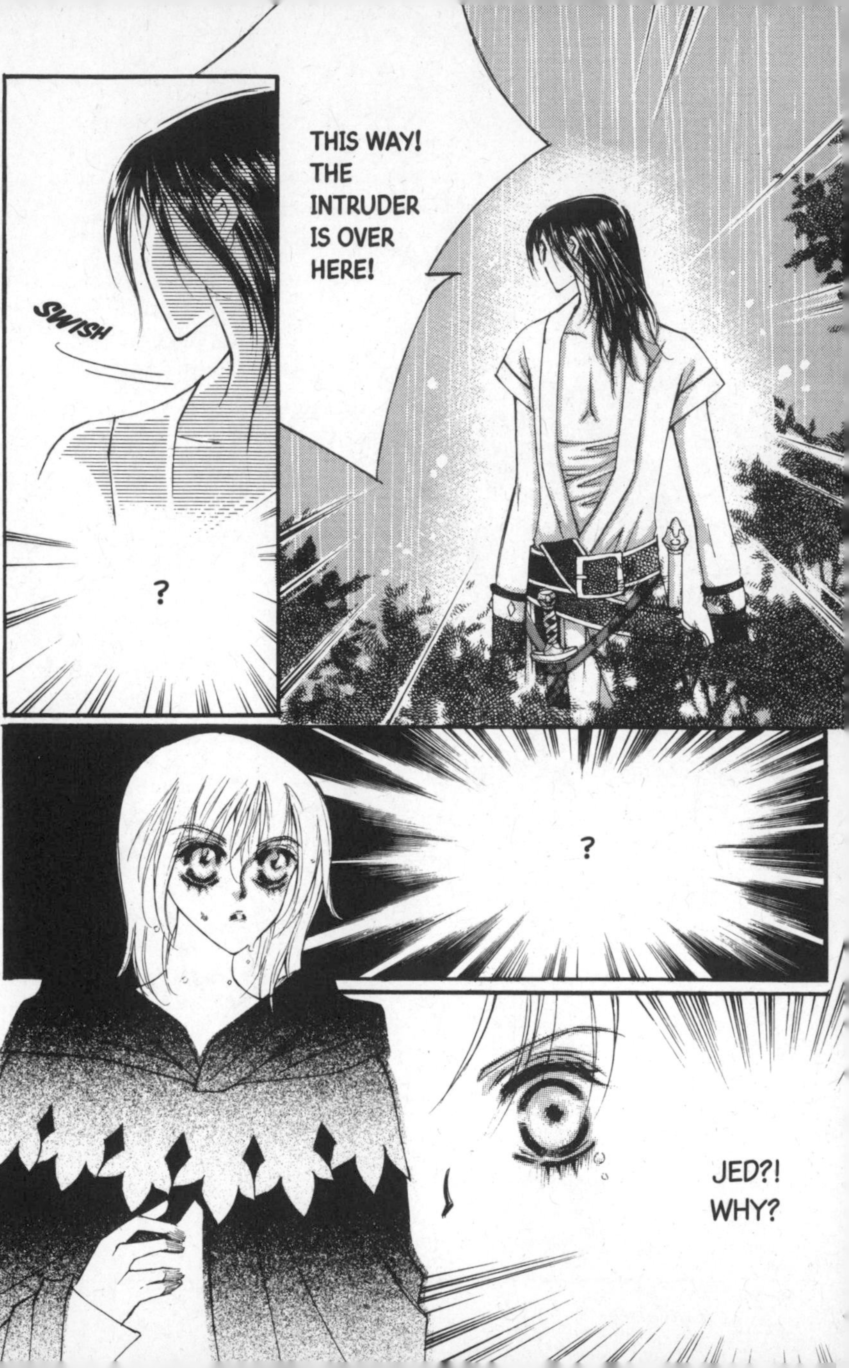
THIS WAY! THE INTRUDER IS OVER HERE!
SWISH
?
?
JED?! WHY?

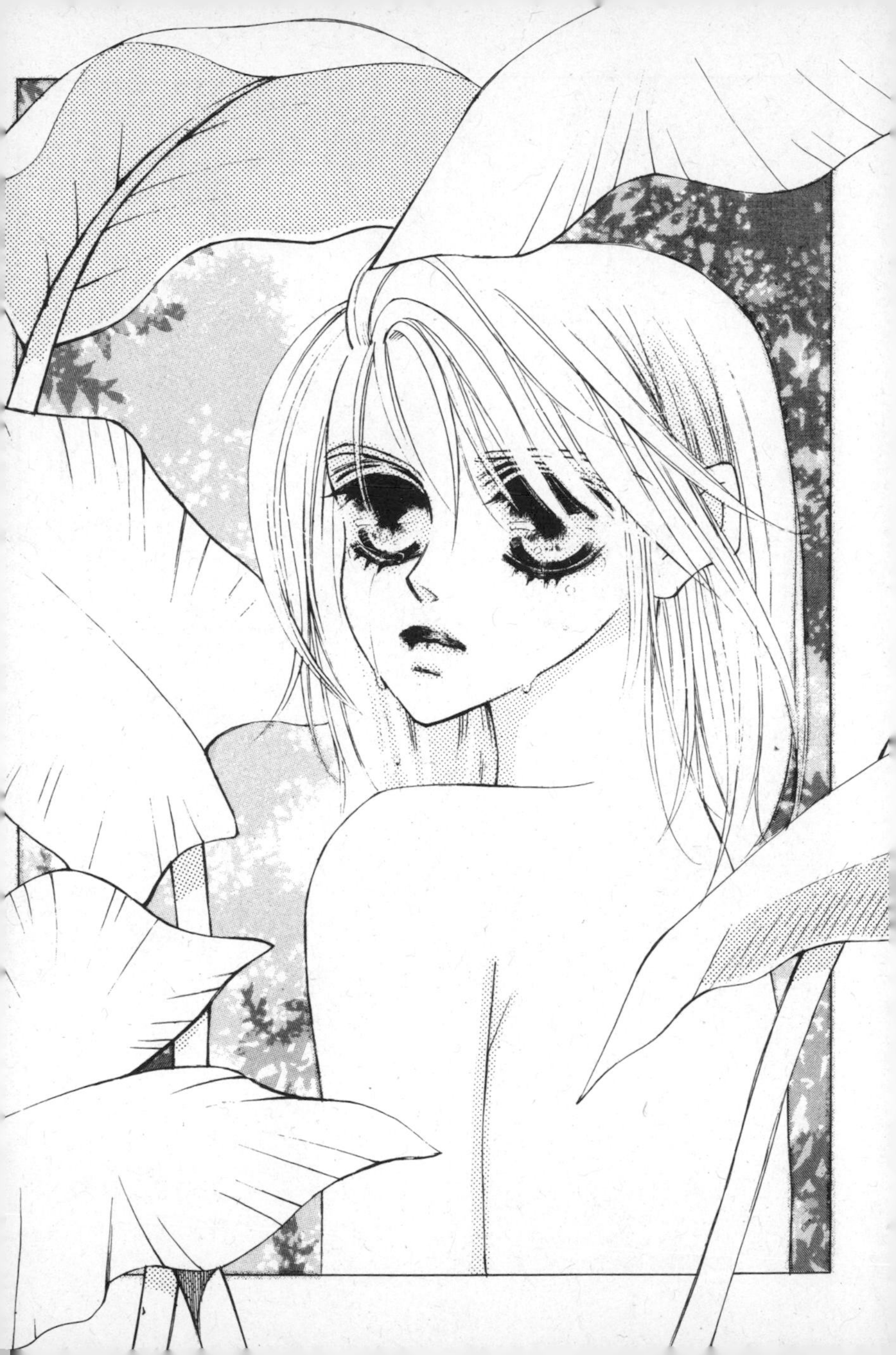

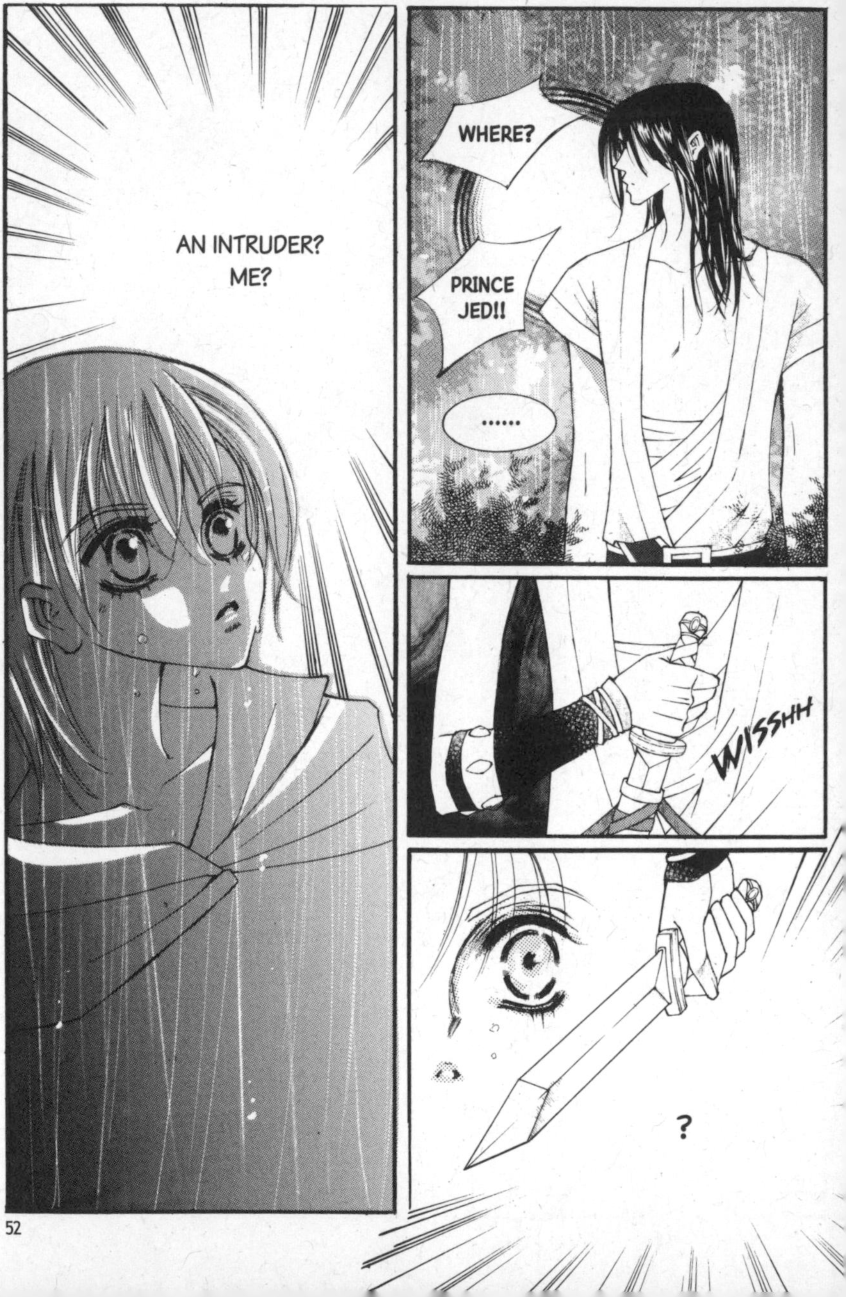
AN INTRUDER? ME?
WHERE?
PRINCE JED!!
......
WISSHH
?

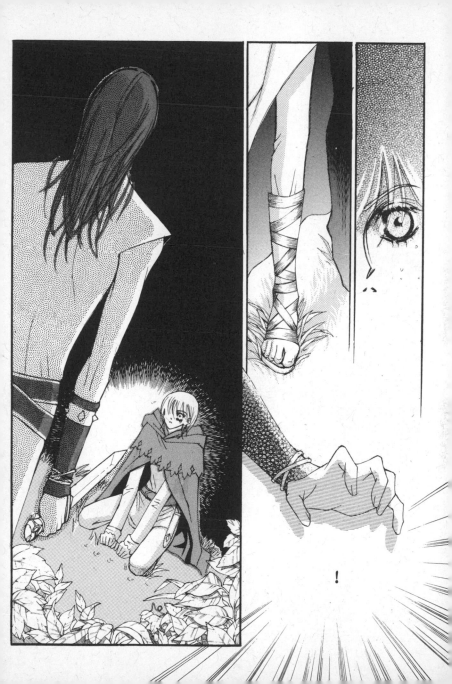

!

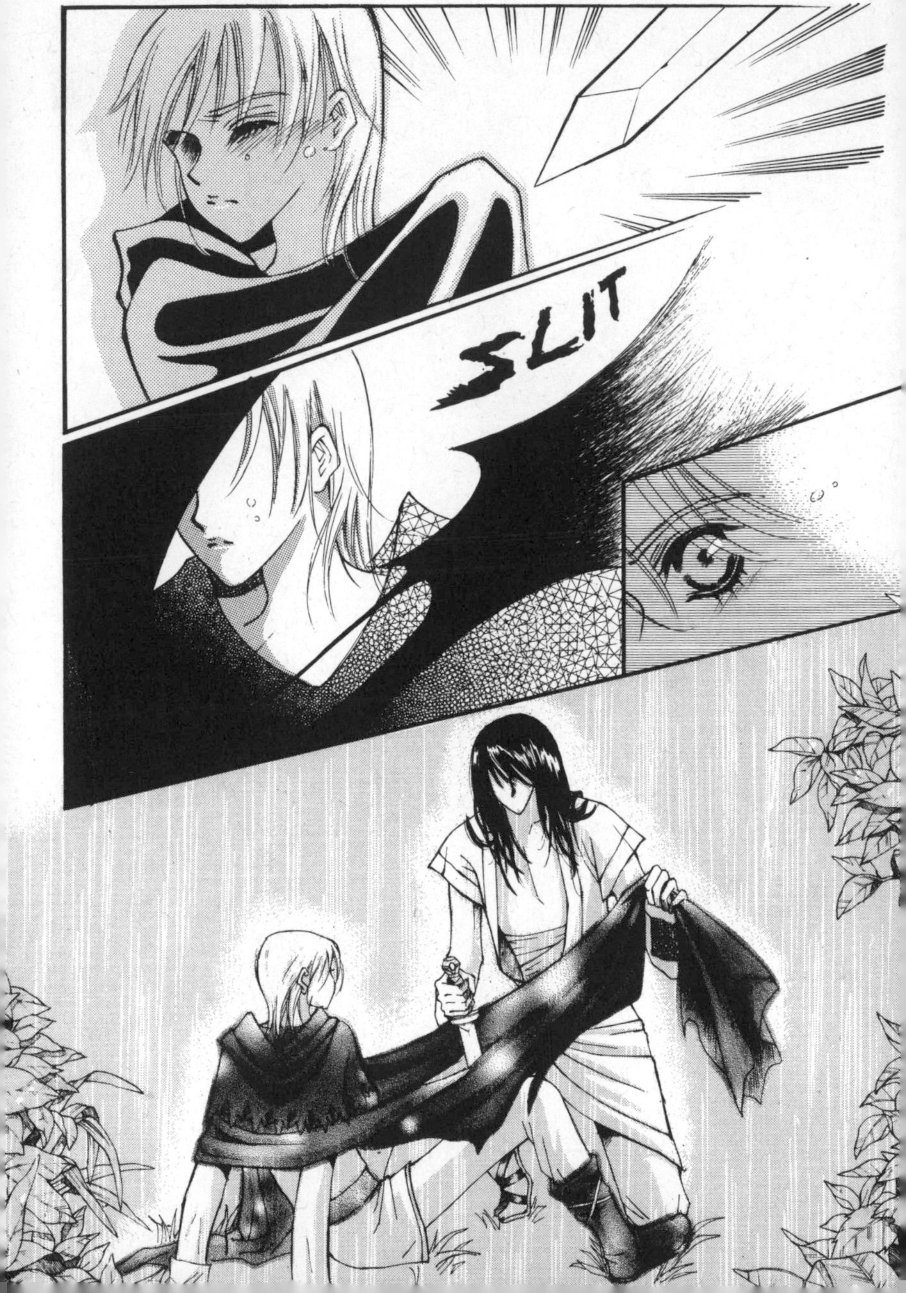
SLIT

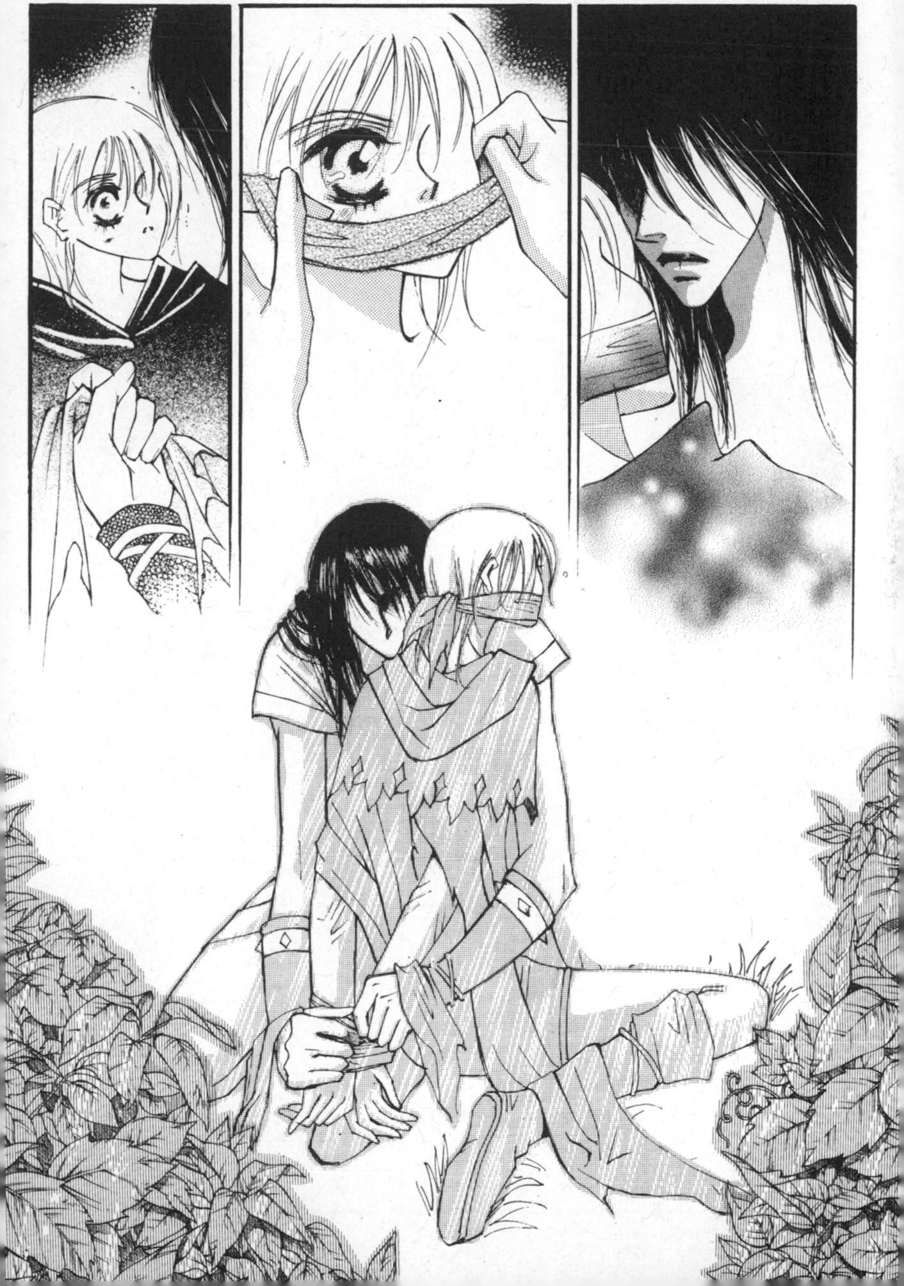

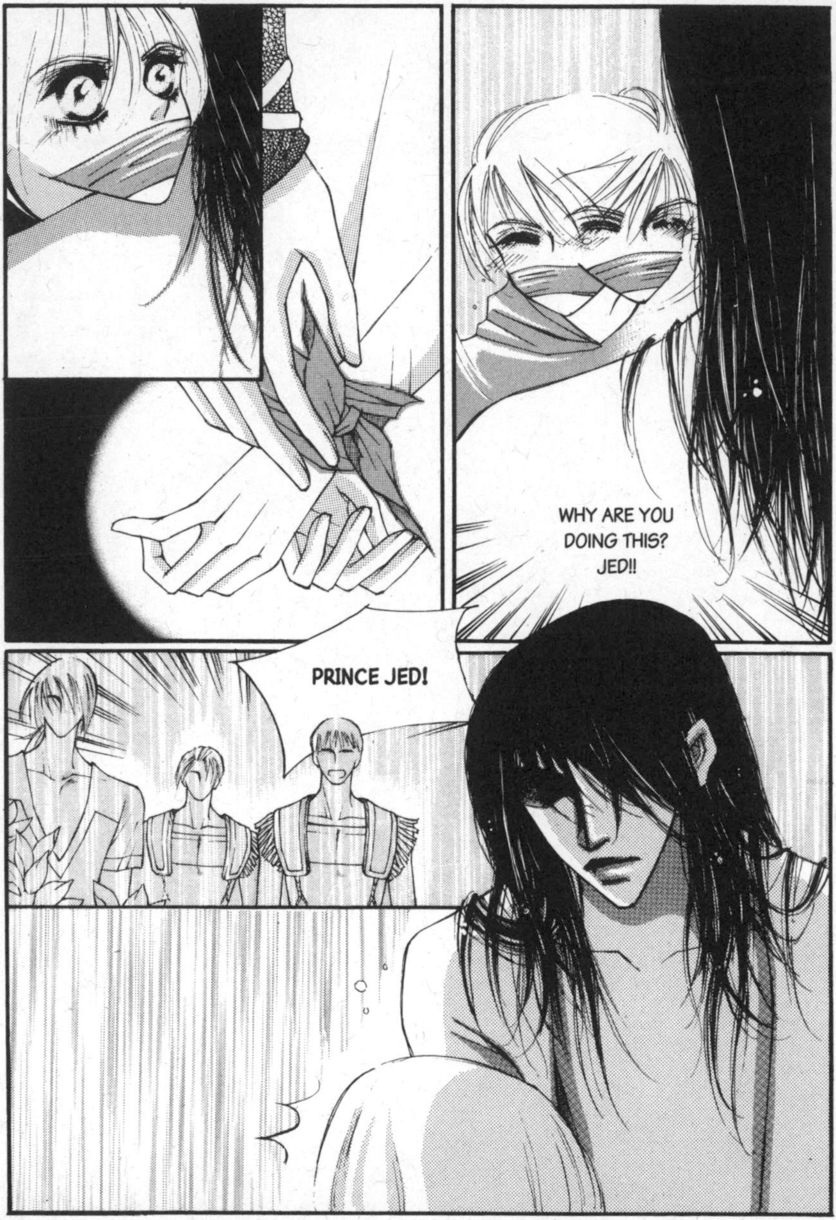
WHY ARE YOU
DOING THIS?
JED!!
PRINCE JED!

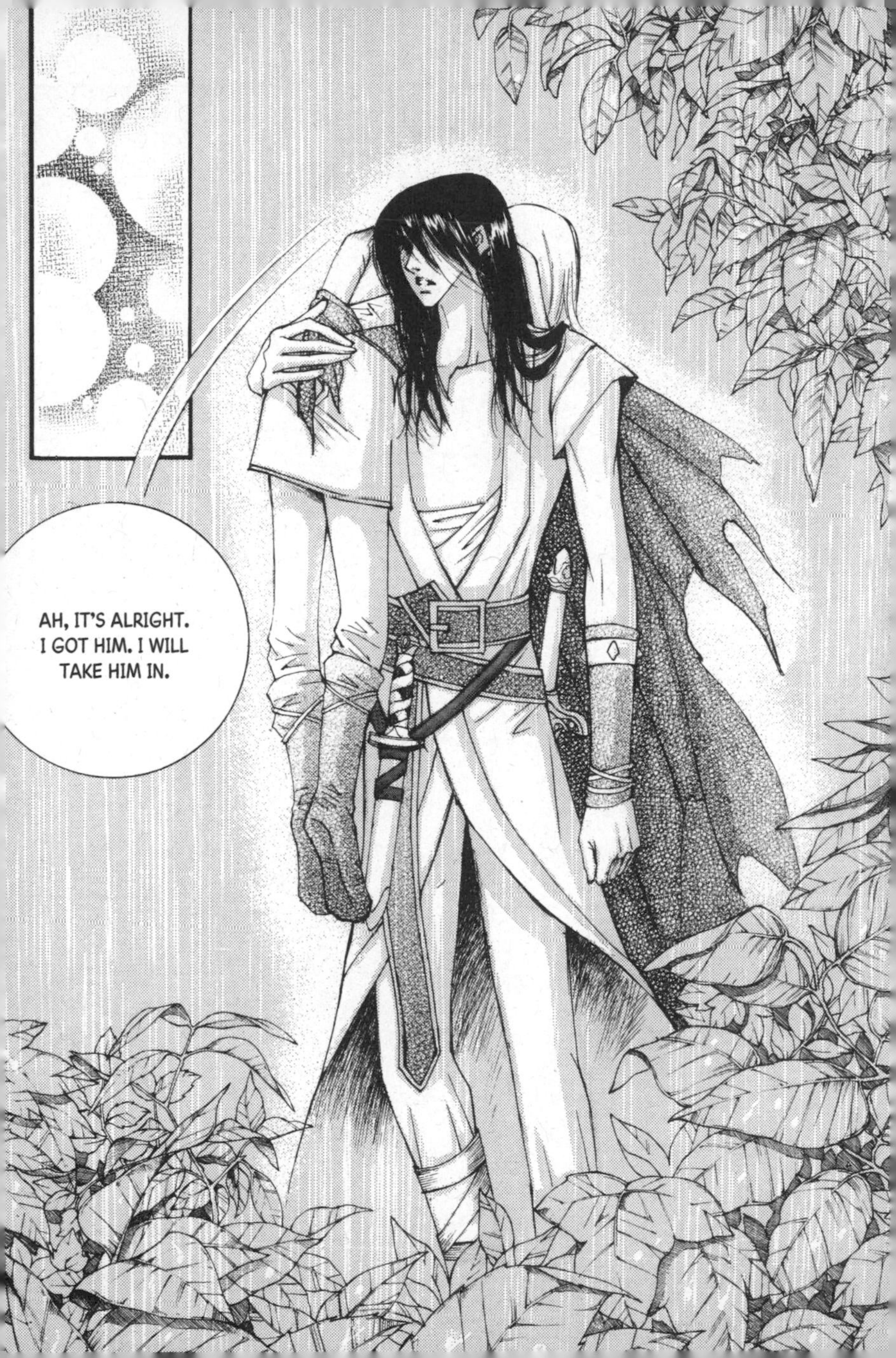
AH, IT'S ALRIGHT. I GOT HIM. I WILL TAKE HIM IN.

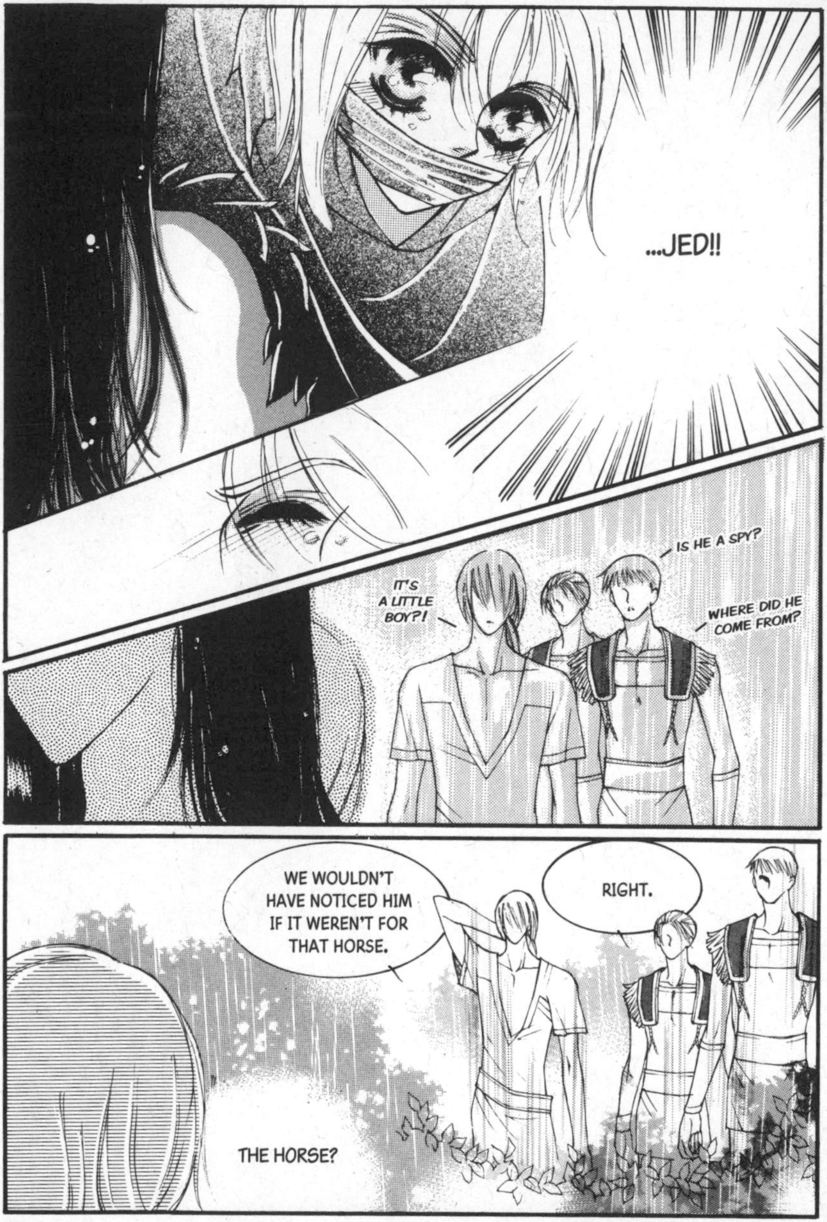
...JED!!
IT'S A LITTLE BOY?!
IS HE A SPY?
WHERE DID HE COME FROM?
WE WOULDN'T HAVE NOTICED HIM IF IT WEREN'T FOR THAT HORSE.
RIGHT.
THE HORSE?

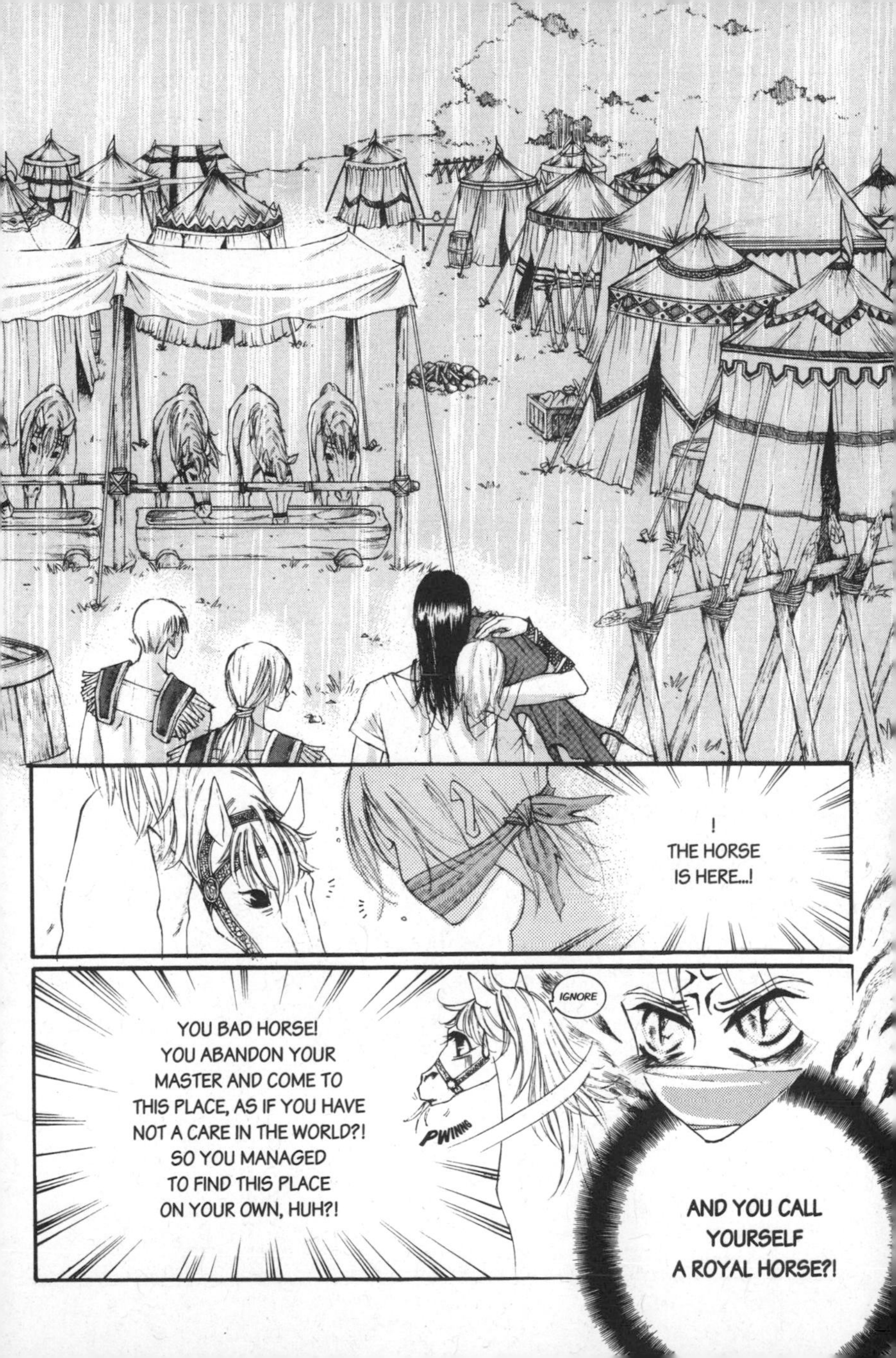
!
THE HORSE IS HERE...!
YOU BAD HORSE! YOU ABANDON YOUR MASTER AND COME TO THIS PLACE, AS IF YOU HAVE NOT A CARE IN THE WORLD?! SO YOU MANAGED TO FIND THIS PLACE ON YOUR OWN, HUH?!
IGNORE
PWING
AND YOU CALL YOURSELF A ROYAL HORSE?!

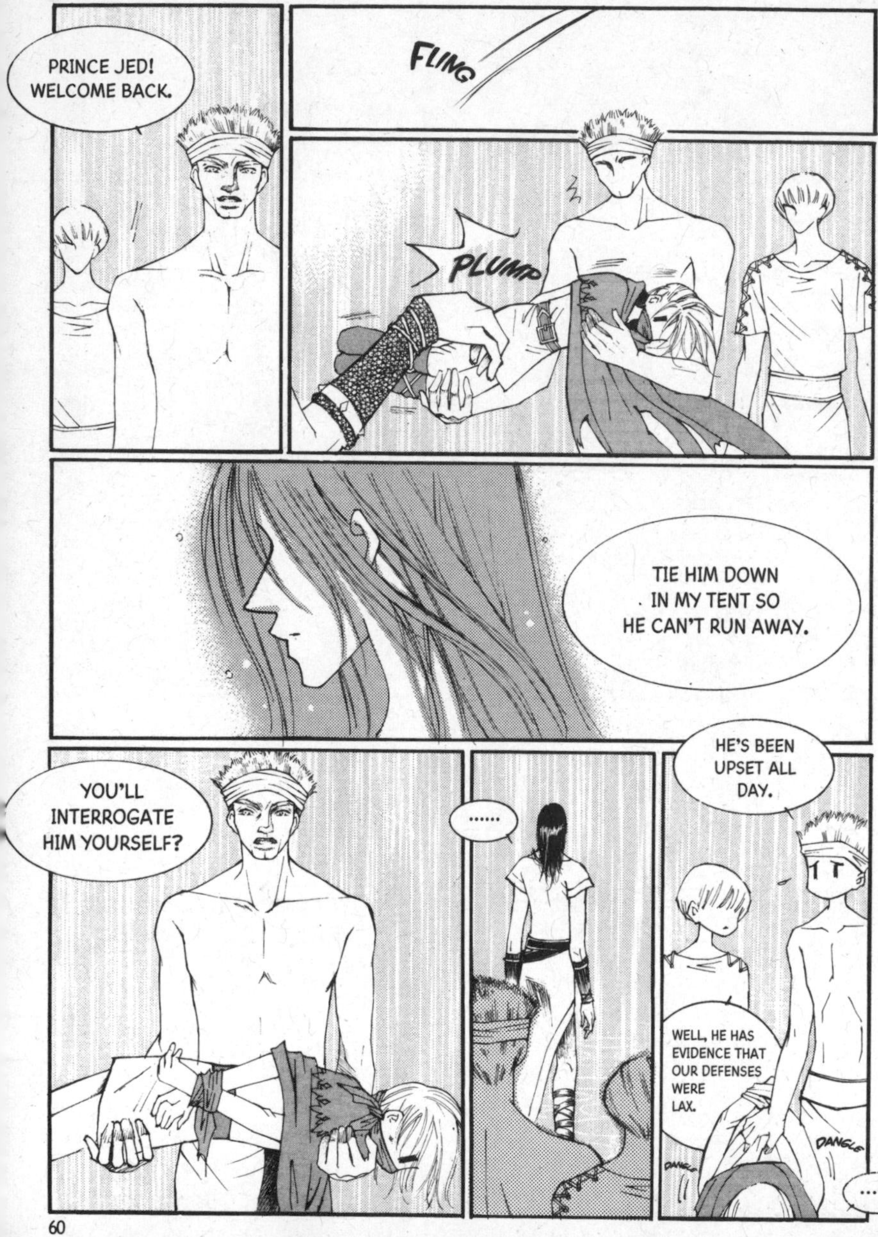
PRINCE JED! WELCOME BACK.
FLING
PLUMP
TIE HIM DOWN IN MY TENT SO HE CAN'T RUN AWAY.
YOU'LL INTERROGATE HIM YOURSELF?
....
HE'S BEEN UPSET ALL DAY.
WELL, HE HAS EVIDENCE THAT OUR DEFENSES WERE LAX.
DANGLE
DANGLE
...

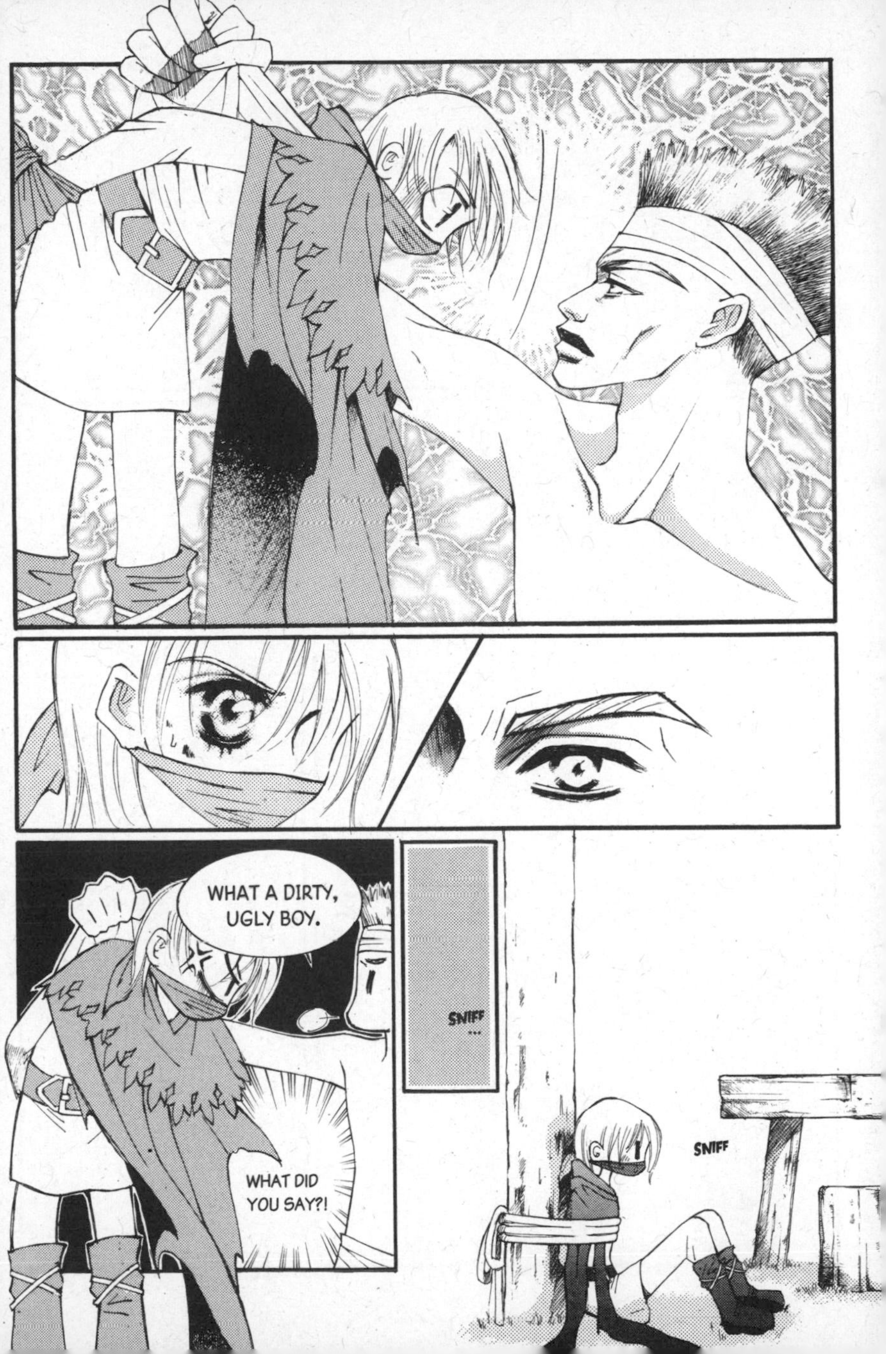
WHAT A DIRTY, UGLY BOY.
WHAT DID YOU SAY?!
SNIFF ...
SNIFF

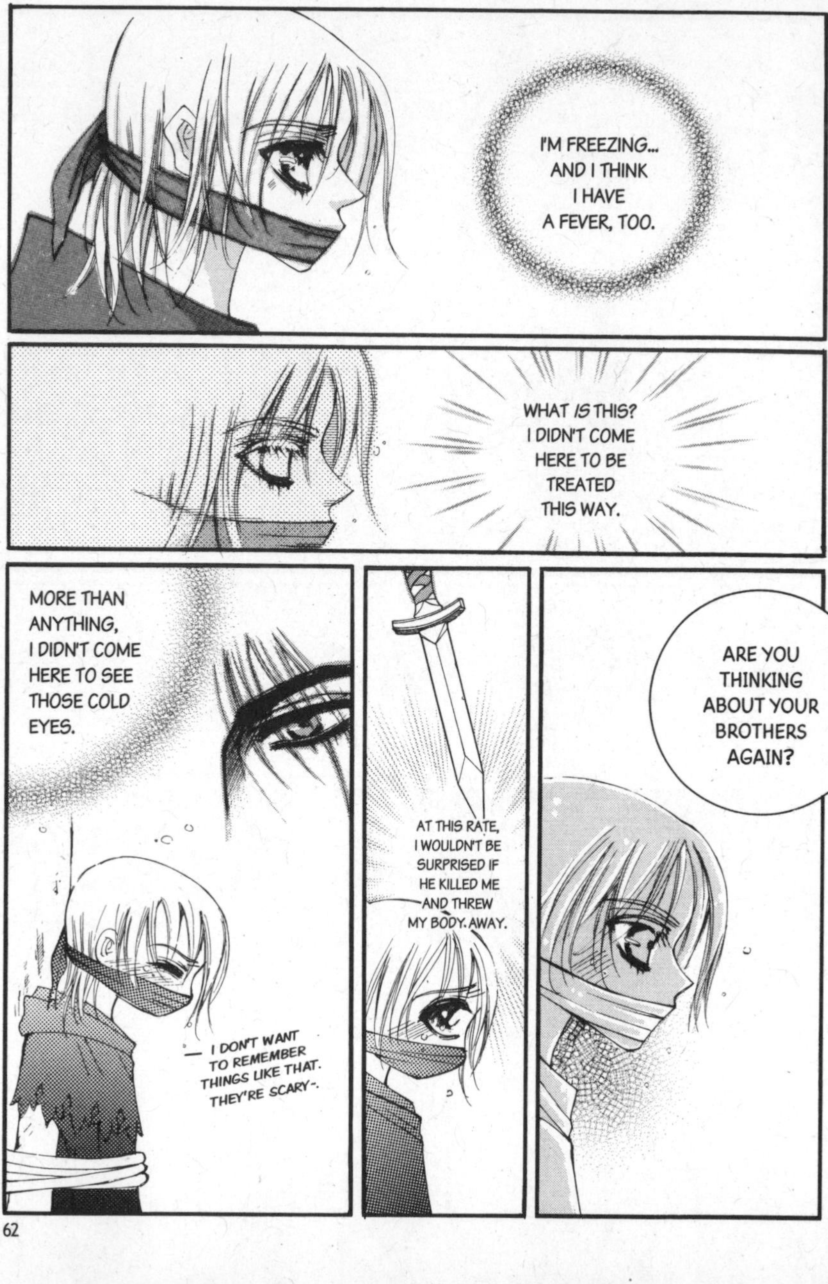
I'M FREEZING... AND I THINK I HAVE A FEVER, TOO.
WHAT *IS* THIS? I DIDN'T COME HERE TO BE TREATED THIS WAY.
MORE THAN ANYTHING, I DIDN'T COME HERE TO SEE THOSE COLD EYES.
— I DON'T WANT TO REMEMBER THINGS LIKE THAT. THEY'RE SCARY-.
AT THIS RATE, I WOULDN'T BE SURPRISED IF HE KILLED ME AND THREW MY BODY AWAY.
ARE YOU THINKING ABOUT YOUR BROTHERS AGAIN?

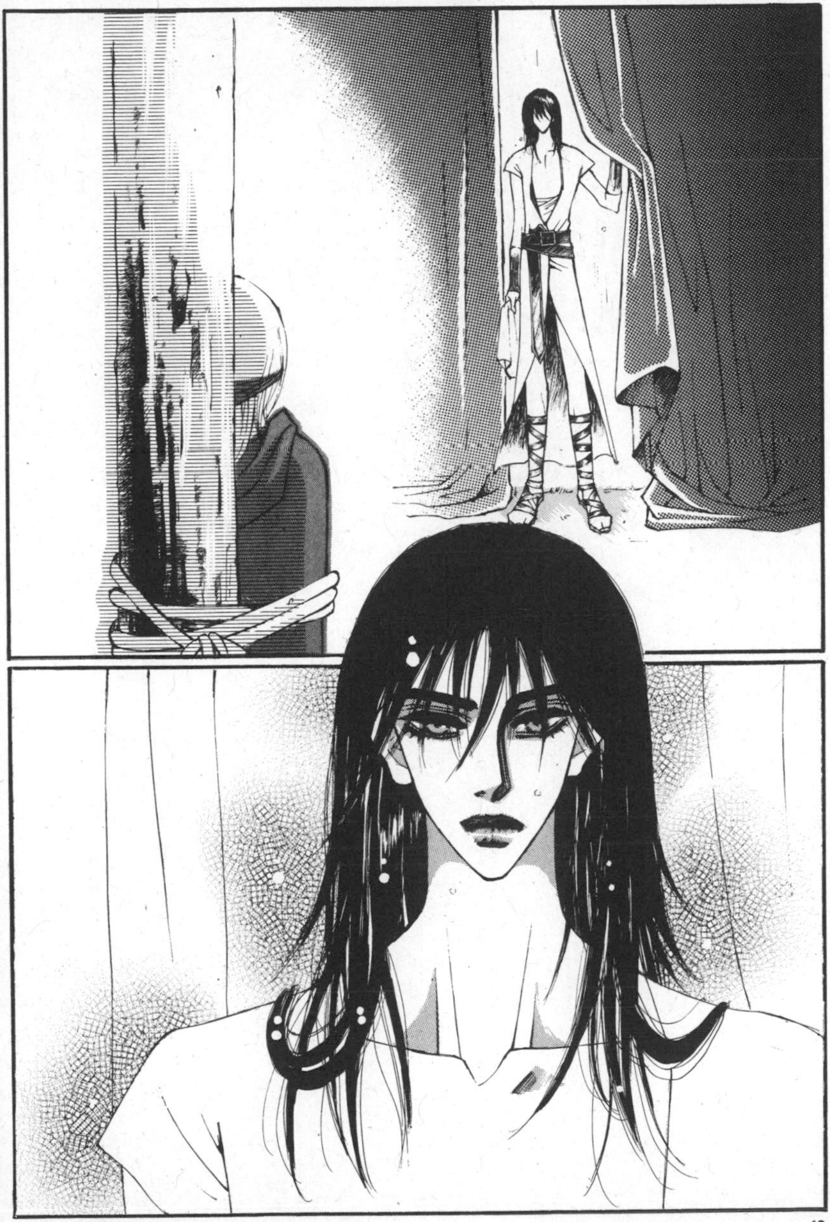

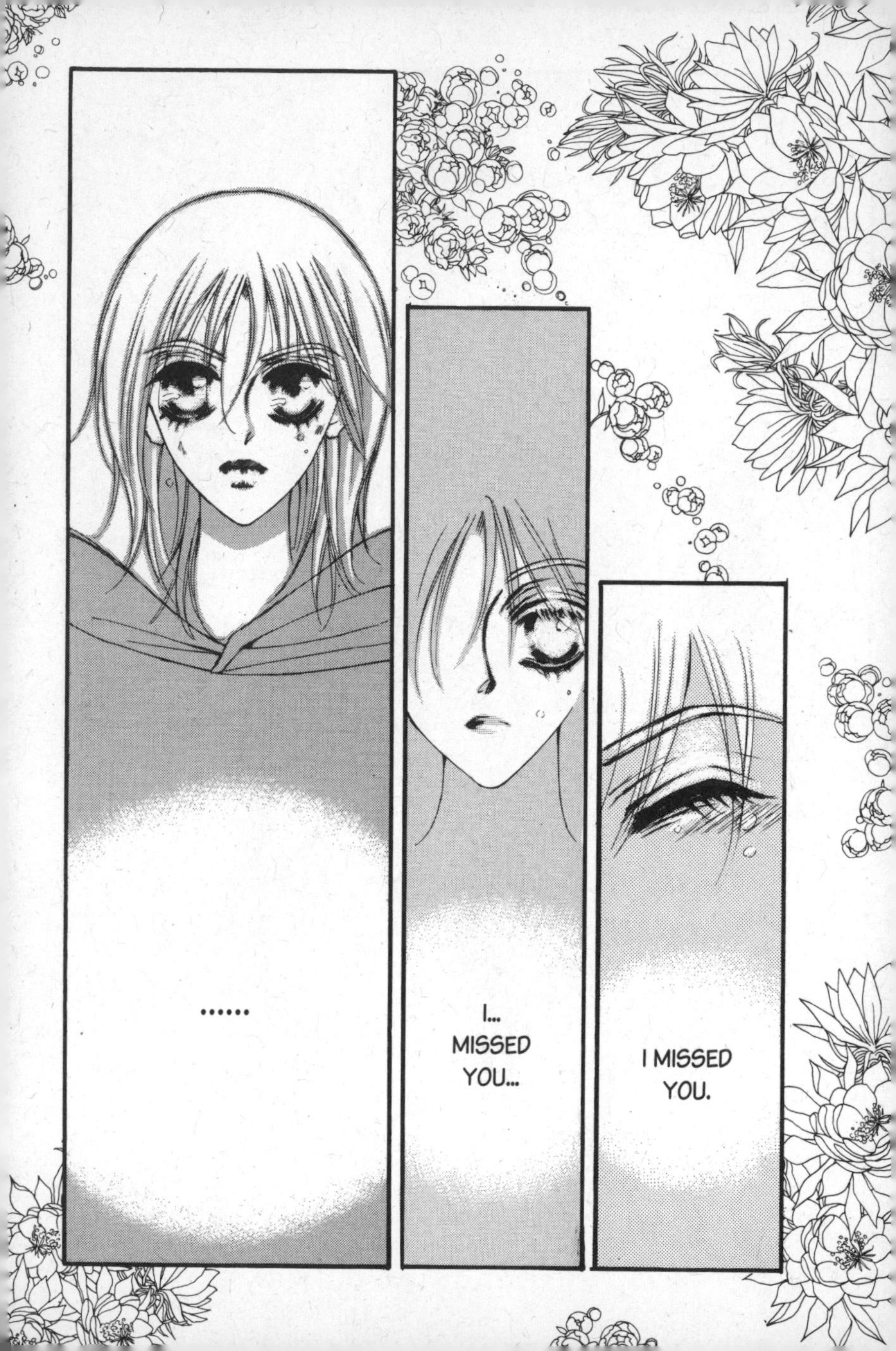
I MISSED YOU.
I... MISSED YOU...
......

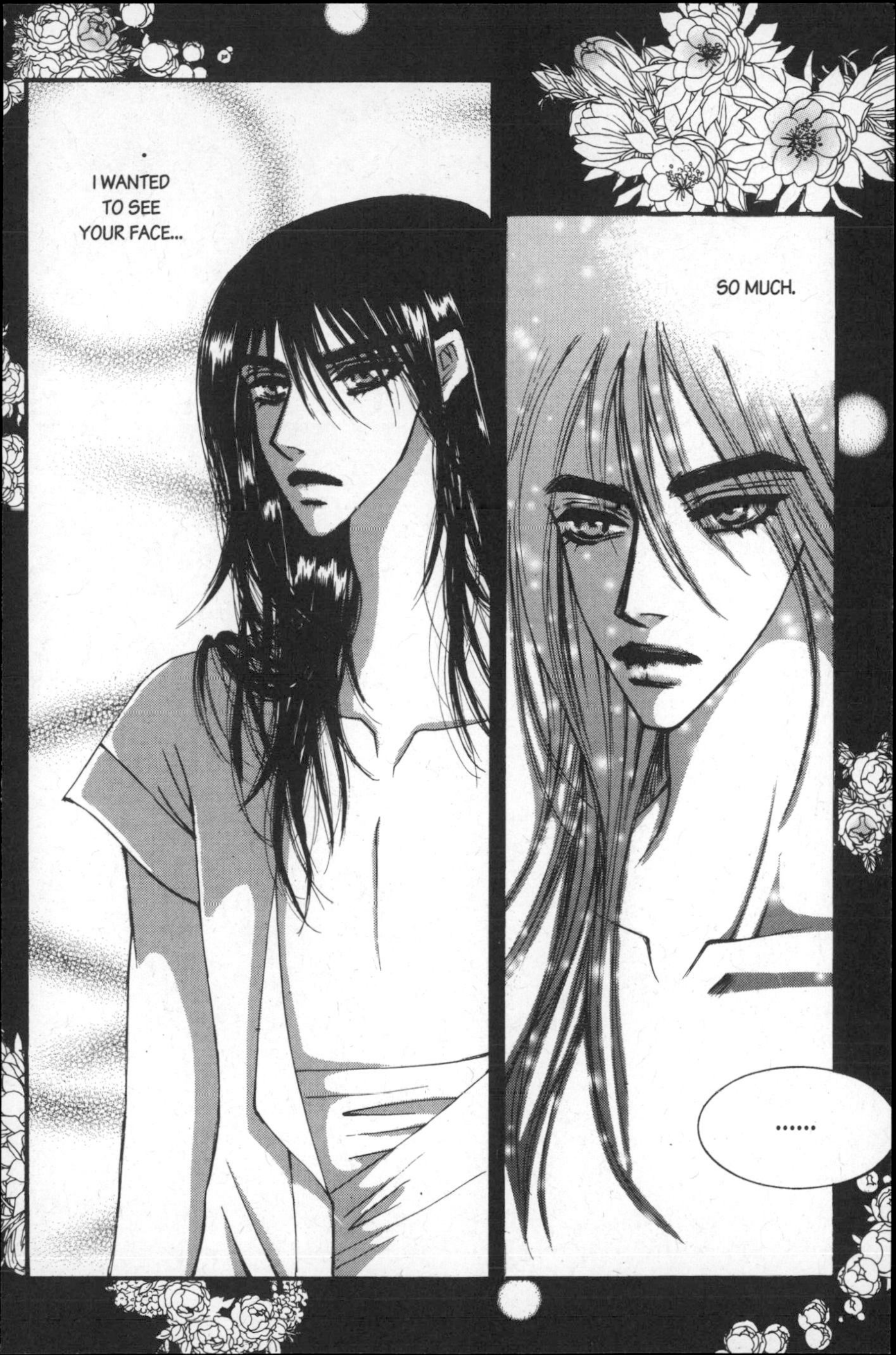

I WANTED TO SEE YOUR FACE...
SO MUCH.
......

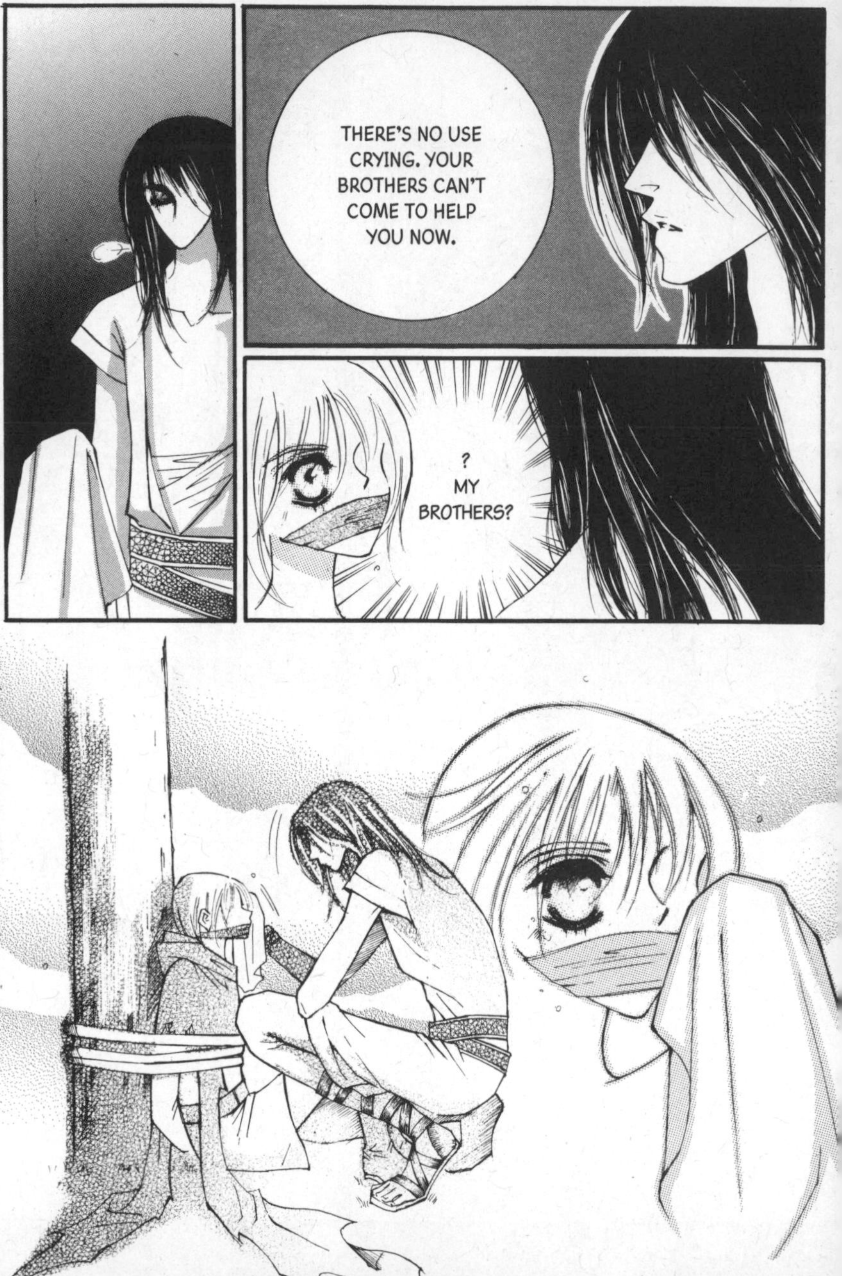
THERE'S NO USE CRYING. YOUR BROTHERS CAN'T COME TO HELP YOU NOW.
? MY BROTHERS?

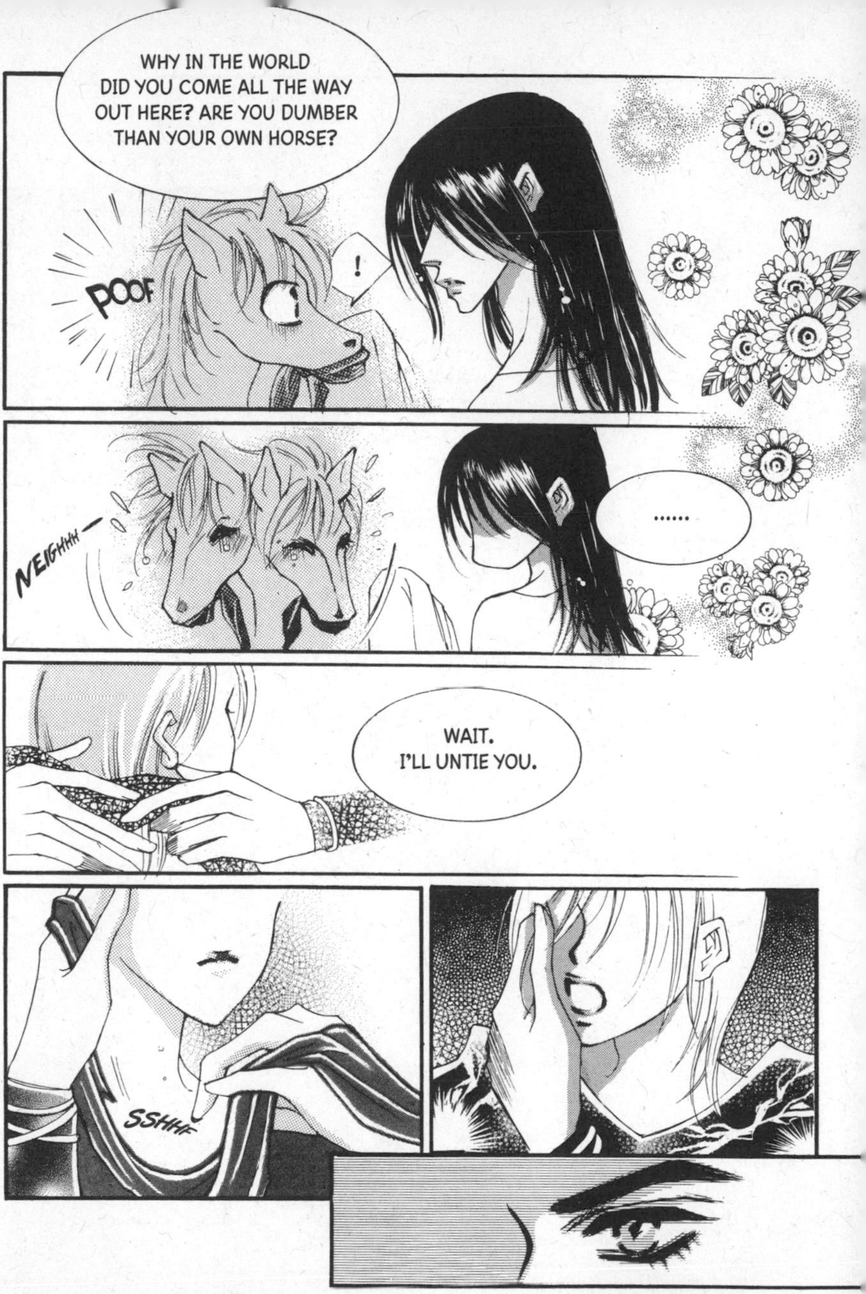
WHY IN THE WORLD DID YOU COME ALL THE WAY OUT HERE? ARE YOU DUMBER THAN YOUR OWN HORSE?
POOF
!
NEIGHHH—
......
WAIT. I'LL UNTIE YOU.
SSHHF

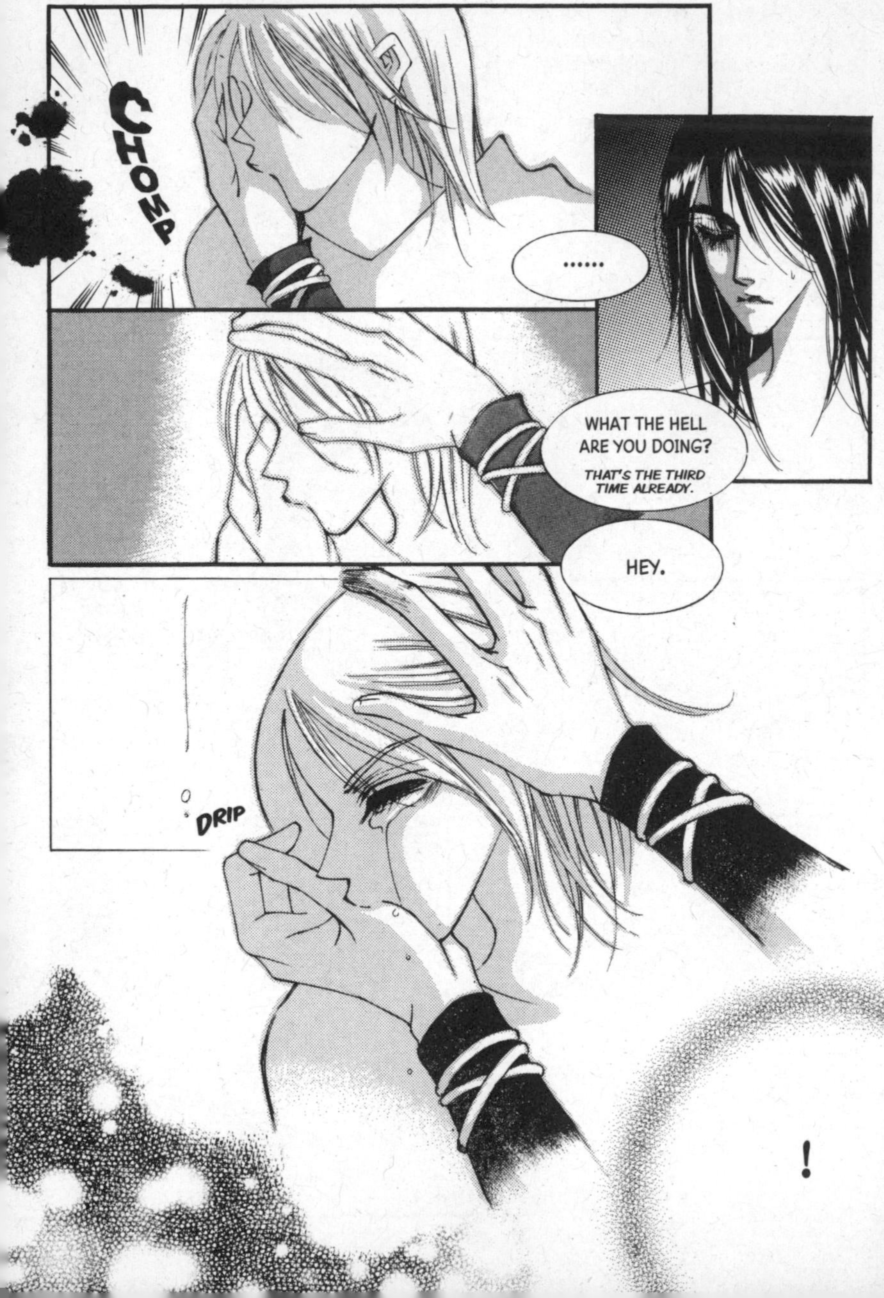
CHOMP
......
WHAT THE HELL ARE YOU DOING?
THAT'S THE THIRD TIME ALREADY.
HEY.
DRIP
!

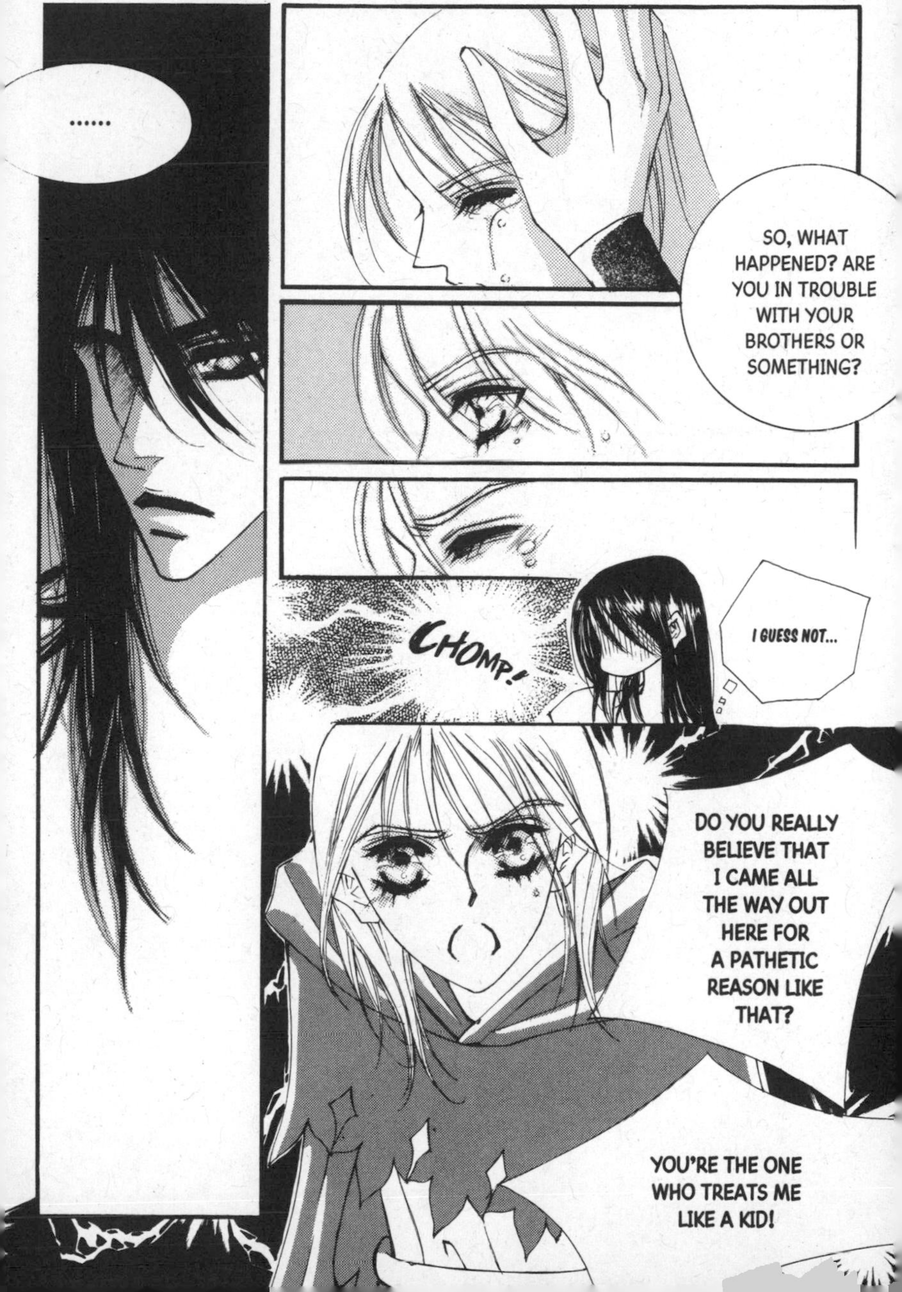
SO, WHAT HAPPENED? ARE YOU IN TROUBLE WITH YOUR BROTHERS OR SOMETHING?
......
I GUESS NOT...
CHOMP!
DO YOU REALLY BELIEVE THAT I CAME ALL THE WAY OUT HERE FOR A PATHETIC REASON LIKE THAT?
YOU'RE THE ONE WHO TREATS ME LIKE A KID!

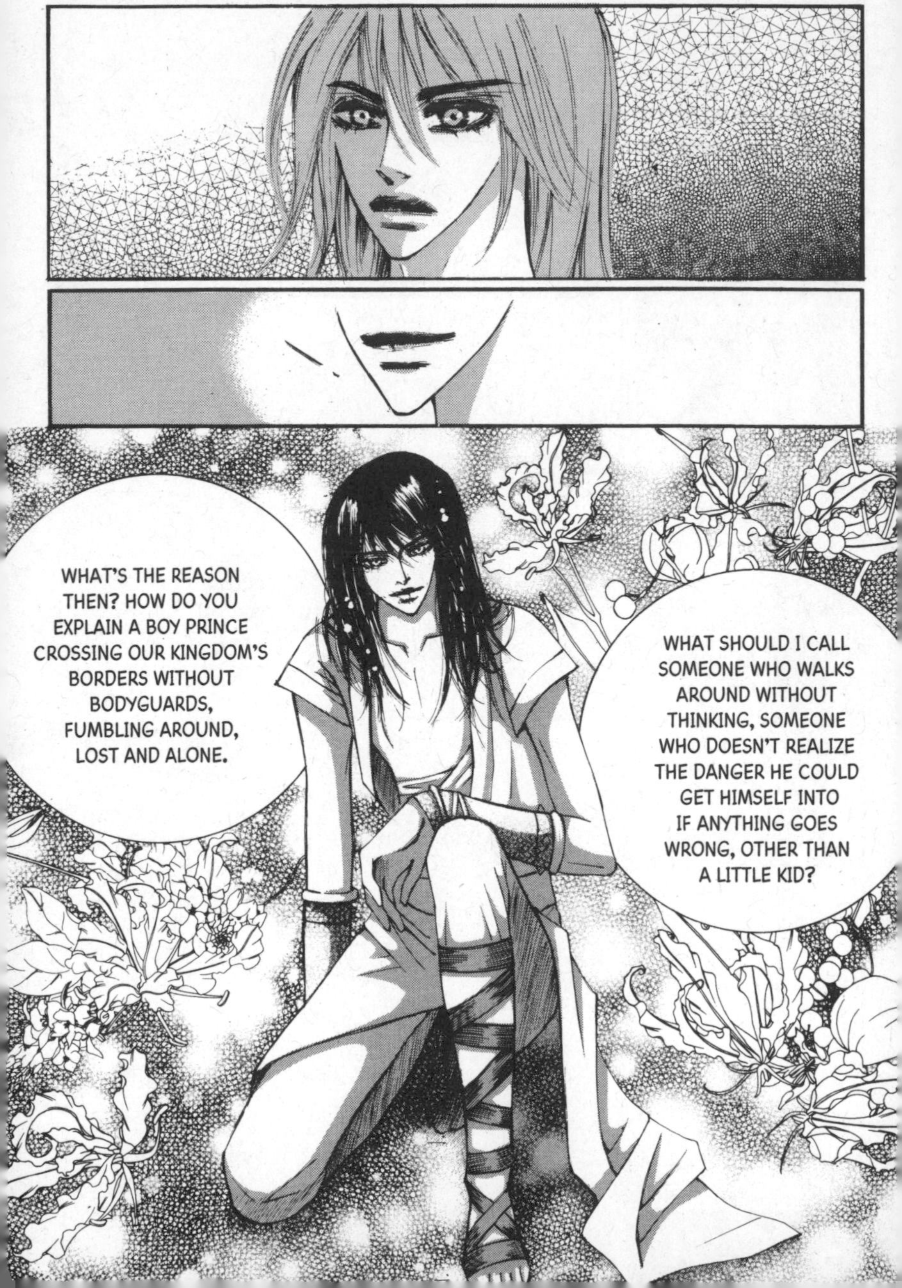

WHAT'S THE REASON THEN? HOW DO YOU EXPLAIN A BOY PRINCE CROSSING OUR KINGDOM'S BORDERS WITHOUT BODYGUARDS, FUMBLING AROUND, LOST AND ALONE.
WHAT SHOULD I CALL SOMEONE WHO WALKS AROUND WITHOUT THINKING, SOMEONE WHO DOESN'T REALIZE THE DANGER HE COULD GET HIMSELF INTO IF ANYTHING GOES WRONG, OTHER THAN A LITTLE KID?

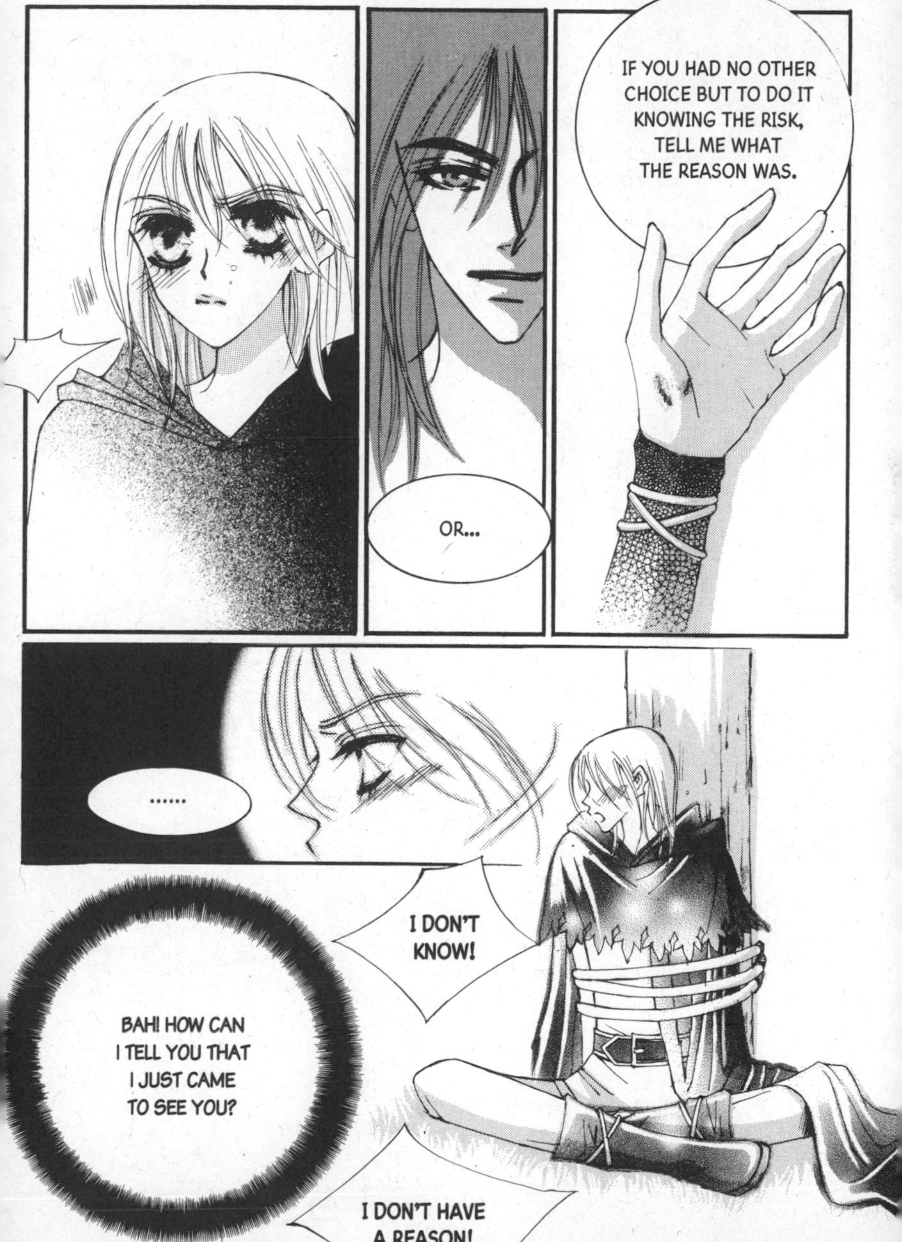

IF YOU HAD NO OTHER CHOICE BUT TO DO IT KNOWING THE RISK, TELL ME WHAT THE REASON WAS.
OR...
......
I DON'T KNOW!
BAH! HOW CAN I TELL YOU THAT I JUST CAME TO SEE YOU?
I DON'T HAVE A REASON!

YOU'RE NO LONGER MY WIFE WHOM I MUST RESPECT.
PERHAPS YOU'RE FORGETTING.
YOU'RE A MERE PRISONER WHOM I CAN TREAT AS I PLEASE.

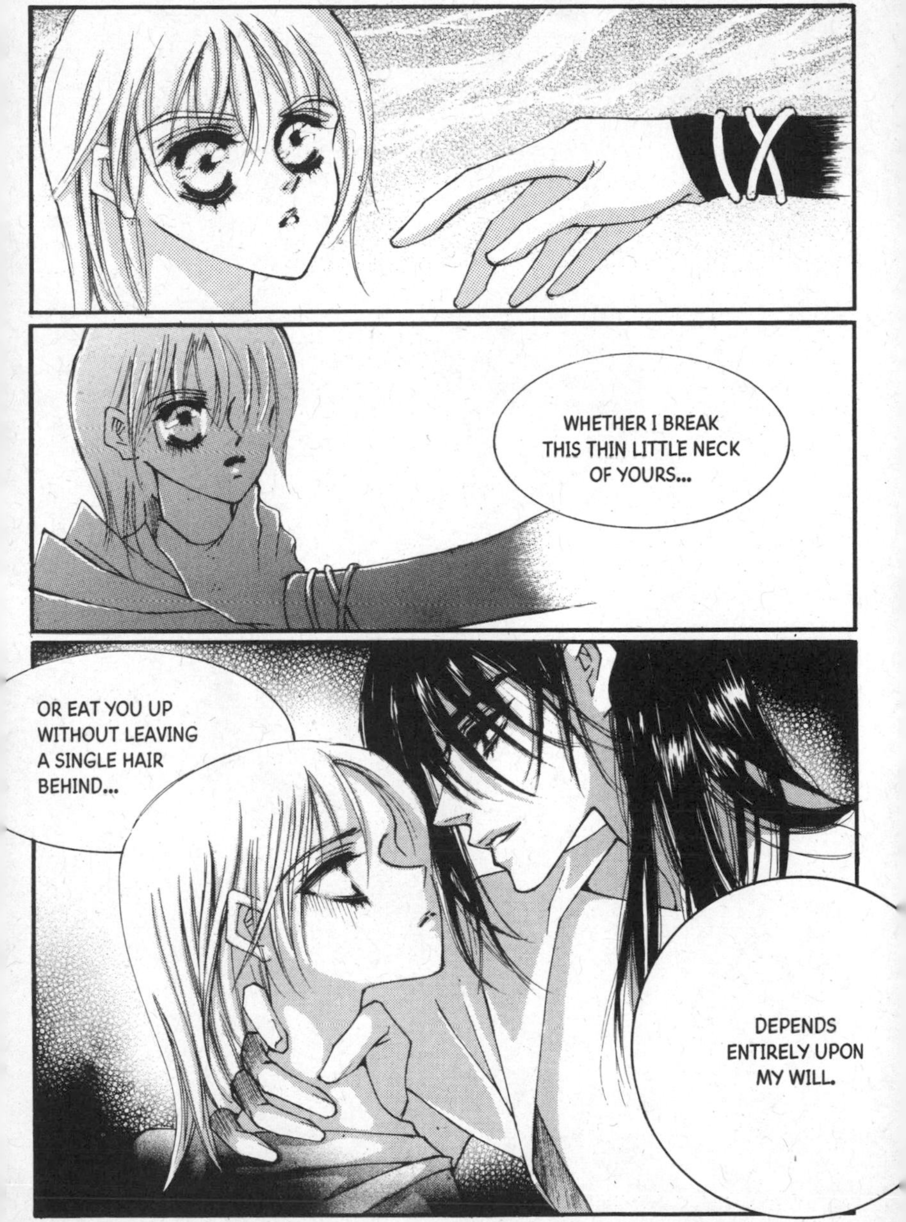
WHETHER I BREAK THIS THIN LITTLE NECK OF YOURS...
OR EAT YOU UP WITHOUT LEAVING A SINGLE HAIR BEHIND...
DEPENDS ENTIRELY UPON MY WILL.

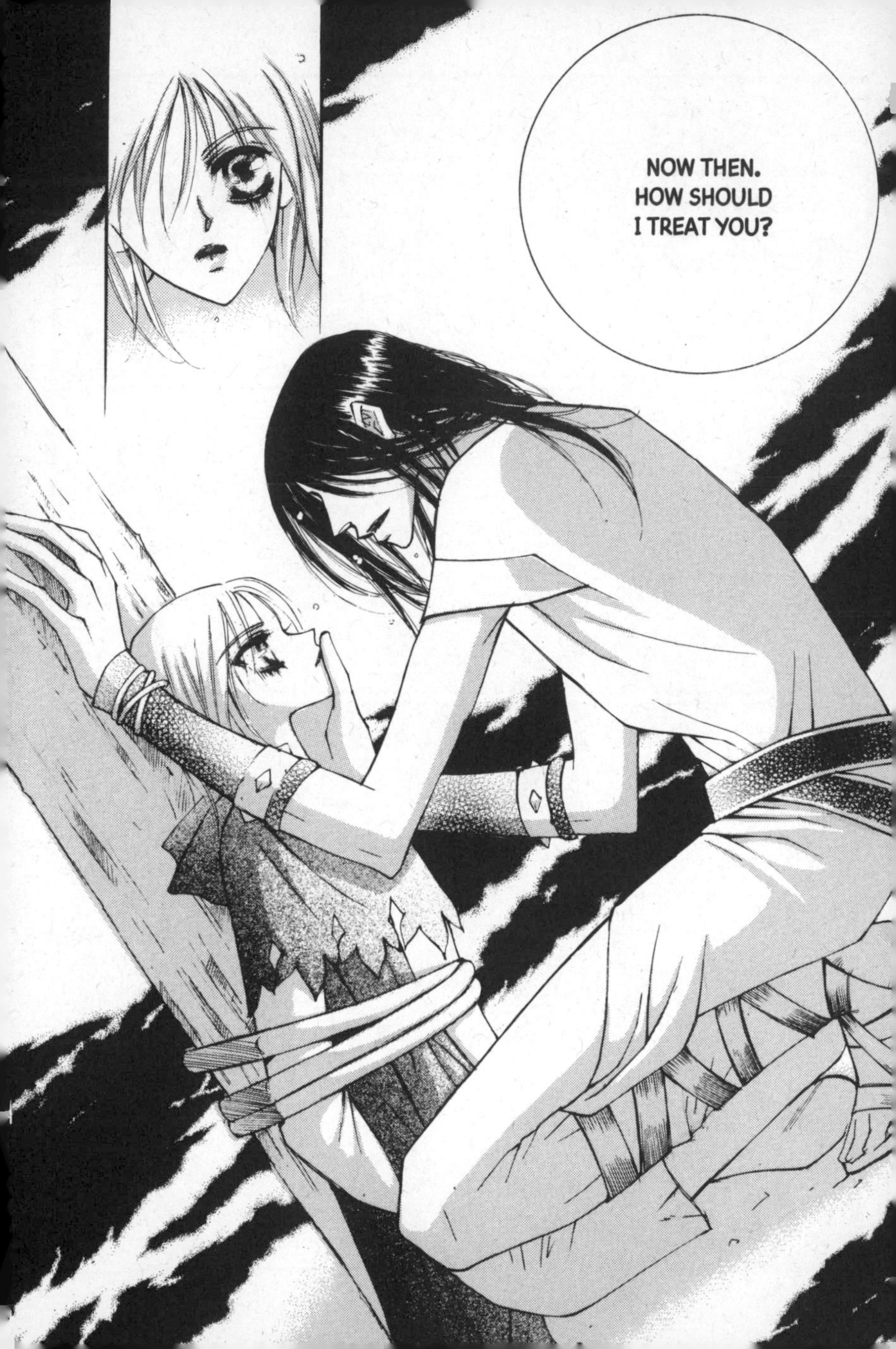
NOW THEN.
HOW SHOULD
I TREAT YOU?

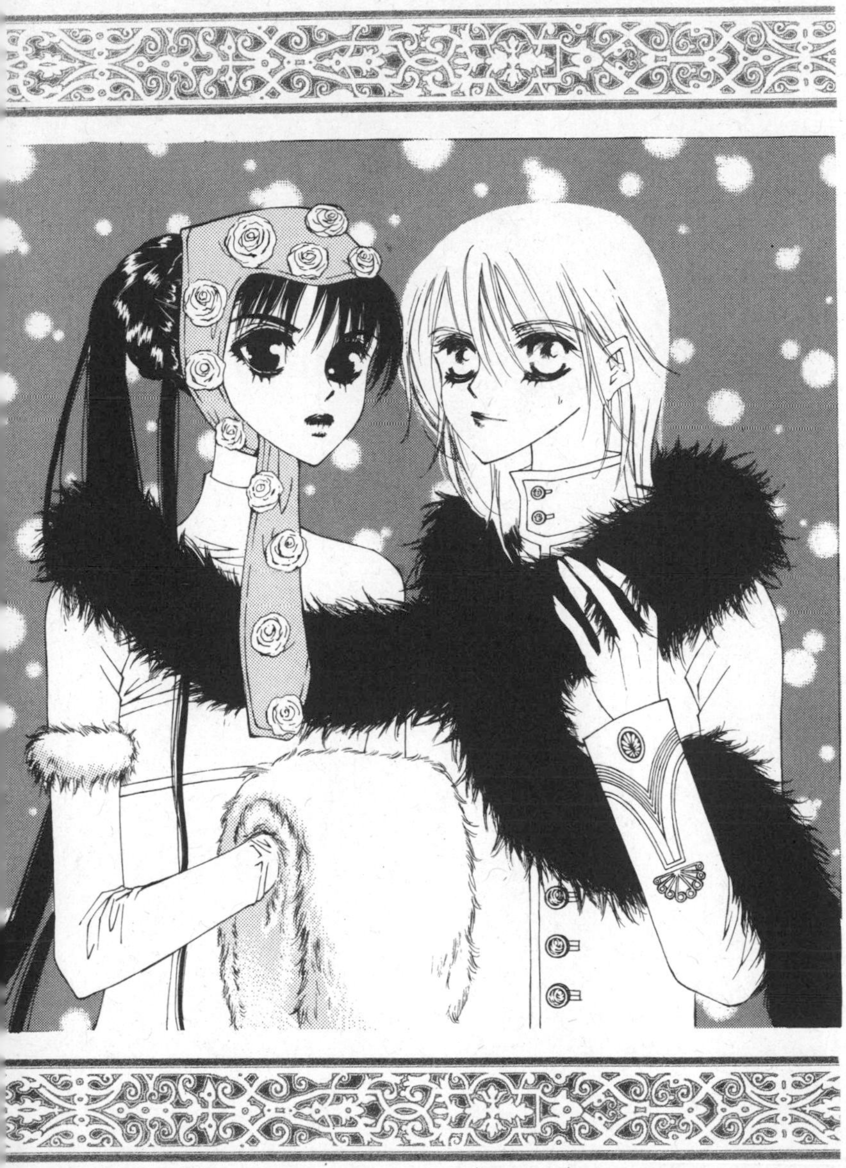

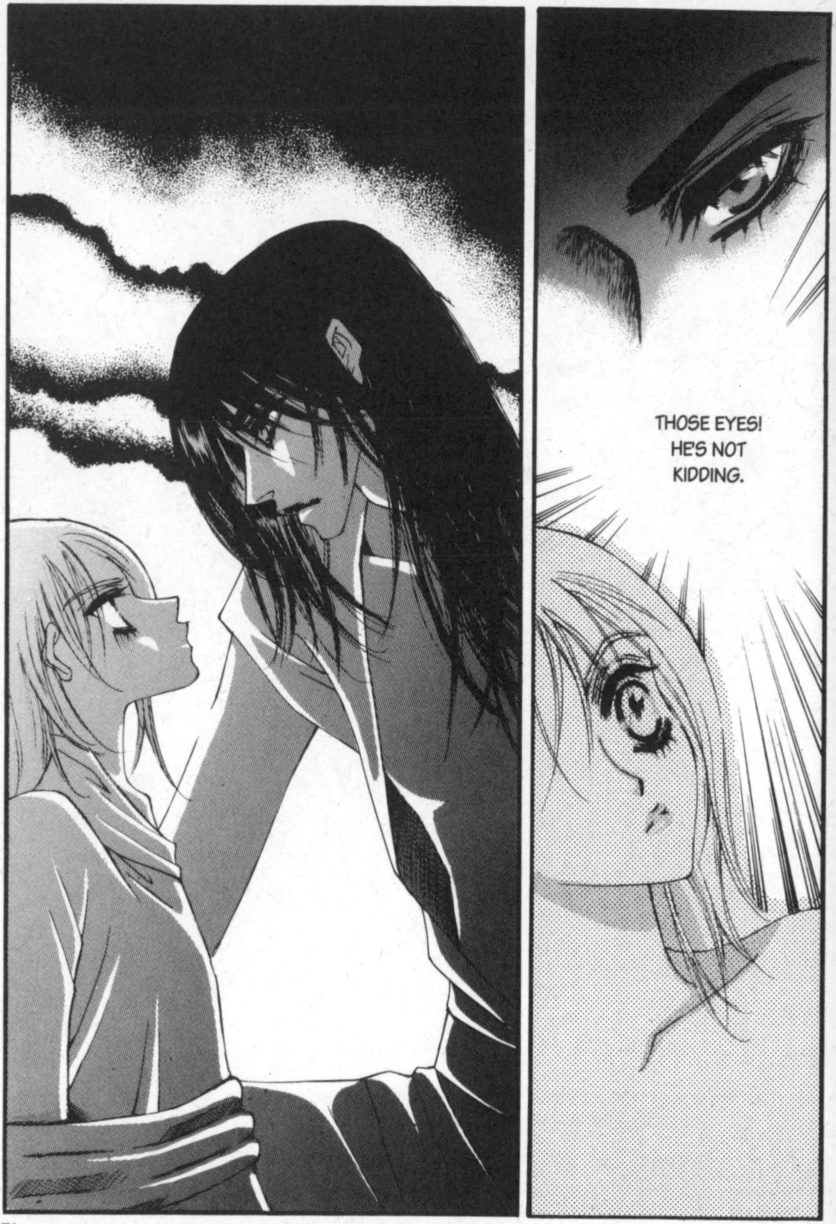
THOSE EYES! HE'S NOT KIDDING.

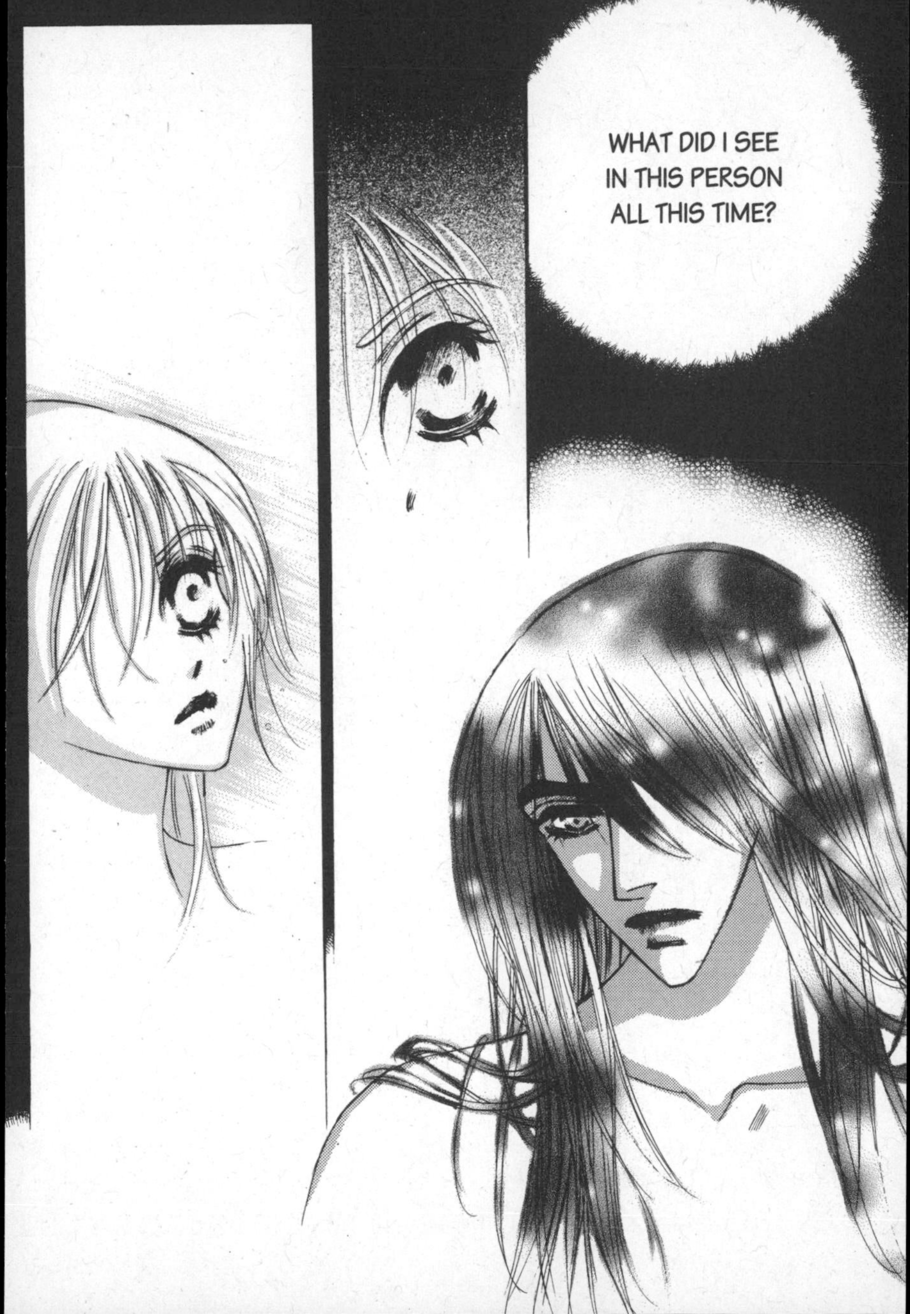
WHAT DID I SEE IN THIS PERSON ALL THIS TIME?

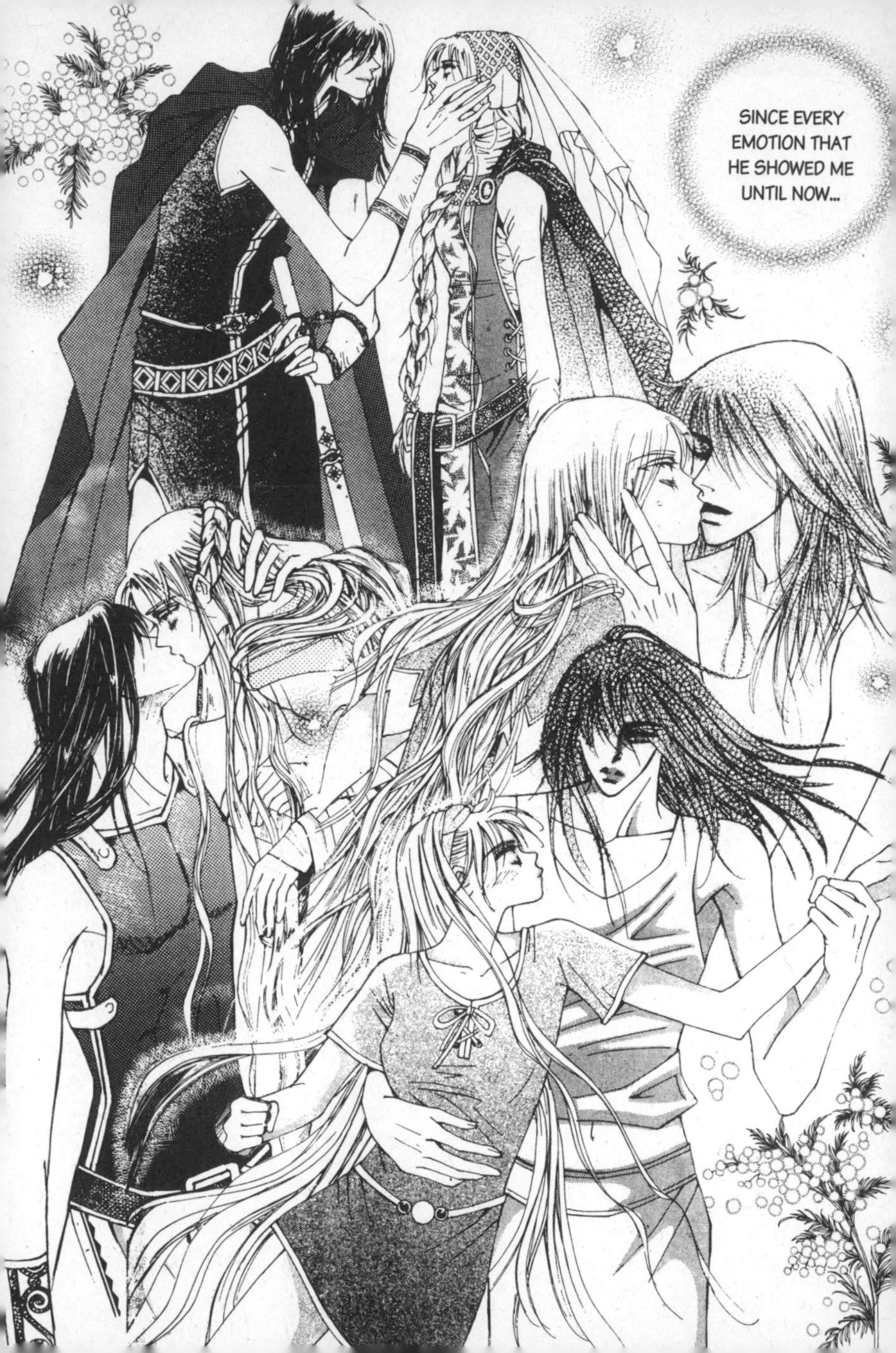
SINCE EVERY
EMOTION THAT
HE SHOWED ME
UNTIL NOW...

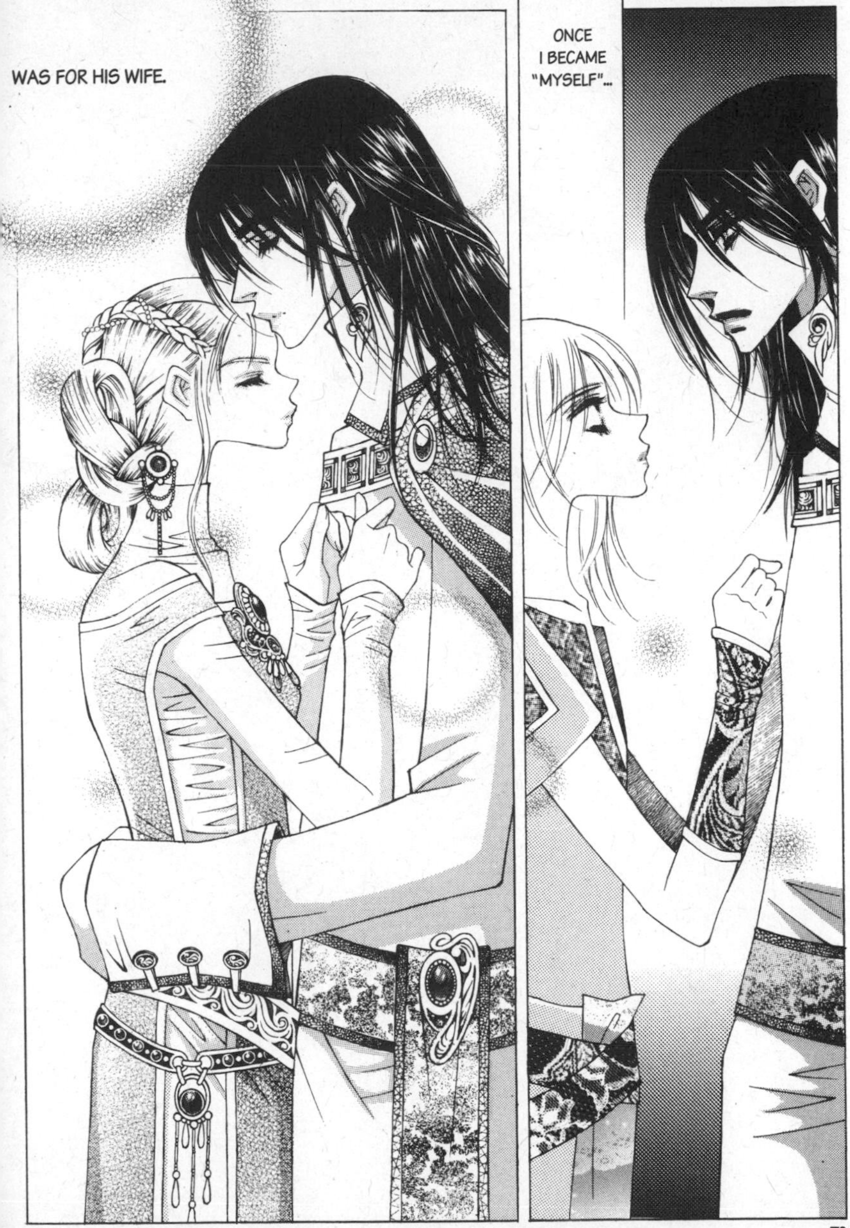
WAS FOR HIS WIFE.
ONCE I BECAME "MYSELF"...

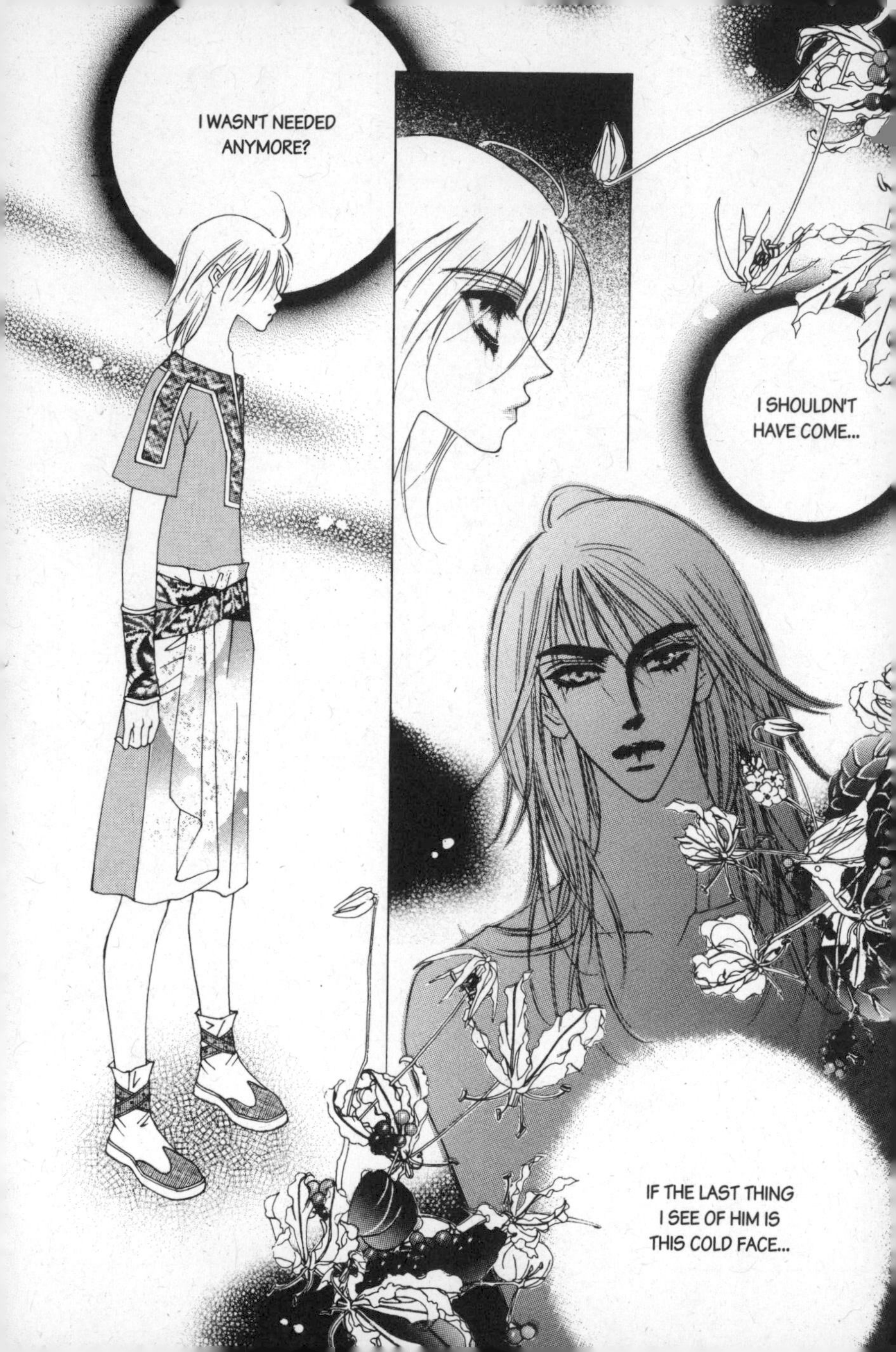
I WASN'T NEEDED ANYMORE?
I SHOULDN'T HAVE COME...
IF THE LAST THING I SEE OF HIM IS THIS COLD FACE...

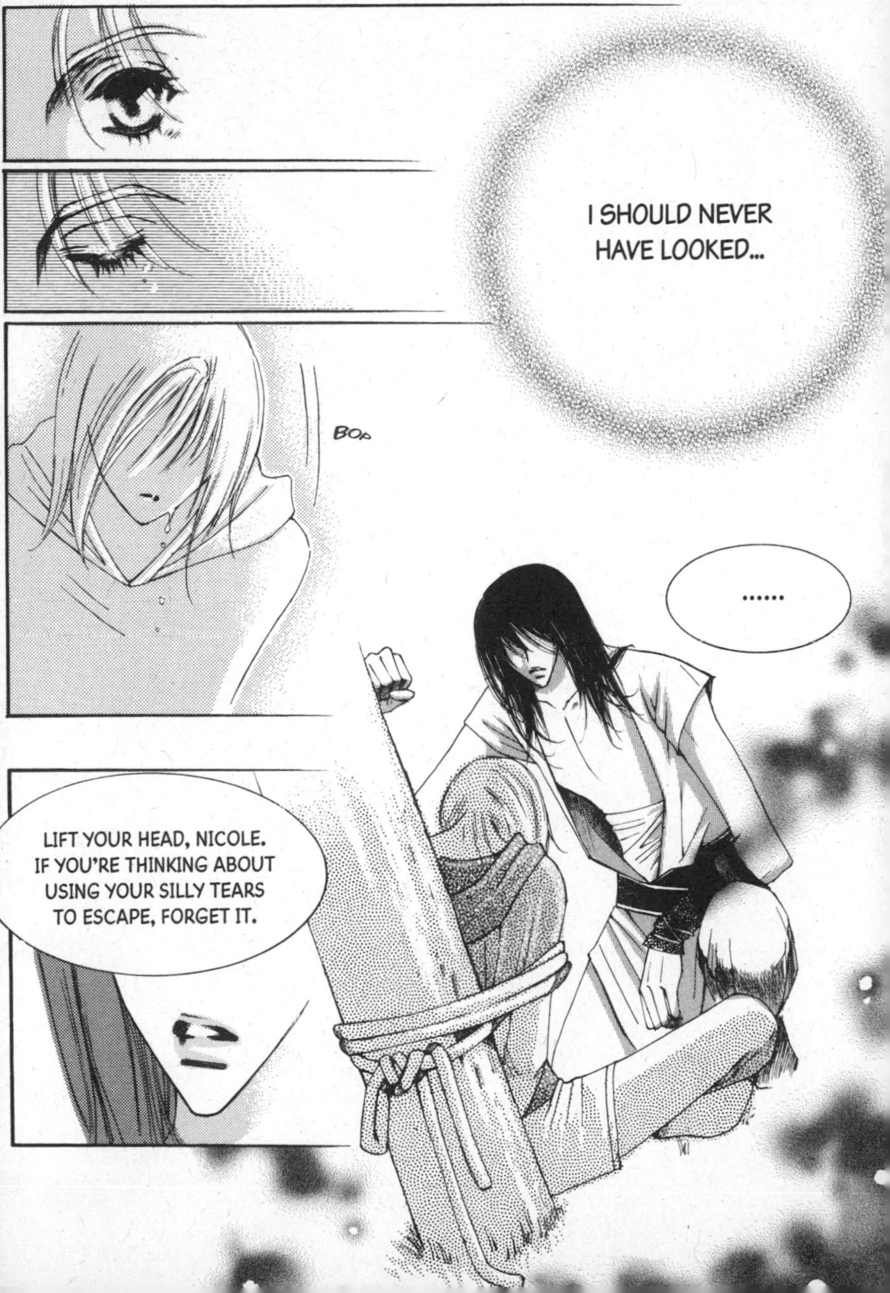
I SHOULD NEVER HAVE LOOKED...
BOP
......
LIFT YOUR HEAD, NICOLE. IF YOU'RE THINKING ABOUT USING YOUR SILLY TEARS TO ESCAPE, FORGET IT.

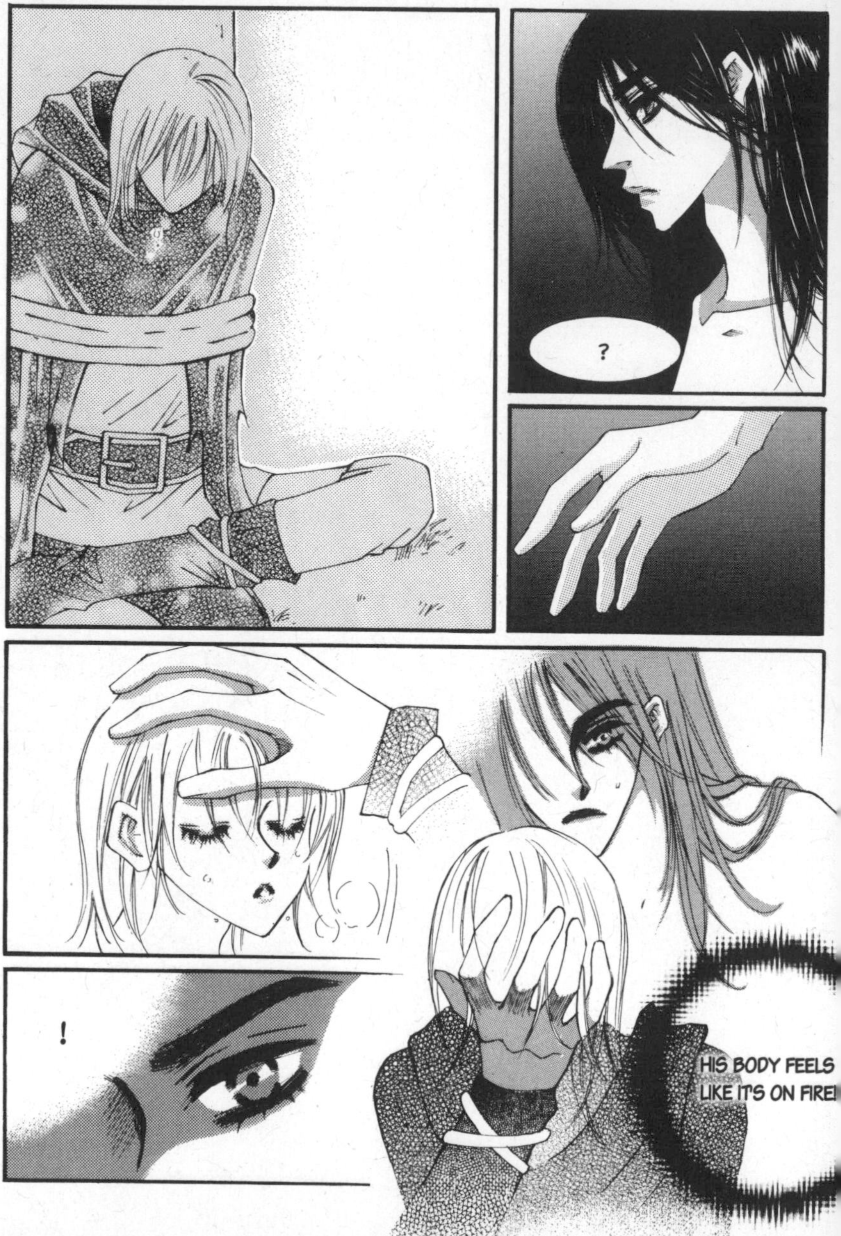
?
!
HIS BODY FEELS
LIKE IT'S ON FIRE!

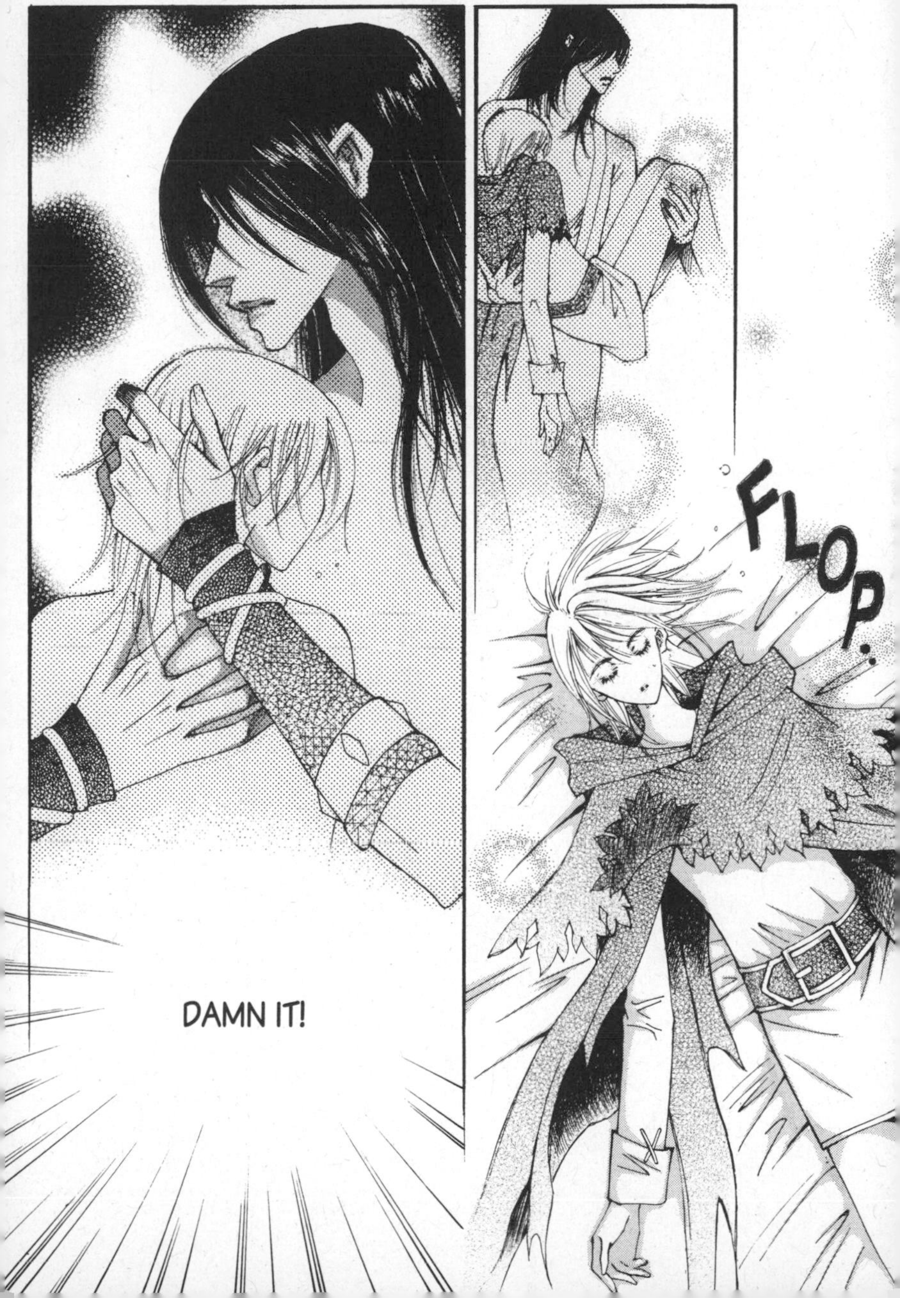
FLOP...
DAMN IT!

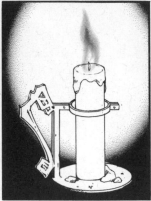

CREAK...

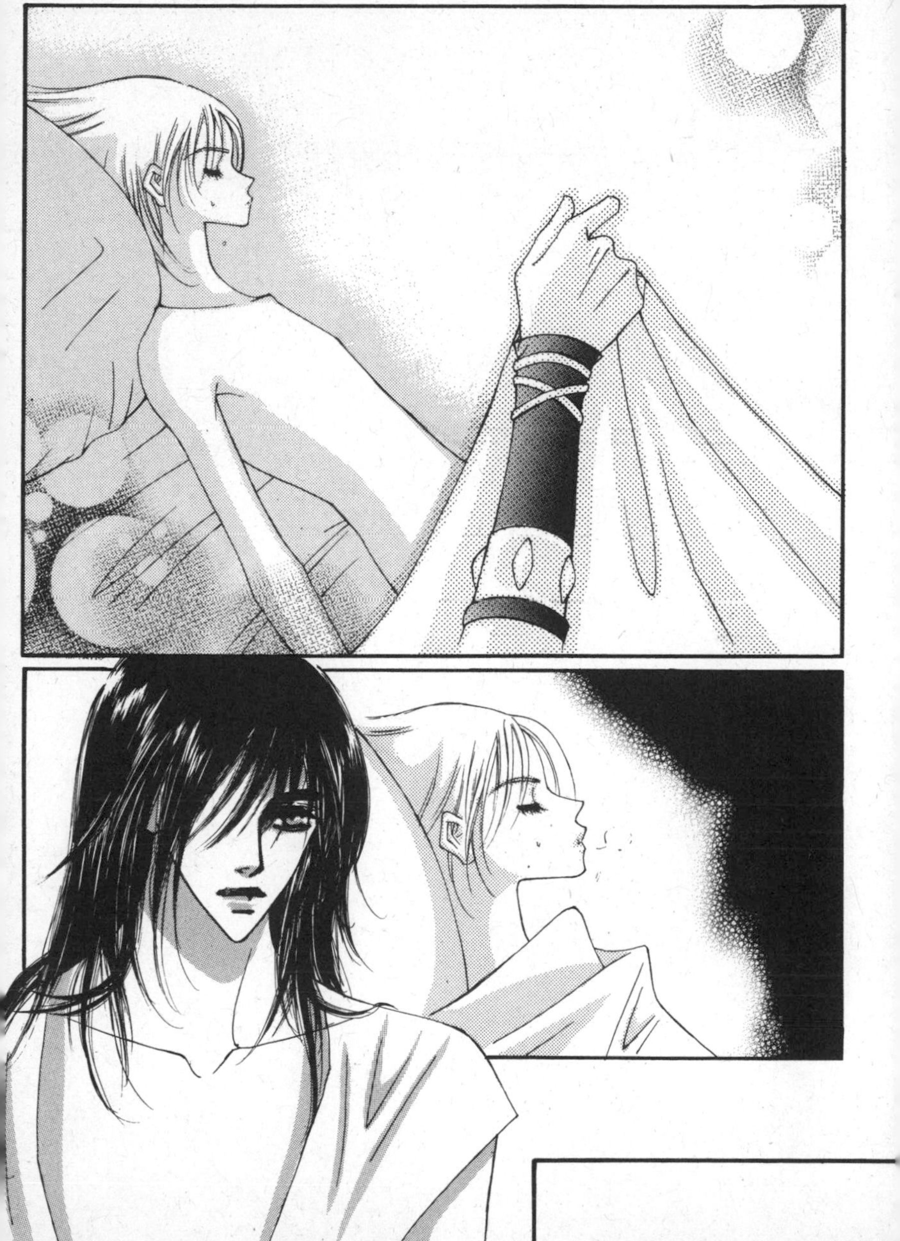

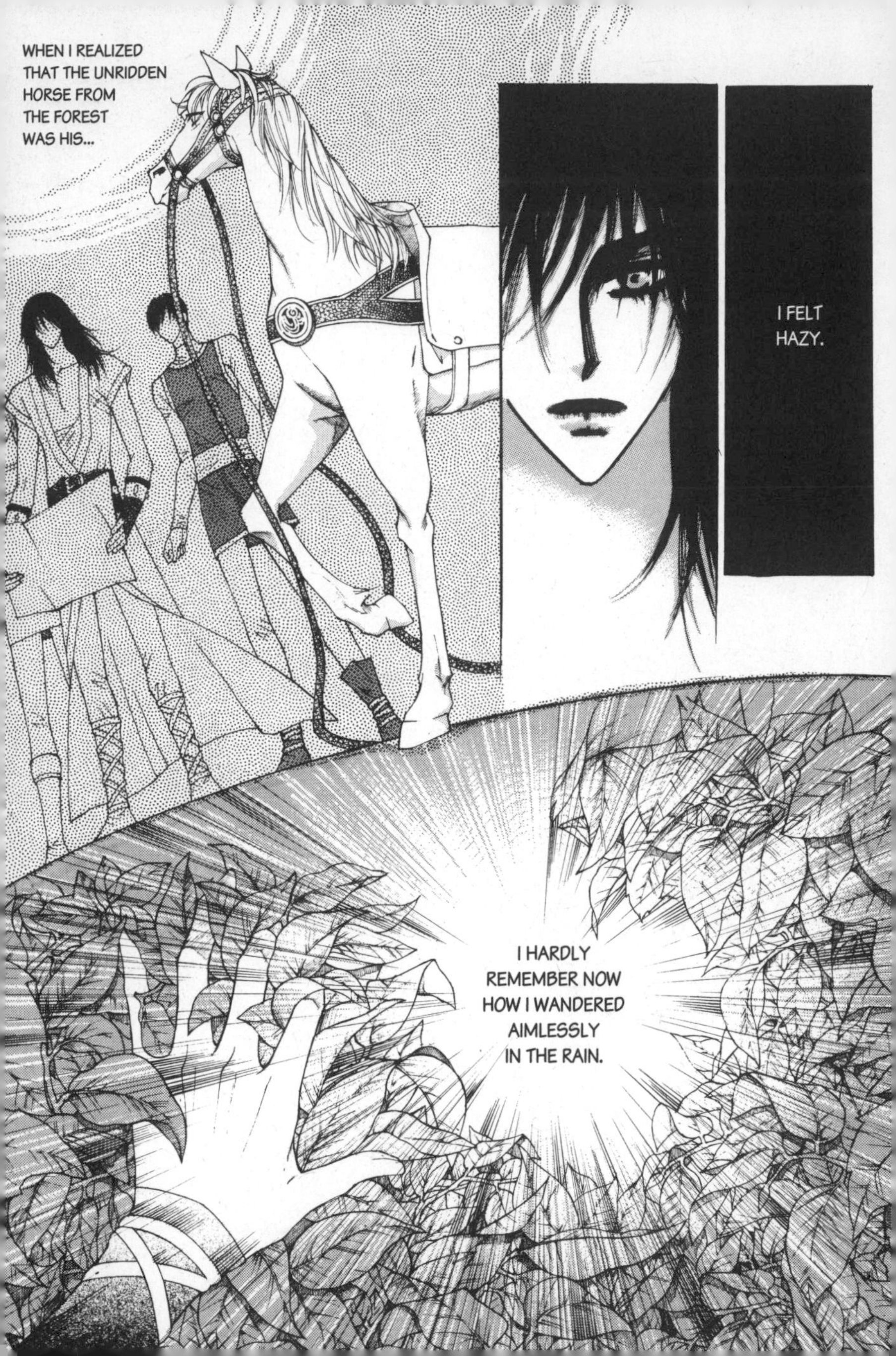

WHEN I REALIZED THAT THE UNRIDDEN HORSE FROM THE FOREST WAS HIS...
I FELT HAZY.
I HARDLY REMEMBER NOW HOW I WANDERED AIMLESSLY IN THE RAIN.

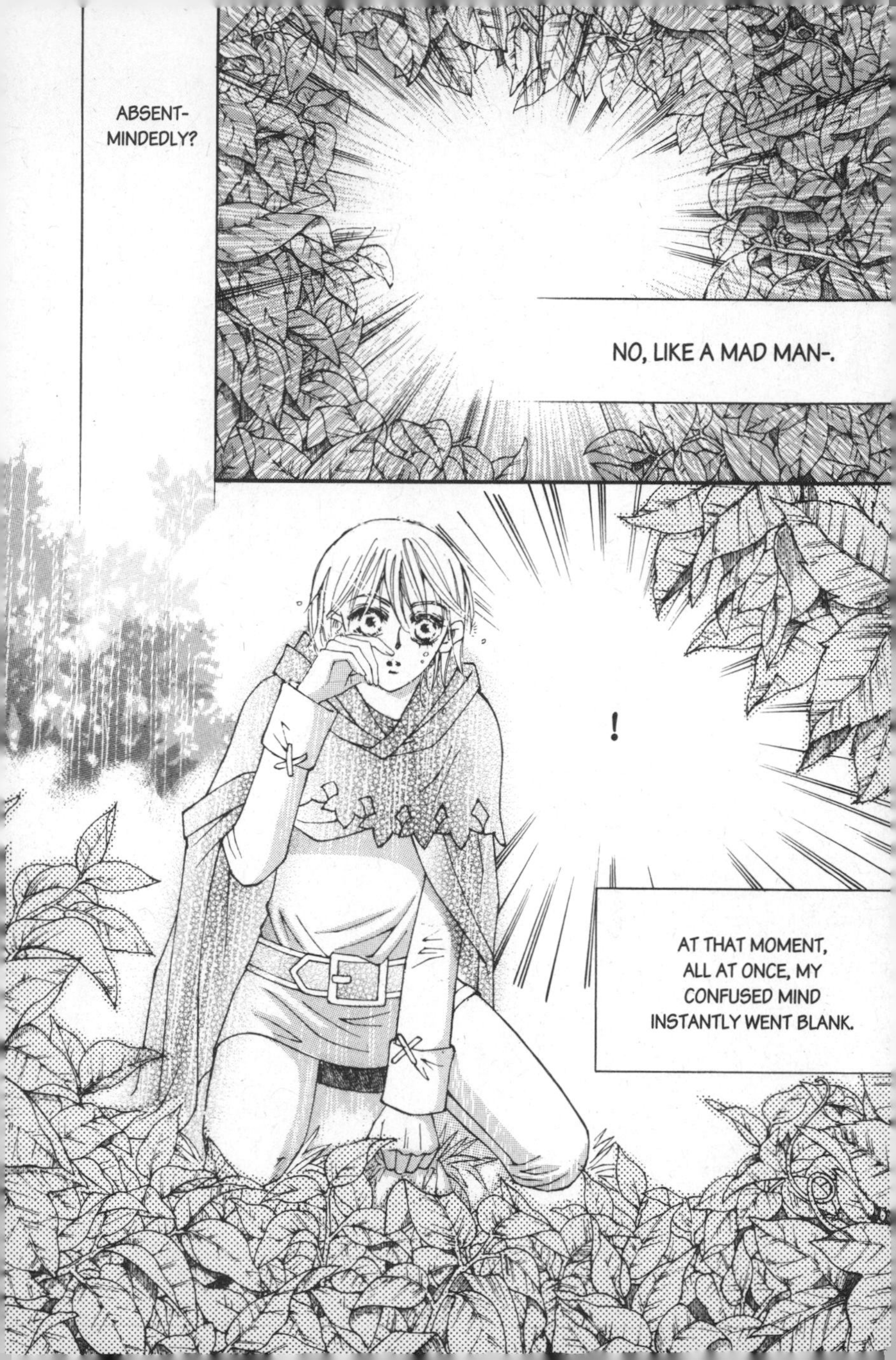
ABSENT-MINDEDLY?
NO, LIKE A MAD MAN-.
!
AT THAT MOMENT, ALL AT ONCE, MY CONFUSED MIND INSTANTLY WENT BLANK.

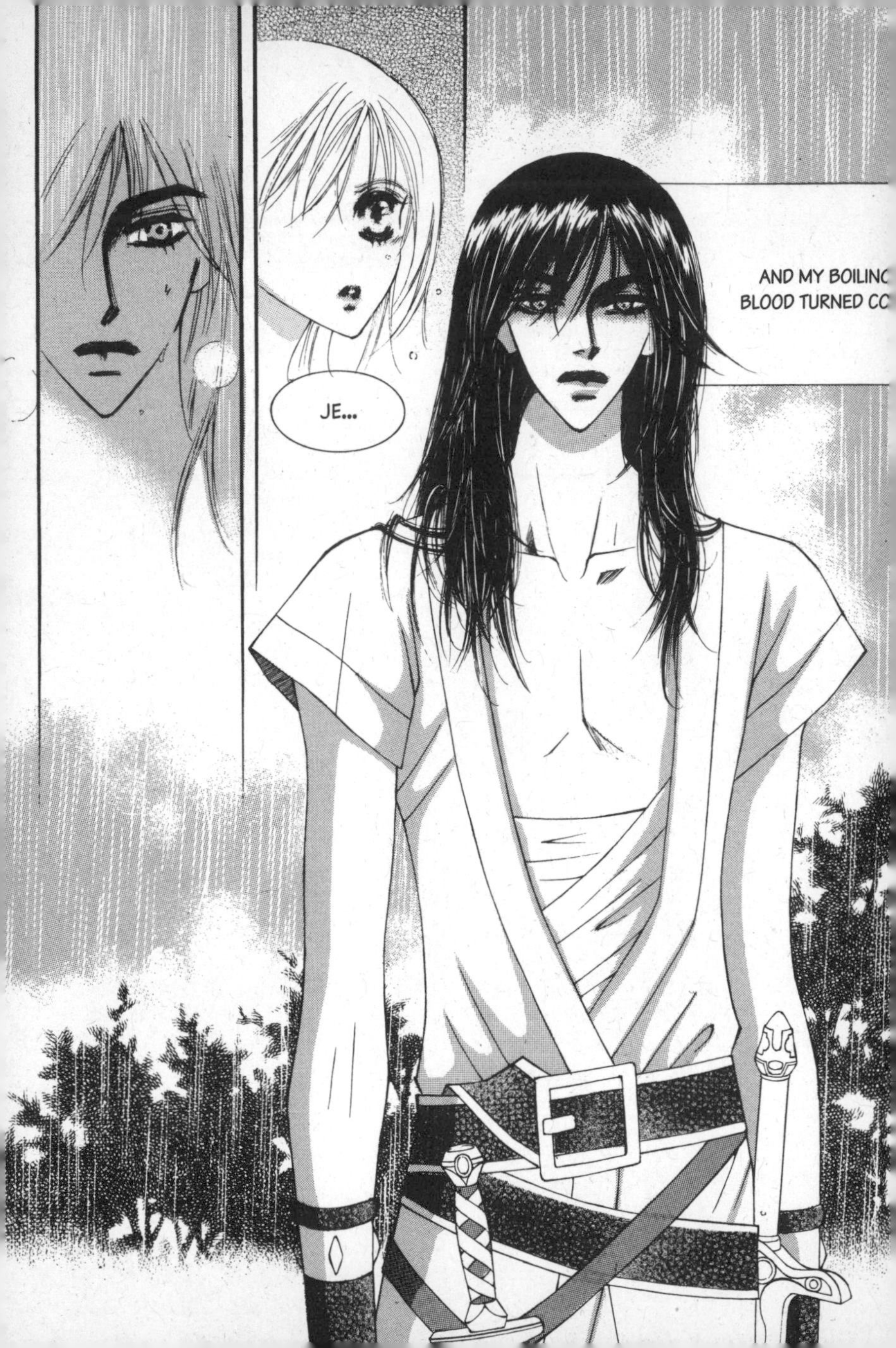
AND MY BOILING
BLOOD TURNED CO
JE...

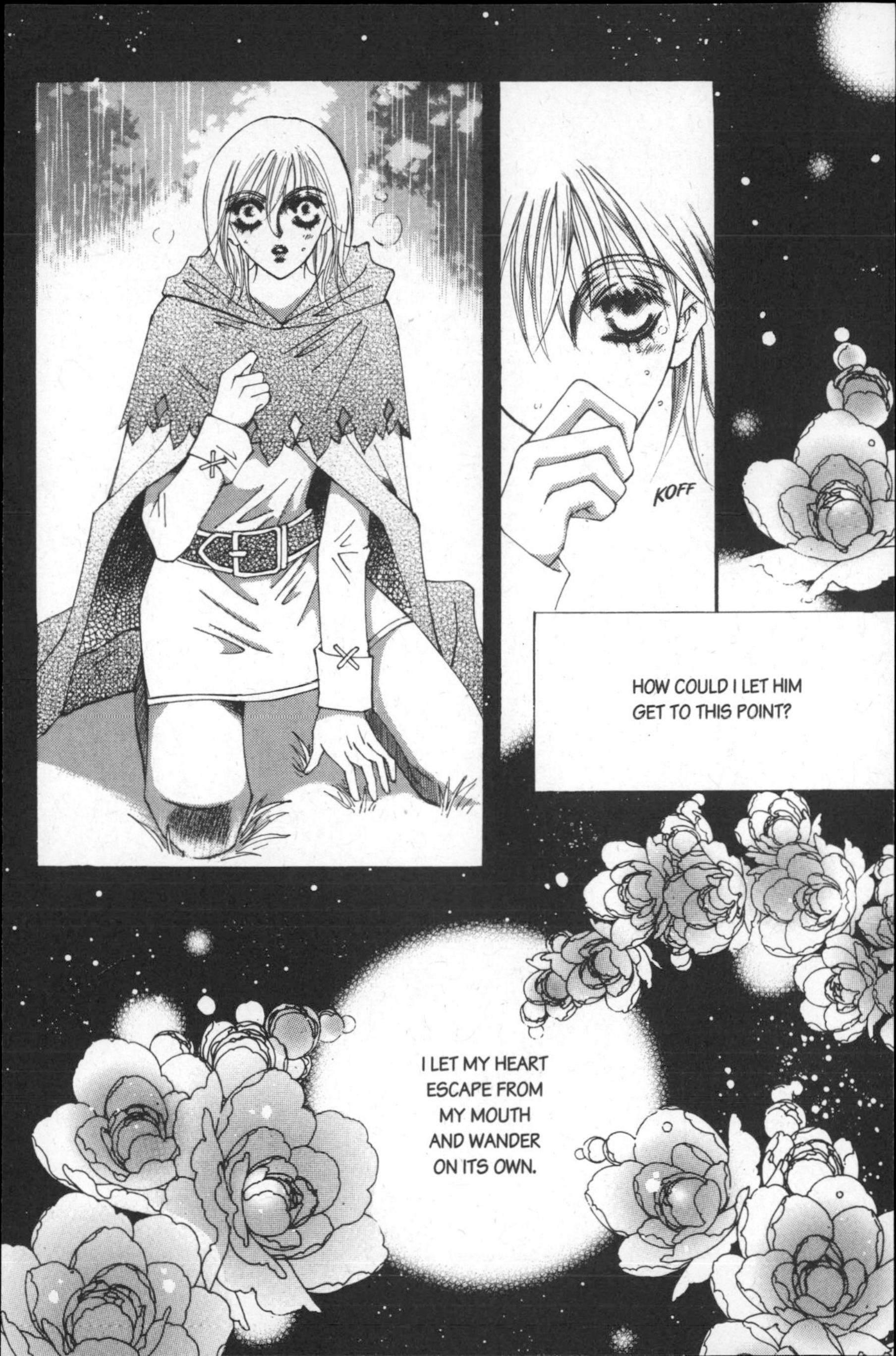
KOFF
HOW COULD I LET HIM GET TO THIS POINT?
I LET MY HEART ESCAPE FROM MY MOUTH AND WANDER ON ITS OWN.

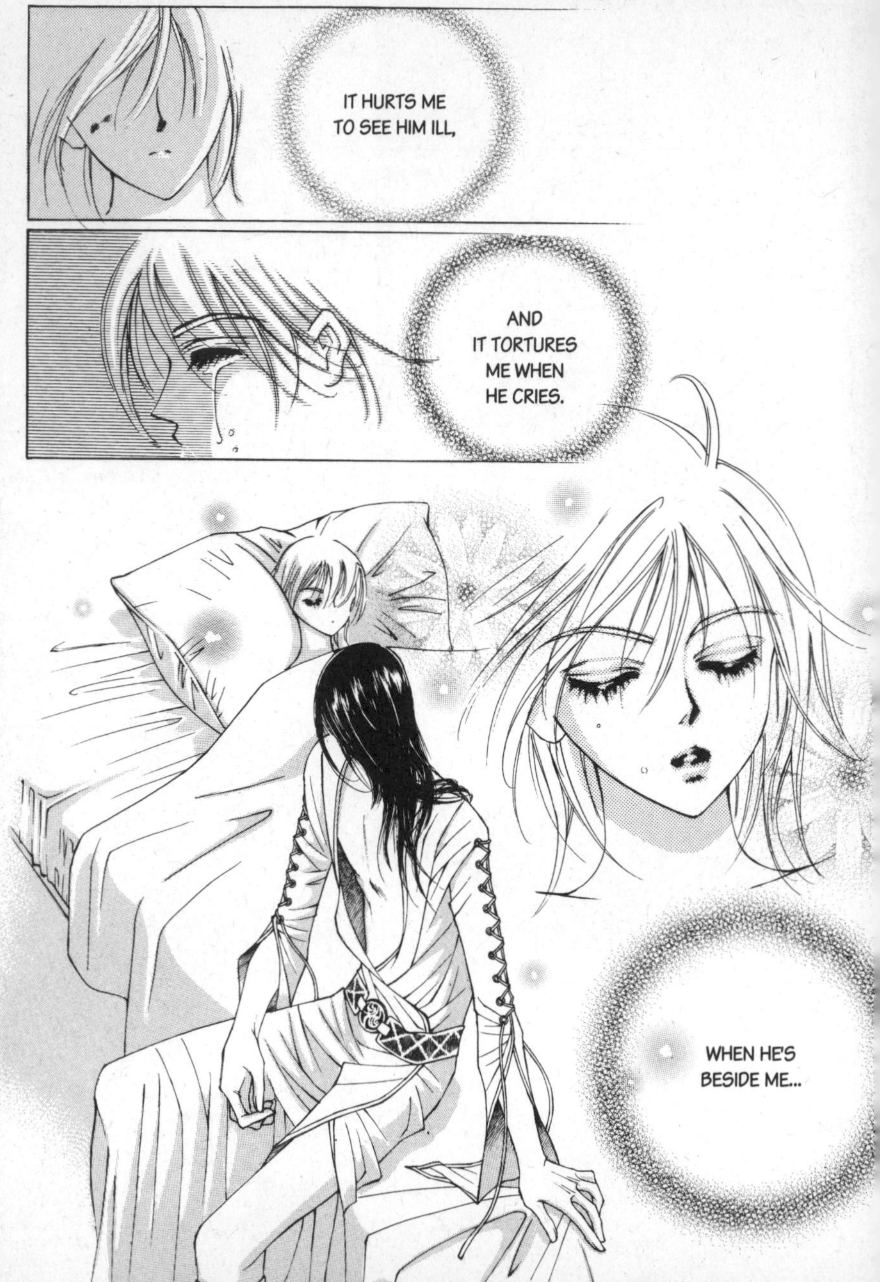
IT HURTS ME
TO SEE HIM ILL,
AND
IT TORTURES
ME WHEN
HE CRIES.
WHEN HE'S
BESIDE ME...

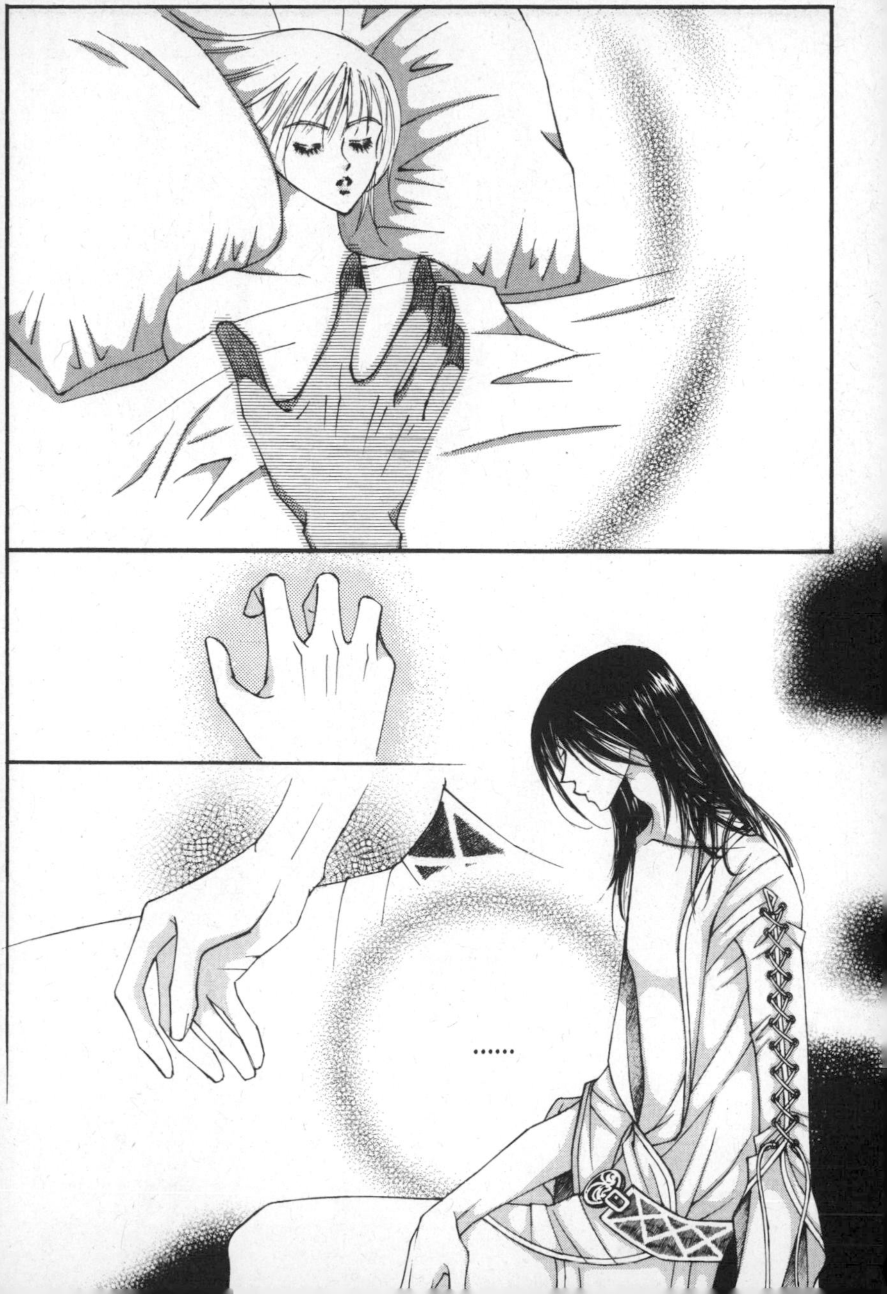
......

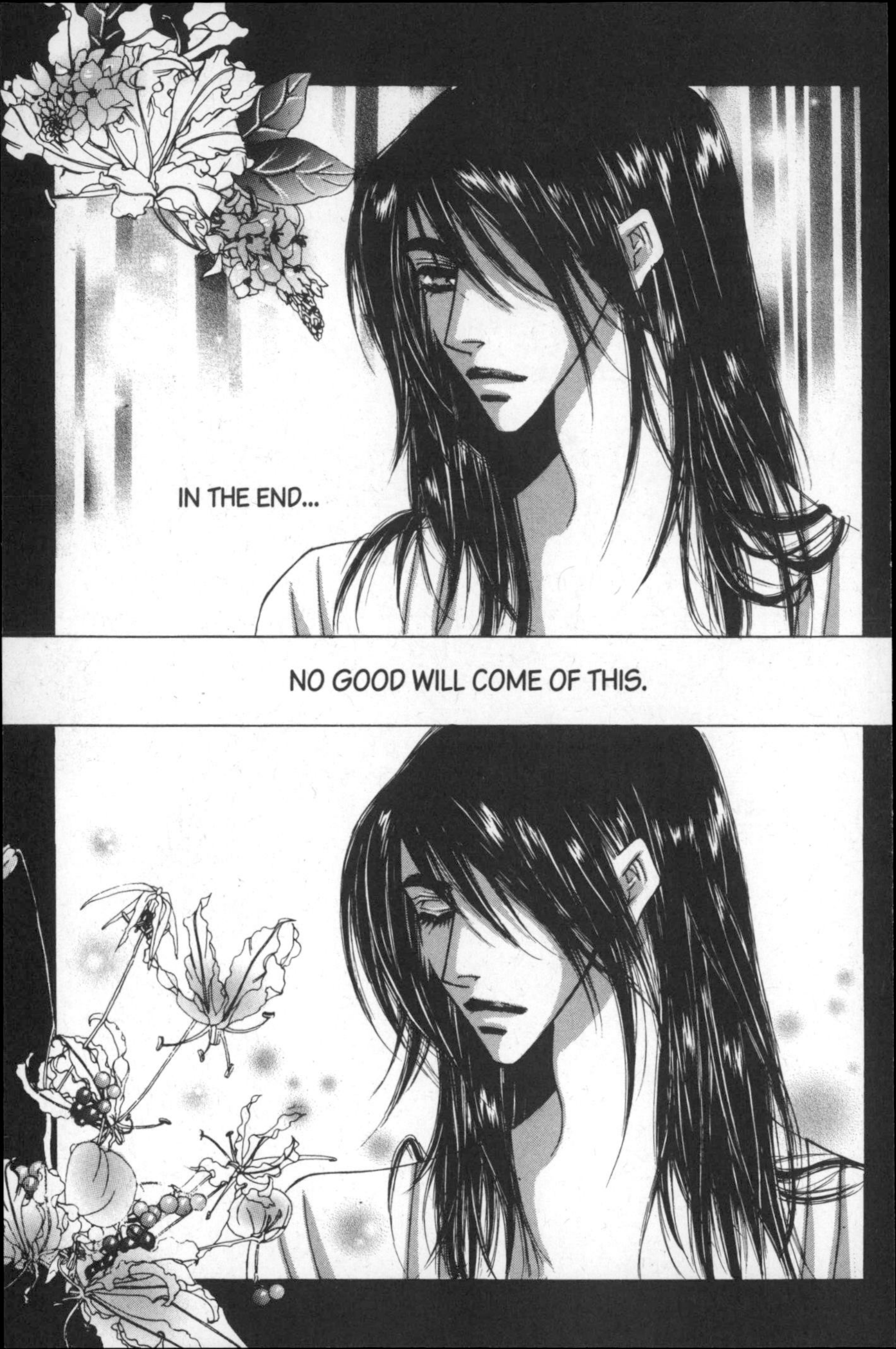
IN THE END...
NO GOOD WILL COME OF THIS.

EVEN THOUGH I'M SURE OF MY FEELINGS, HE'S TOO YOUNG IN HIS.
HE'S VERY RASH.
AND IF HE HAD KNOWN THE STATE I'M IN, HE NEVER WOULD HAVE FLOWN ACROSS THE BORDER SO DEFENSELESSLY.

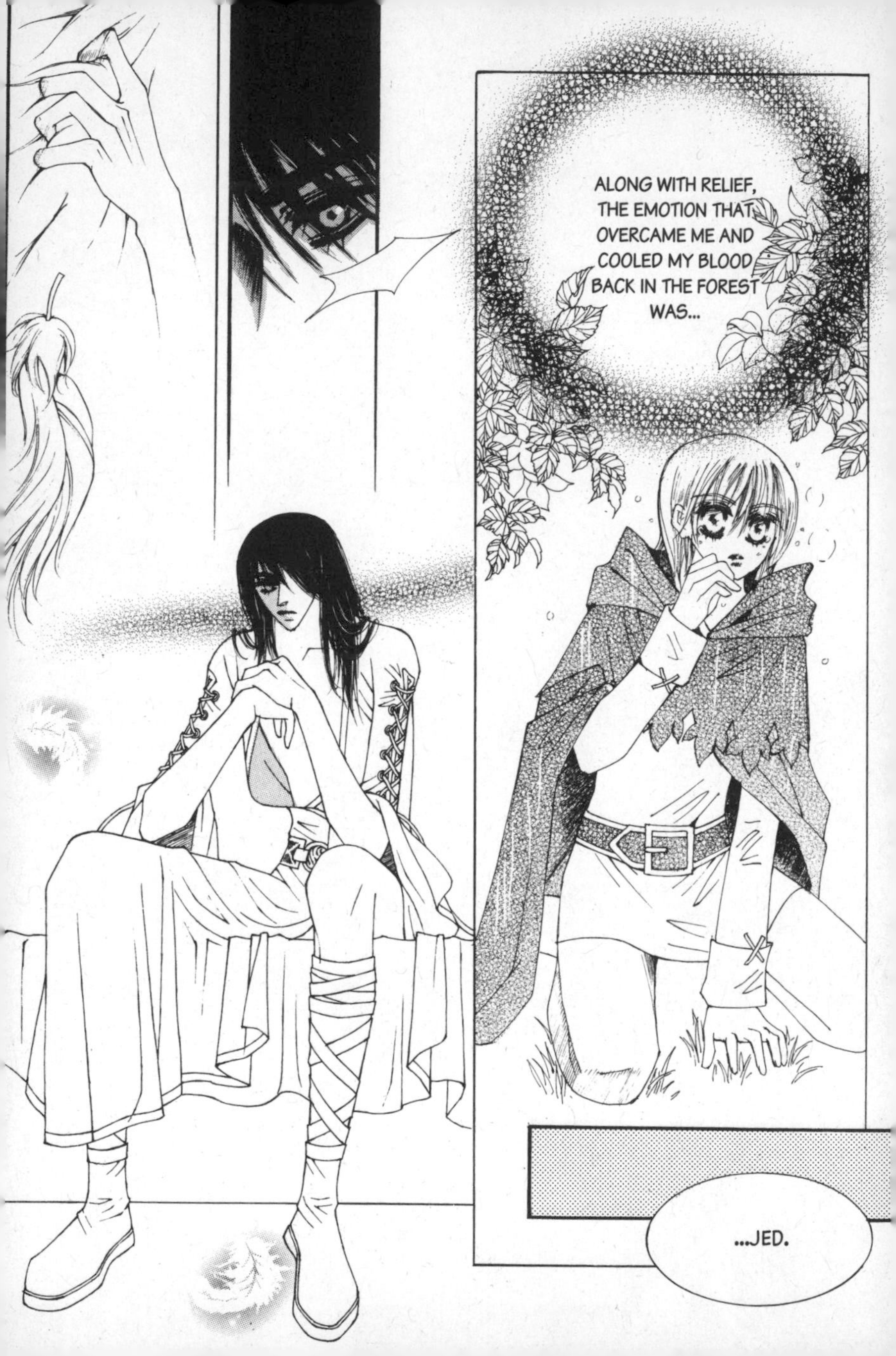
ALONG WITH RELIEF, THE EMOTION THAT OVERCAME ME AND COOLED MY BLOOD BACK IN THE FOREST WAS...
...JED.

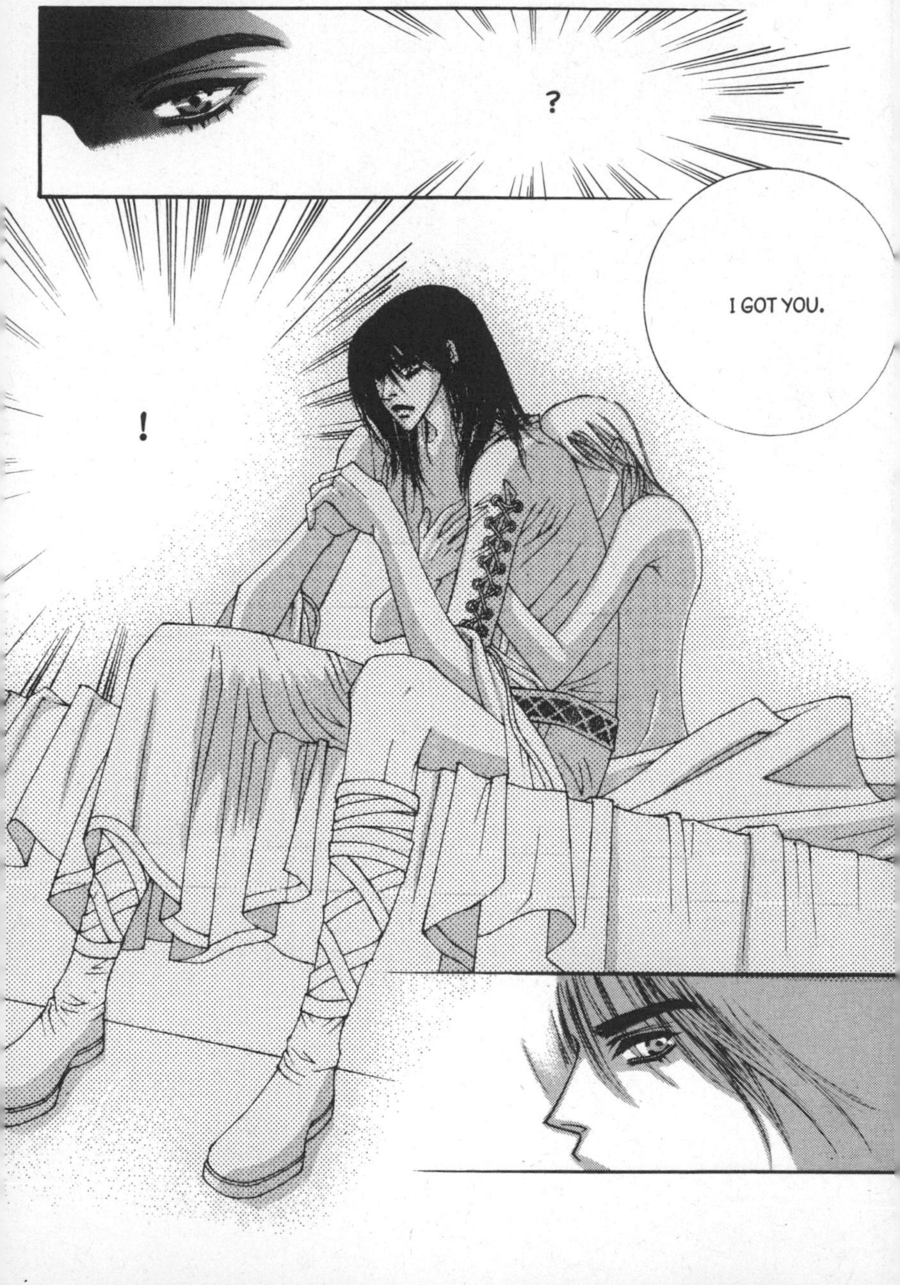
?
I GOT YOU.
!

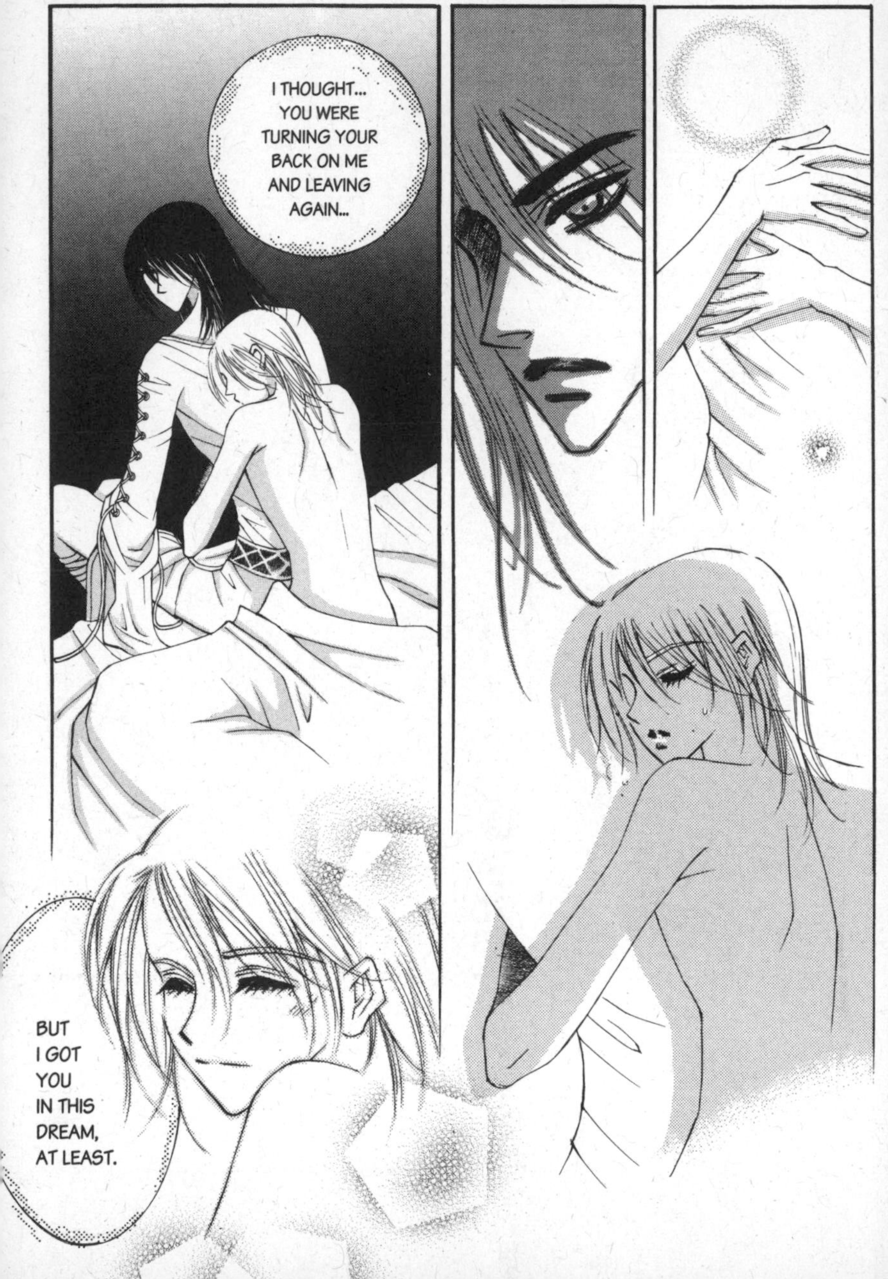
I THOUGHT... YOU WERE TURNING YOUR BACK ON ME AND LEAVING AGAIN...
BUT I GOT YOU IN THIS DREAM, AT LEAST.

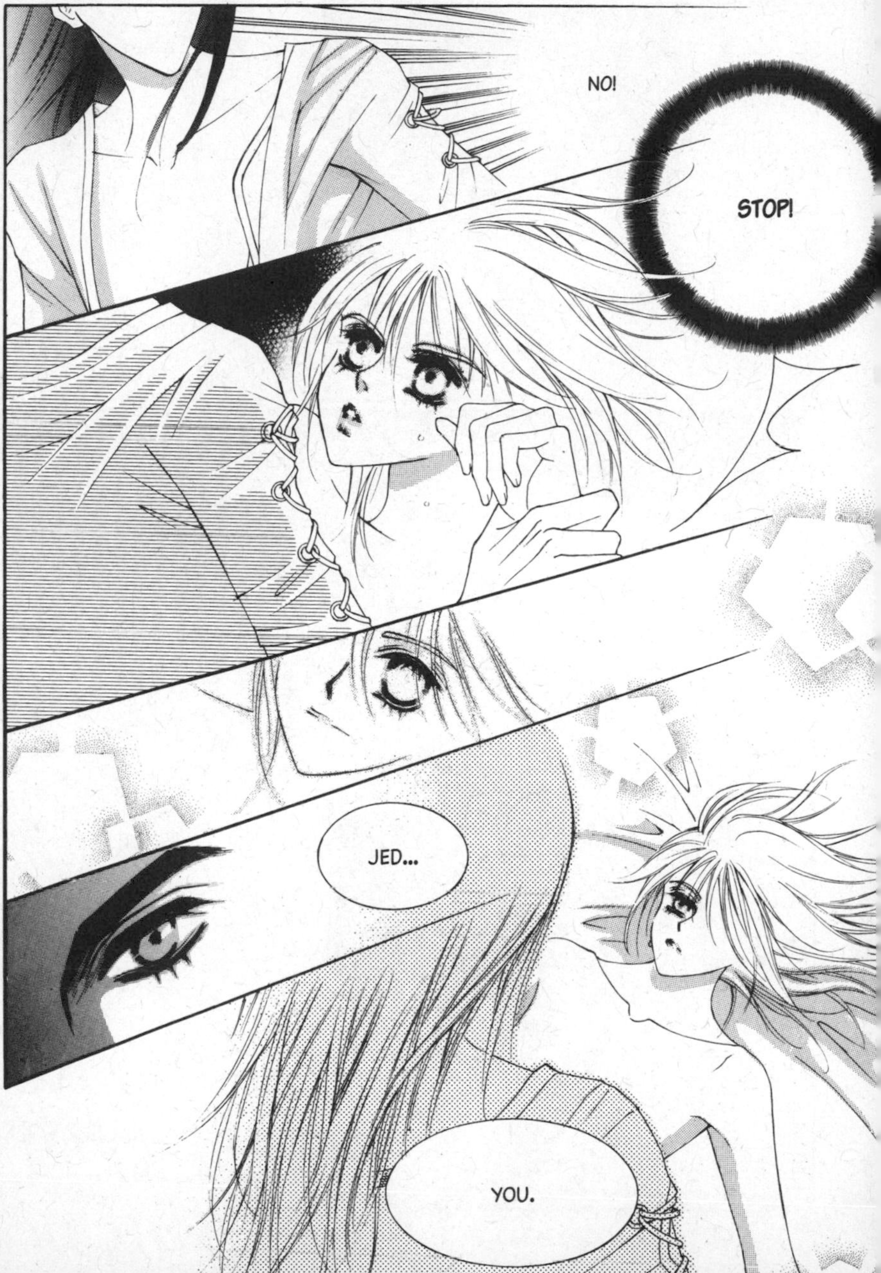
NO!
STOP!
JED...
YOU.

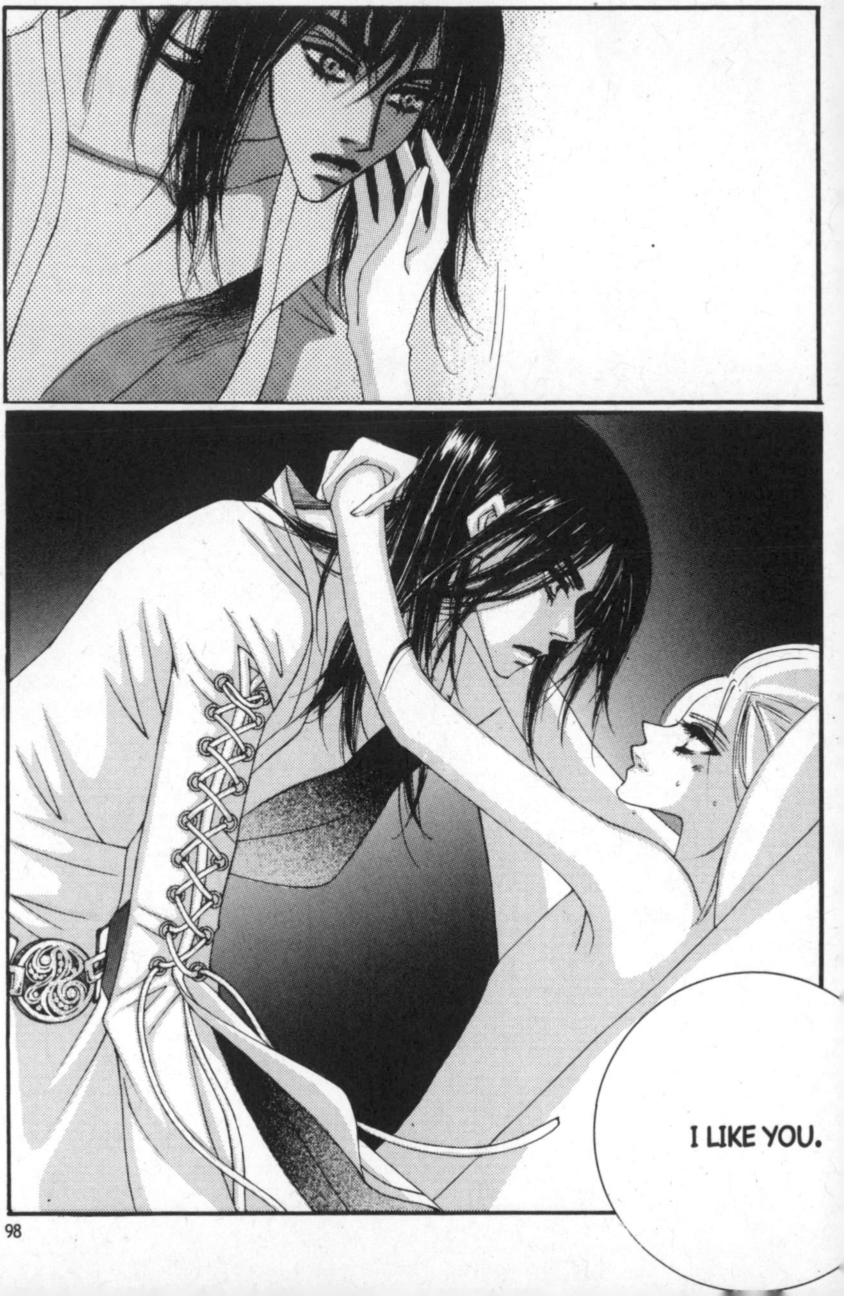
I LIKE YOU.

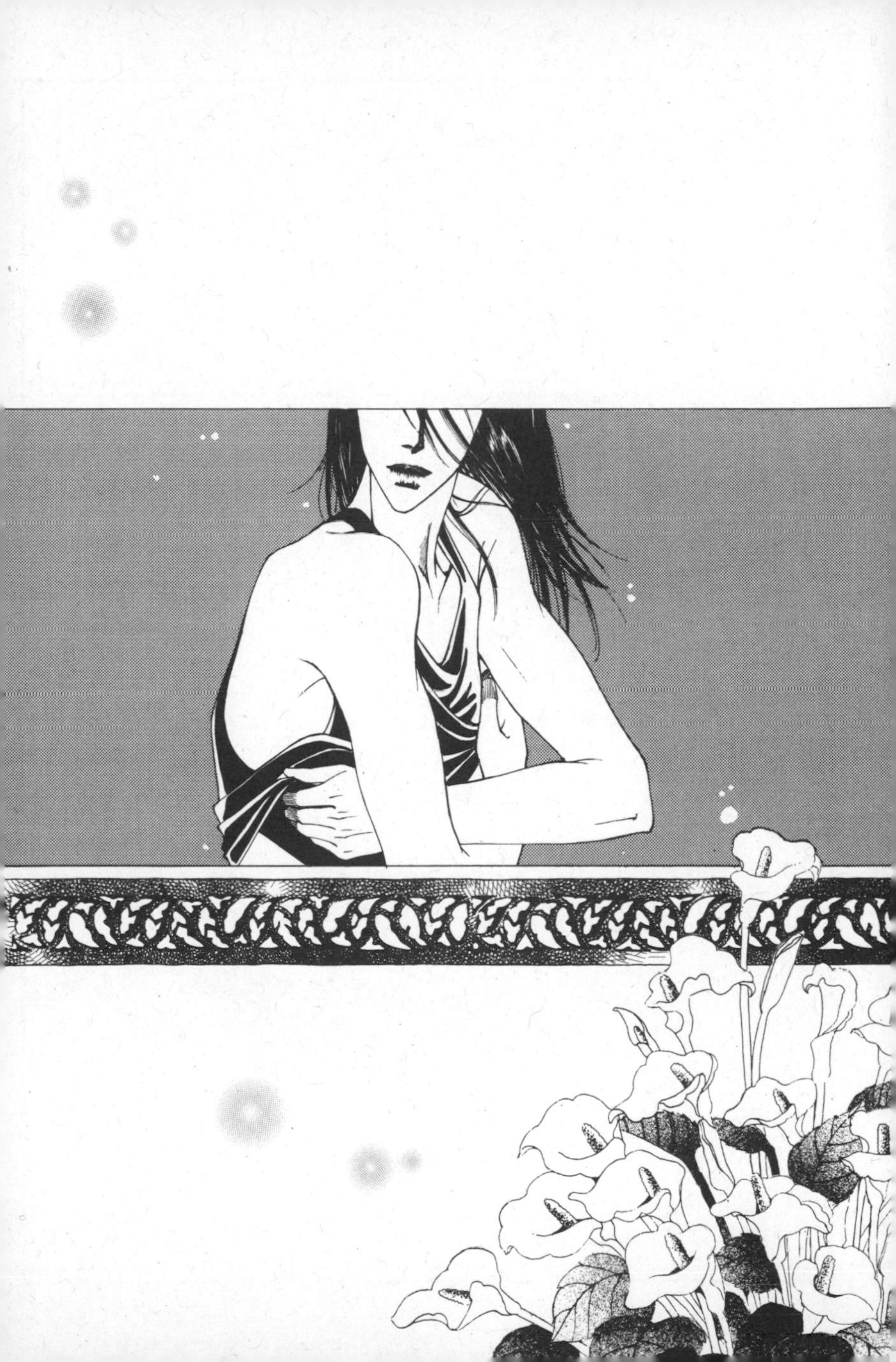

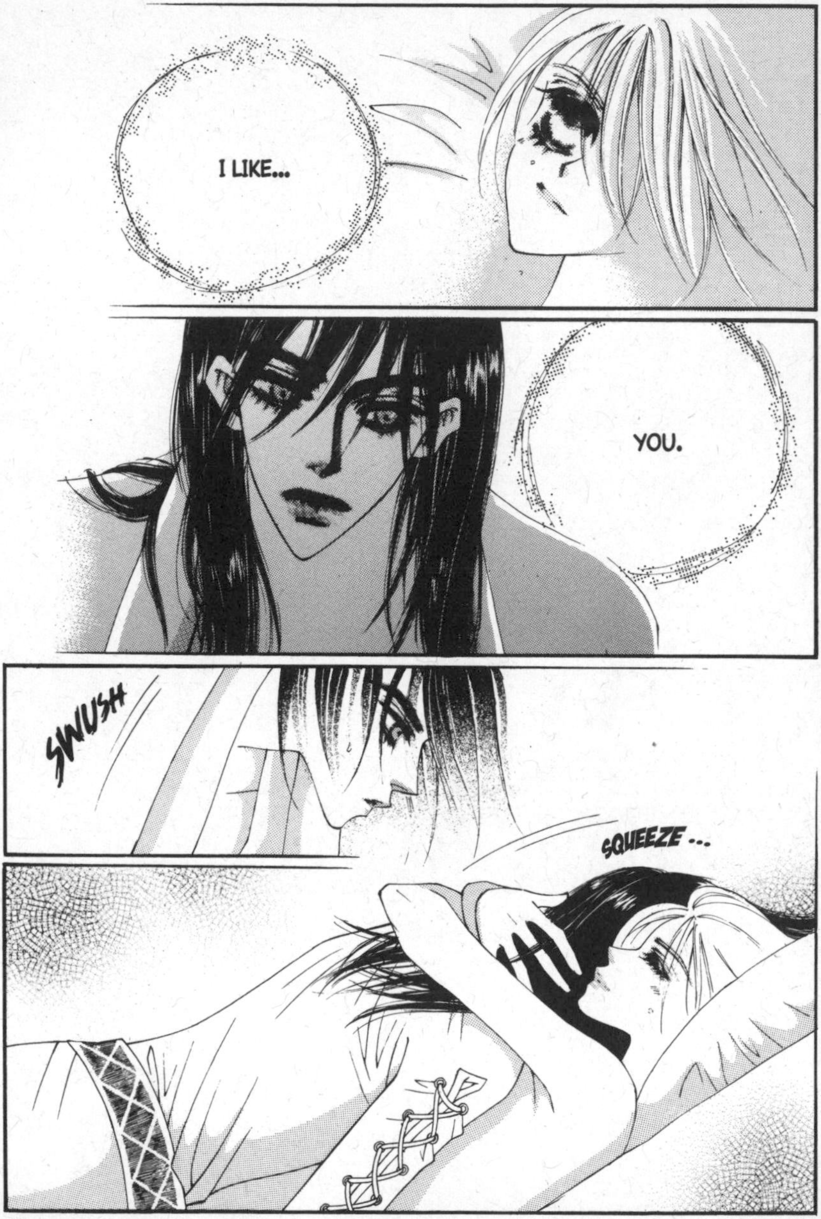
I LIKE...
YOU.
SWUSH
SQUEEZE ...

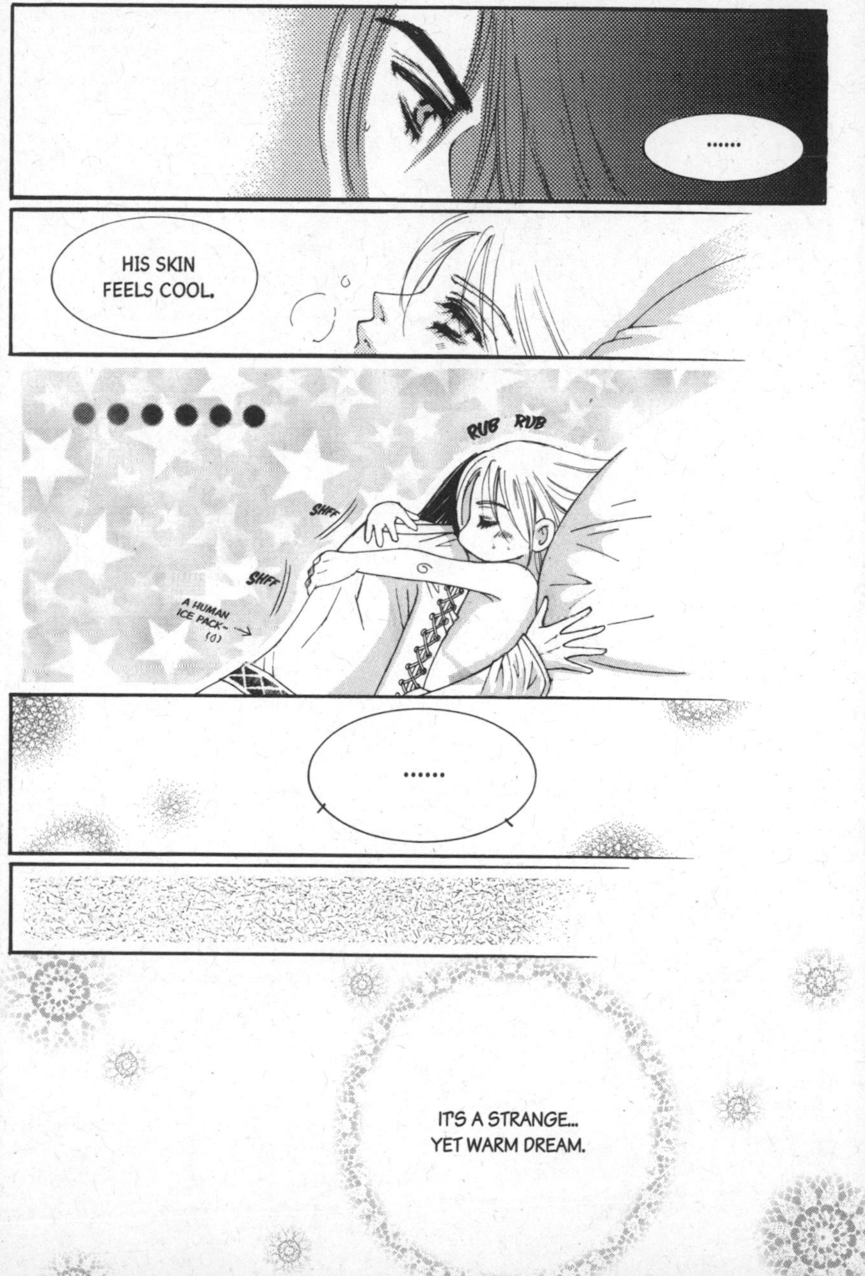
......
HIS SKIN FEELS COOL.
●●●●●●
RUB RUB
SHFF
SHFF
A HUMAN ICE PACK~
......
IT'S A STRANGE... YET WARM DREAM.

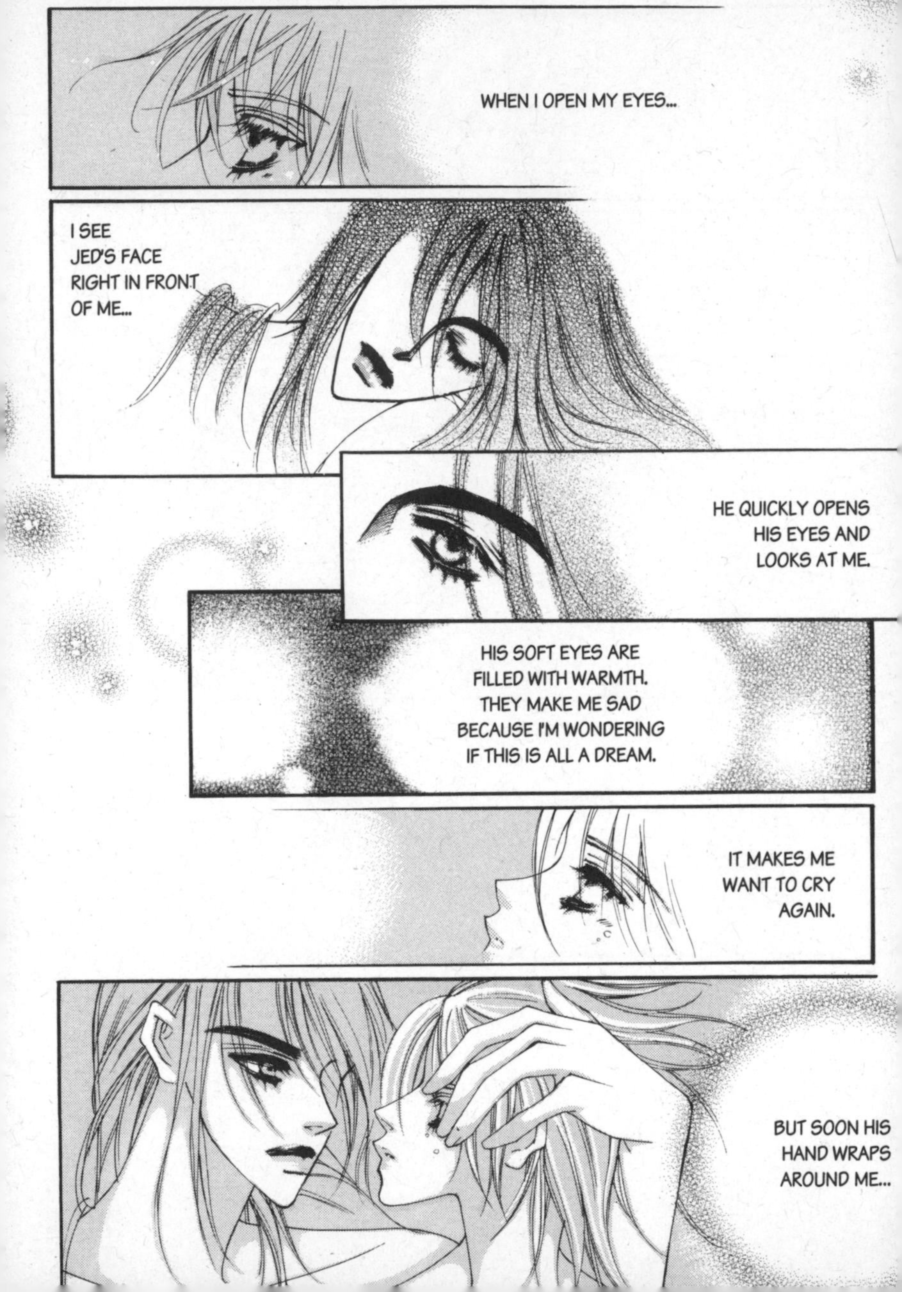
WHEN I OPEN MY EYES...
I SEE
JED'S FACE
RIGHT IN FRONT
OF ME...
HE QUICKLY OPENS
HIS EYES AND
LOOKS AT ME.
HIS SOFT EYES ARE
FILLED WITH WARMTH.
THEY MAKE ME SAD
BECAUSE I'M WONDERING
IF THIS IS ALL A DREAM.
IT MAKES ME
WANT TO CRY
AGAIN.
BUT SOON HIS
HAND WRAPS
AROUND ME...

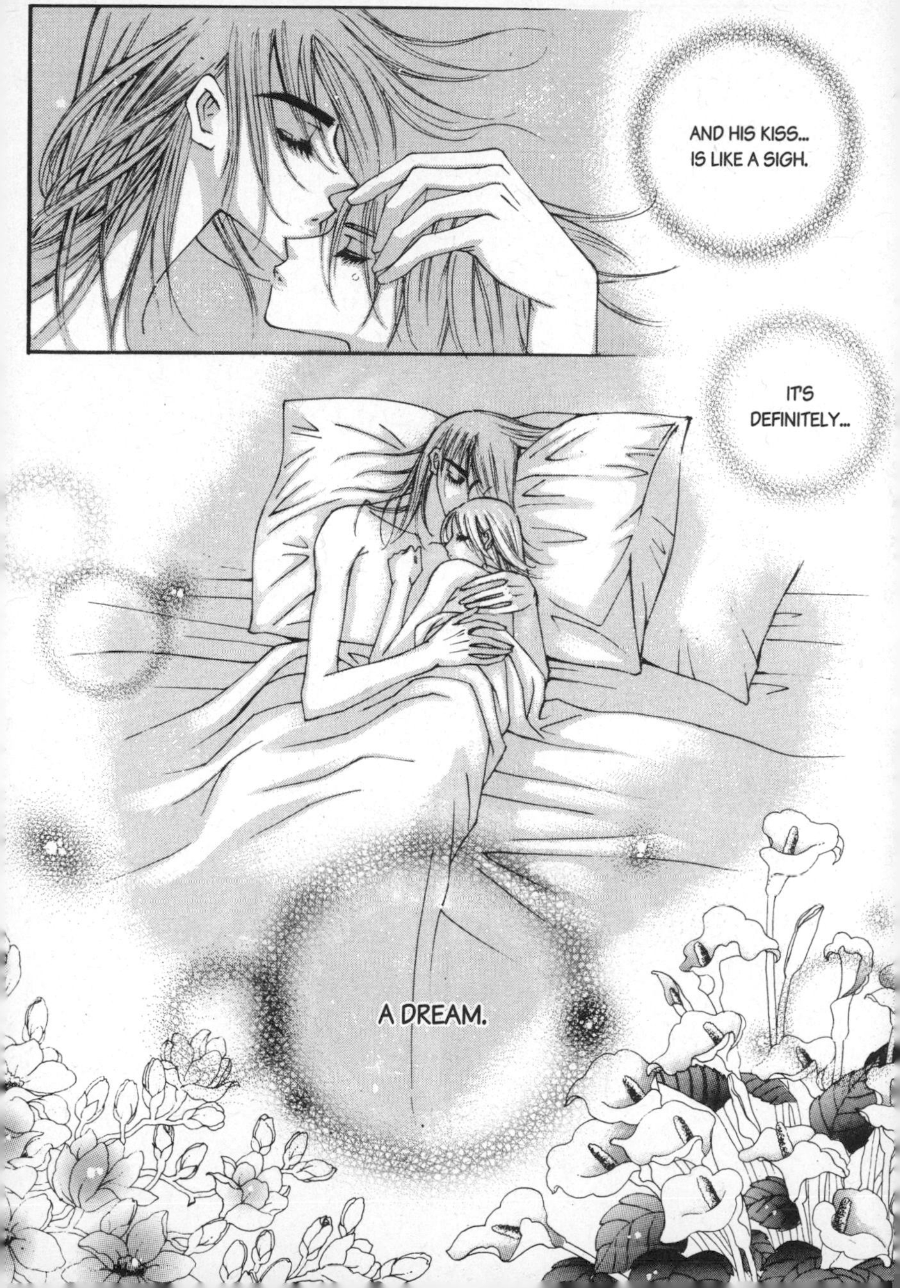
AND HIS KISS...
IS LIKE A SIGH.
IT'S
DEFINITELY...
A DREAM.

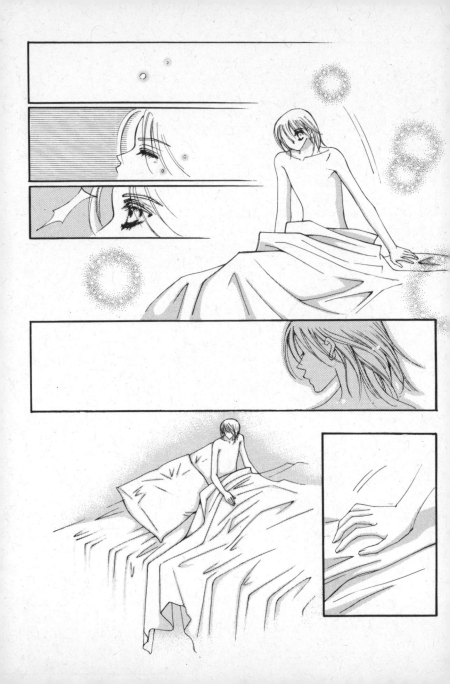

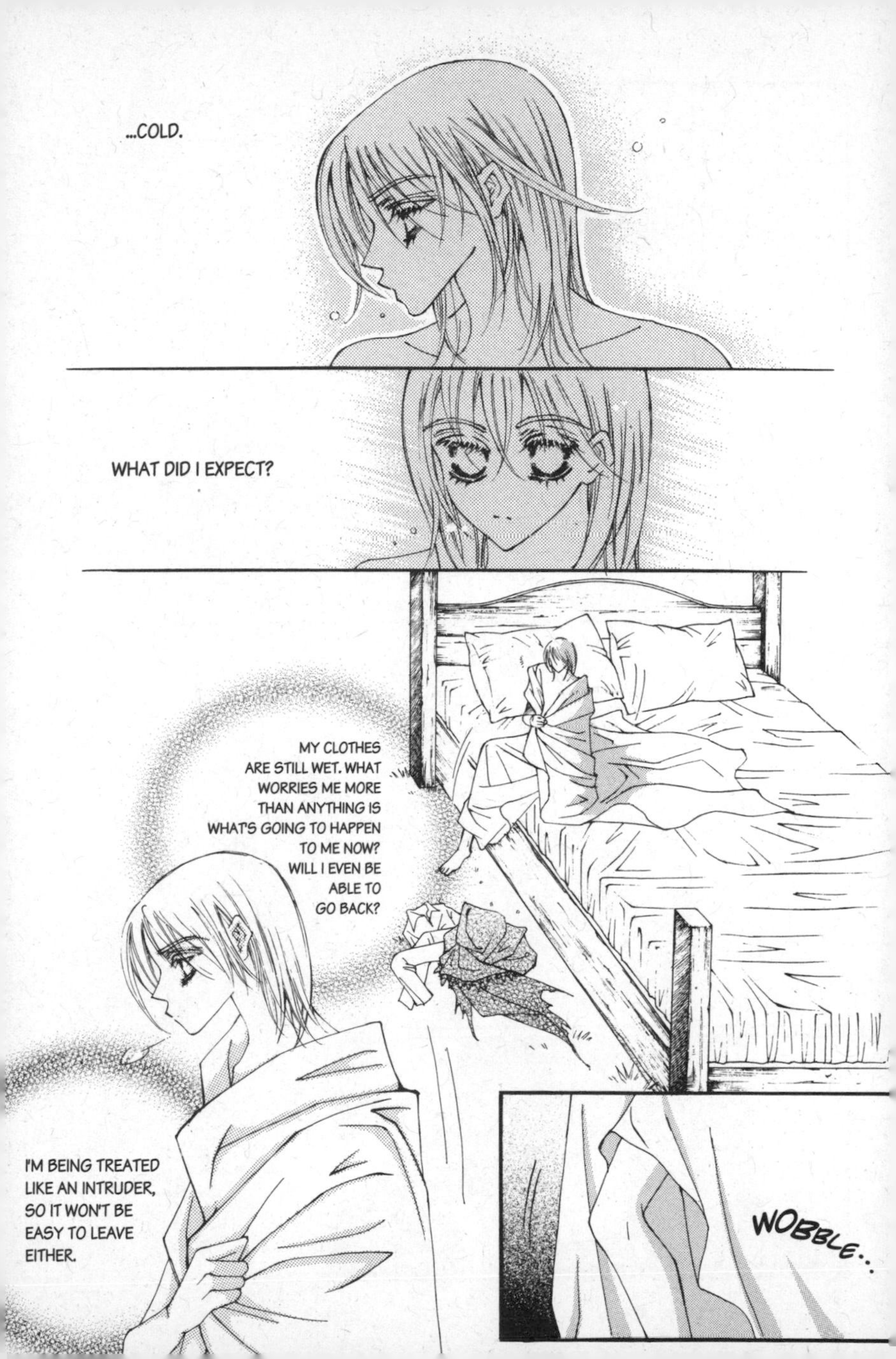
...COLD.
WHAT DID I EXPECT?
MY CLOTHES ARE STILL WET. WHAT WORRIES ME MORE THAN ANYTHING IS WHAT'S GOING TO HAPPEN TO ME NOW? WILL I EVEN BE ABLE TO GO BACK?
I'M BEING TREATED LIKE AN INTRUDER, SO IT WON'T BE EASY TO LEAVE EITHER.
WOBBLE...

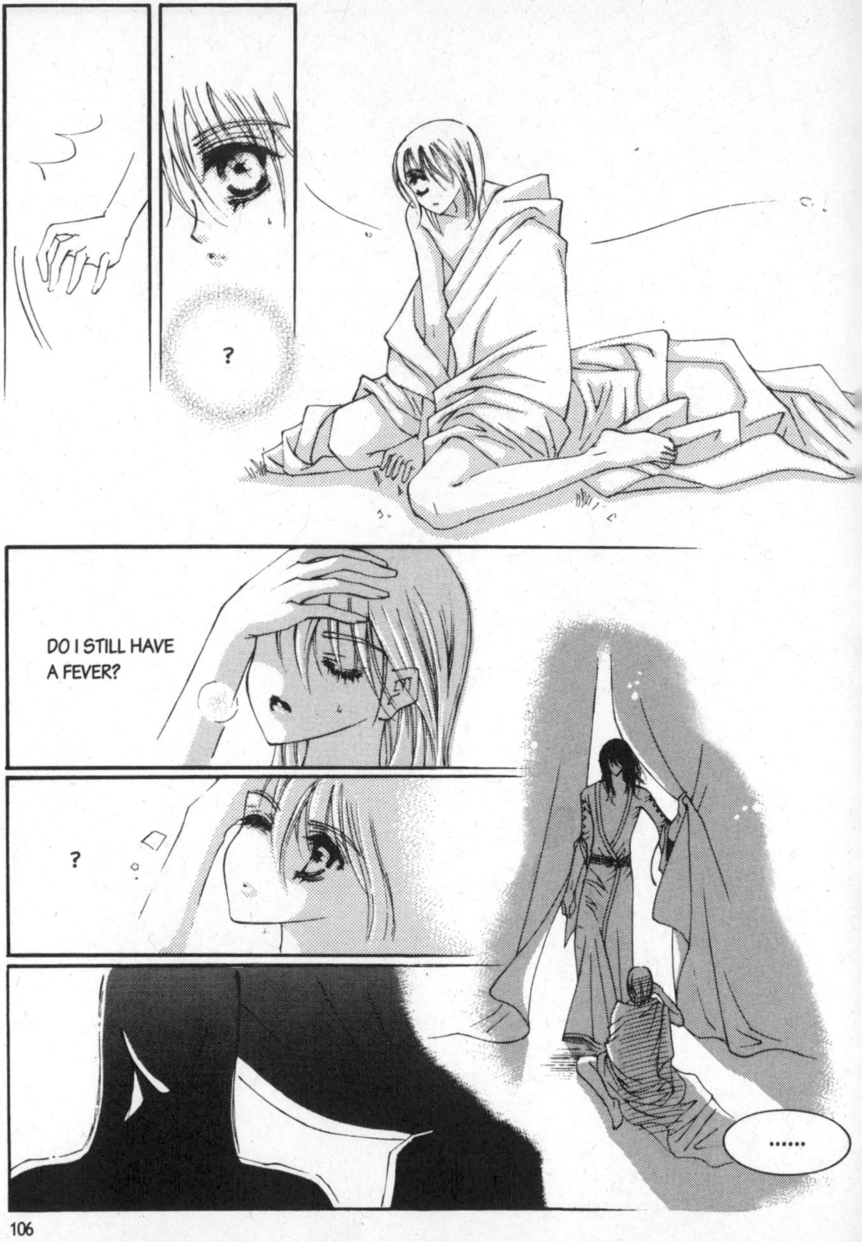
?
DO I STILL HAVE A FEVER?
?
......

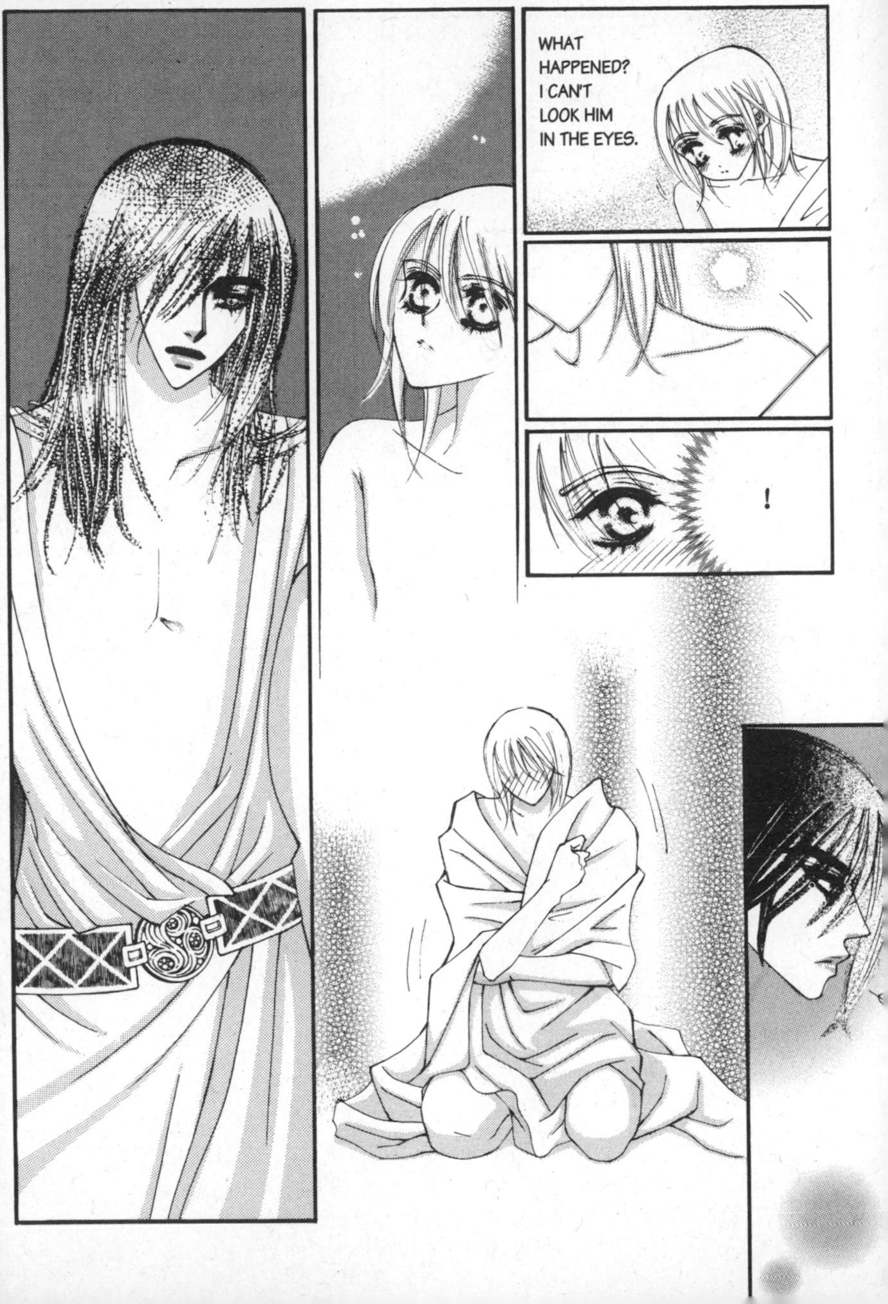
WHAT HAPPENED? I CAN'T LOOK HIM IN THE EYES.
!

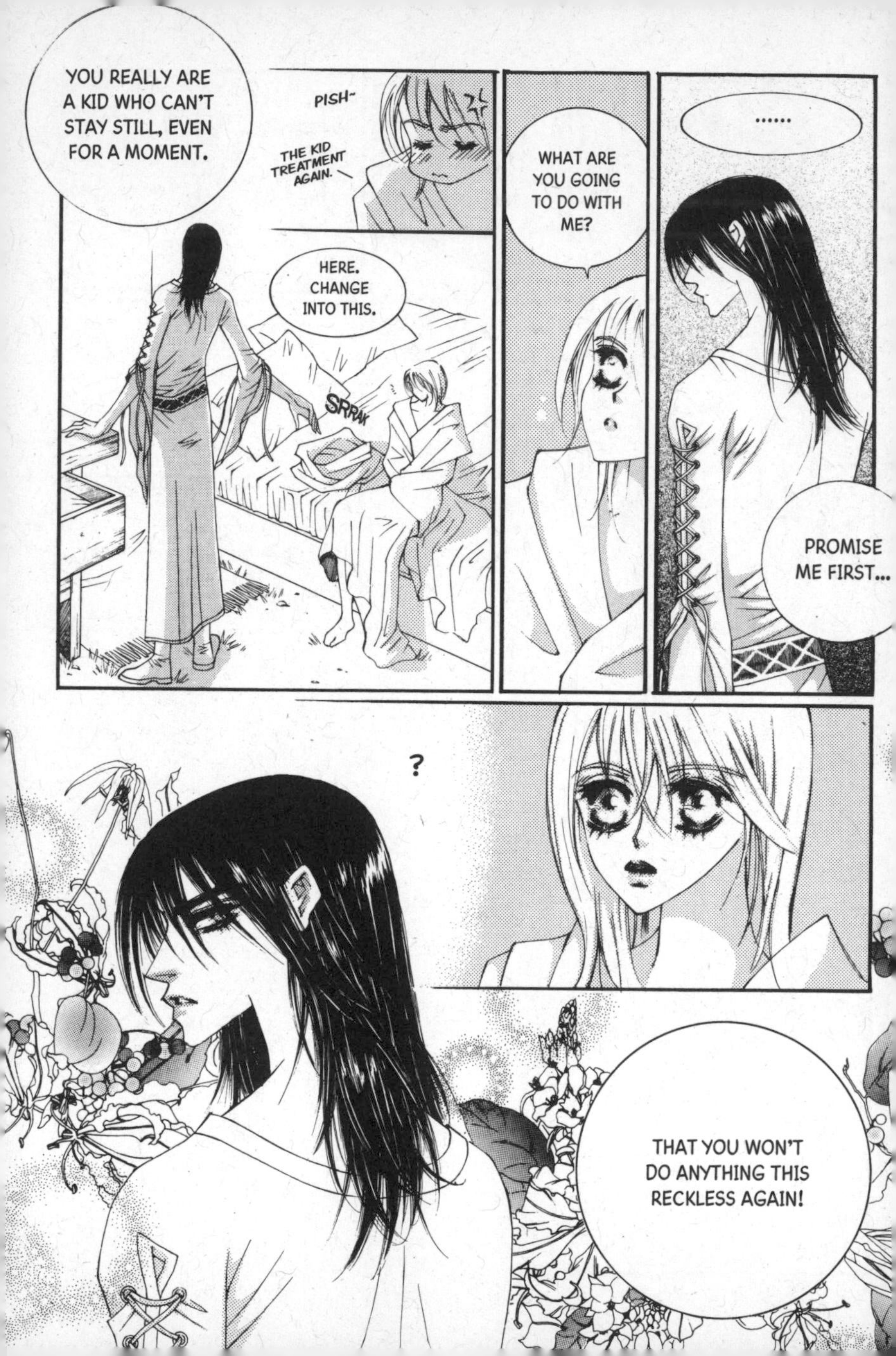

YOU REALLY ARE A KID WHO CAN'T STAY STILL, EVEN FOR A MOMENT.
PISH~
THE KID TREATMENT AGAIN.
HERE. CHANGE INTO THIS.
SRRAK
WHAT ARE YOU GOING TO DO WITH ME?
......
PROMISE ME FIRST...
?
THAT YOU WON'T DO ANYTHING THIS RECKLESS AGAIN!

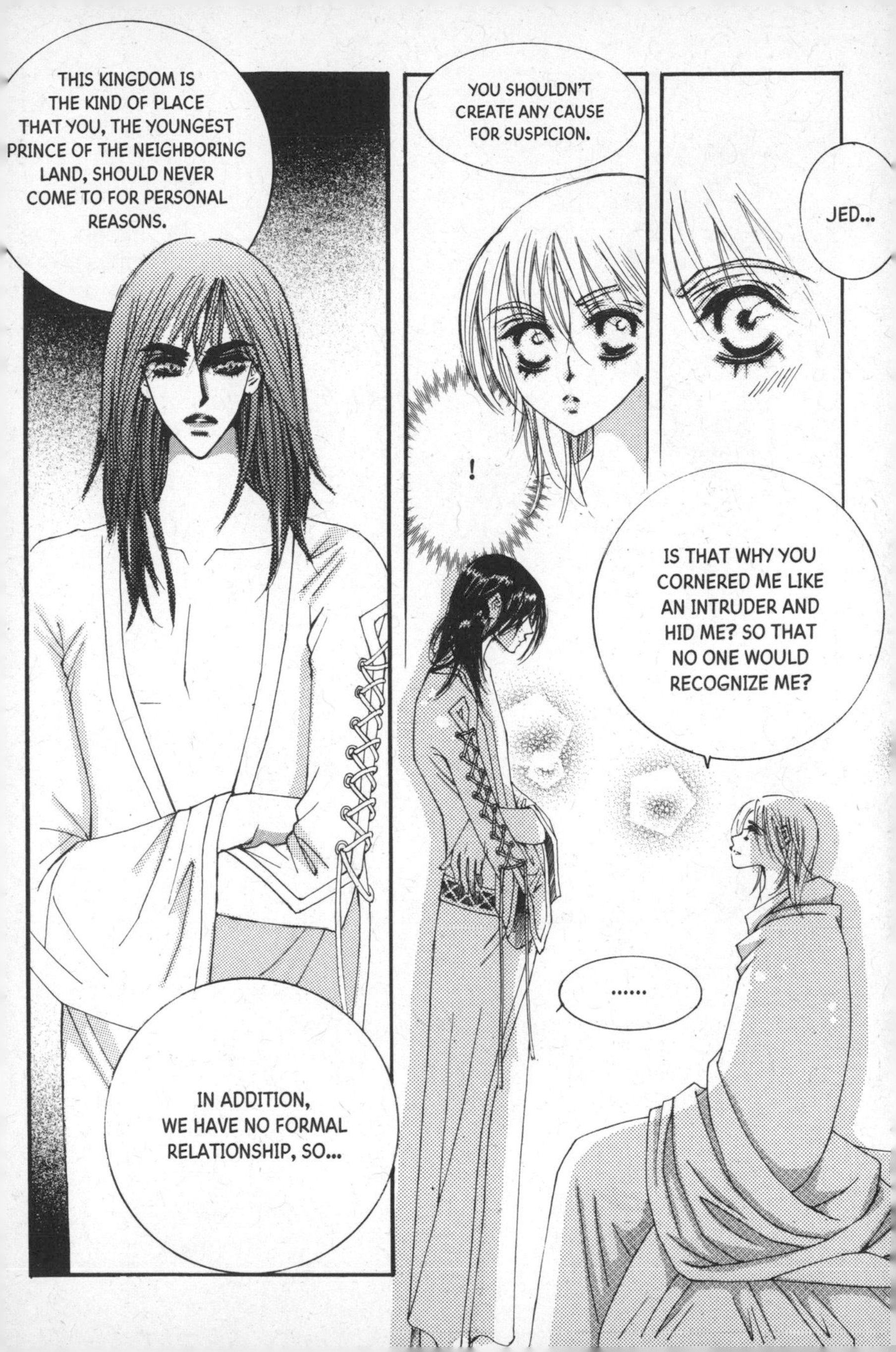
THIS KINGDOM IS THE KIND OF PLACE THAT YOU, THE YOUNGEST PRINCE OF THE NEIGHBORING LAND, SHOULD NEVER COME TO FOR PERSONAL REASONS.
IN ADDITION, WE HAVE NO FORMAL RELATIONSHIP, SO...
YOU SHOULDN'T CREATE ANY CAUSE FOR SUSPICION.
JED...
!
IS THAT WHY YOU CORNERED ME LIKE AN INTRUDER AND HID ME? SO THAT NO ONE WOULD RECOGNIZE ME?
......

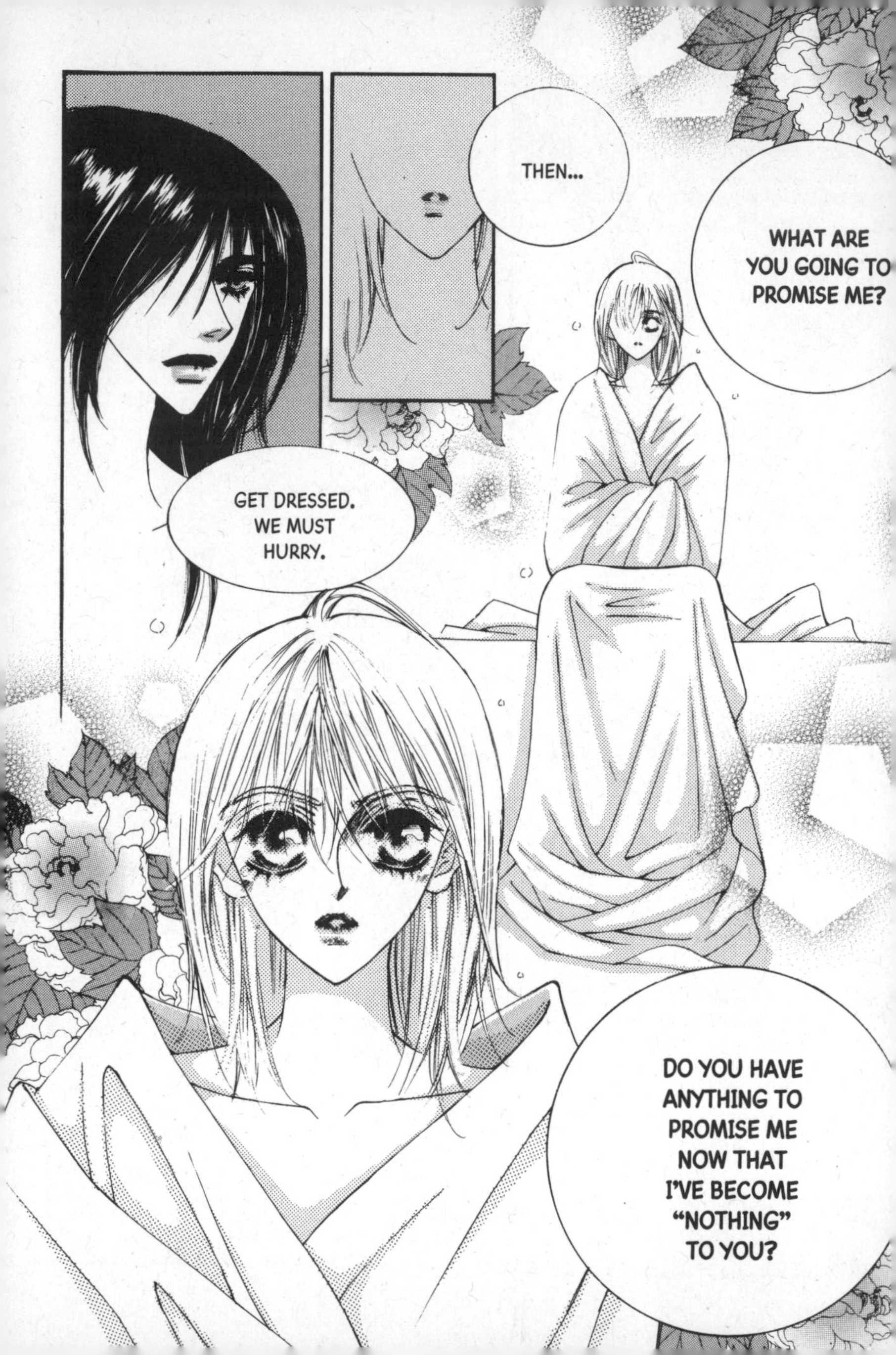
THEN...
WHAT ARE YOU GOING TO PROMISE ME?
GET DRESSED. WE MUST HURRY.
DO YOU HAVE ANYTHING TO PROMISE ME NOW THAT I'VE BECOME "NOTHING" TO YOU?

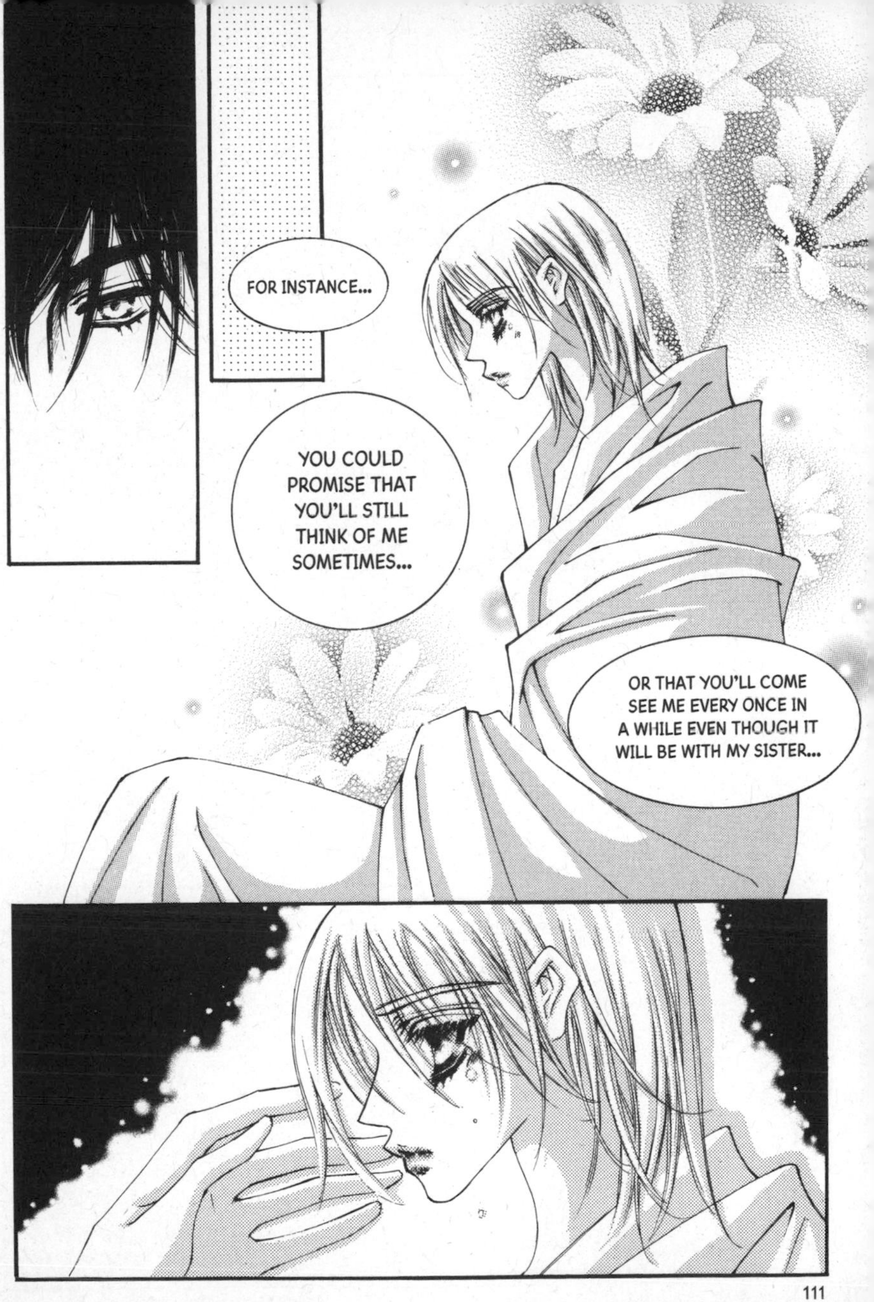
FOR INSTANCE...
YOU COULD PROMISE THAT YOU'LL STILL THINK OF ME SOMETIMES...
OR THAT YOU'LL COME SEE ME EVERY ONCE IN A WHILE EVEN THOUGH IT WILL BE WITH MY SISTER...

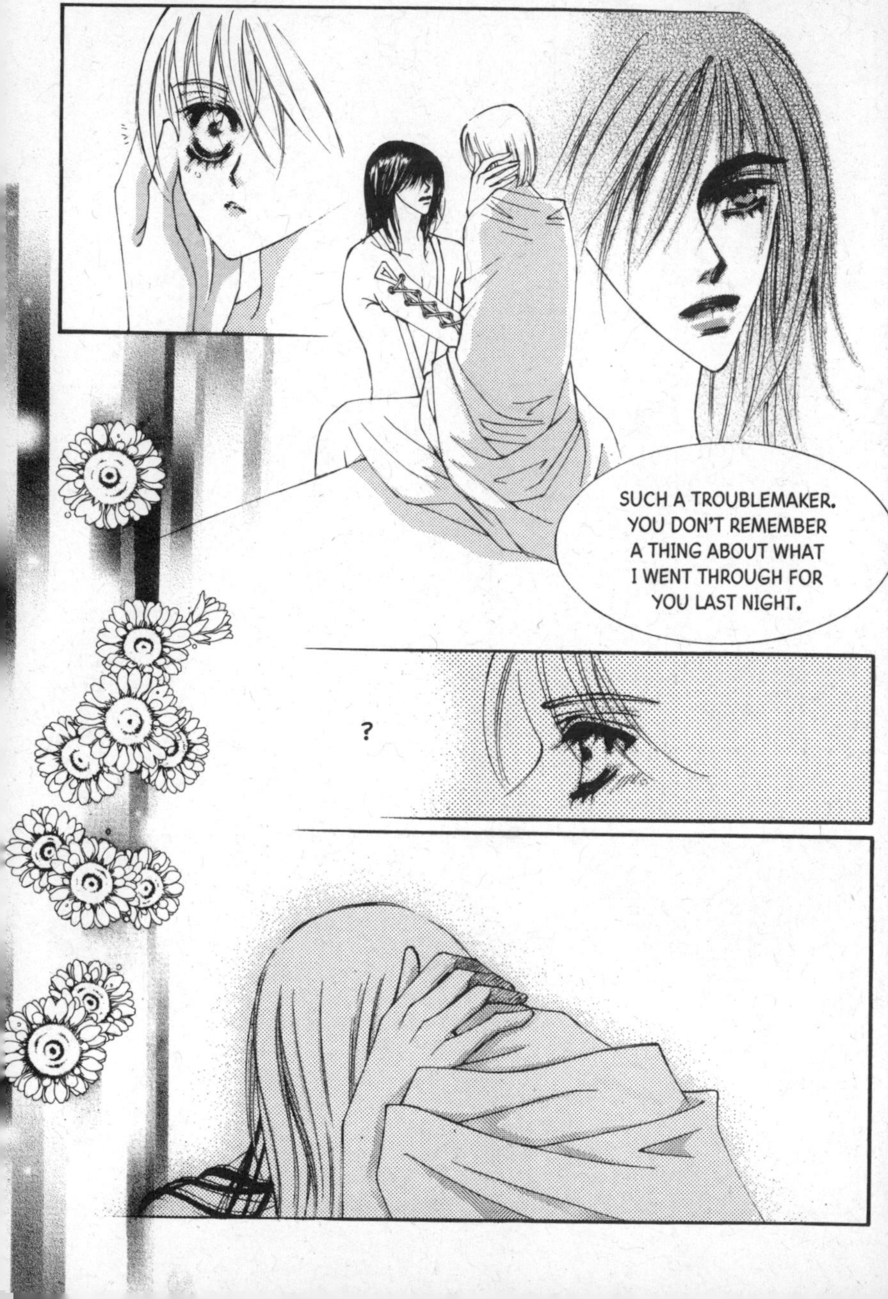
SUCH A TROUBLEMAKER. YOU DON'T REMEMBER A THING ABOUT WHAT I WENT THROUGH FOR YOU LAST NIGHT.
?

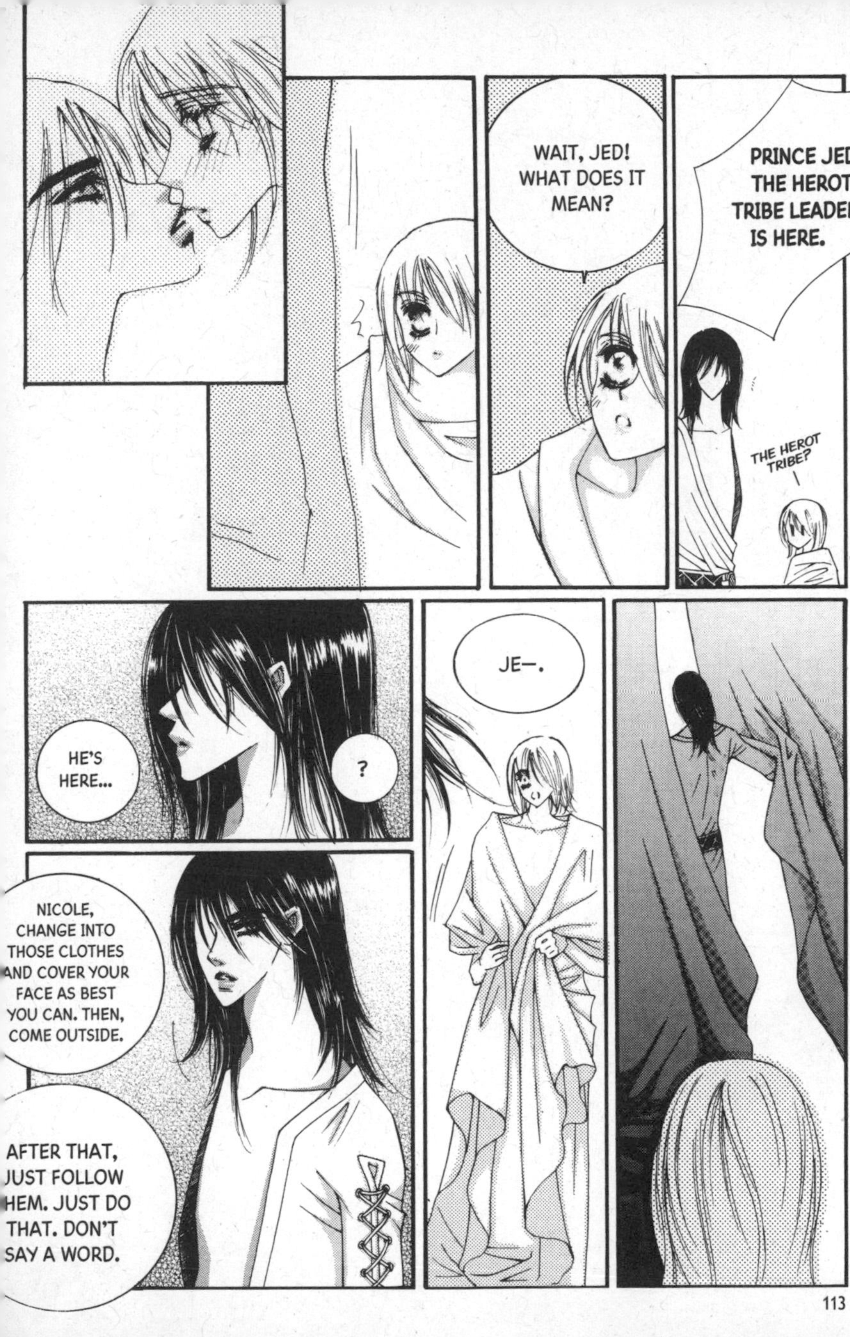
WAIT, JED! WHAT DOES IT MEAN?
PRINCE JED! THE HEROT TRIBE LEADER IS HERE.
THE HEROT TRIBE?
HE'S HERE...
?
JE—.
NICOLE, CHANGE INTO THOSE CLOTHES AND COVER YOUR FACE AS BEST YOU CAN. THEN, COME OUTSIDE.
AFTER THAT, JUST FOLLOW HEM. JUST DO THAT. DON'T SAY A WORD.

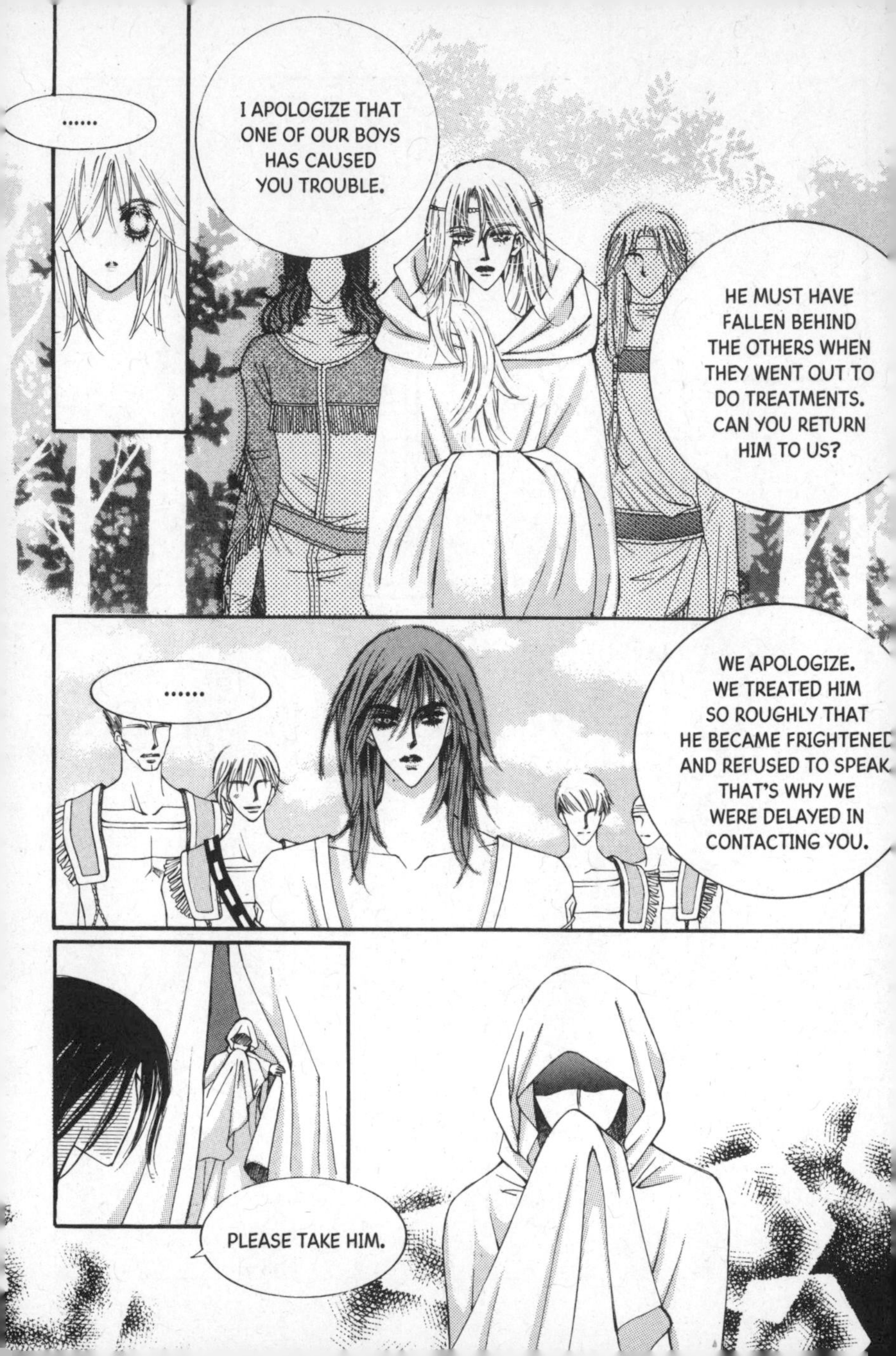
I APOLOGIZE THAT ONE OF OUR BOYS HAS CAUSED YOU TROUBLE.
......
HE MUST HAVE FALLEN BEHIND THE OTHERS WHEN THEY WENT OUT TO DO TREATMENTS. CAN YOU RETURN HIM TO US?
WE APOLOGIZE. WE TREATED HIM SO ROUGHLY THAT HE BECAME FRIGHTENED AND REFUSED TO SPEAK. THAT'S WHY WE WERE DELAYED IN CONTACTING YOU.
......
PLEASE TAKE HIM.

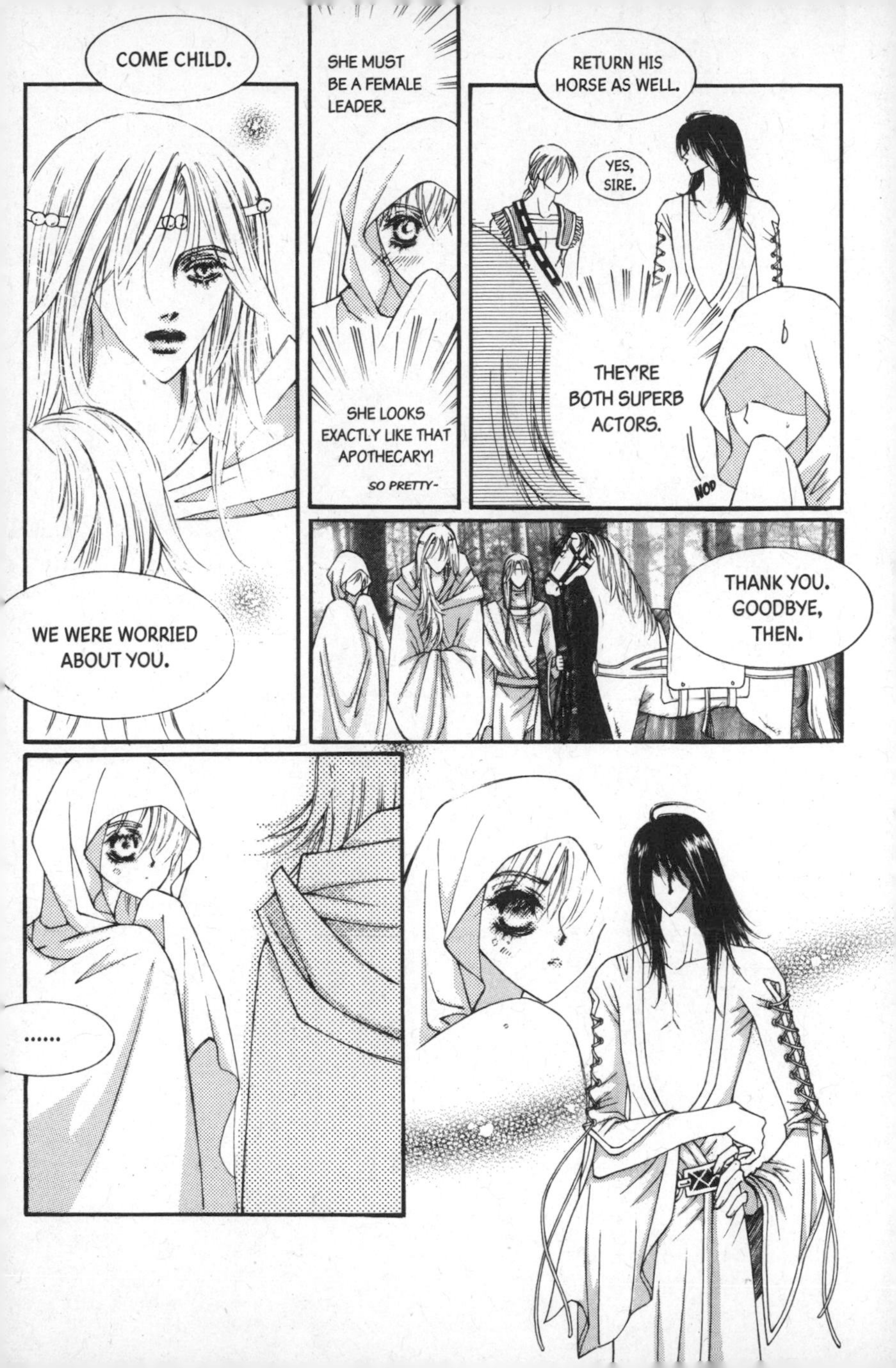
COME CHILD.
SHE MUST BE A FEMALE LEADER.
SHE LOOKS EXACTLY LIKE THAT APOTHECARY!
SO PRETTY-
RETURN HIS HORSE AS WELL.
YES, SIRE.
THEY'RE BOTH SUPERB ACTORS.
NOD
WE WERE WORRIED ABOUT YOU.
THANK YOU. GOODBYE, THEN.
....

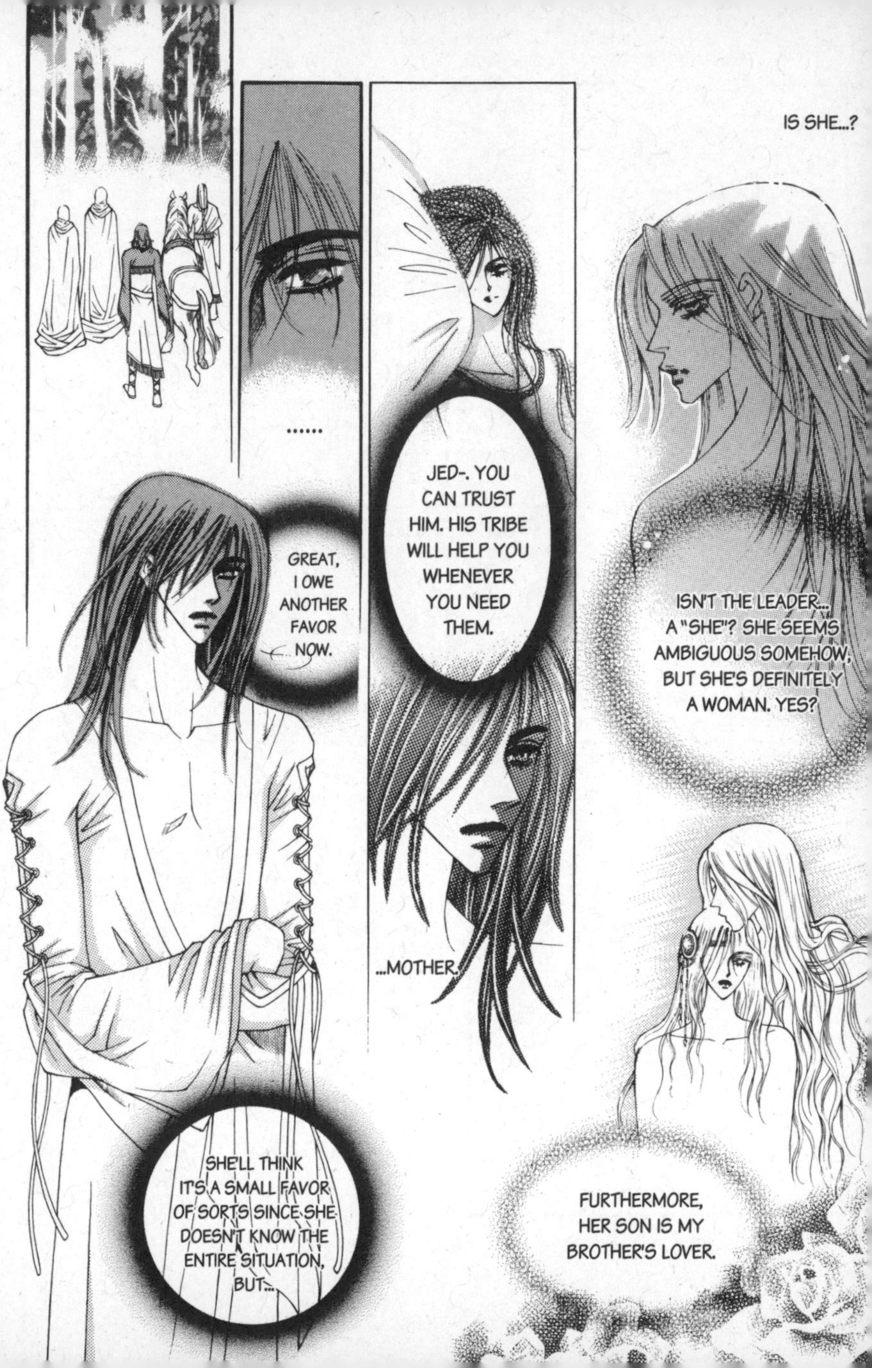
......
GREAT, I OWE ANOTHER FAVOR NOW.
JED-. YOU CAN TRUST HIM. HIS TRIBE WILL HELP YOU WHENEVER YOU NEED THEM.
...MOTHER.
IS SHE...?
ISN'T THE LEADER... A "SHE"? SHE SEEMS AMBIGUOUS SOMEHOW, BUT SHE'S DEFINITELY A WOMAN. YES?
SHE'LL THINK IT'S A SMALL FAVOR OF SORTS SINCE SHE DOESN'T KNOW THE ENTIRE SITUATION, BUT...
FURTHERMORE, HER SON IS MY BROTHER'S LOVER.

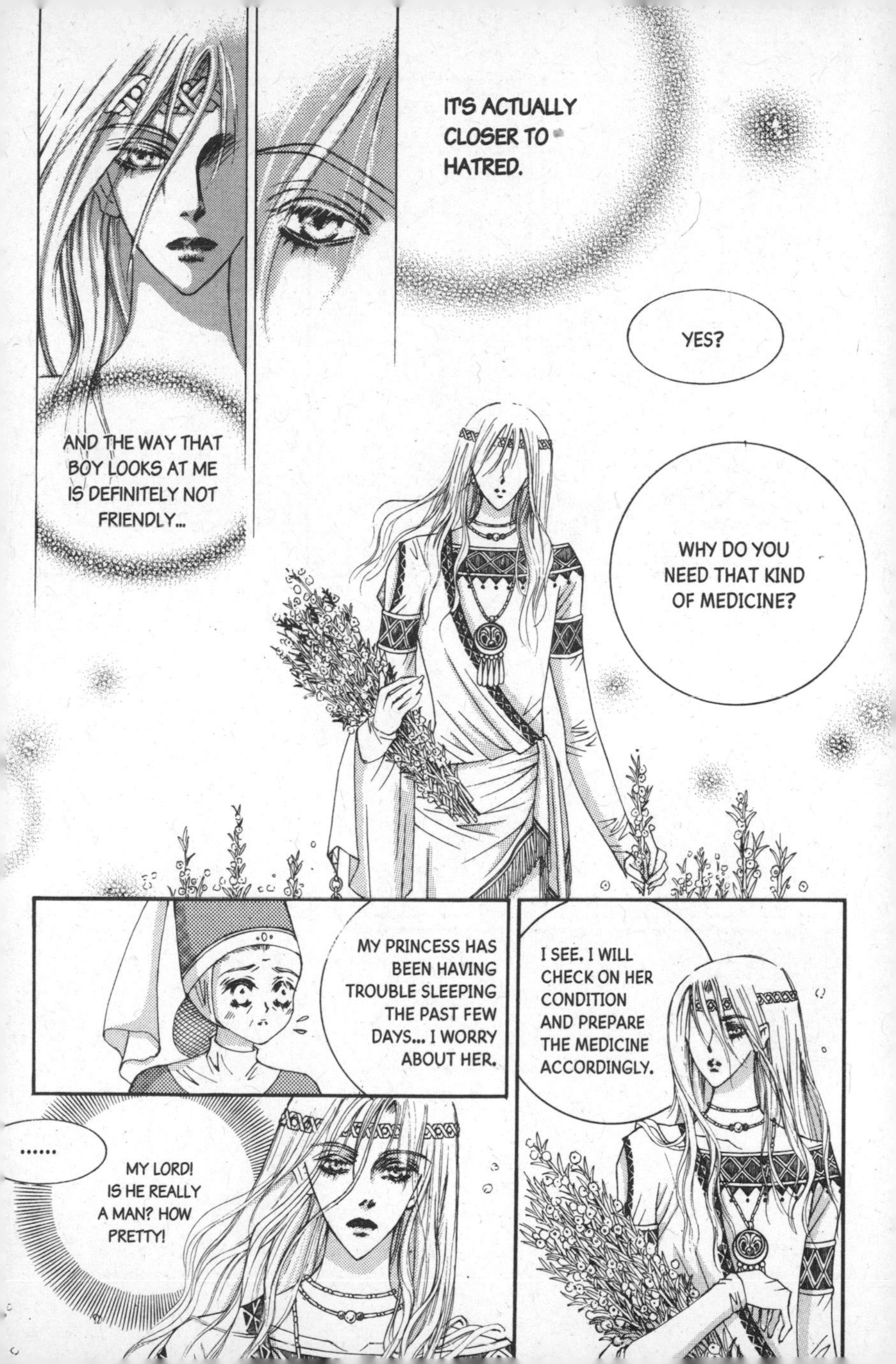
IT'S ACTUALLY CLOSER TO HATRED.
AND THE WAY THAT BOY LOOKS AT ME IS DEFINITELY NOT FRIENDLY...
YES?
WHY DO YOU NEED THAT KIND OF MEDICINE?
MY PRINCESS HAS BEEN HAVING TROUBLE SLEEPING THE PAST FEW DAYS... I WORRY ABOUT HER.
I SEE. I WILL CHECK ON HER CONDITION AND PREPARE THE MEDICINE ACCORDINGLY.
......
MY LORD! IS HE REALLY A MAN? HOW PRETTY!

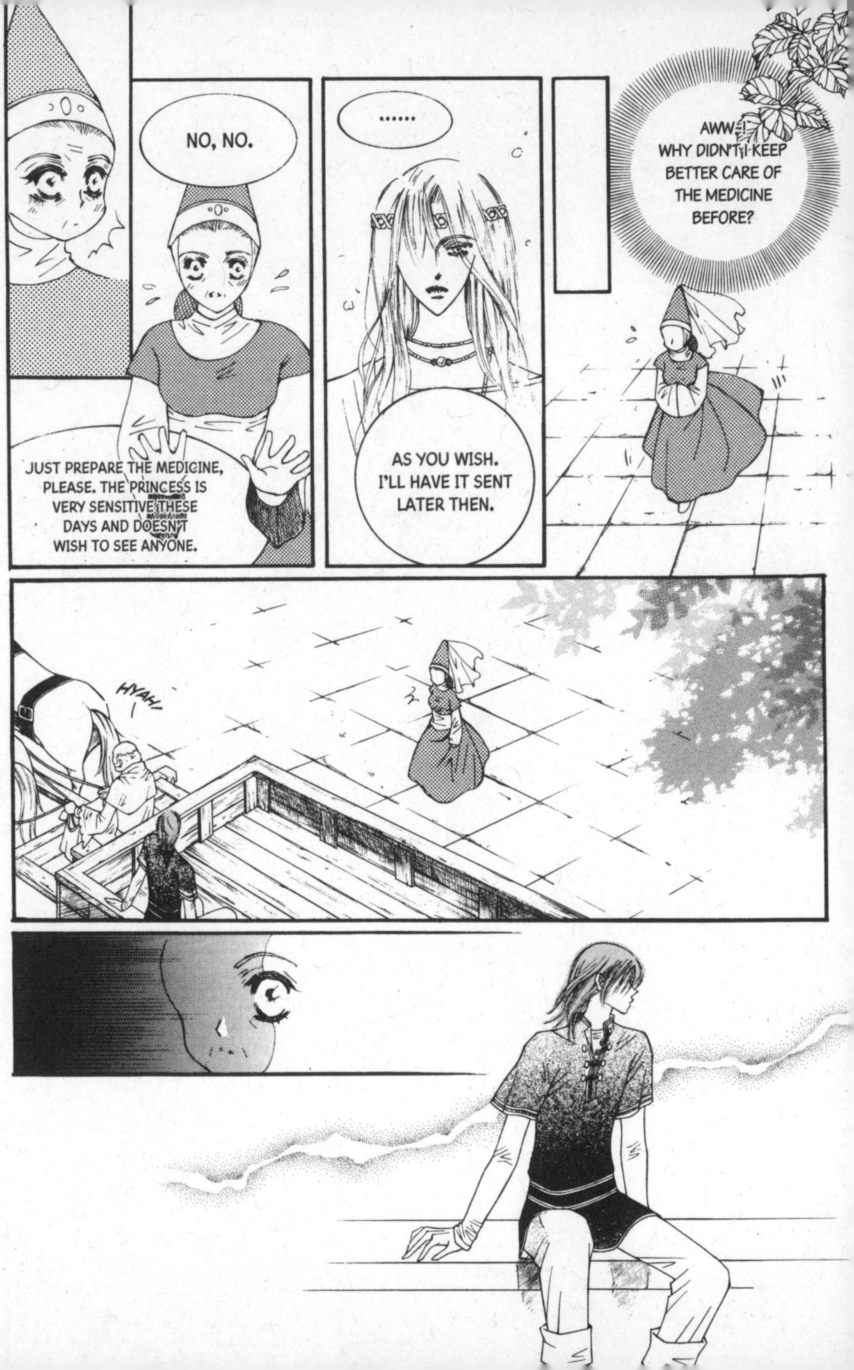
NO, NO.
JUST PREPARE THE MEDICINE, PLEASE. THE PRINCESS IS VERY SENSITIVE THESE DAYS AND DOESN'T WISH TO SEE ANYONE.
......
AS YOU WISH. I'LL HAVE IT SENT LATER THEN.
AWW...! WHY DIDN'T I KEEP BETTER CARE OF THE MEDICINE BEFORE?
HYAH!

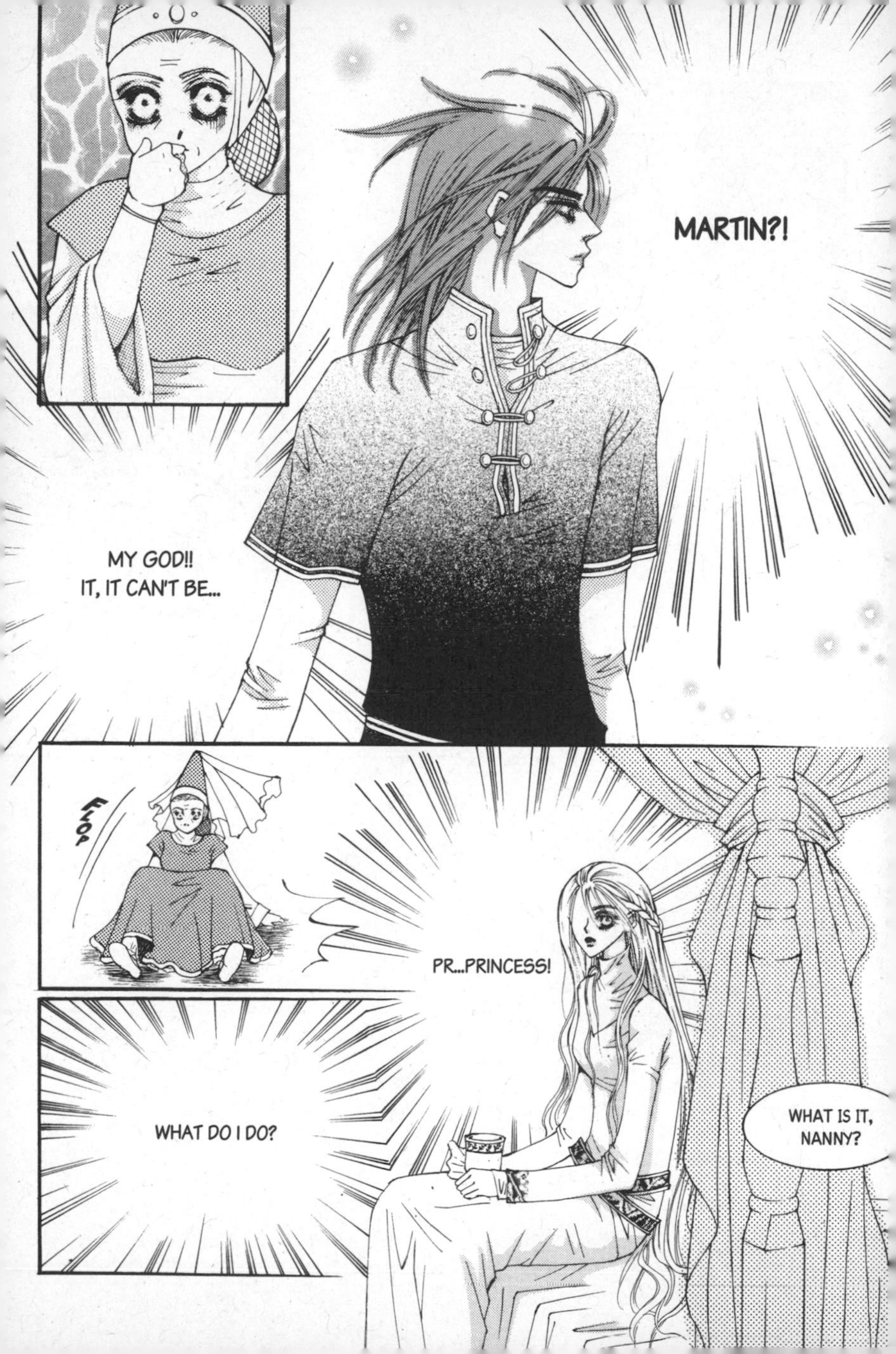
MARTIN?!
MY GOD!! IT, IT CAN'T BE...
FLOP
PR...PRINCESS!
WHAT DO I DO?
WHAT IS IT, NANNY?

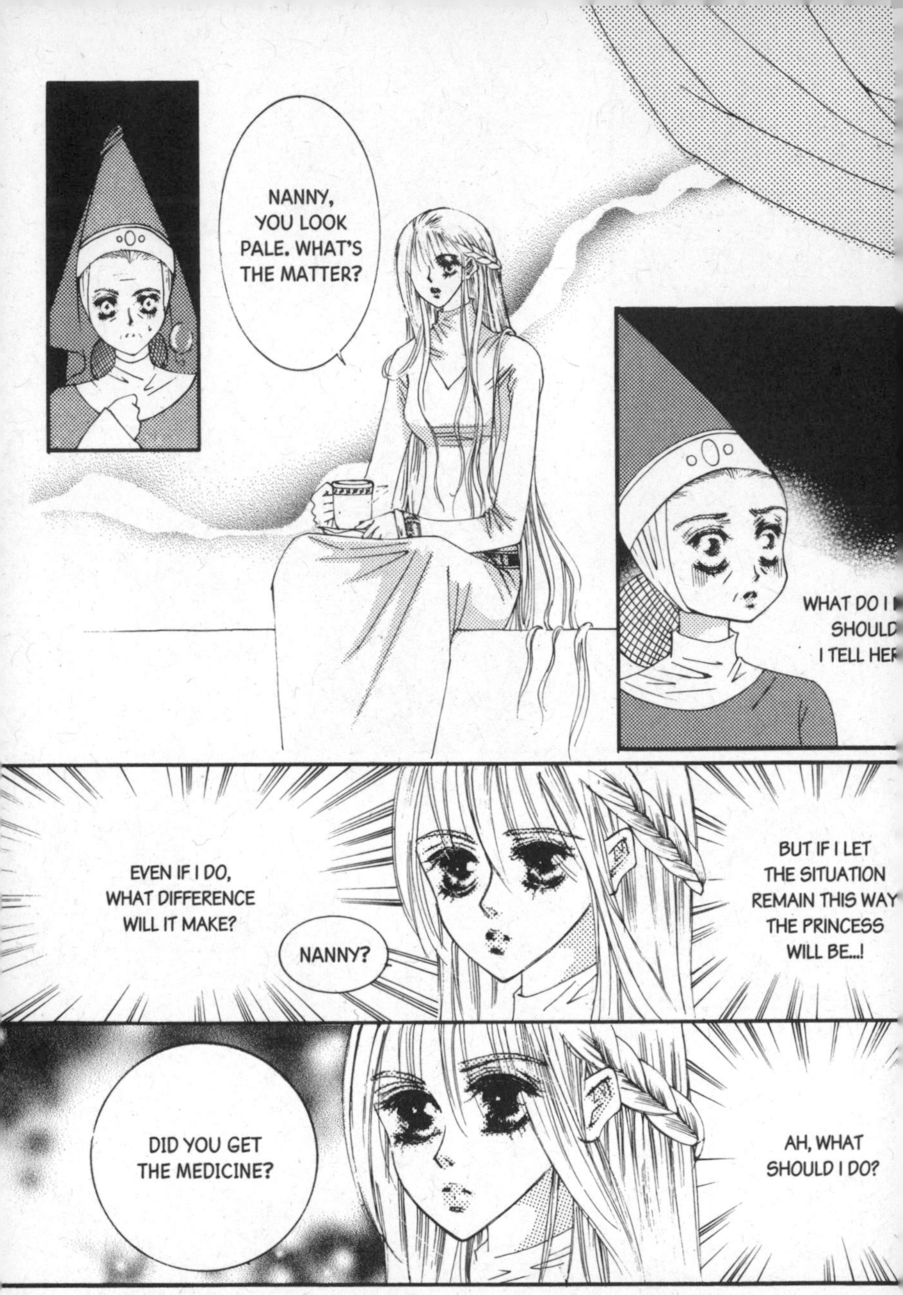
NANNY, YOU LOOK PALE. WHAT'S THE MATTER?
WHAT DO I
SHOULD
I TELL HE
EVEN IF I DO, WHAT DIFFERENCE WILL IT MAKE?
NANNY?
BUT IF I LET THE SITUATION REMAIN THIS WAY THE PRINCESS WILL BE...!
DID YOU GET THE MEDICINE?
AH, WHAT SHOULD I DO?

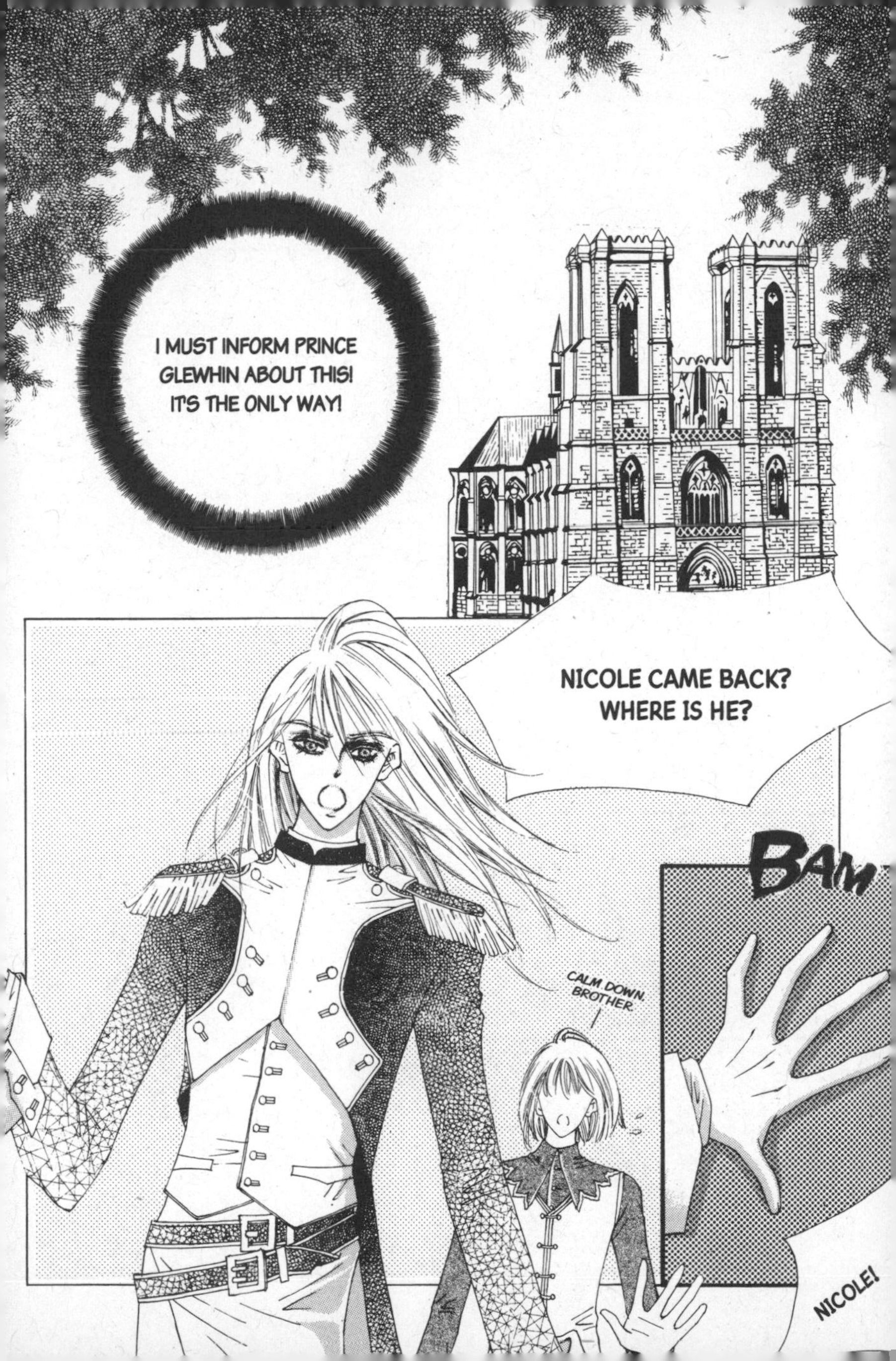
I MUST INFORM PRINCE GLEWHIN ABOUT THIS! IT'S THE ONLY WAY!
NICOLE CAME BACK? WHERE IS HE?
BAM
CALM DOWN, BROTHER.
NICOLE!

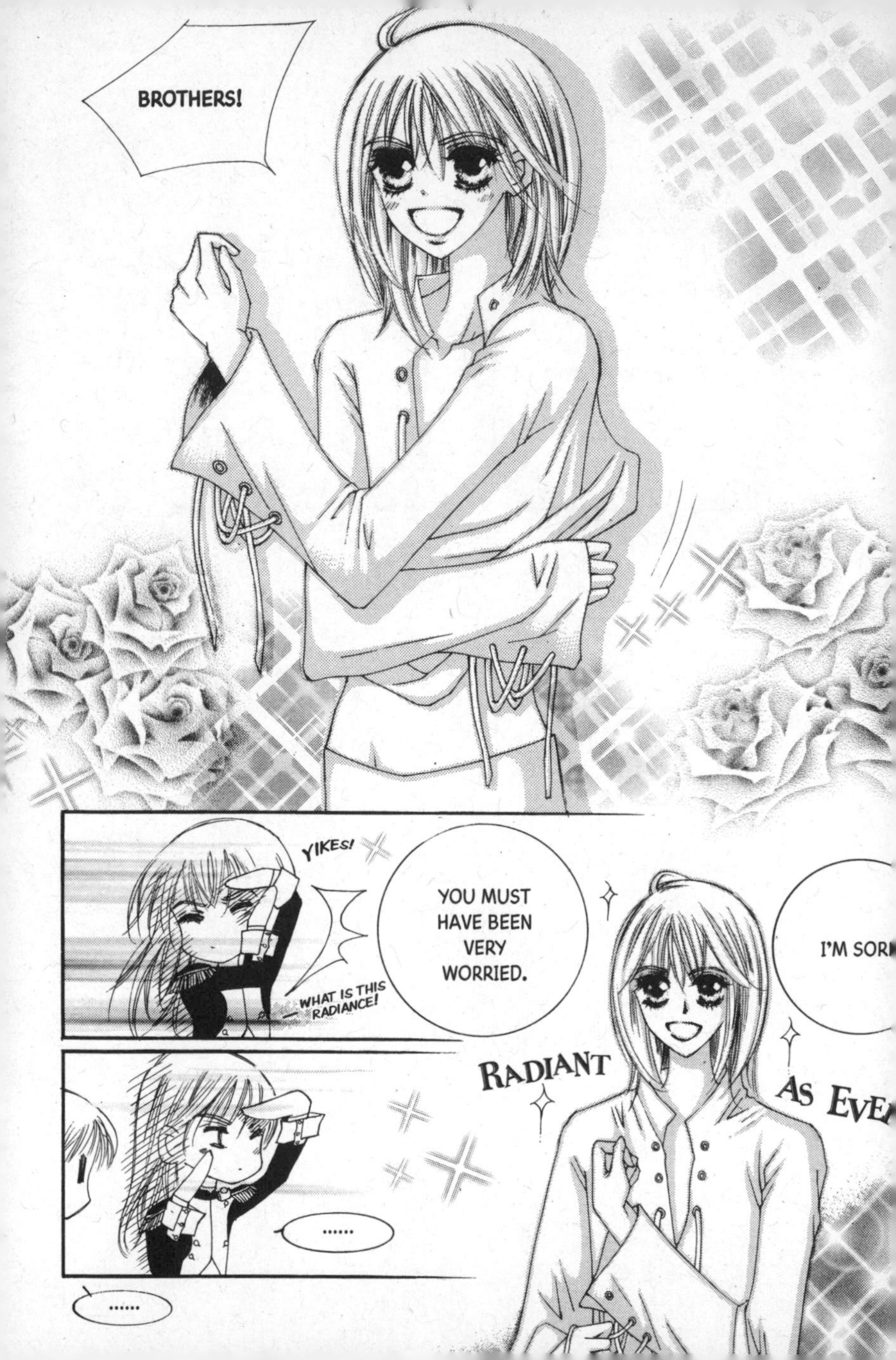

BROTHERS!
I'M SOR
YOU MUST HAVE BEEN VERY WORRIED.
YIKES!
WHAT IS THIS RADIANCE!
RADIANT
AS EVE
......
......

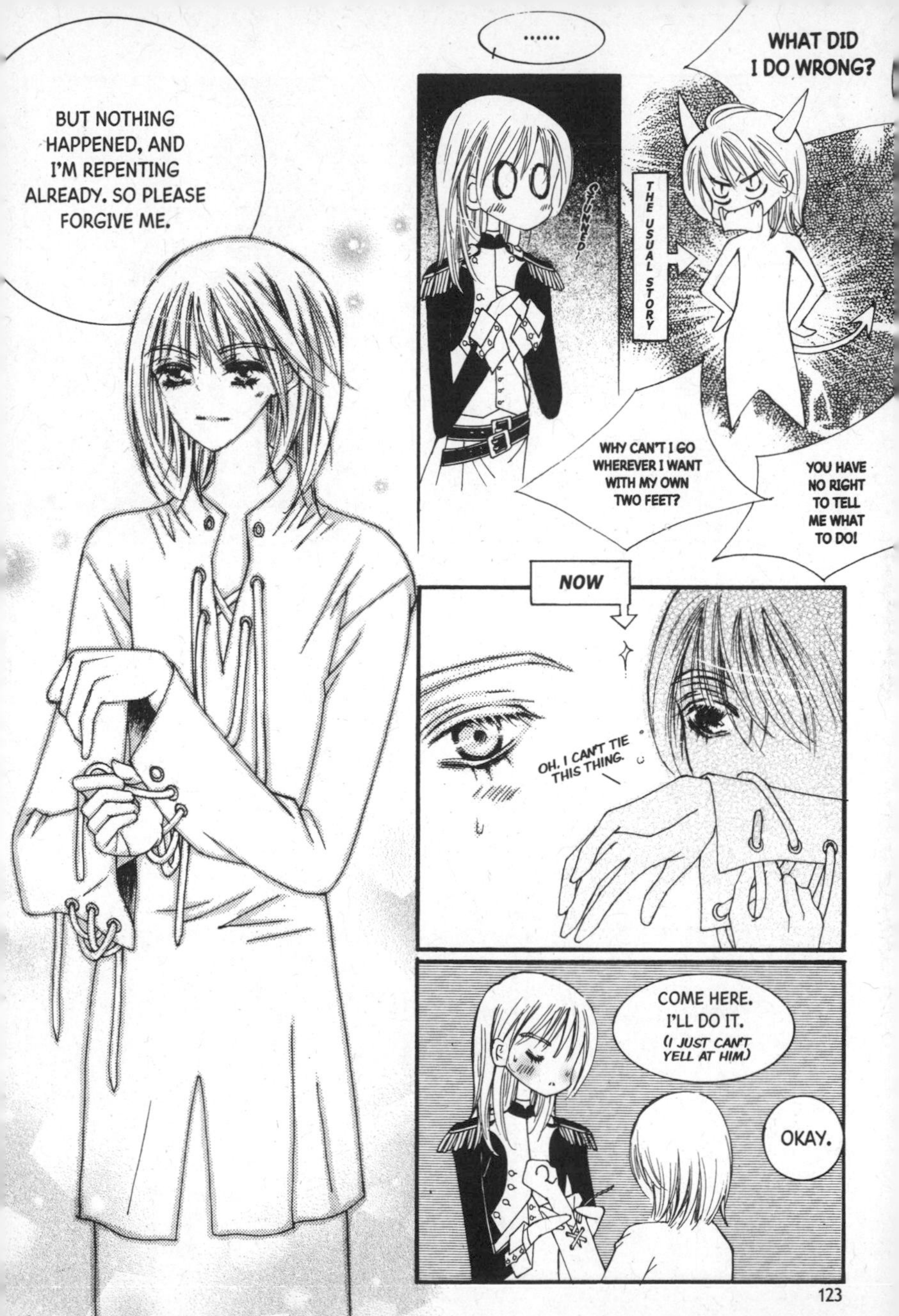
BUT NOTHING HAPPENED, AND I'M REPENTING ALREADY. SO PLEASE FORGIVE ME.
......
WHAT DID I DO WRONG?
STUNNED!
THE USUAL STORY
WHY CAN'T I GO WHEREVER I WANT WITH MY OWN TWO FEET?
YOU HAVE NO RIGHT TO TELL ME WHAT TO DO!
NOW
OH, I CAN'T TIE THIS THING.
COME HERE. I'LL DO IT.
(I JUST CAN'T YELL AT HIM)
OKAY.

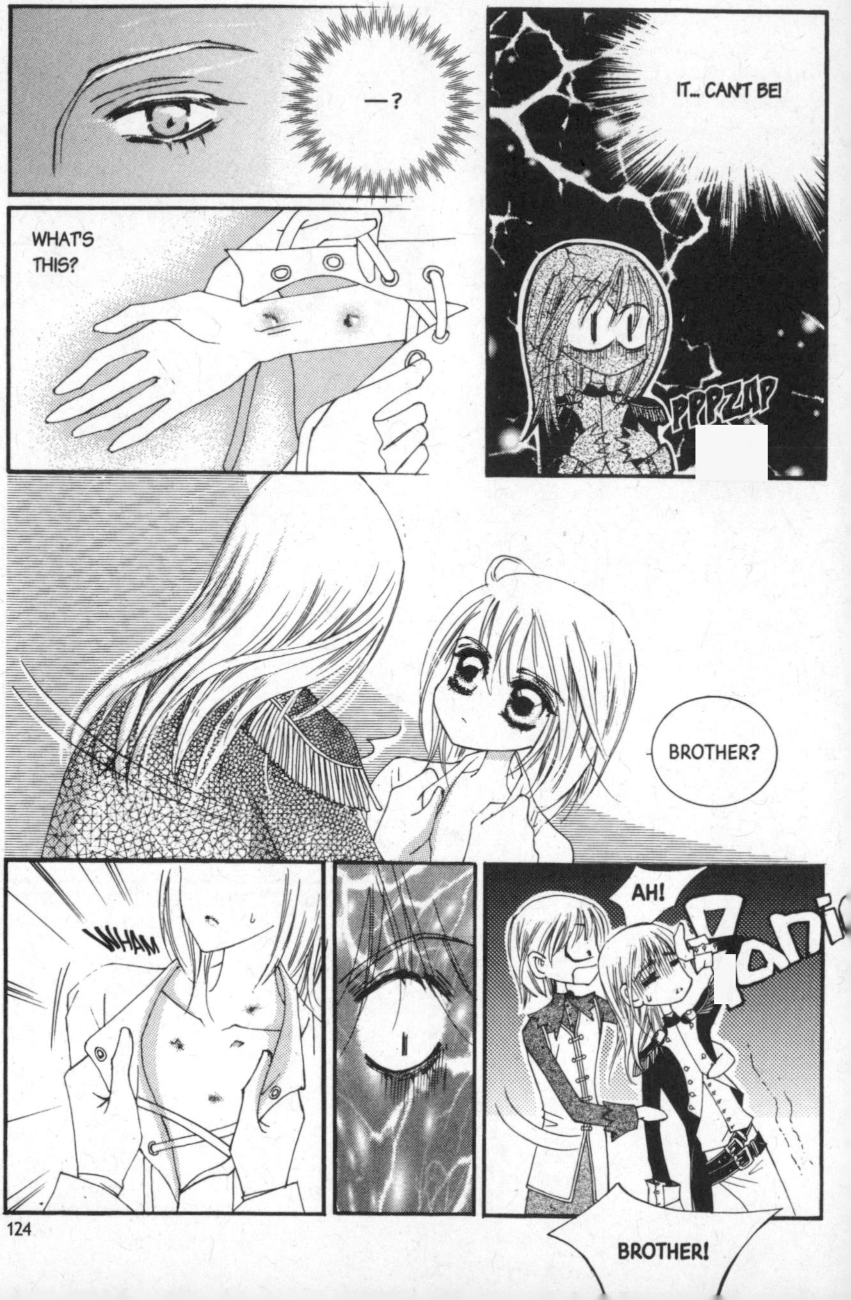
—?
WHAT'S THIS?
IT... CAN'T BE!
PPPZAP
BROTHER?
WHAM
AH!
BROTHER!

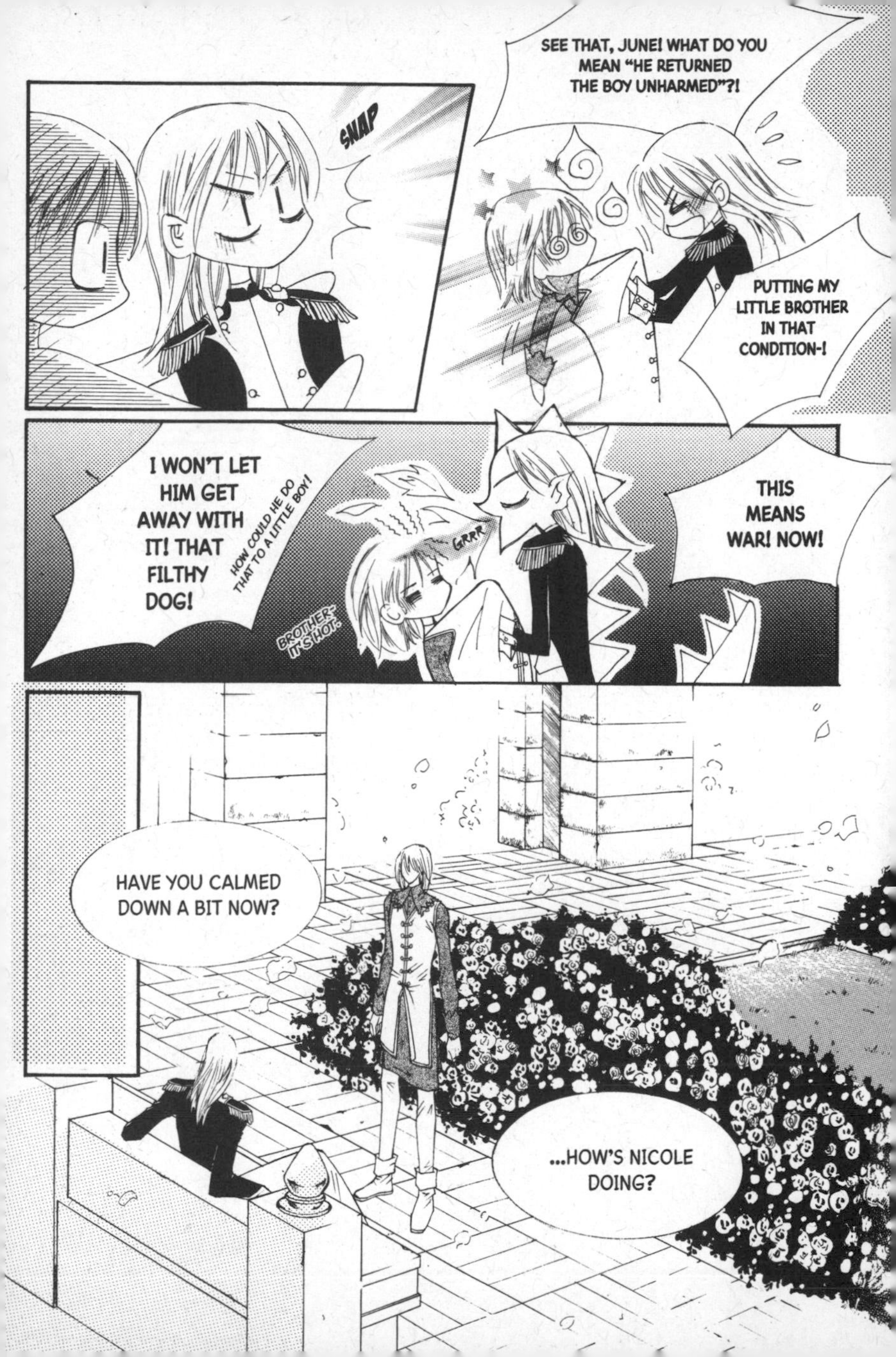
SNAP
SEE THAT, JUNE! WHAT DO YOU MEAN "HE RETURNED THE BOY UNHARMED"?!
PUTTING MY LITTLE BROTHER IN THAT CONDITION-!
I WON'T LET HIM GET AWAY WITH IT! THAT FILTHY DOG!
HOW COULD HE DO THAT TO A LITTLE BOY!
GRRR
BROTHER- IT'S HOT.
THIS MEANS WAR! NOW!
HAVE YOU CALMED DOWN A BIT NOW?
...HOW'S NICOLE DOING?

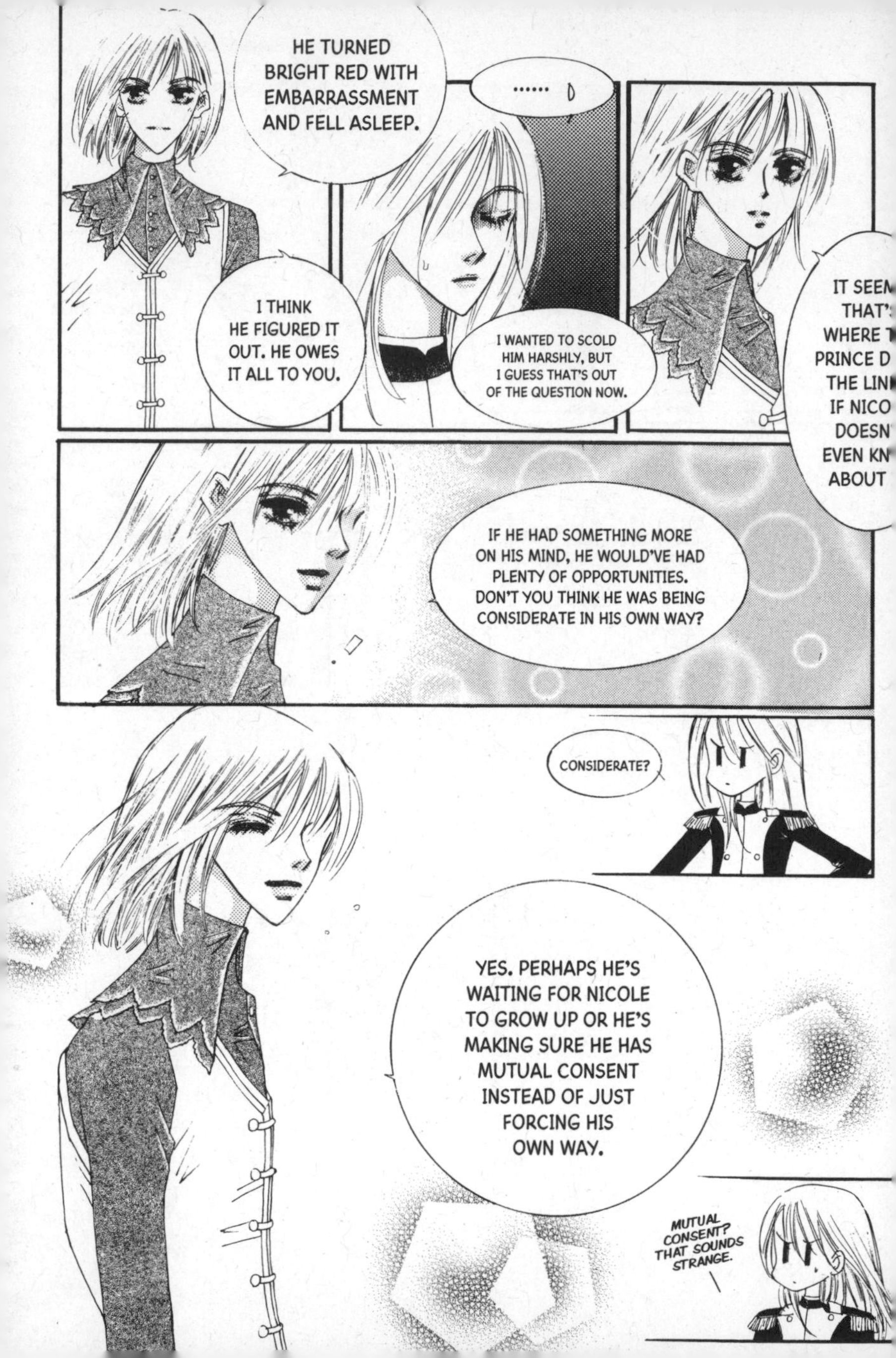
HE TURNED BRIGHT RED WITH EMBARRASSMENT AND FELL ASLEEP.
I THINK HE FIGURED IT OUT. HE OWES IT ALL TO YOU.
......
I WANTED TO SCOLD HIM HARSHLY, BUT I GUESS THAT'S OUT OF THE QUESTION NOW.
IT SEEM THAT' WHERE T PRINCE D THE LIN IF NICO DOESN EVEN KN ABOUT
IF HE HAD SOMETHING MORE ON HIS MIND, HE WOULD'VE HAD PLENTY OF OPPORTUNITIES. DON'T YOU THINK HE WAS BEING CONSIDERATE IN HIS OWN WAY?
CONSIDERATE?
YES. PERHAPS HE'S WAITING FOR NICOLE TO GROW UP OR HE'S MAKING SURE HE HAS MUTUAL CONSENT INSTEAD OF JUST FORCING HIS OWN WAY.
MUTUAL CONSENT? THAT SOUNDS STRANGE.

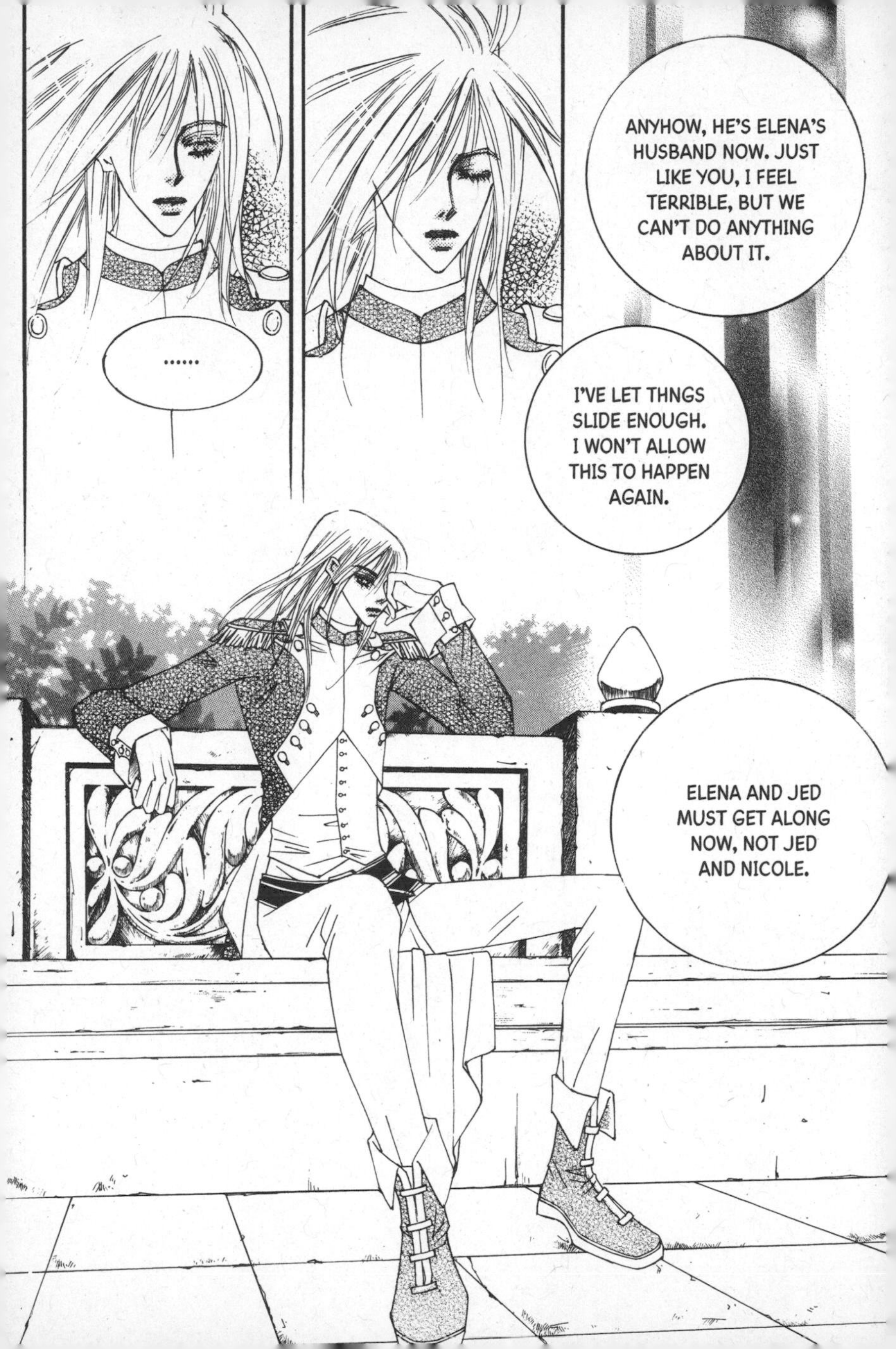
ANYHOW, HE'S ELENA'S HUSBAND NOW. JUST LIKE YOU, I FEEL TERRIBLE, BUT WE CAN'T DO ANYTHING ABOUT IT.
......
I'VE LET THNGS SLIDE ENOUGH. I WON'T ALLOW THIS TO HAPPEN AGAIN.
ELENA AND JED MUST GET ALONG NOW, NOT JED AND NICOLE.

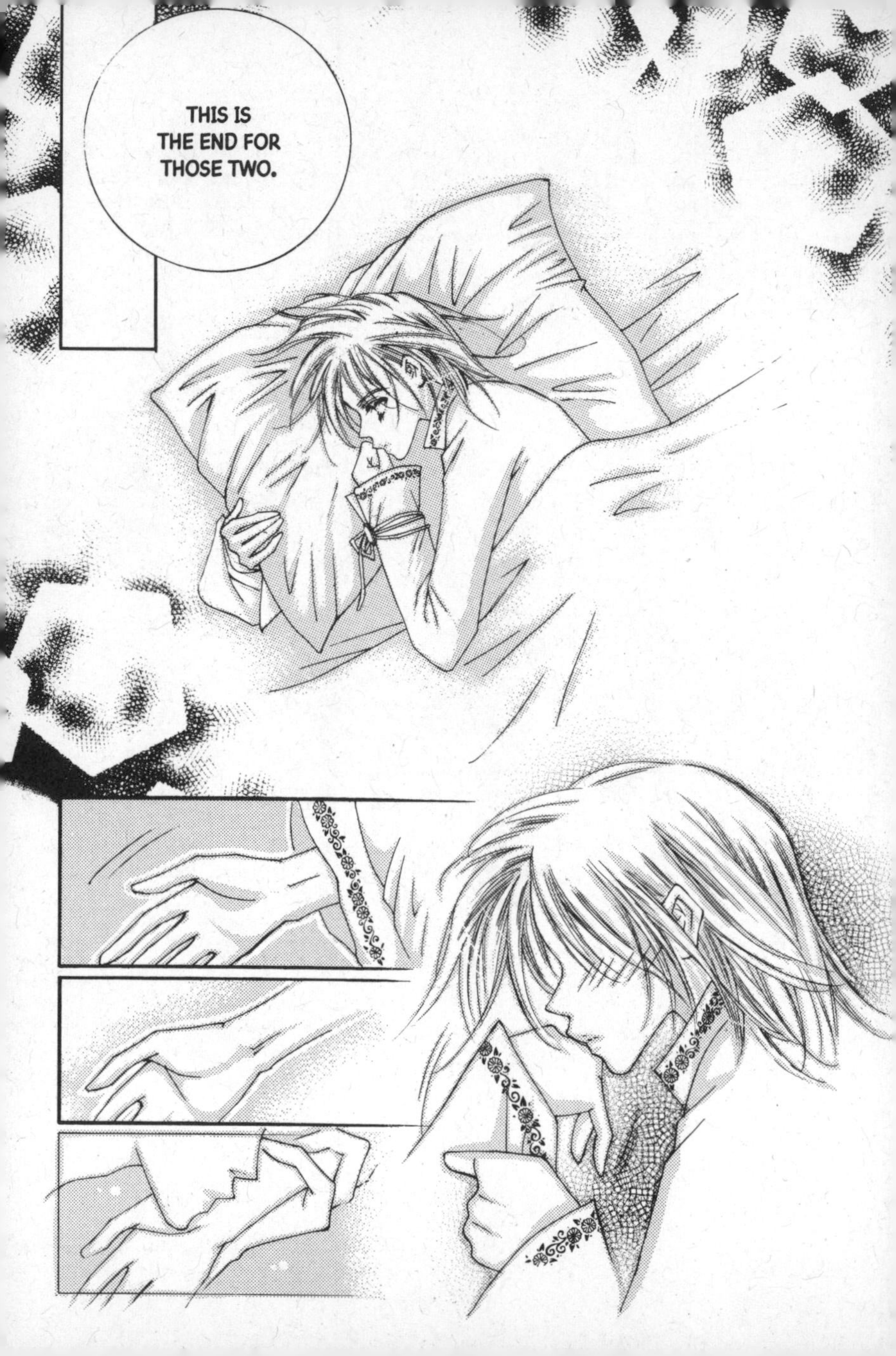
THIS IS THE END FOR THOSE TWO.

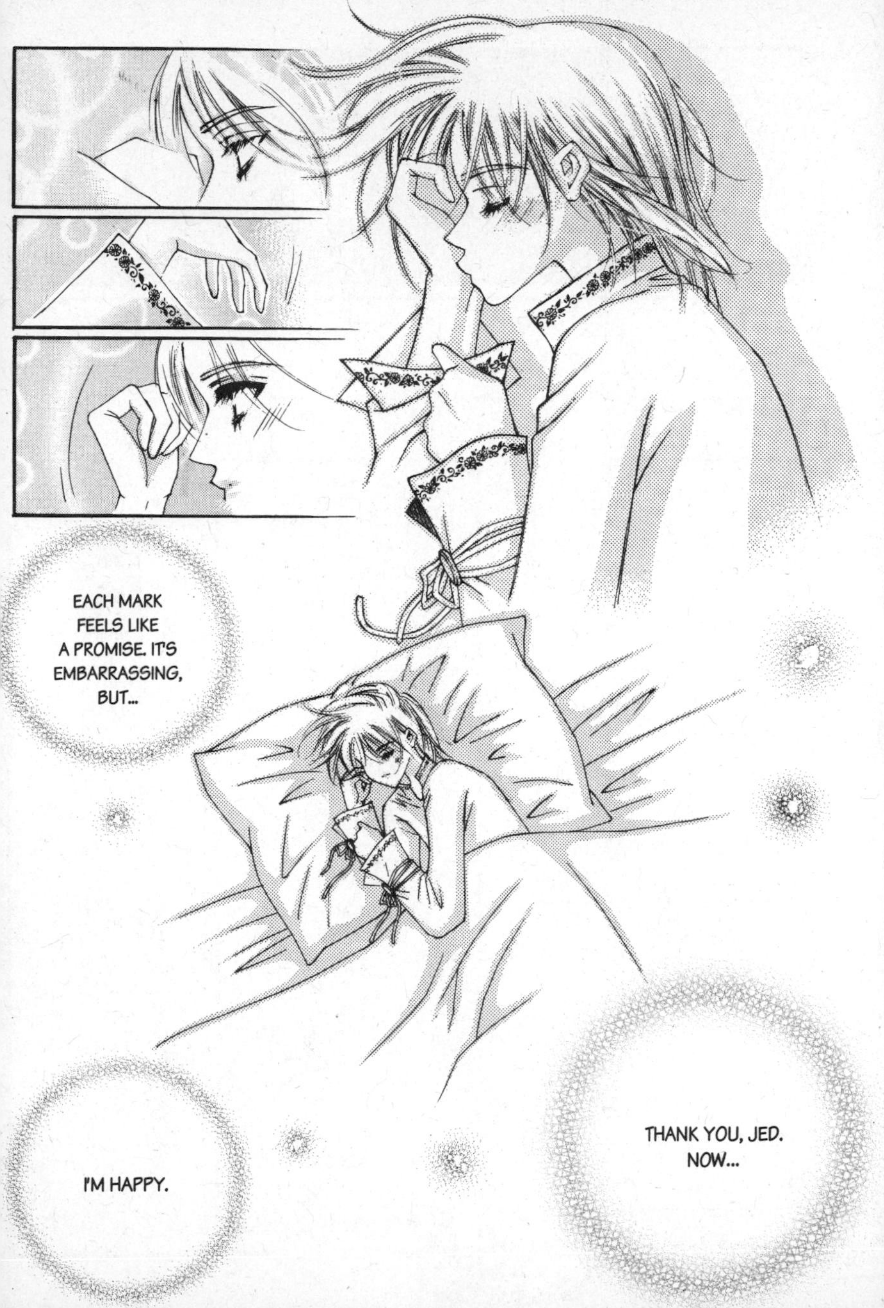
EACH MARK FEELS LIKE A PROMISE. IT'S EMBARRASSING, BUT...
I'M HAPPY.
THANK YOU, JED. NOW...

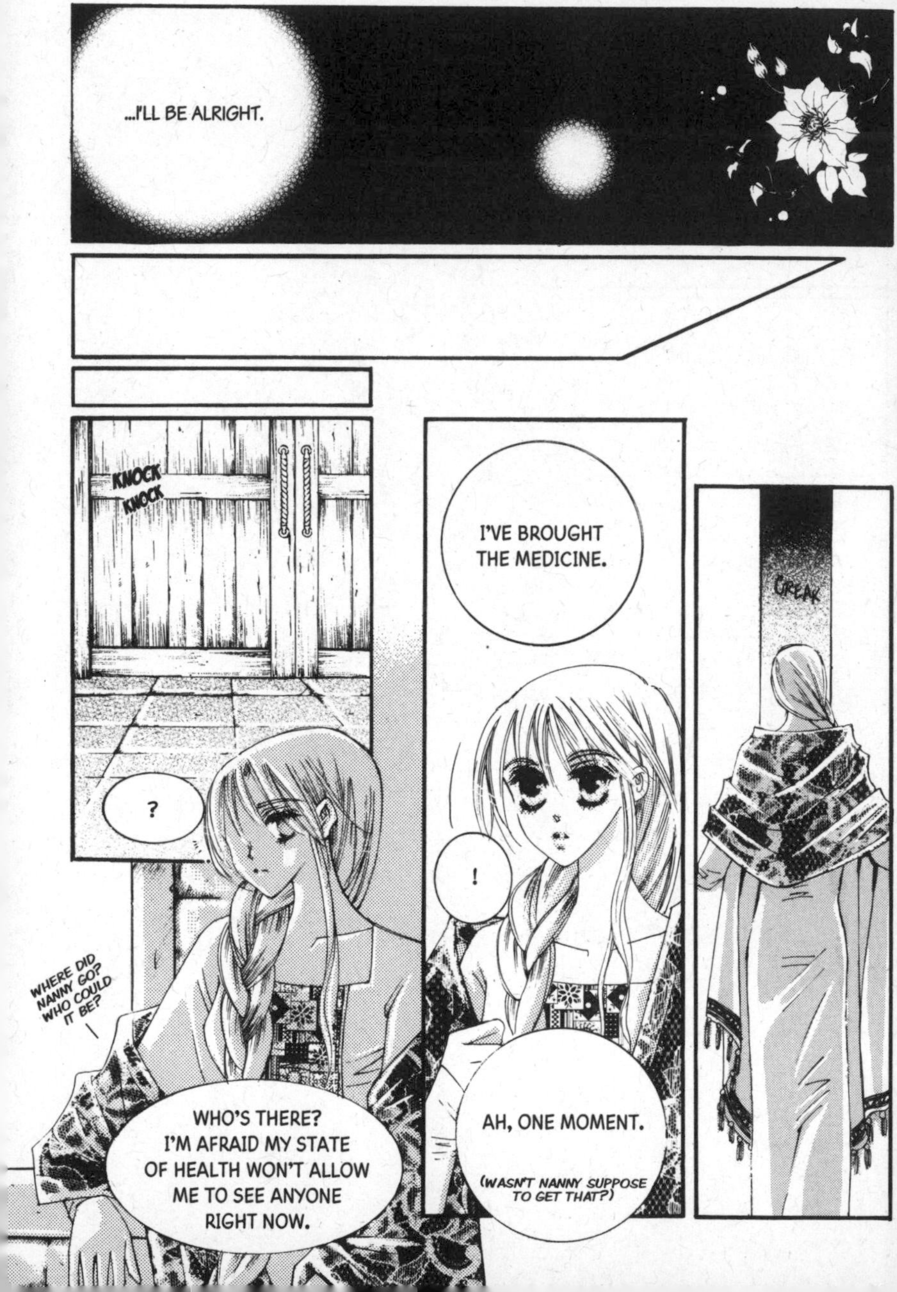
...I'LL BE ALRIGHT.
KNOCK KNOCK
?
WHERE DID NANNY GO? WHO COULD IT BE?
WHO'S THERE? I'M AFRAID MY STATE OF HEALTH WON'T ALLOW ME TO SEE ANYONE RIGHT NOW.
I'VE BROUGHT THE MEDICINE.
!
AH, ONE MOMENT.
(WASN'T NANNY SUPPOSE TO GET THAT?)
CREAK

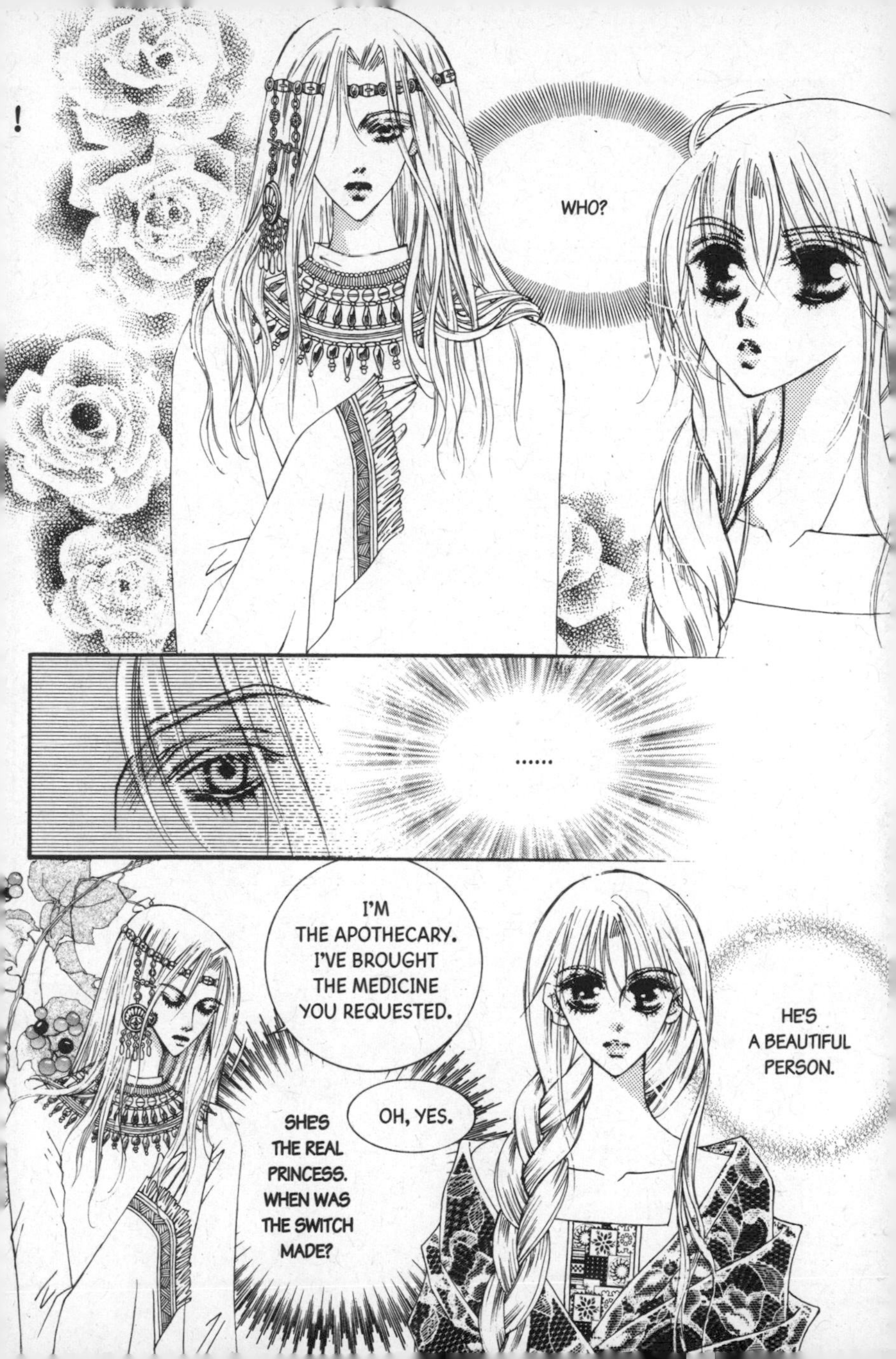
!
WHO?
......
I'M THE APOTHECARY. I'VE BROUGHT THE MEDICINE YOU REQUESTED.
HE'S A BEAUTIFUL PERSON.
OH, YES.
SHE'S THE REAL PRINCESS. WHEN WAS THE SWITCH MADE?

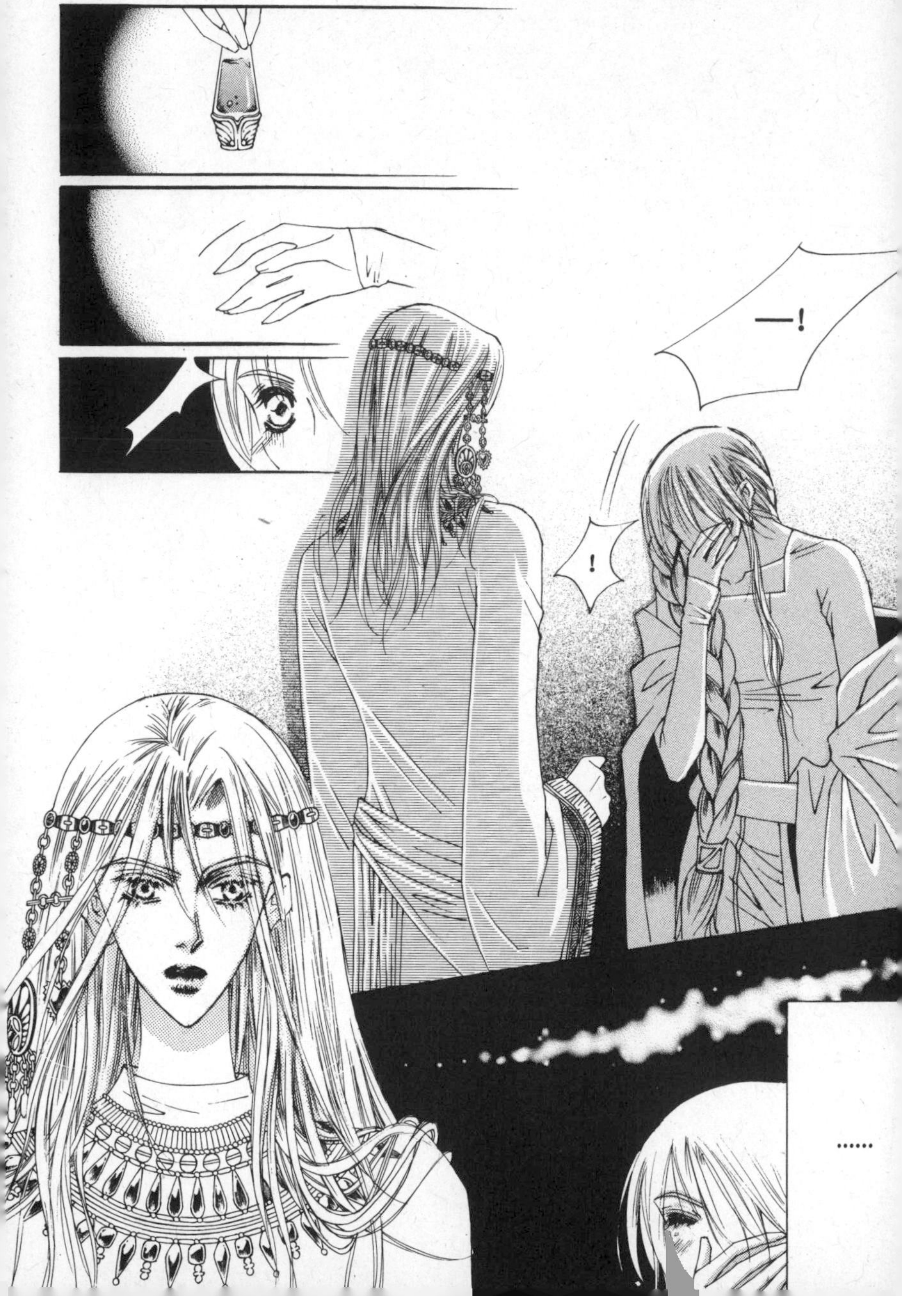

—!
!
......

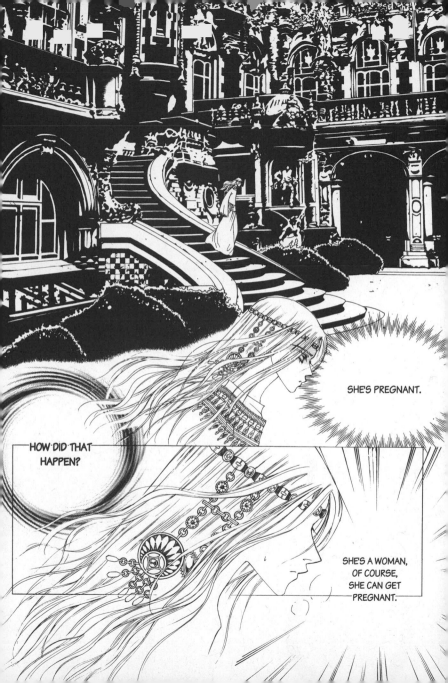

SHE'S PREGNANT.

HOW DID THAT HAPPEN?

SHE'S A WOMAN, OF COURSE, SHE CAN GET PREGNANT.

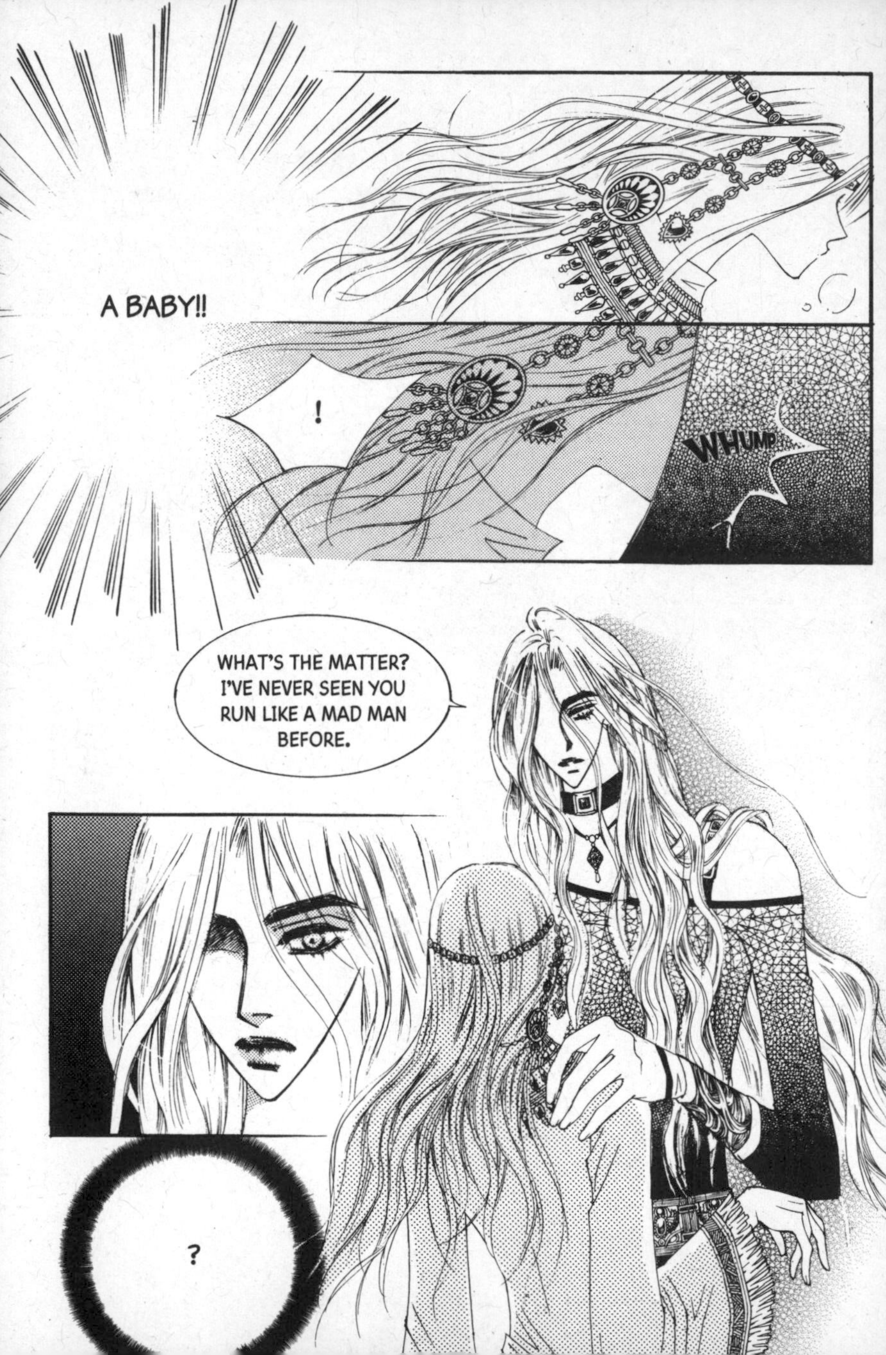
A BABY!!
!
WHUMP
WHAT'S THE MATTER? I'VE NEVER SEEN YOU RUN LIKE A MAD MAN BEFORE.
?

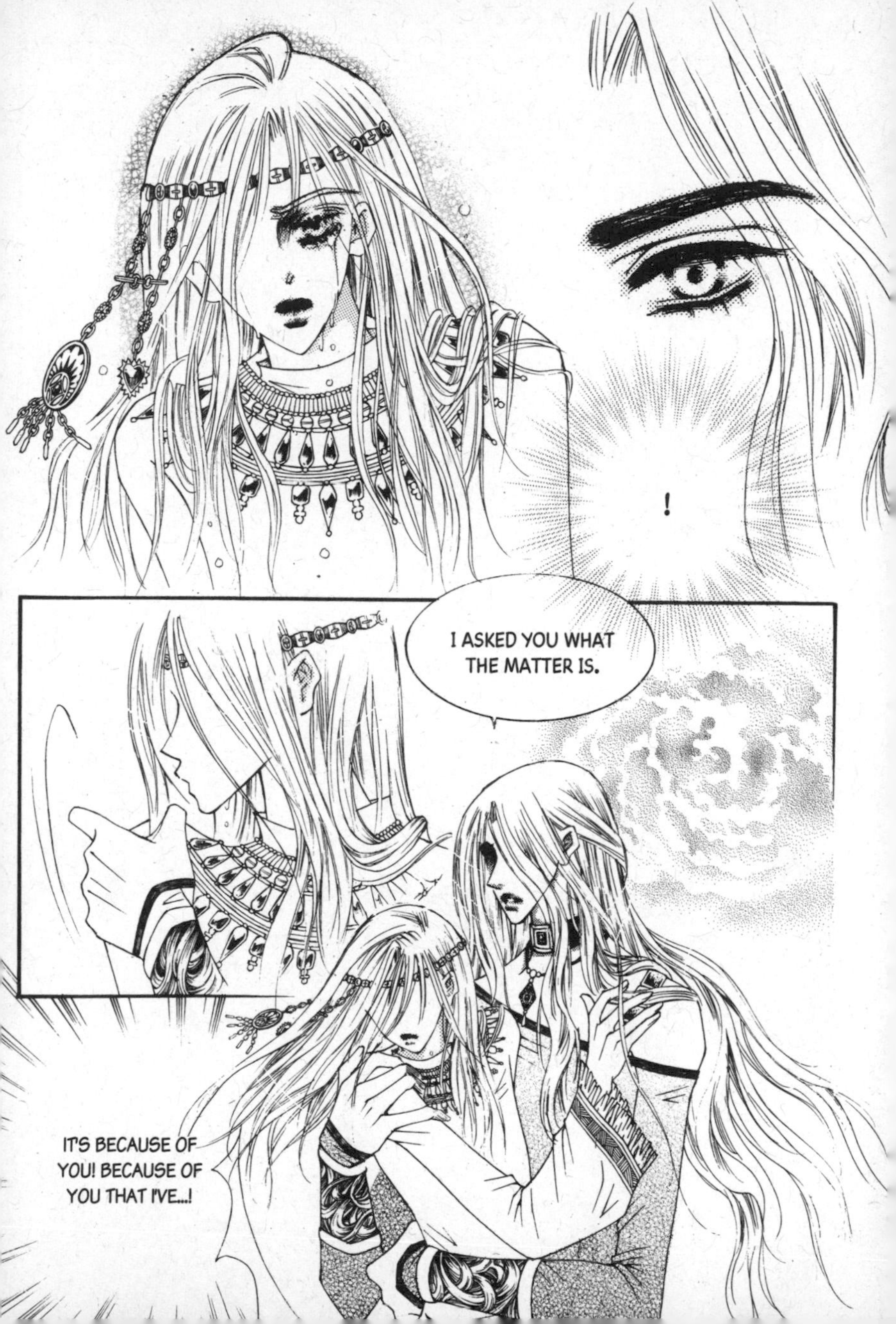
!
I ASKED YOU WHAT THE MATTER IS.
IT'S BECAUSE OF YOU! BECAUSE OF YOU THAT I'VE...!

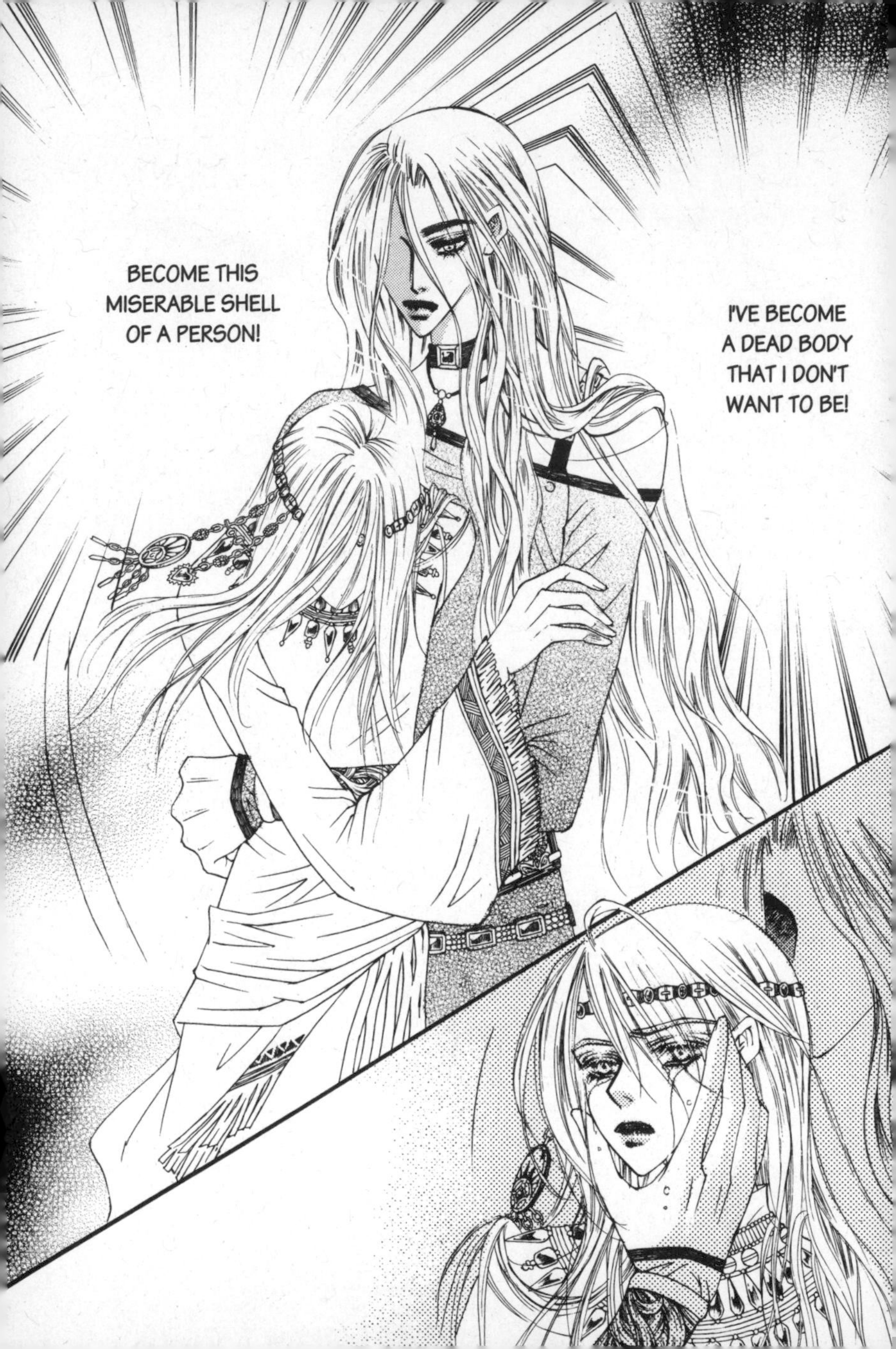
I'VE BECOME A DEAD BODY THAT I DON'T WANT TO BE!
BECOME THIS MISERABLE SHELL OF A PERSON!

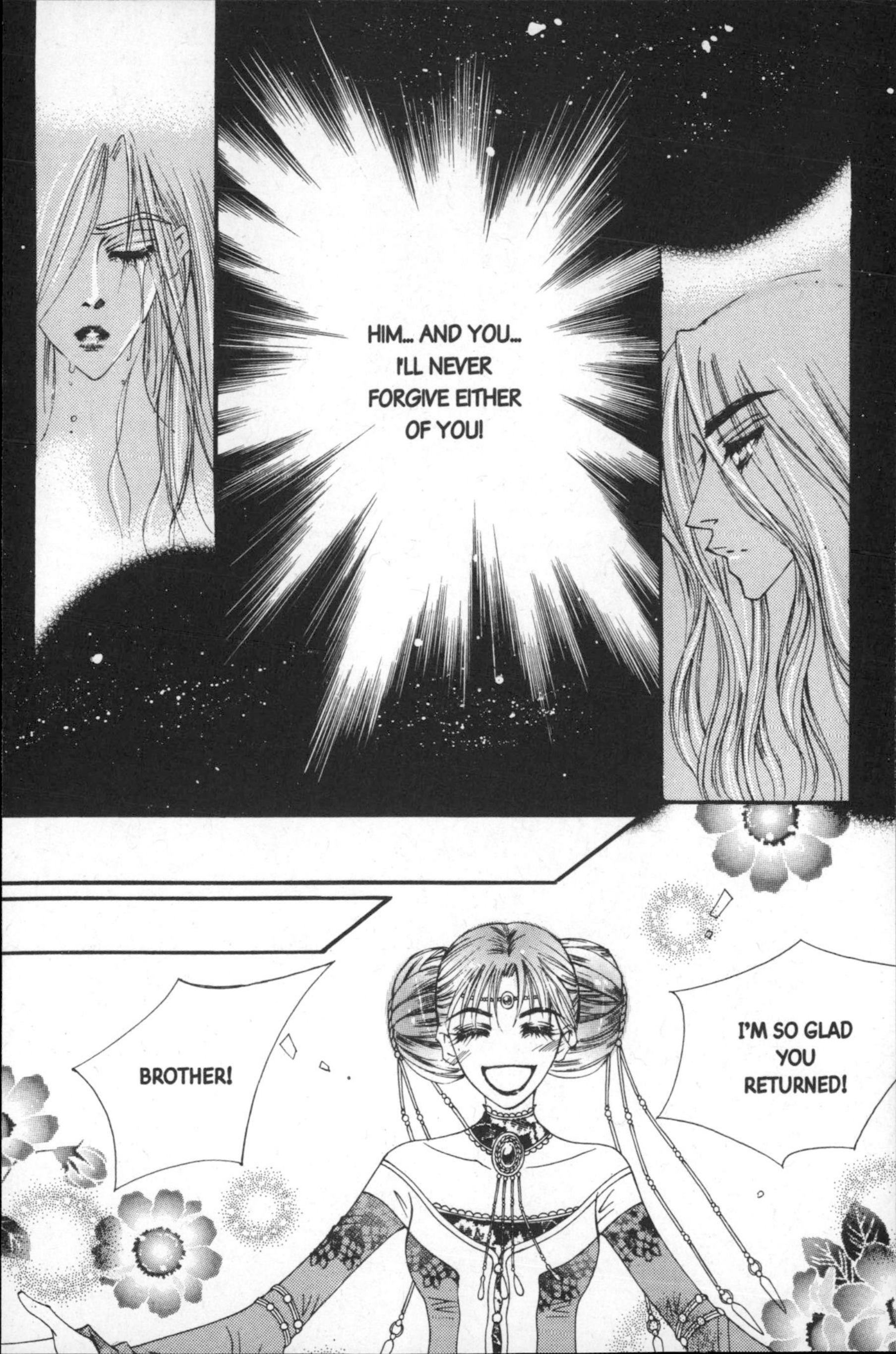
HIM... AND YOU... I'LL NEVER FORGIVE EITHER OF YOU!
I'M SO GLAD YOU RETURNED!
BROTHER!

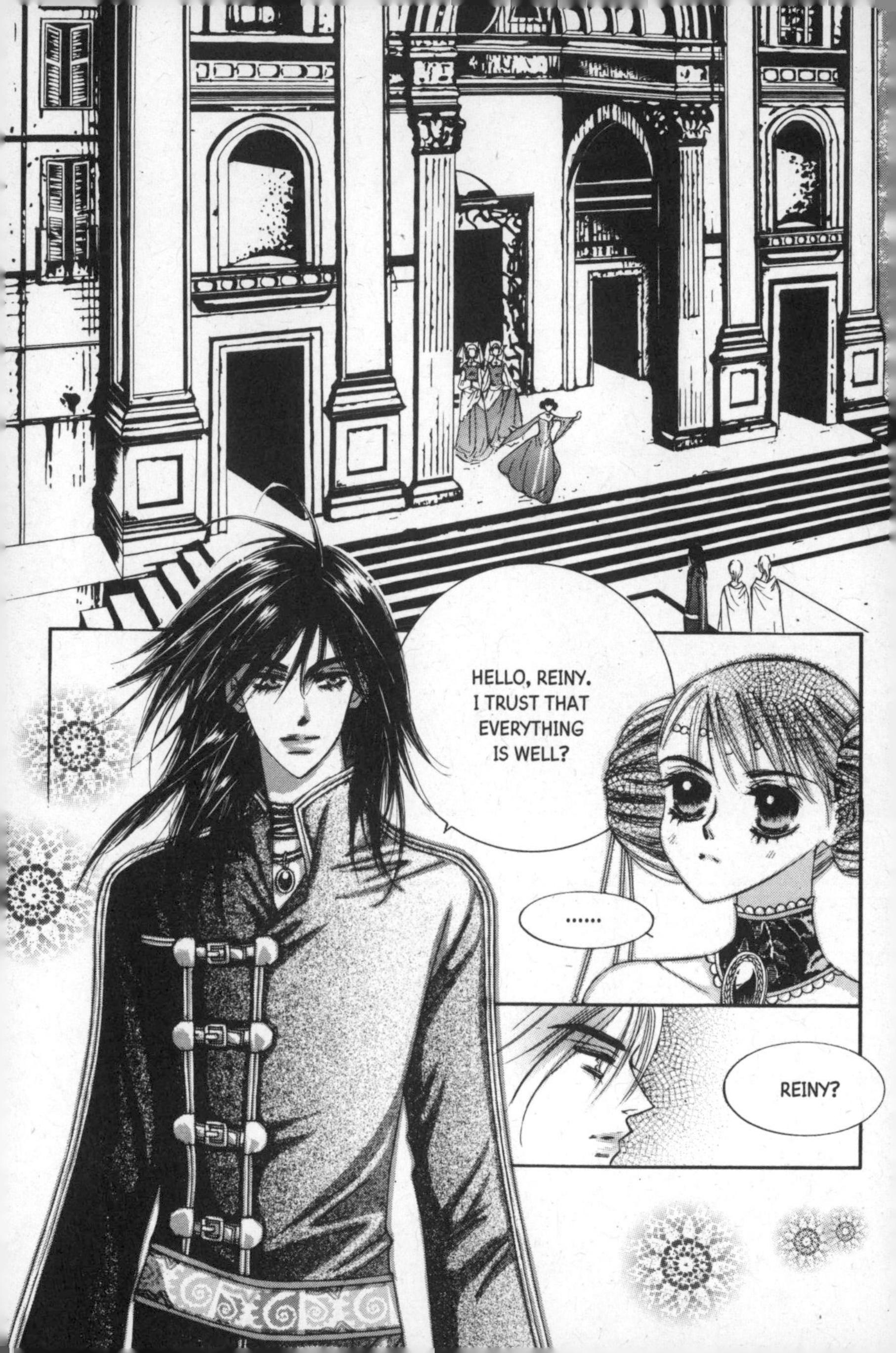
HELLO, REINY. I TRUST THAT EVERYTHING IS WELL?
......
REINY?

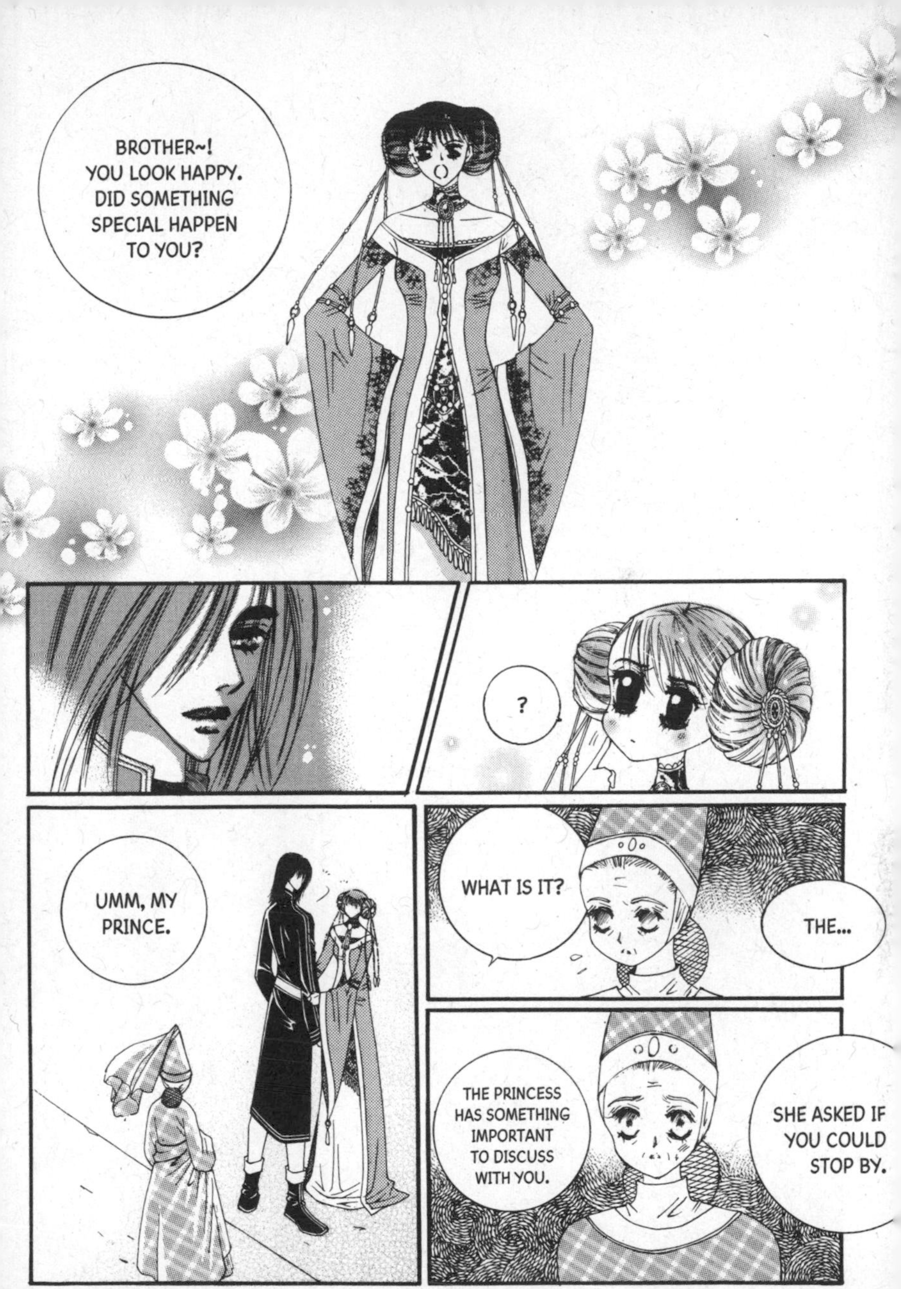
BROTHER~! YOU LOOK HAPPY. DID SOMETHING SPECIAL HAPPEN TO YOU?
?
UMM, MY PRINCE.
WHAT IS IT?
THE...
THE PRINCESS HAS SOMETHING IMPORTANT TO DISCUSS WITH YOU.
SHE ASKED IF YOU COULD STOP BY.

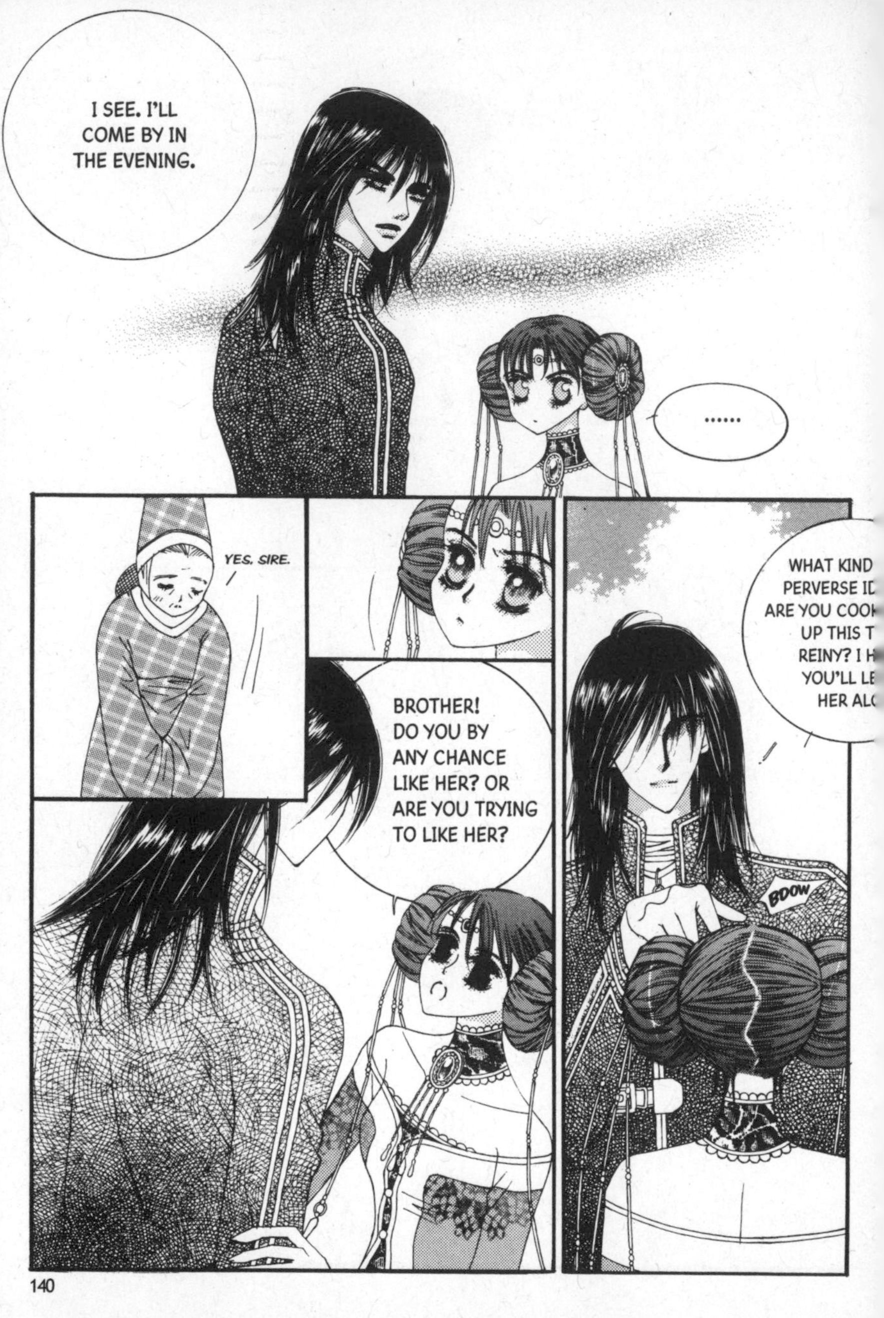
I SEE. I'LL COME BY IN THE EVENING.
......
YES, SIRE.
BROTHER! DO YOU BY ANY CHANCE LIKE HER? OR ARE YOU TRYING TO LIKE HER?
WHAT KIND PERVERSE ID ARE YOU COOK UP THIS T REINY? I H YOU'LL LE HER ALC
BOOW

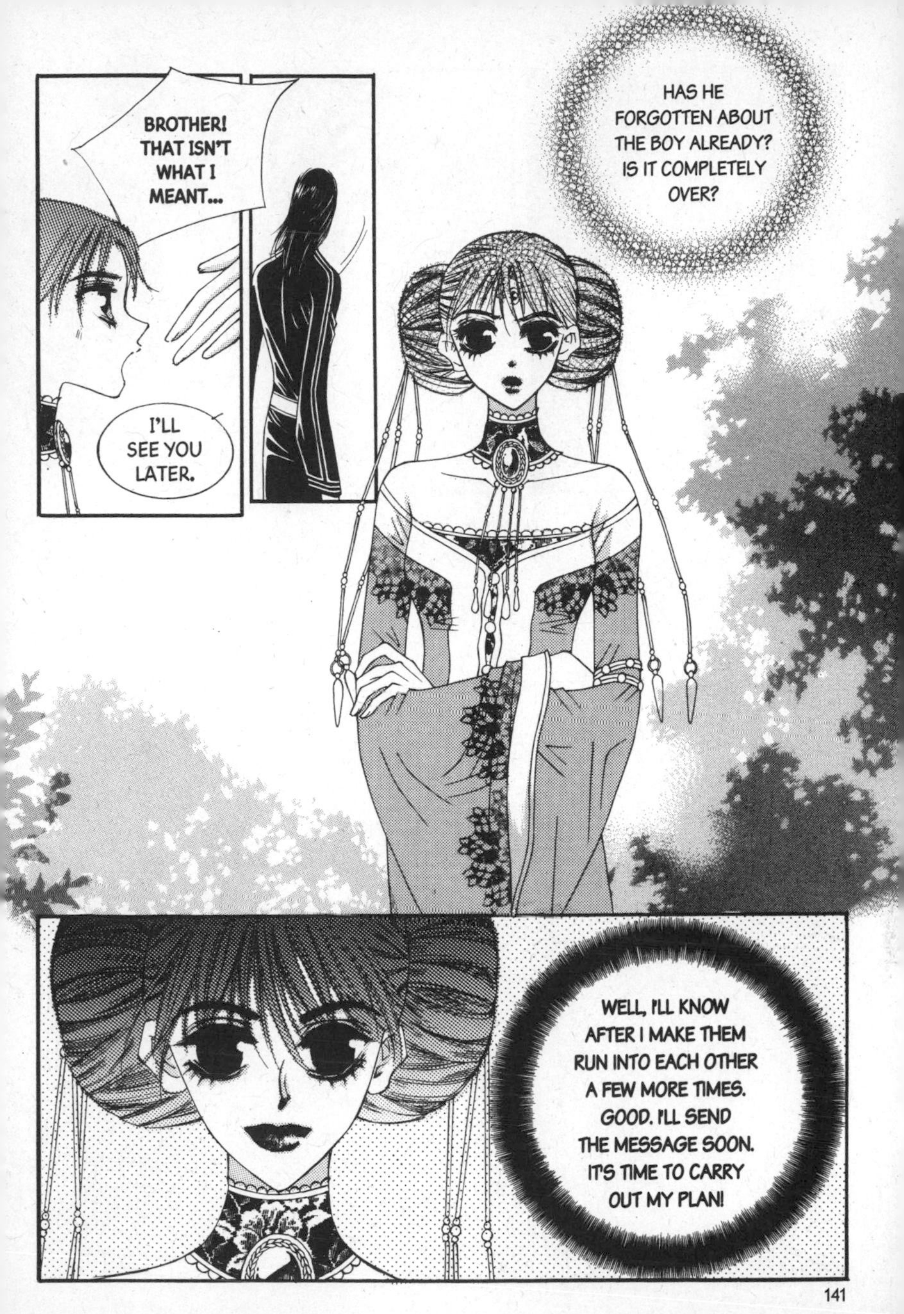
HAS HE FORGOTTEN ABOUT THE BOY ALREADY? IS IT COMPLETELY OVER?
BROTHER! THAT ISN'T WHAT I MEANT...
I'LL SEE YOU LATER.
WELL, I'LL KNOW AFTER I MAKE THEM RUN INTO EACH OTHER A FEW MORE TIMES. GOOD. I'LL SEND THE MESSAGE SOON. IT'S TIME TO CARRY OUT MY PLAN!

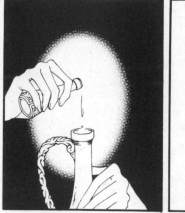

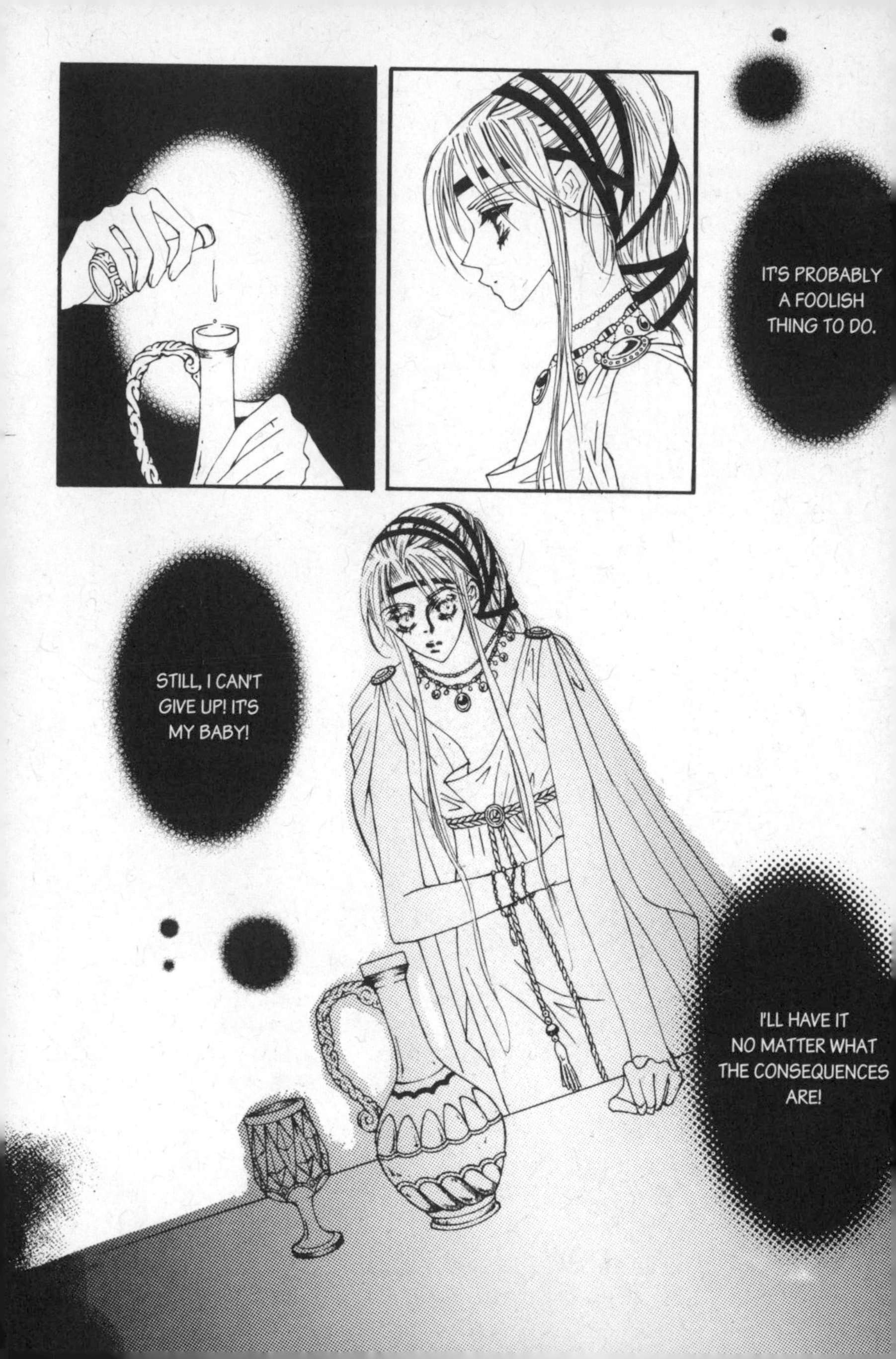

IT'S PROBABLY
A FOOLISH
THING TO DO.

STILL, I CAN'T
GIVE UP! IT'S
MY BABY!

I'LL HAVE IT
NO MATTER WHAT
THE CONSEQUENCES
ARE!

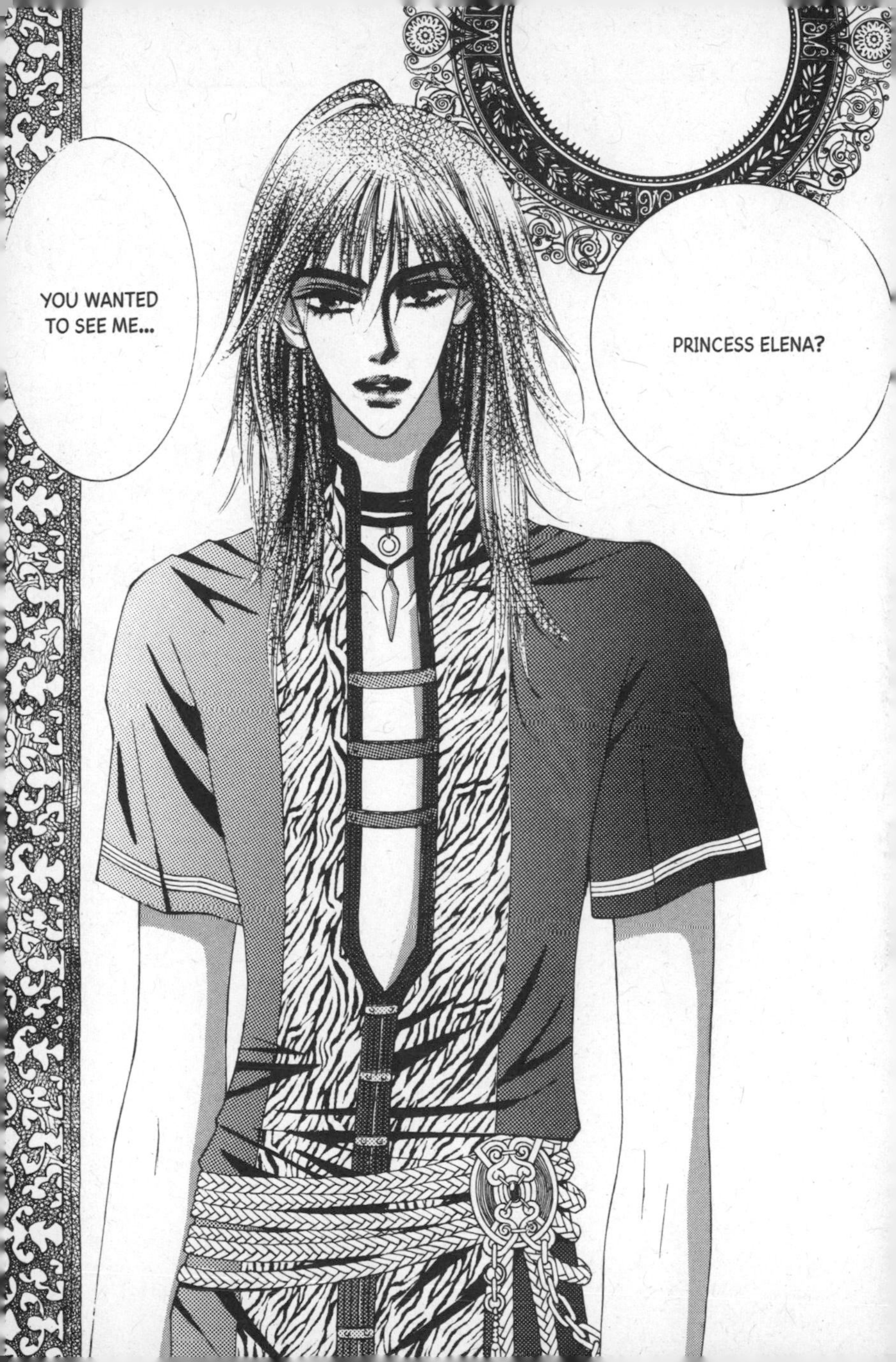
YOU WANTED TO SEE ME...
PRINCESS ELENA?

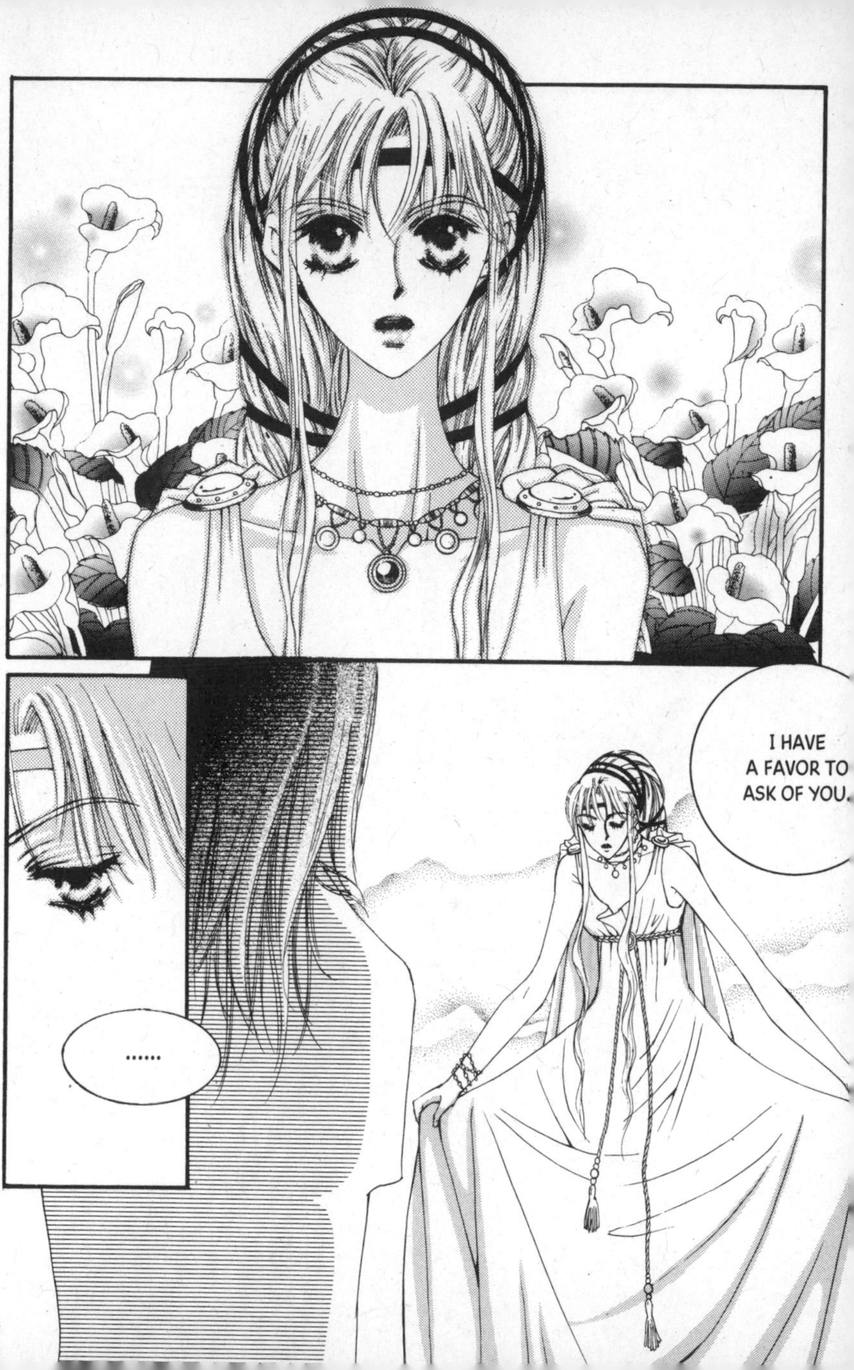
I HAVE A FAVOR TO ASK OF YOU.
......

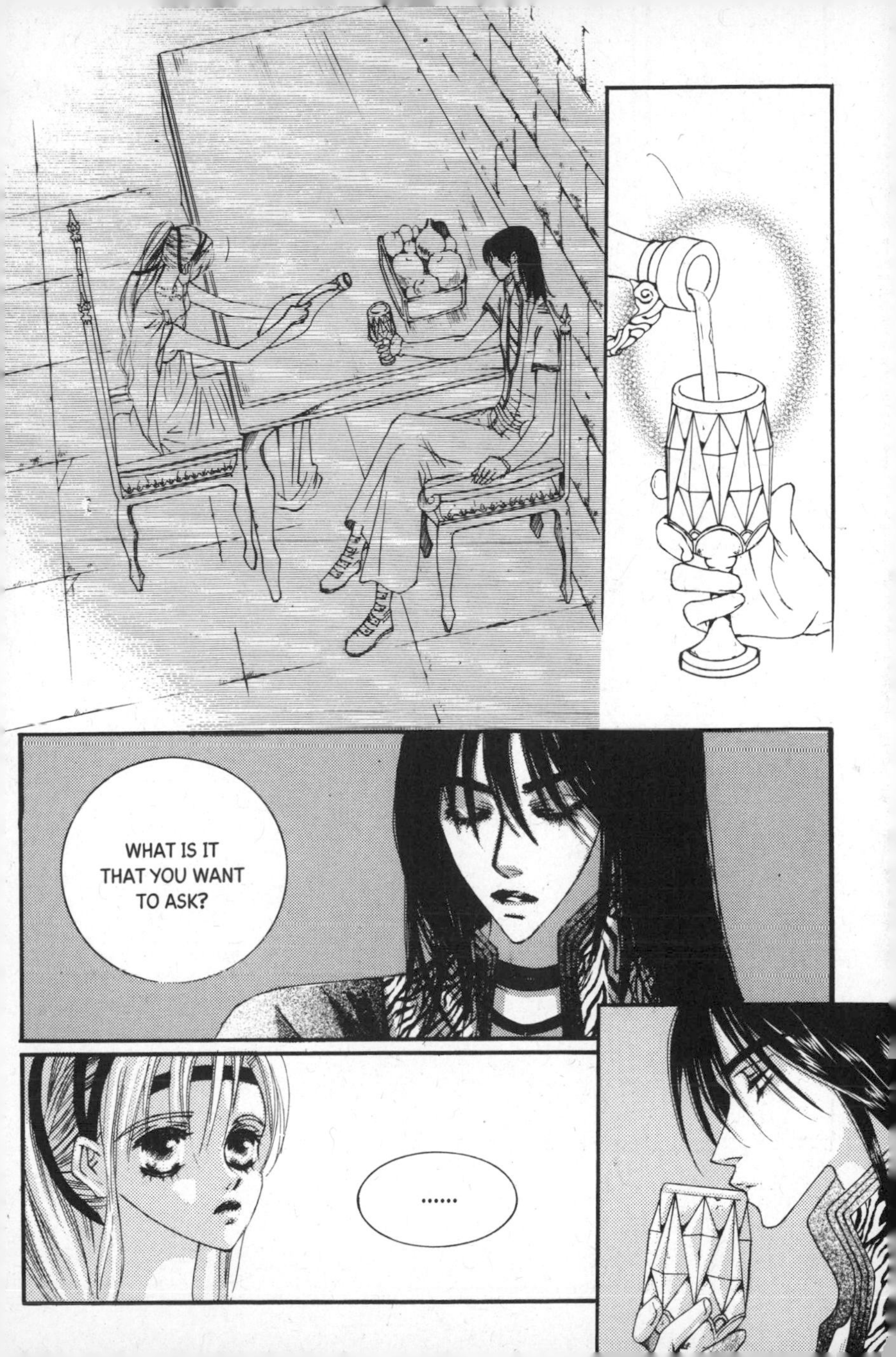

WHAT IS IT THAT YOU WANT TO ASK?
......

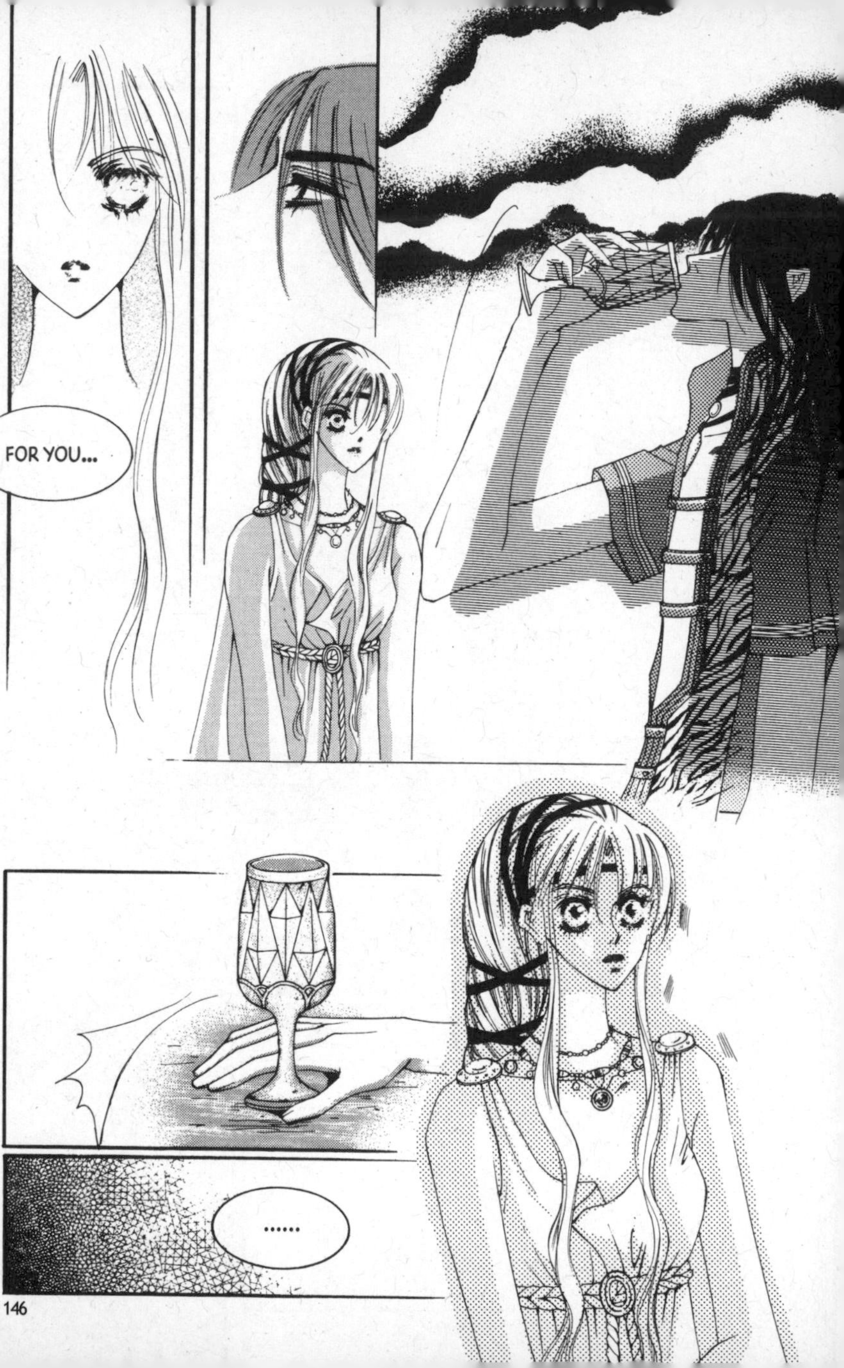
FOR YOU...
......

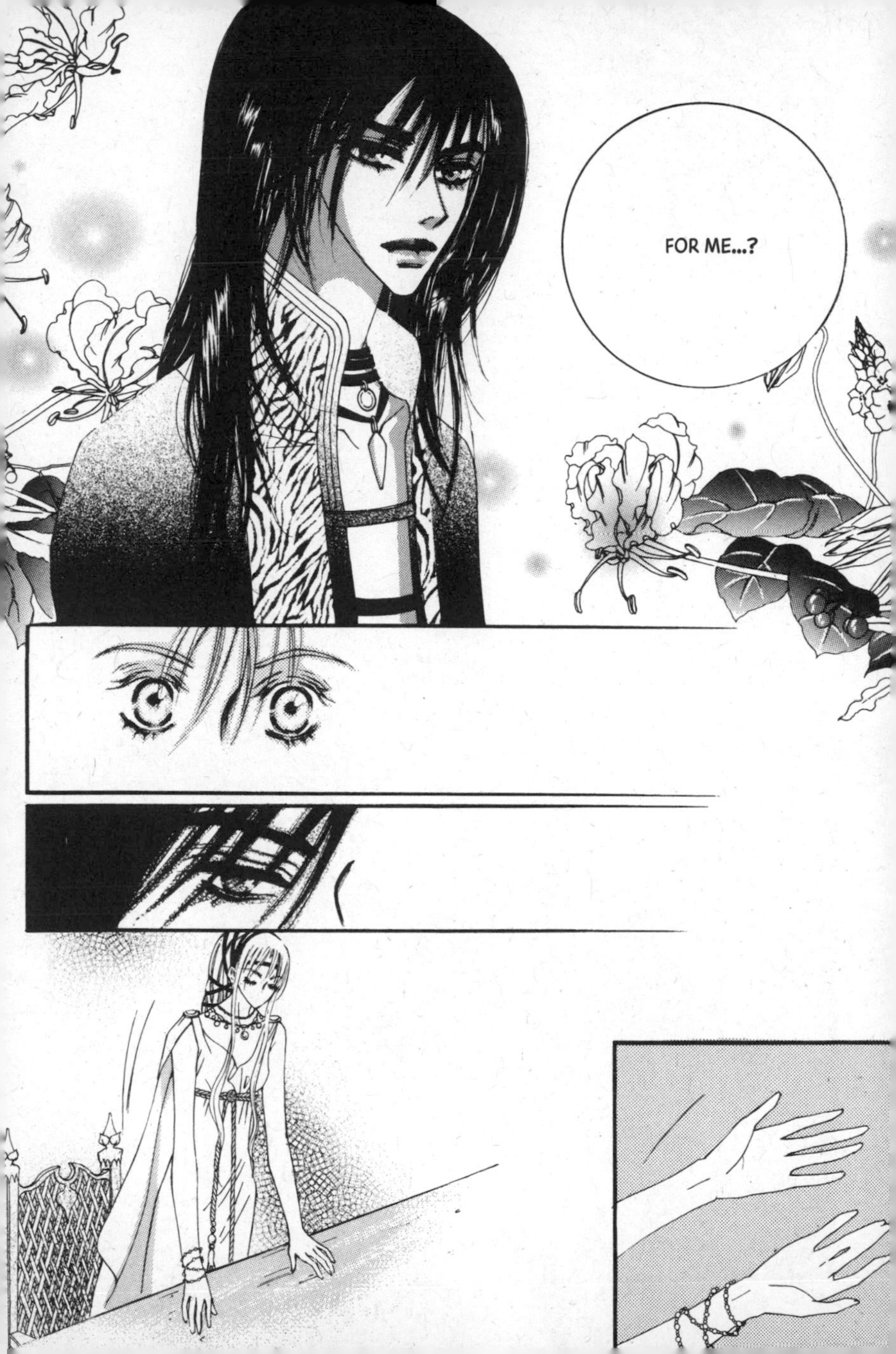
FOR ME...?

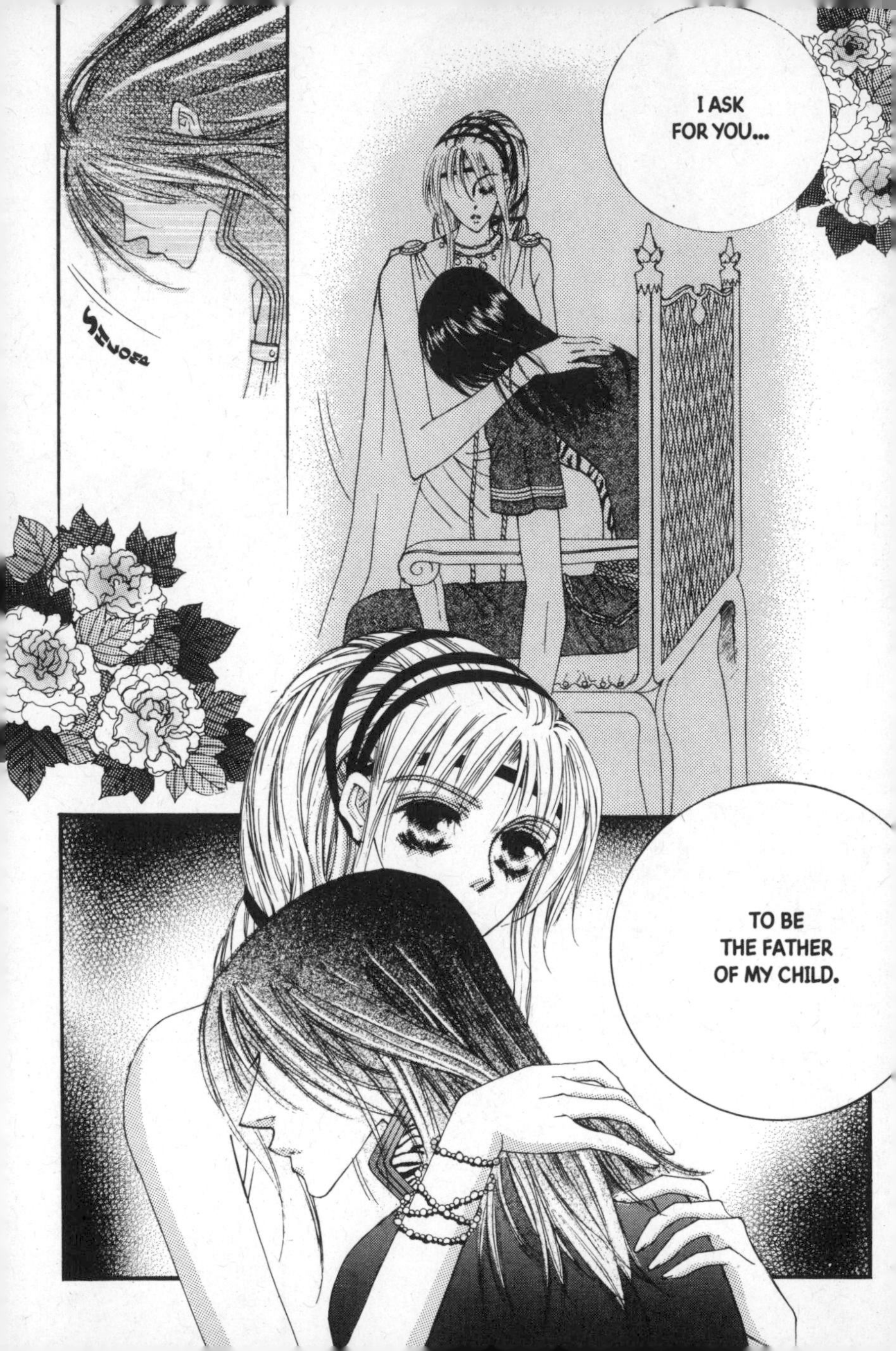
I ASK FOR YOU...
TO BE THE FATHER OF MY CHILD.

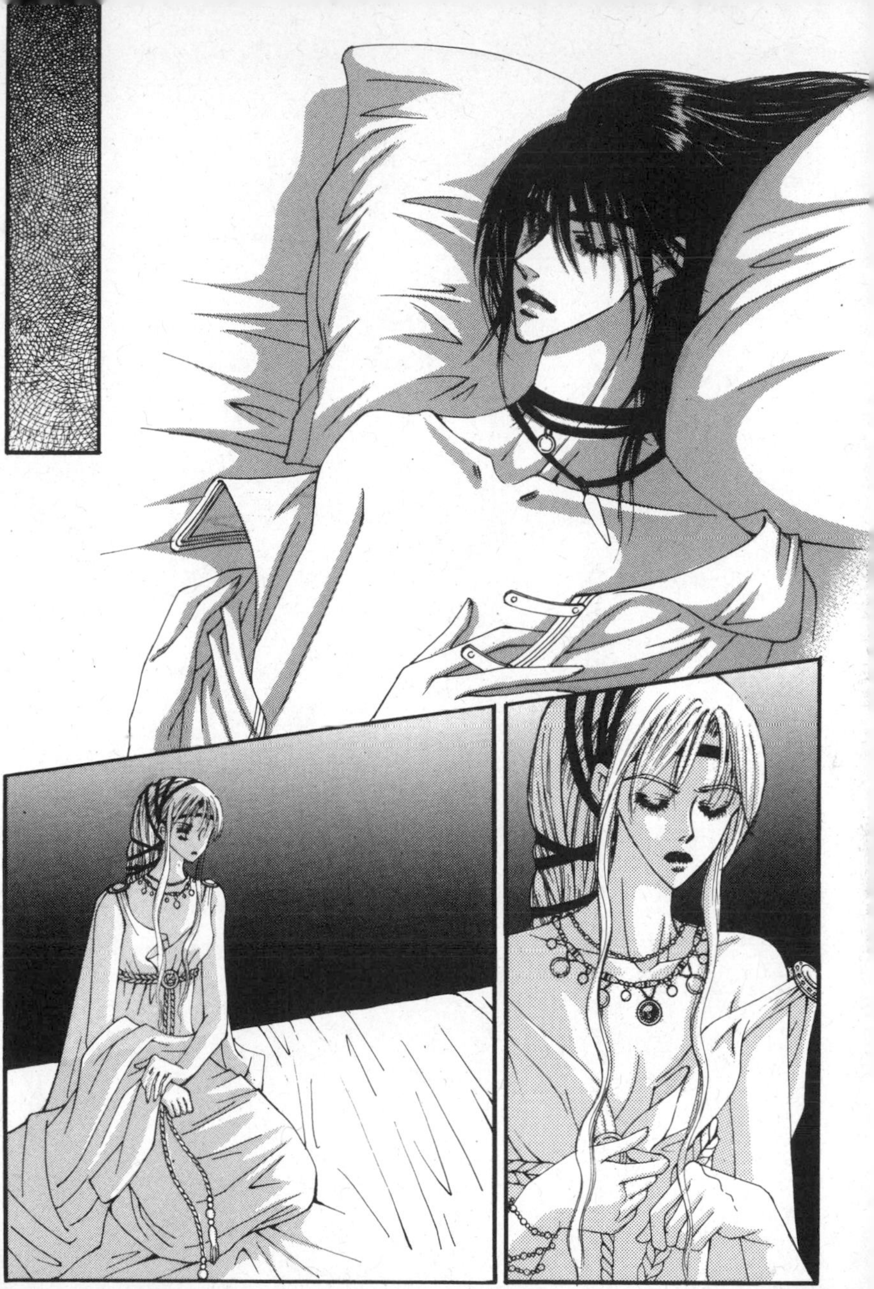

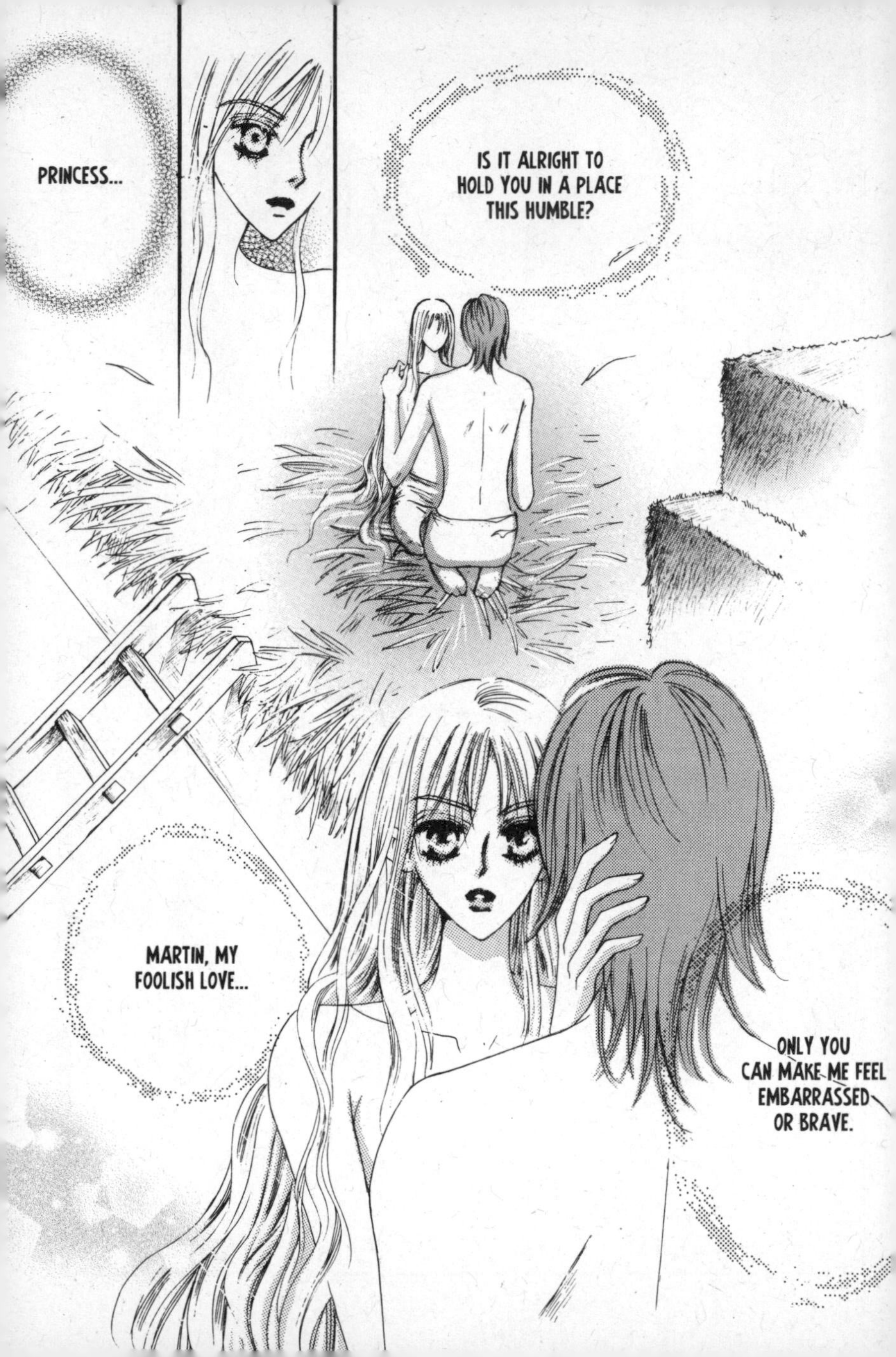
PRINCESS...
IS IT ALRIGHT TO HOLD YOU IN A PLACE THIS HUMBLE?
ONLY YOU CAN MAKE ME FEEL EMBARRASSED OR BRAVE.
MARTIN, MY FOOLISH LOVE...

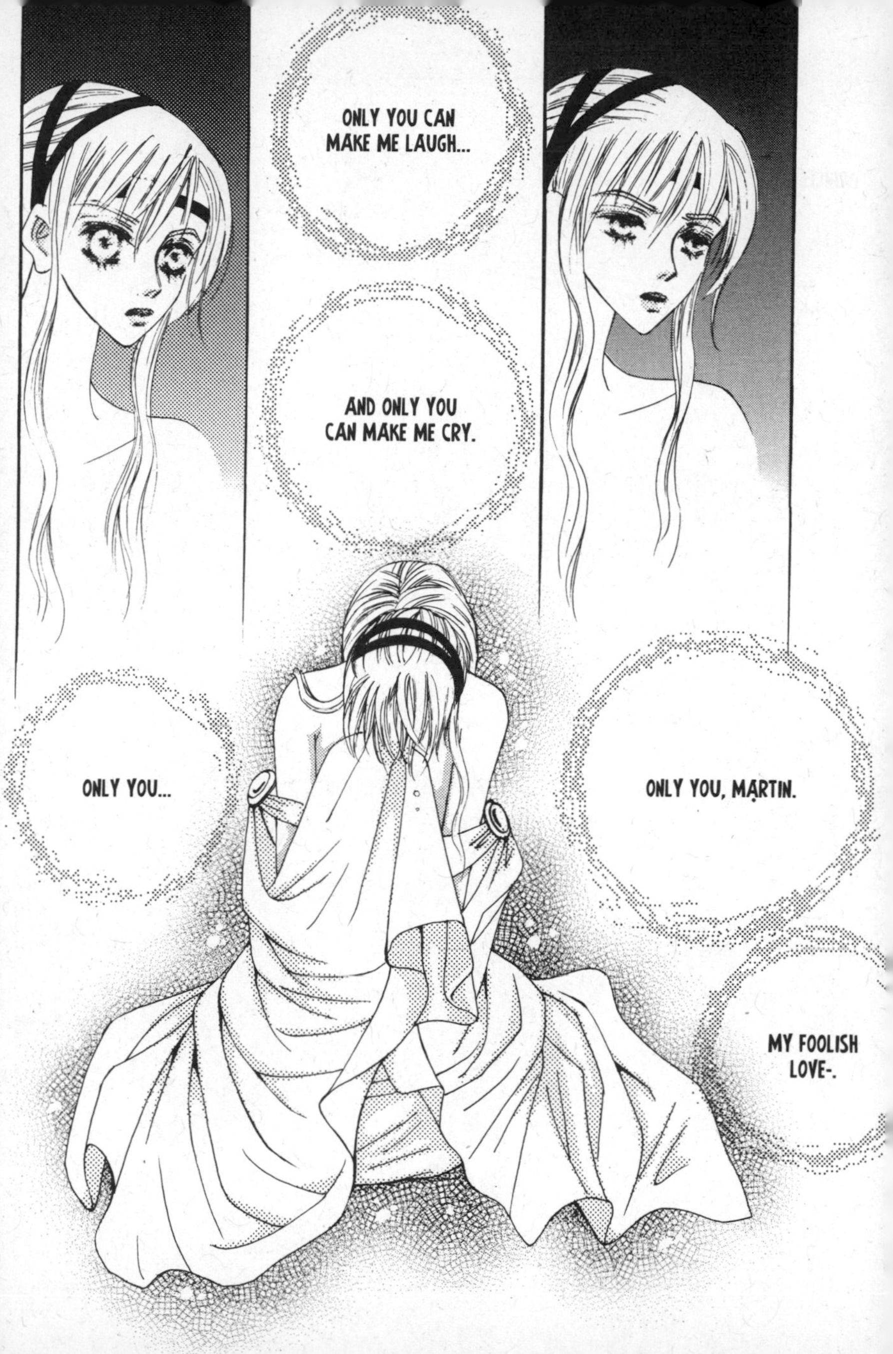
ONLY YOU CAN MAKE ME LAUGH...
AND ONLY YOU CAN MAKE ME CRY.
ONLY YOU, MARTIN.
ONLY YOU...
MY FOOLISH LOVE-.

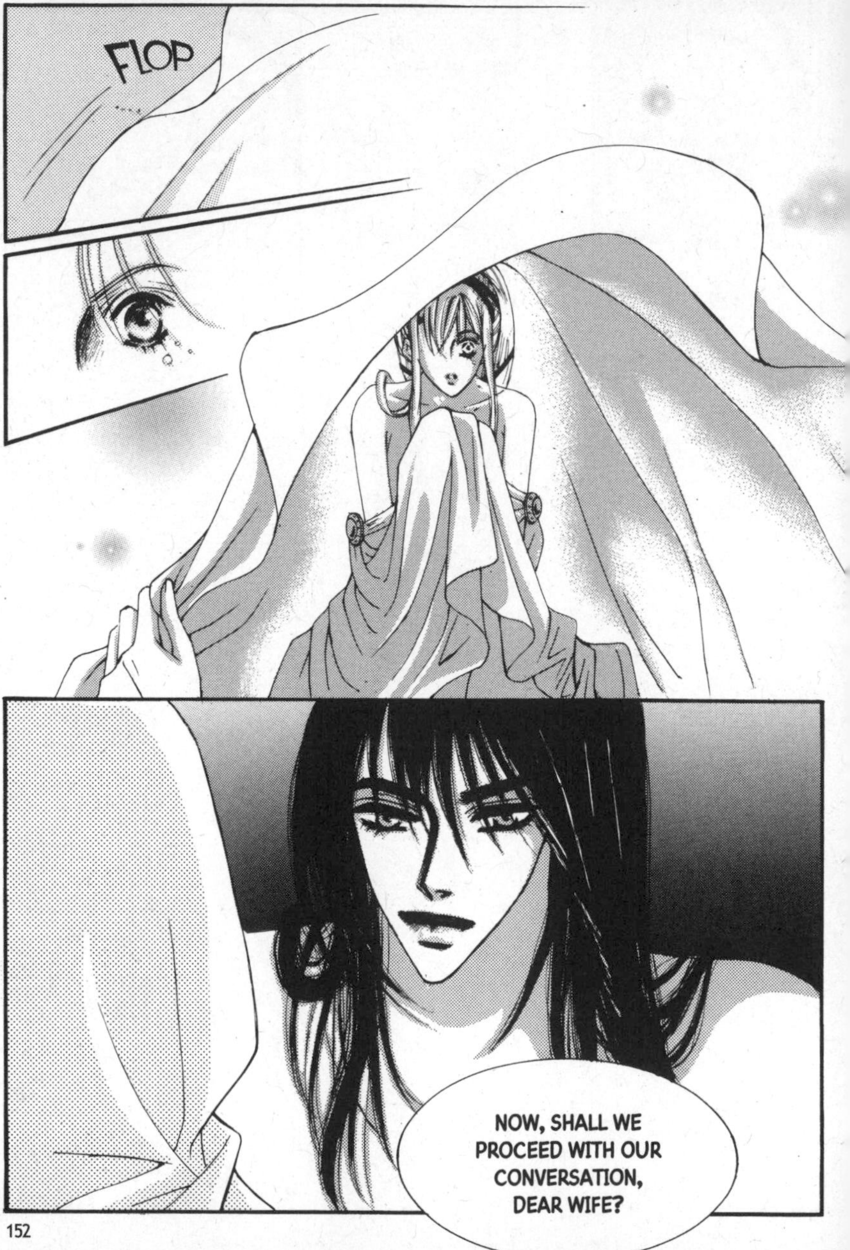
FLOP
NOW, SHALL WE PROCEED WITH OUR CONVERSATION, DEAR WIFE?

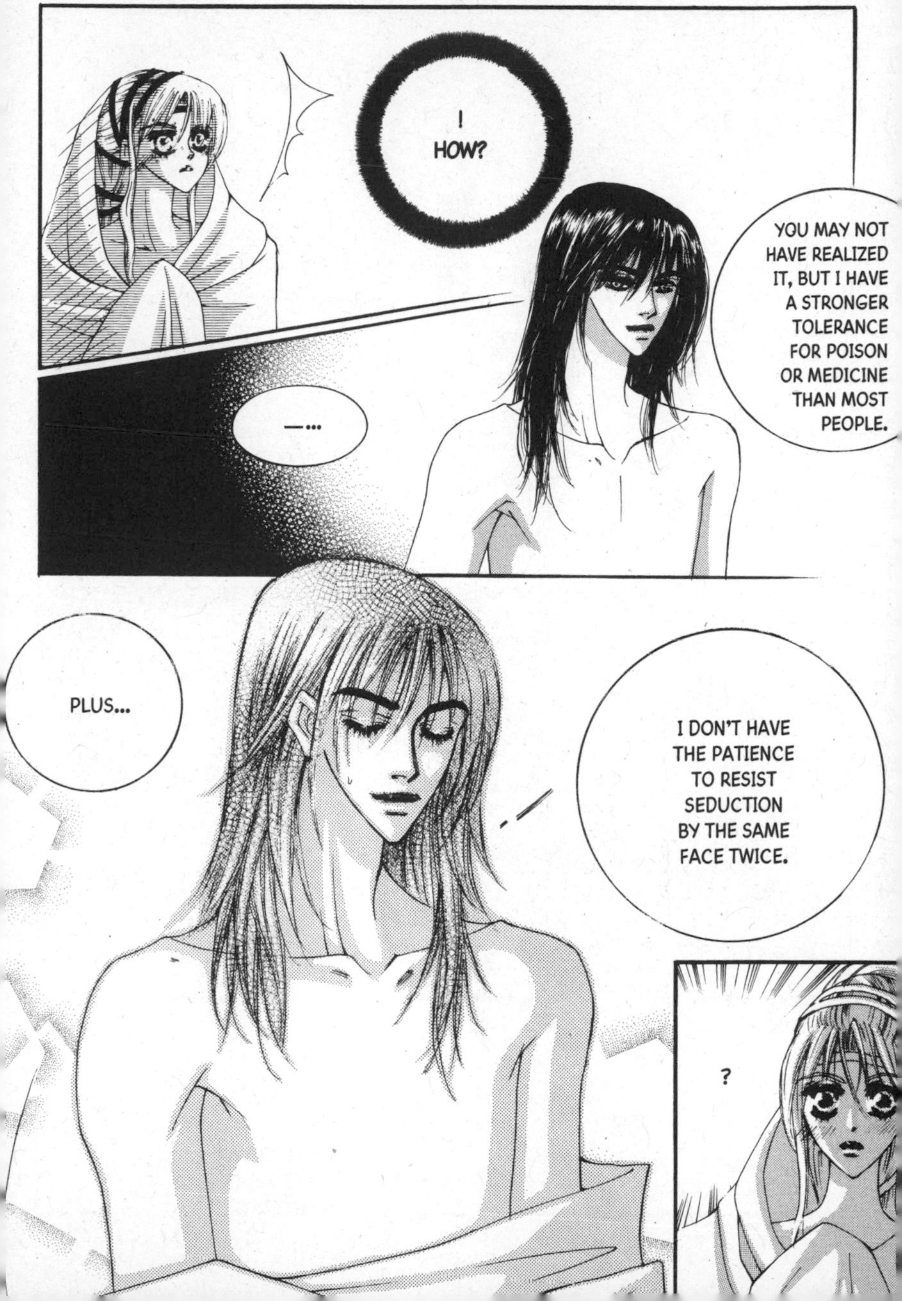
I
HOW?
YOU MAY NOT HAVE REALIZED IT, BUT I HAVE A STRONGER TOLERANCE FOR POISON OR MEDICINE THAN MOST PEOPLE.
—...
I DON'T HAVE THE PATIENCE TO RESIST SEDUCTION BY THE SAME FACE TWICE.
PLUS...
?

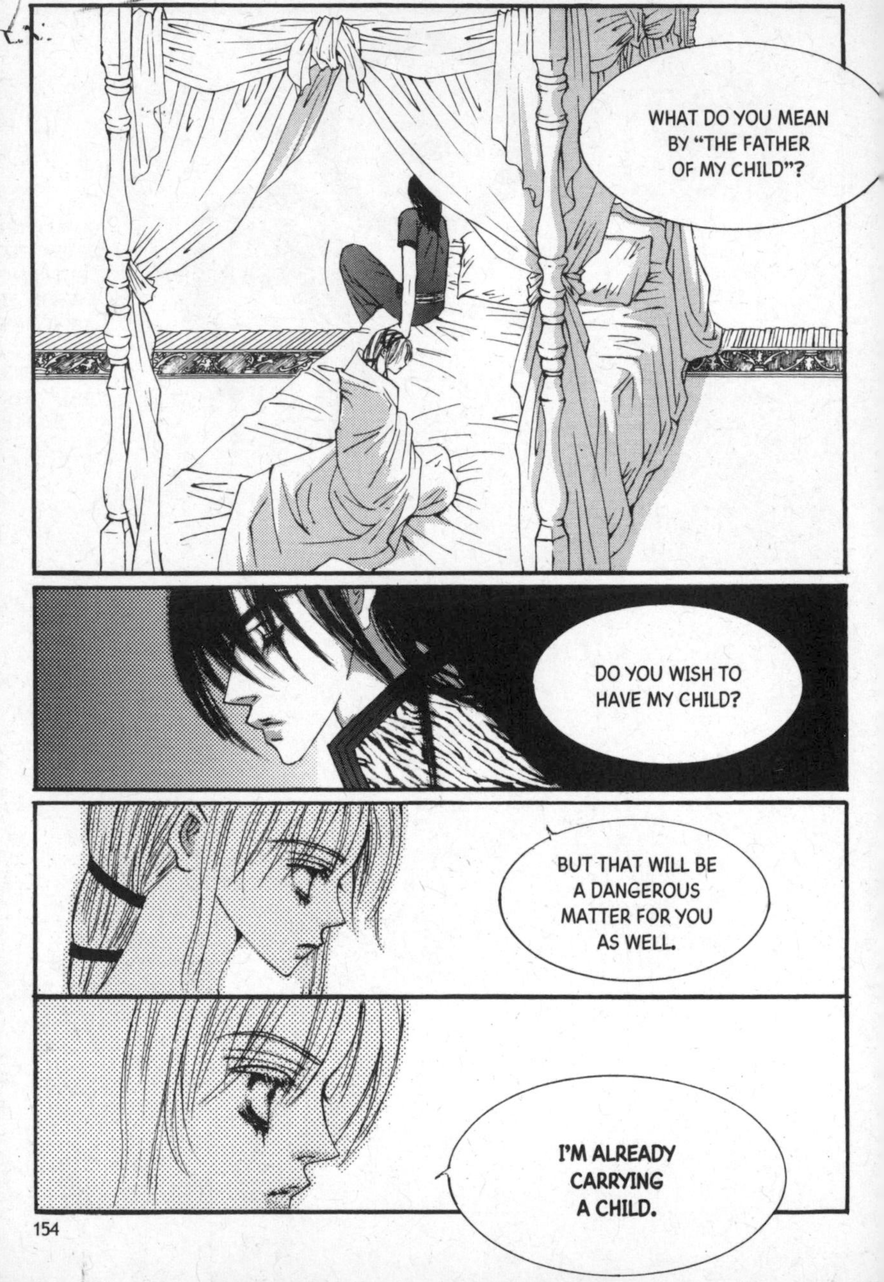
WHAT DO YOU MEAN BY "THE FATHER OF MY CHILD"?
DO YOU WISH TO HAVE MY CHILD?
BUT THAT WILL BE A DANGEROUS MATTER FOR YOU AS WELL.
I'M ALREADY CARRYING A CHILD.

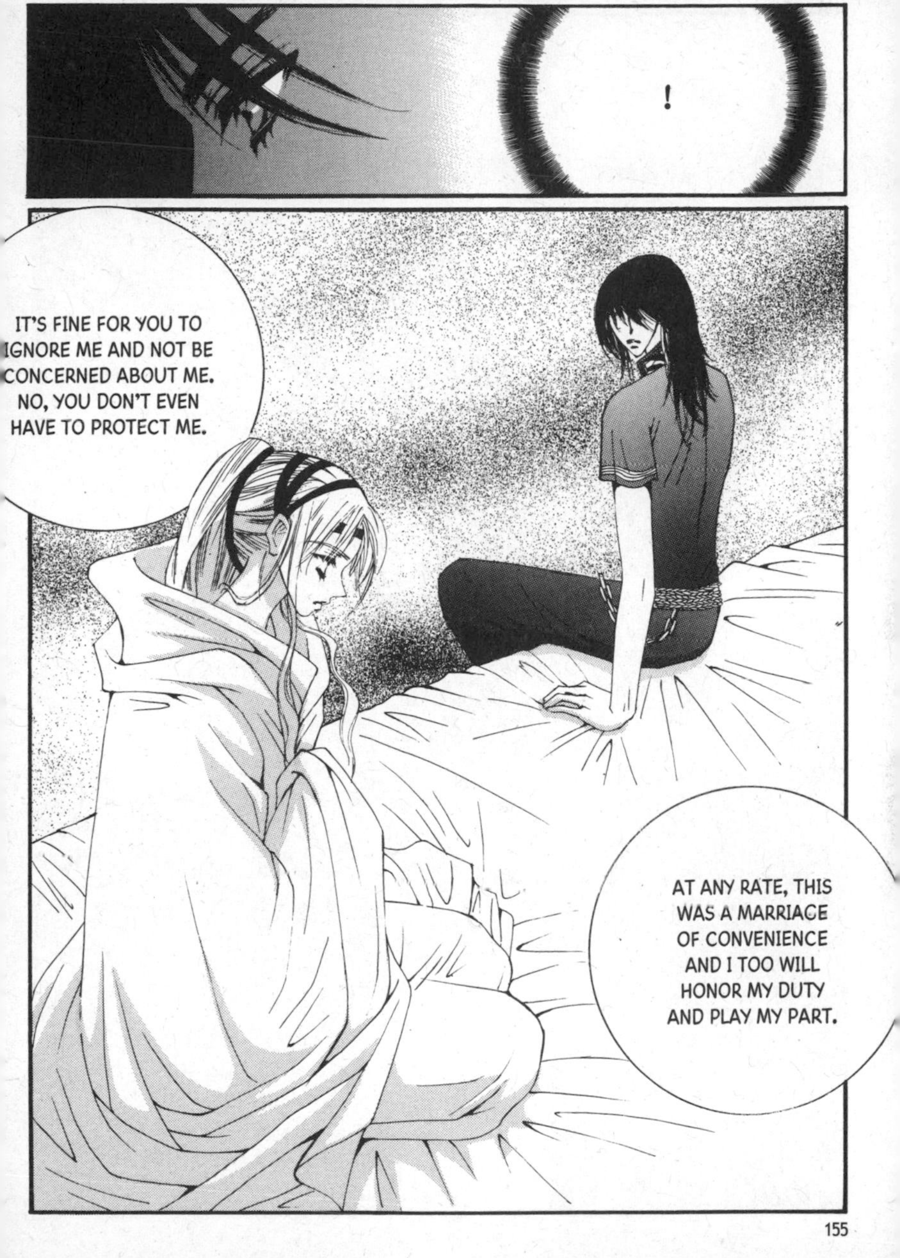
!
IT'S FINE FOR YOU TO IGNORE ME AND NOT BE CONCERNED ABOUT ME. NO, YOU DON'T EVEN HAVE TO PROTECT ME.
AT ANY RATE, THIS WAS A MARRIAGE OF CONVENIENCE AND I TOO WILL HONOR MY DUTY AND PLAY MY PART.

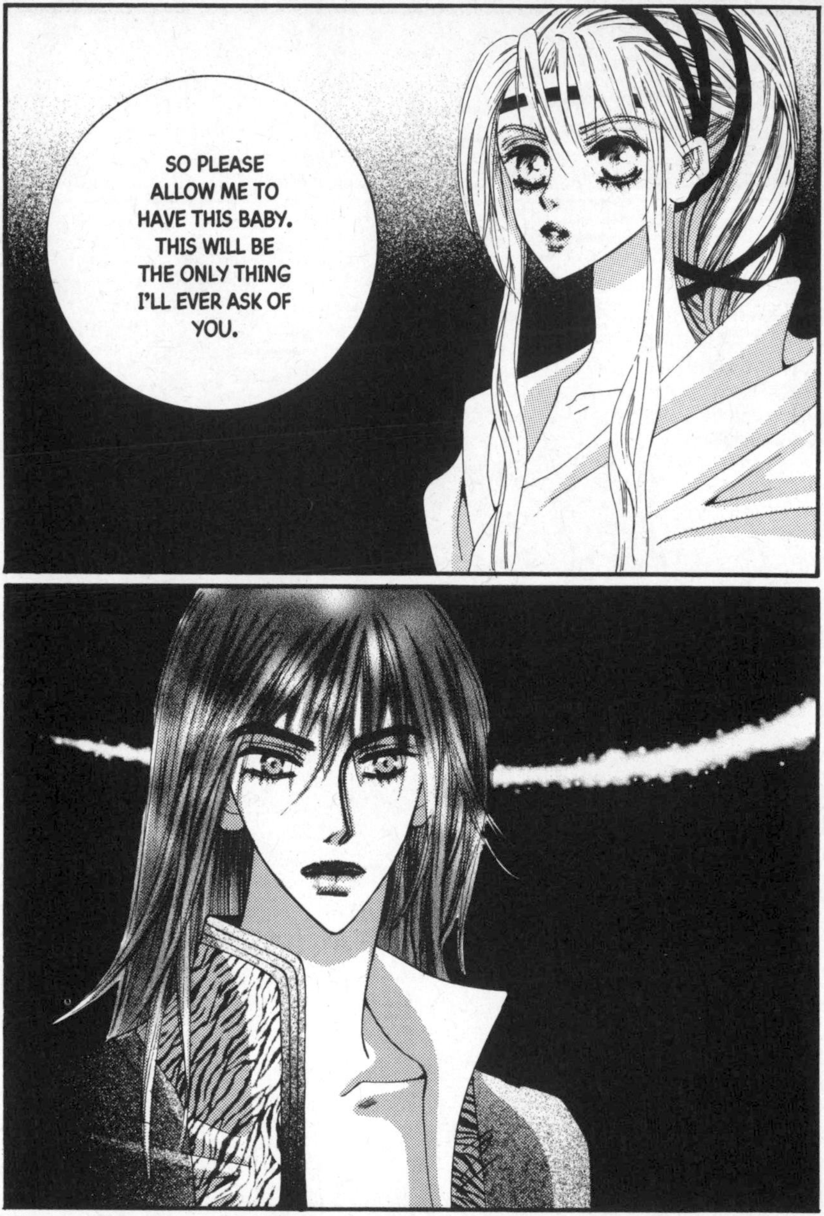
SO PLEASE ALLOW ME TO HAVE THIS BABY. THIS WILL BE THE ONLY THING I'LL EVER ASK OF YOU.

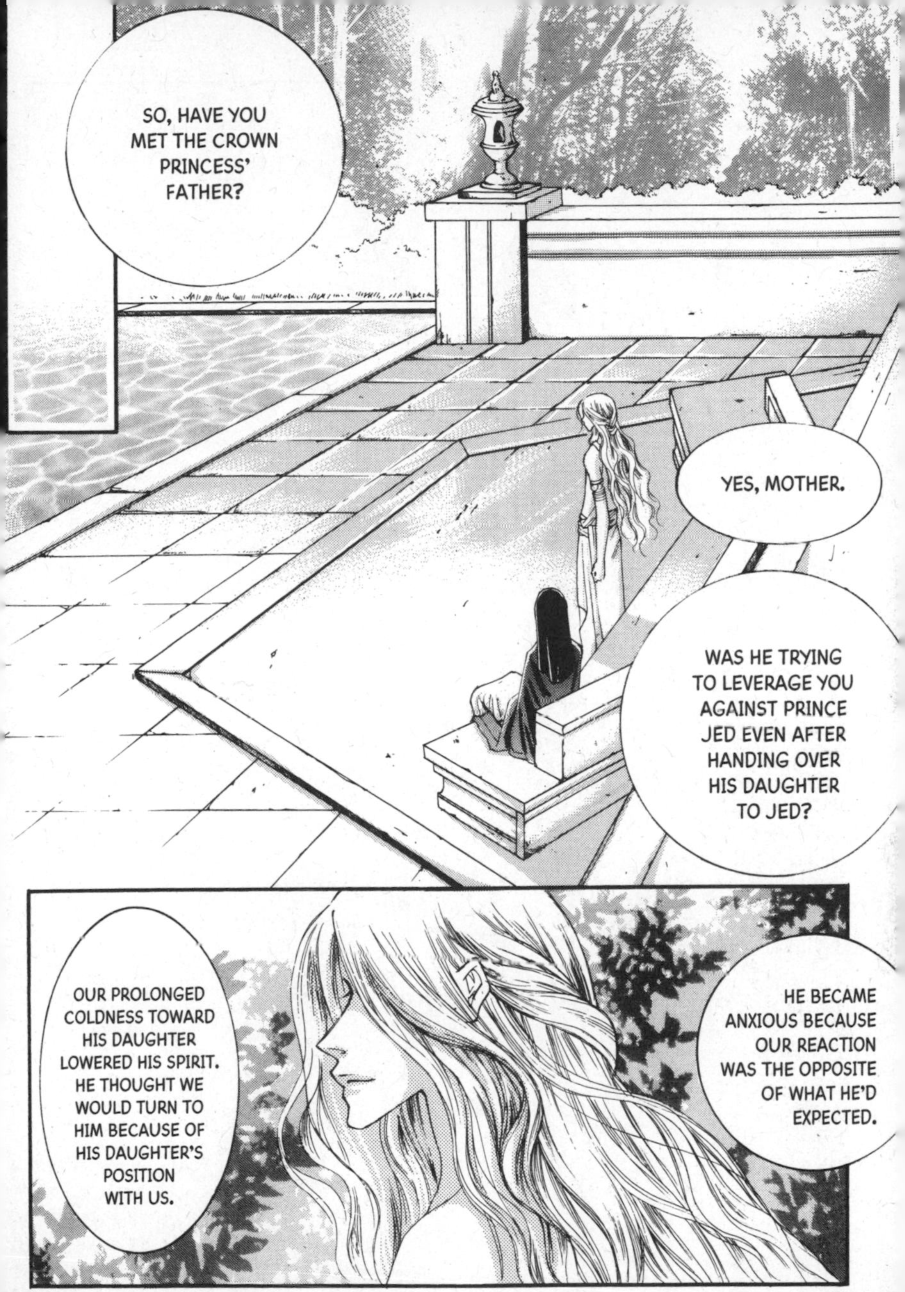
SO, HAVE YOU MET THE CROWN PRINCESS' FATHER?
YES, MOTHER.
WAS HE TRYING TO LEVERAGE YOU AGAINST PRINCE JED EVEN AFTER HANDING OVER HIS DAUGHTER TO JED?
HE BECAME ANXIOUS BECAUSE OUR REACTION WAS THE OPPOSITE OF WHAT HE'D EXPECTED.
OUR PROLONGED COLDNESS TOWARD HIS DAUGHTER LOWERED HIS SPIRIT. HE THOUGHT WE WOULD TURN TO HIM BECAUSE OF HIS DAUGHTER'S POSITION WITH US.

WELL DONE. AS LONG AS YOU HAVE THAT OLD MAN IN YOUR HANDS...
HE'LL BE INVALUABLE HELPING US TO DISPOS OF JED'S POWERLESS AND NOISY SUPPORTER WHO CLAIM THEY'RE FOLLOWING THE RIGHT CAUSE.
THAT WON'T BE ENOUGH. HE ISN'T THE TYPE TO WIGGLE UNLESS WE CUT OFF HIS ARMS AND LEGS.
AND REINY HAS NOW BECOME TOO DANGEROUS TO HANDLE CARELESSLY. WE NEED A SAFER AND BETTER STIMULANT THAN HER.

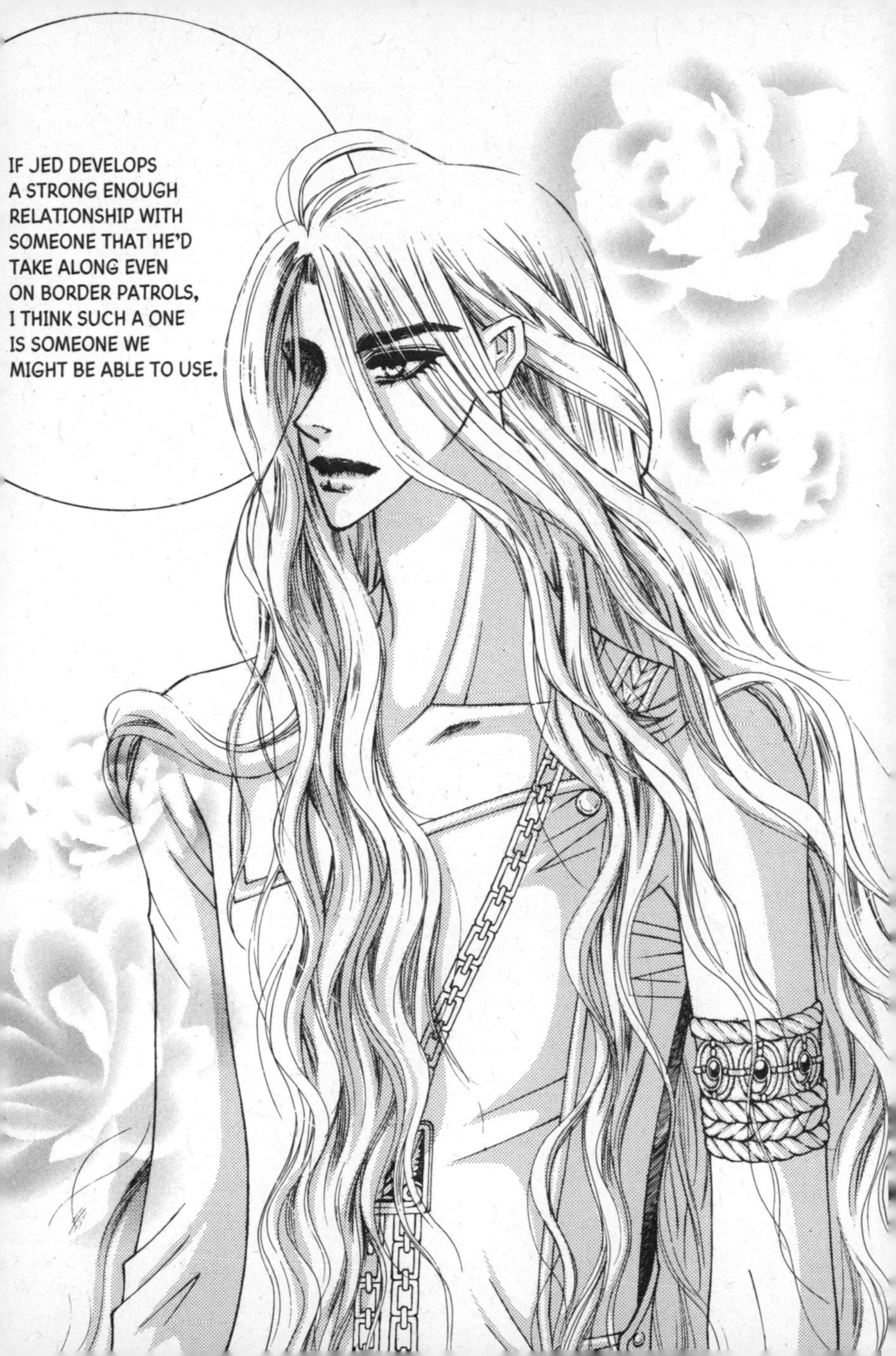
IF JED DEVELOPS A STRONG ENOUGH RELATIONSHIP WITH SOMEONE THAT HE'D TAKE ALONG EVEN ON BORDER PATROLS, I THINK SUCH A ONE IS SOMEONE WE MIGHT BE ABLE TO USE.

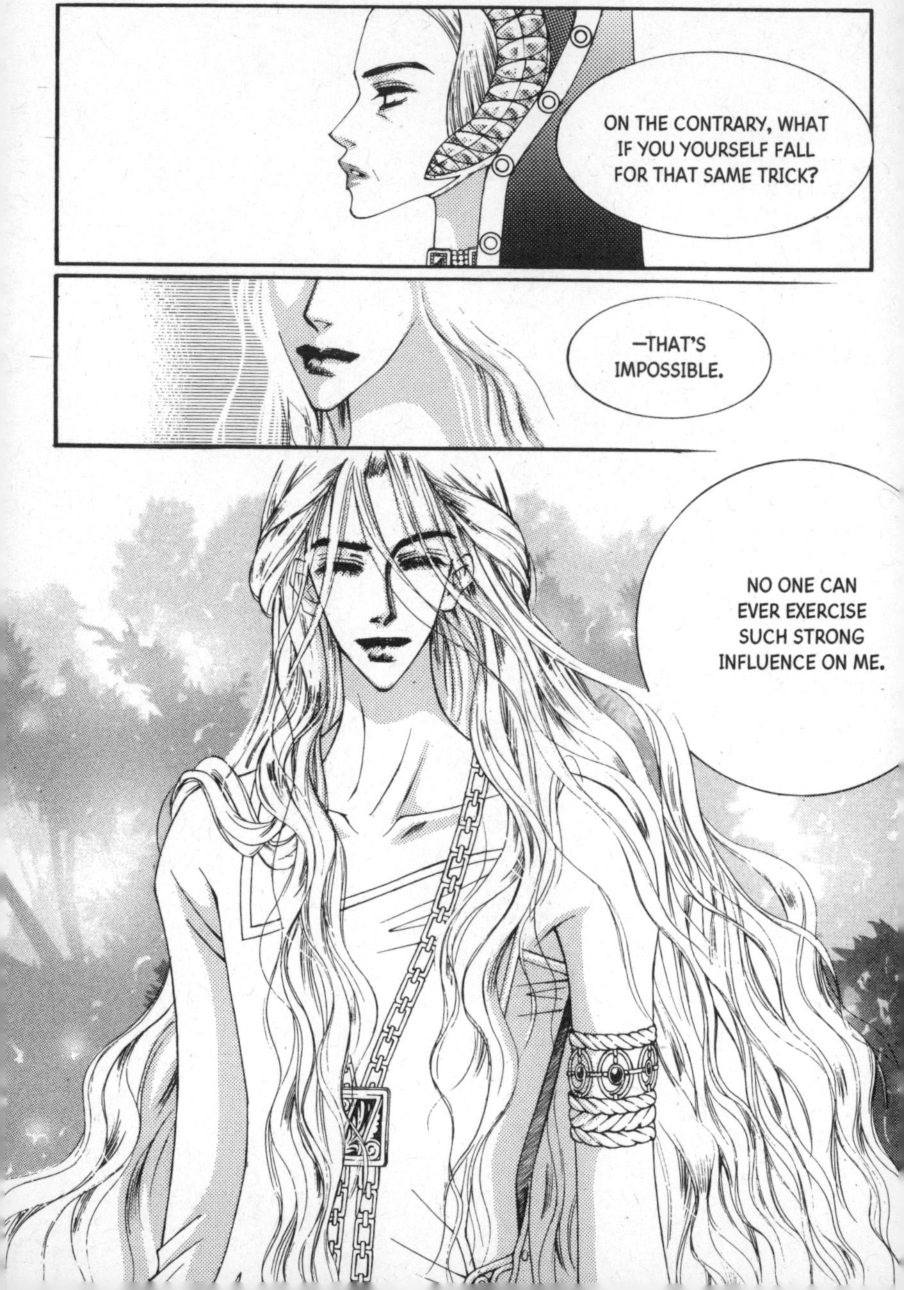
ON THE CONTRARY, WHAT IF YOU YOURSELF FALL FOR THAT SAME TRICK?
—THAT'S IMPOSSIBLE.
NO ONE CAN EVER EXERCISE SUCH STRONG INFLUENCE ON ME.

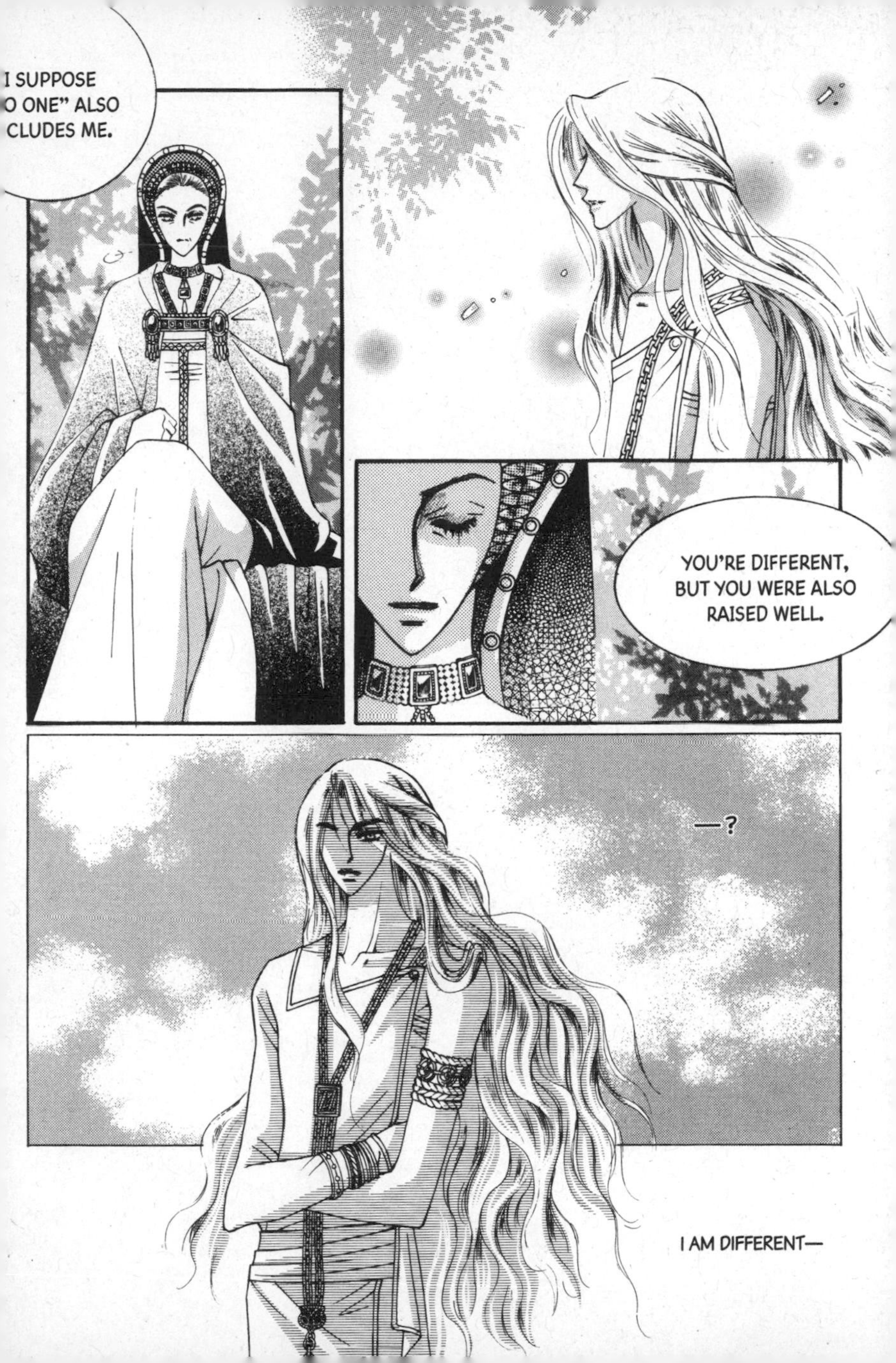
I SUPPOSE
O ONE" ALSO
CLUDES ME.
YOU'RE DIFFERENT, BUT YOU WERE ALSO RAISED WELL.
—?
I AM DIFFERENT—

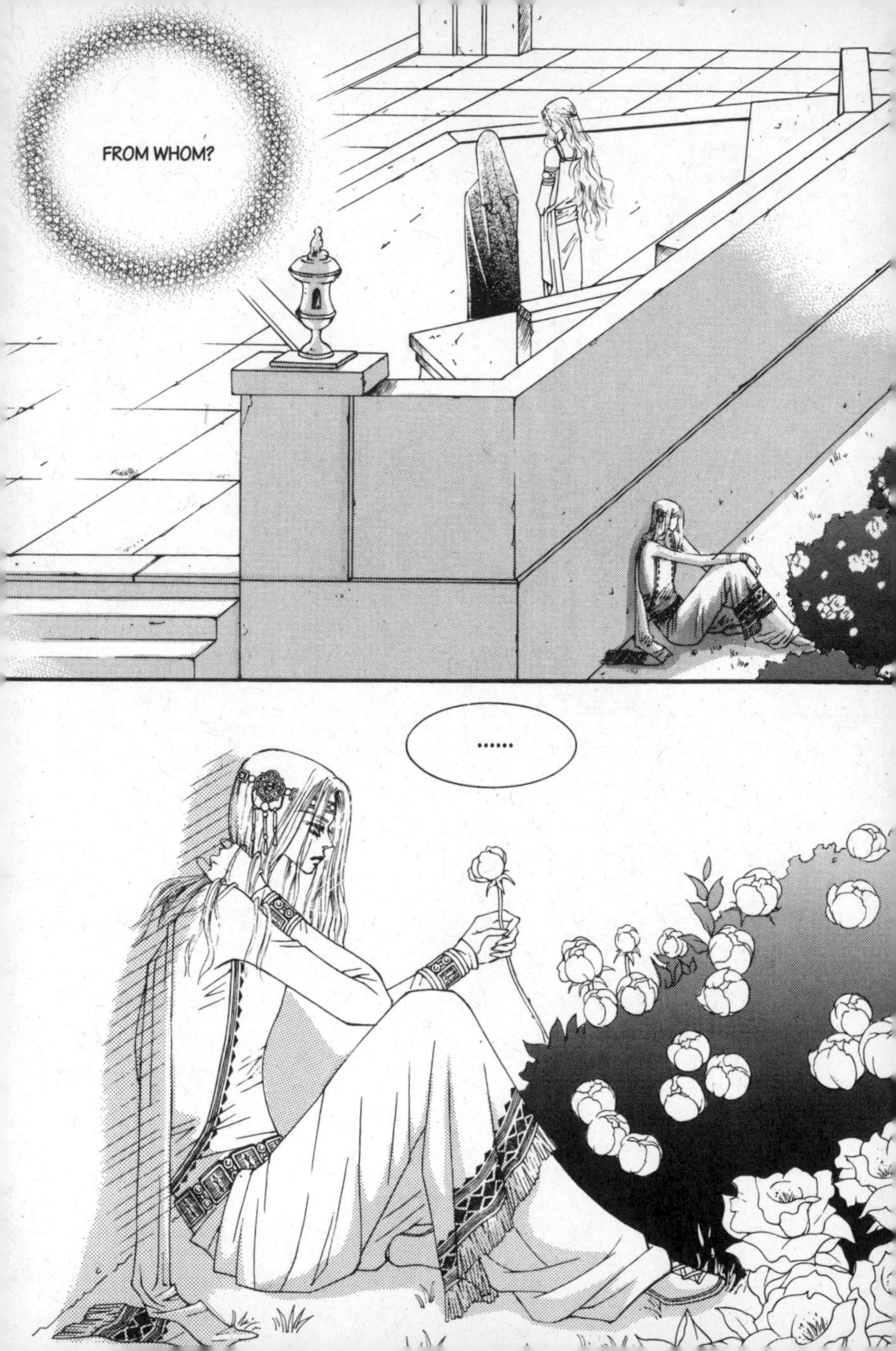
FROM WHOM?
......

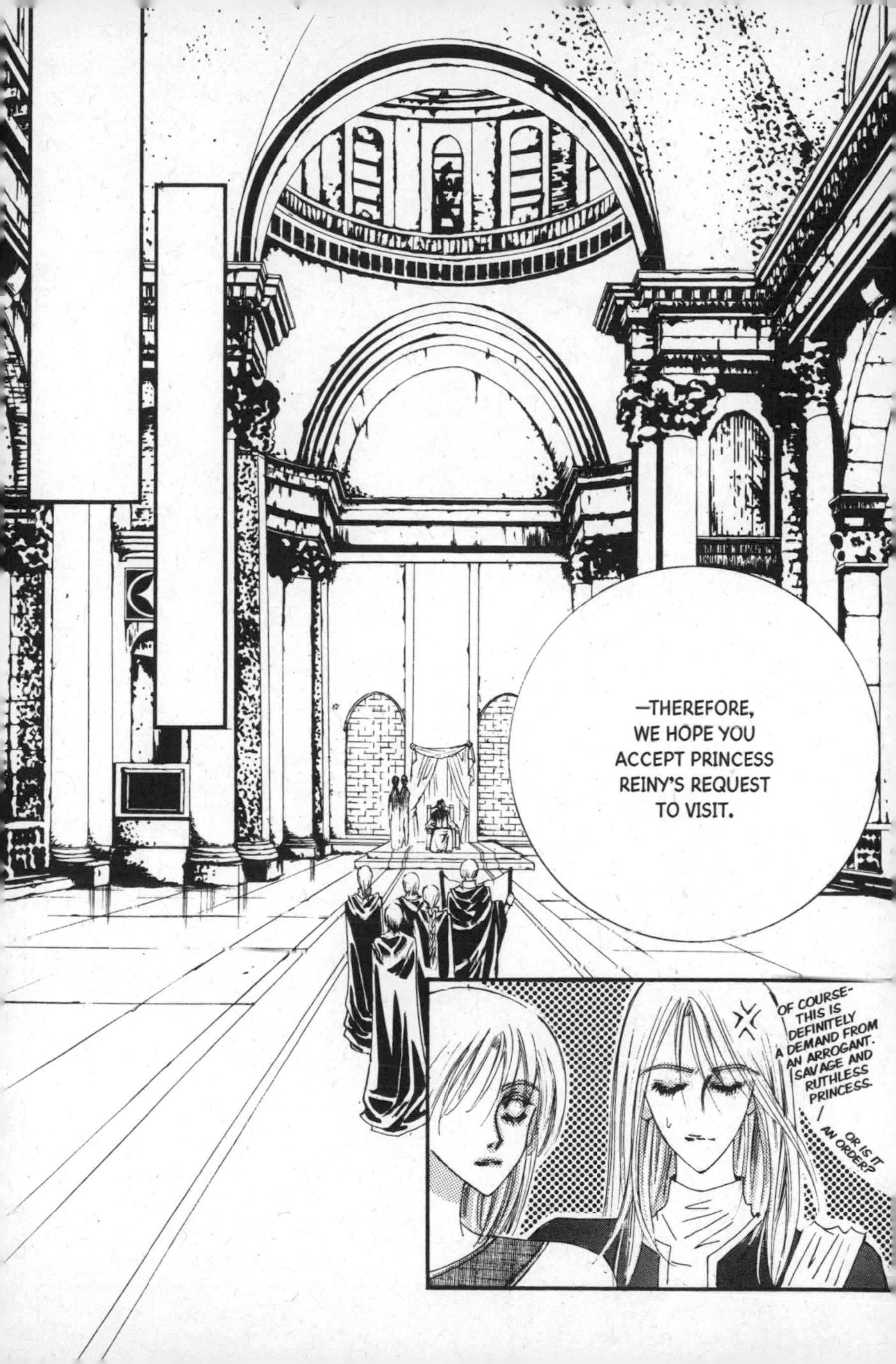
—THEREFORE, WE HOPE YOU ACCEPT PRINCESS REINY'S REQUEST TO VISIT.
OF COURSE-THIS IS DEFINITELY A DEMAND FROM AN ARROGANT, SAVAGE AND RUTHLESS PRINCESS.
OR IS IT AN ORDER?

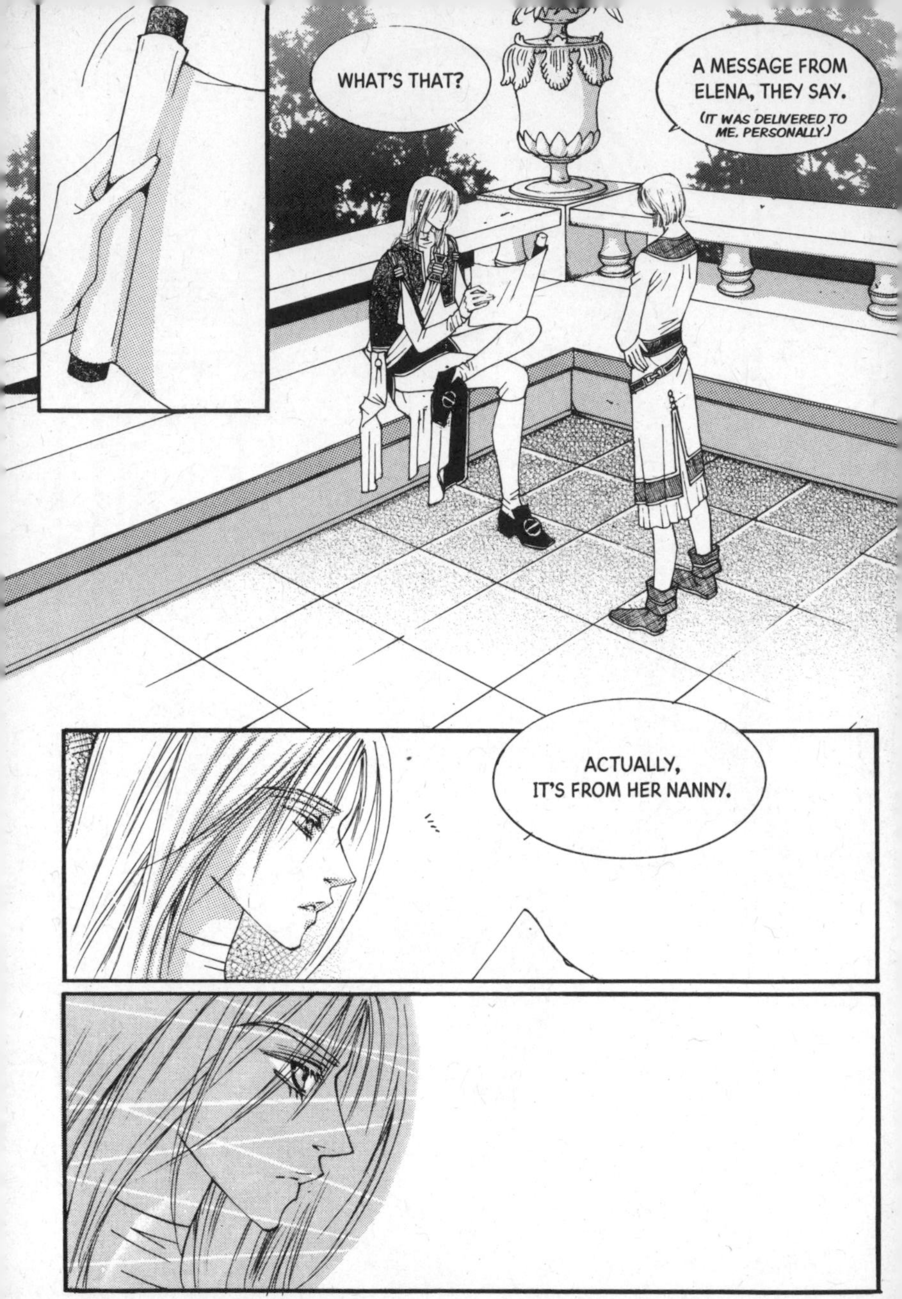
WHAT'S THAT?
A MESSAGE FROM ELENA, THEY SAY.
(IT WAS DELIVERED TO ME. PERSONALLY.)
ACTUALLY, IT'S FROM HER NANNY.

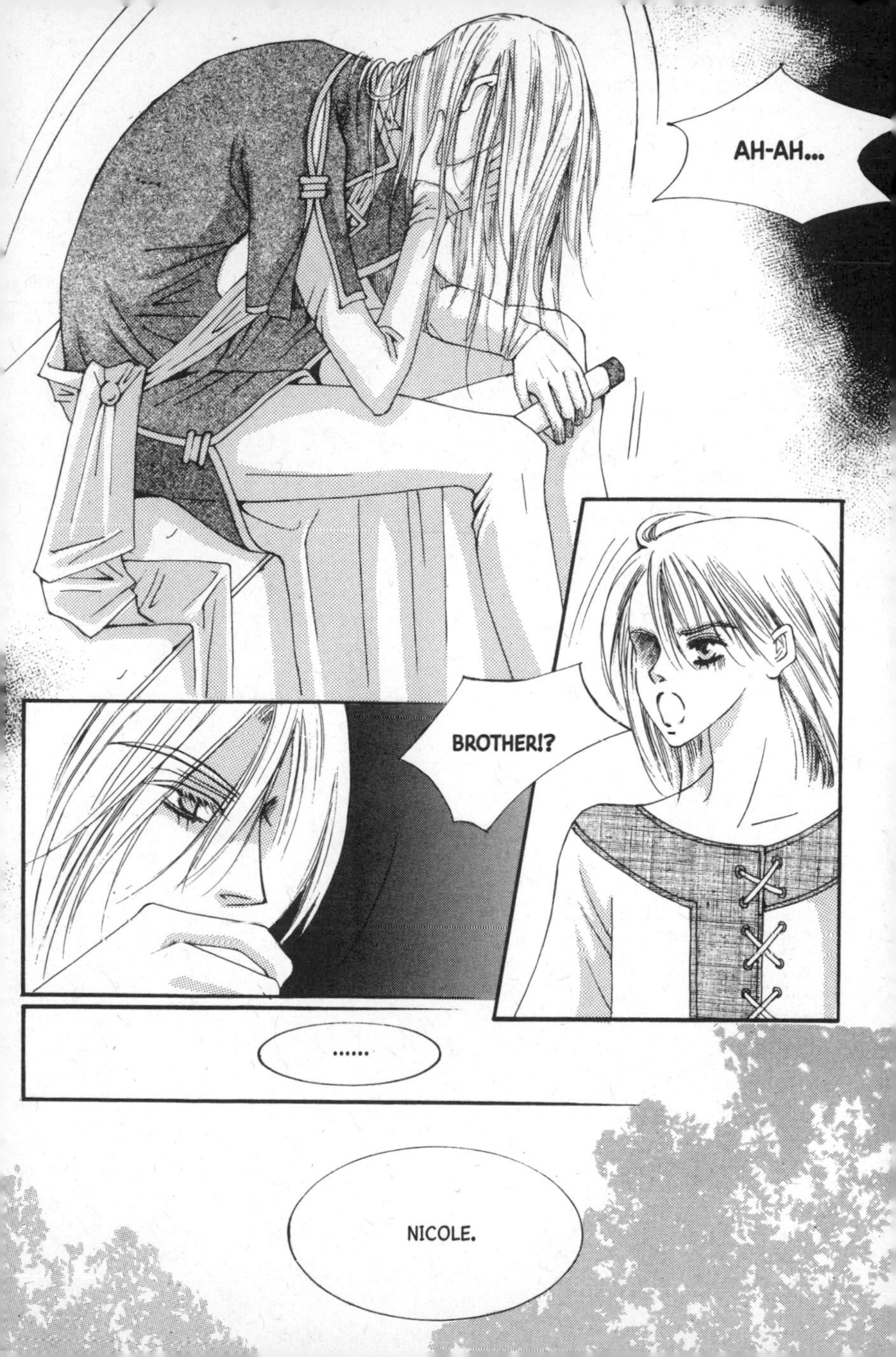
AH-AH...
BROTHER!?
......
NICOLE.

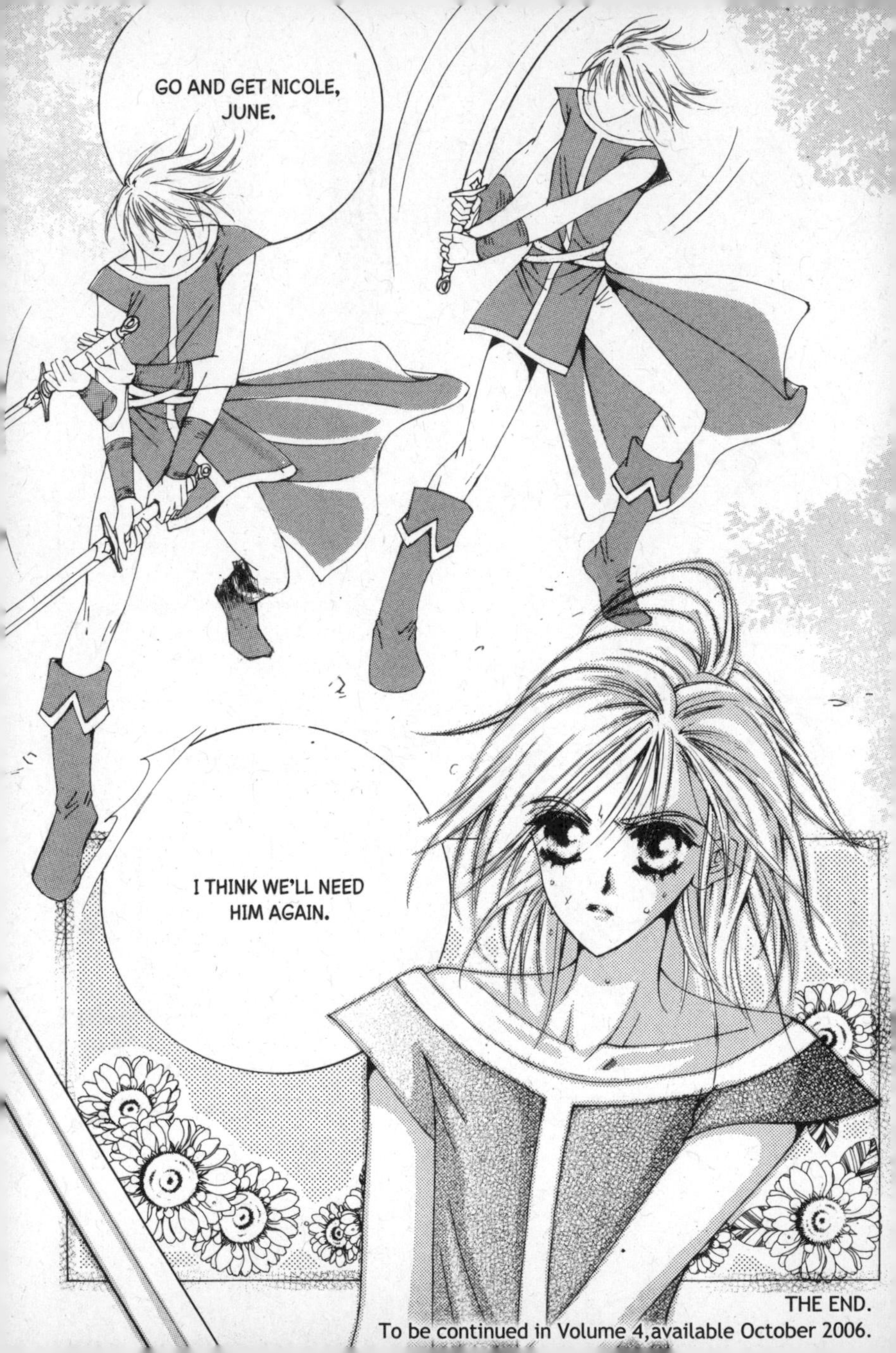
GO AND GET NICOLE, JUNE.
I THINK WE'LL NEED HIM AGAIN.
THE END.
To be continued in Volume 4, available October 2006.

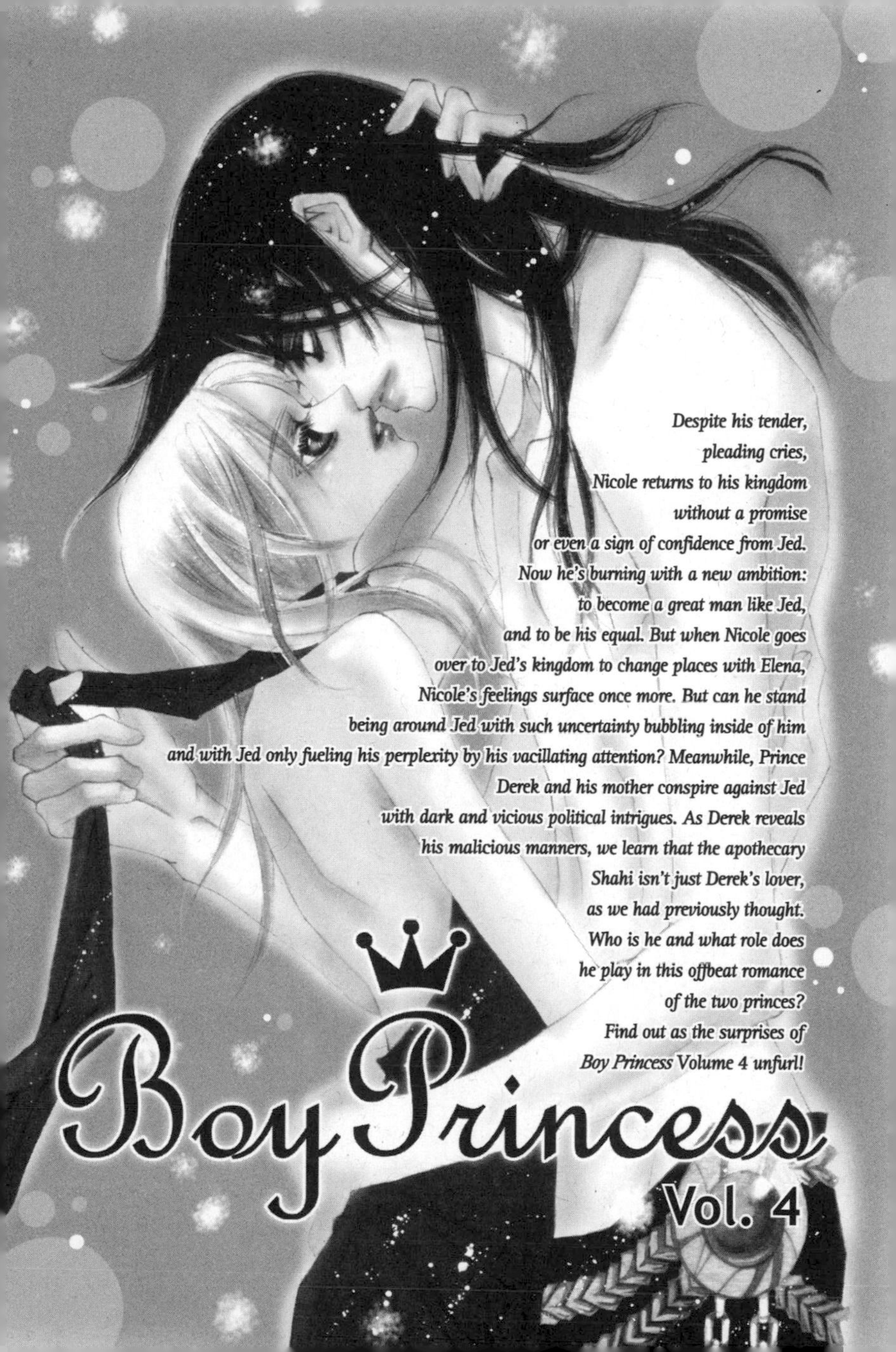
Despite his tender,
pleading cries,
Nicole returns to his kingdom
without a promise
or even a sign of confidence from Jed.
Now he's burning with a new ambition:
to become a great man like Jed,
and to be his equal. But when Nicole goes
over to Jed's kingdom to change places with Elena,
Nicole's feelings surface once more. But can he stand
being around Jed with such uncertainty bubbling inside of him
and with Jed only fueling his perplexity by his vacillating attention? Meanwhile, Prince
Derek and his mother conspire against Jed
with dark and vicious political intrigues. As Derek reveals
his malicious manners, we learn that the apothecary
Shahi isn't just Derek's lover,
as we had previously thought.
Who is he and what role does
he play in this offbeat romance
of the two princes?
Find out as the surprises of
Boy Princess Volume 4 unfurl!
Boy Princess
Vol. 4

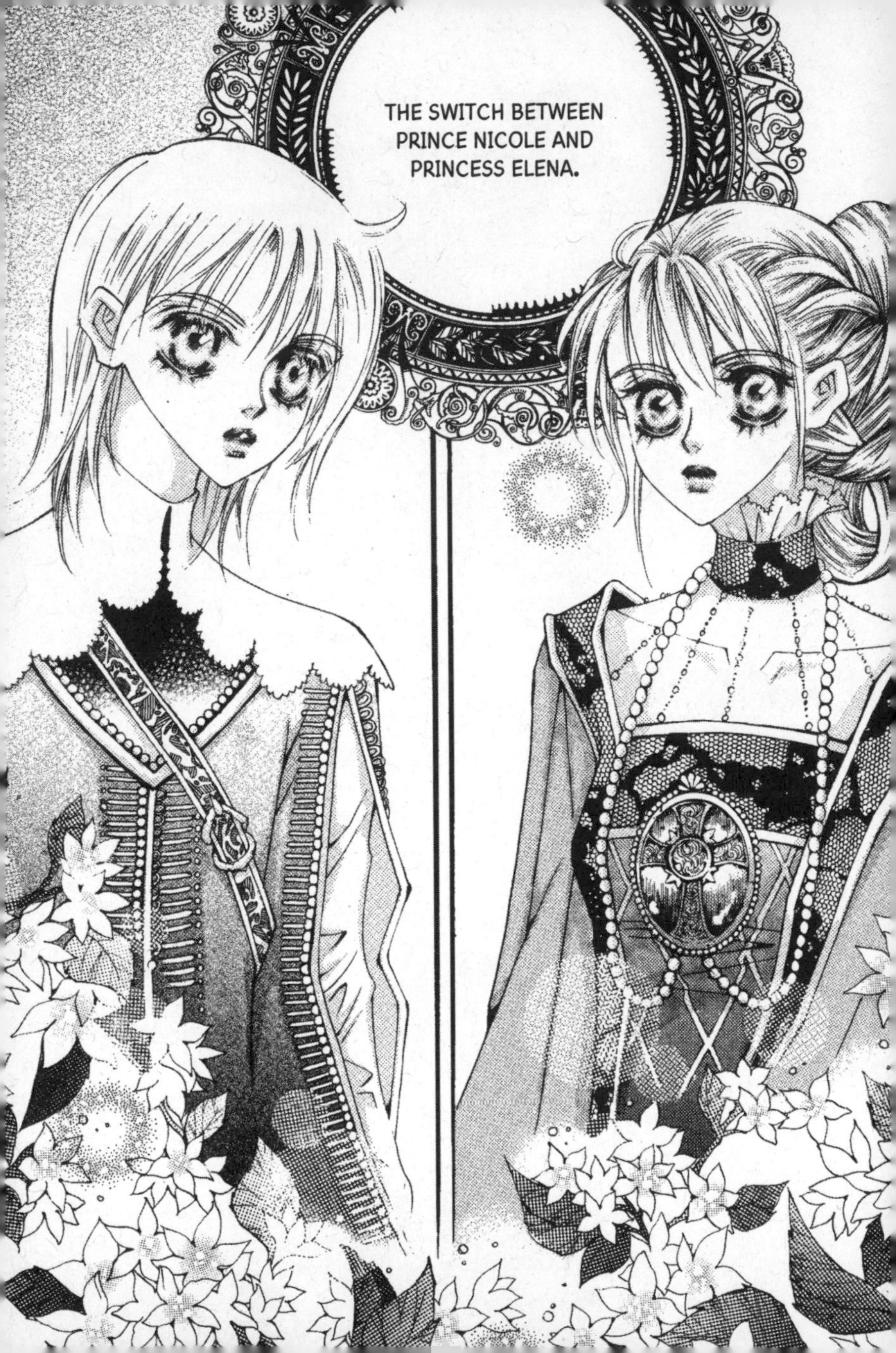
THE SWITCH BETWEEN PRINCE NICOLE AND PRINCESS ELENA.

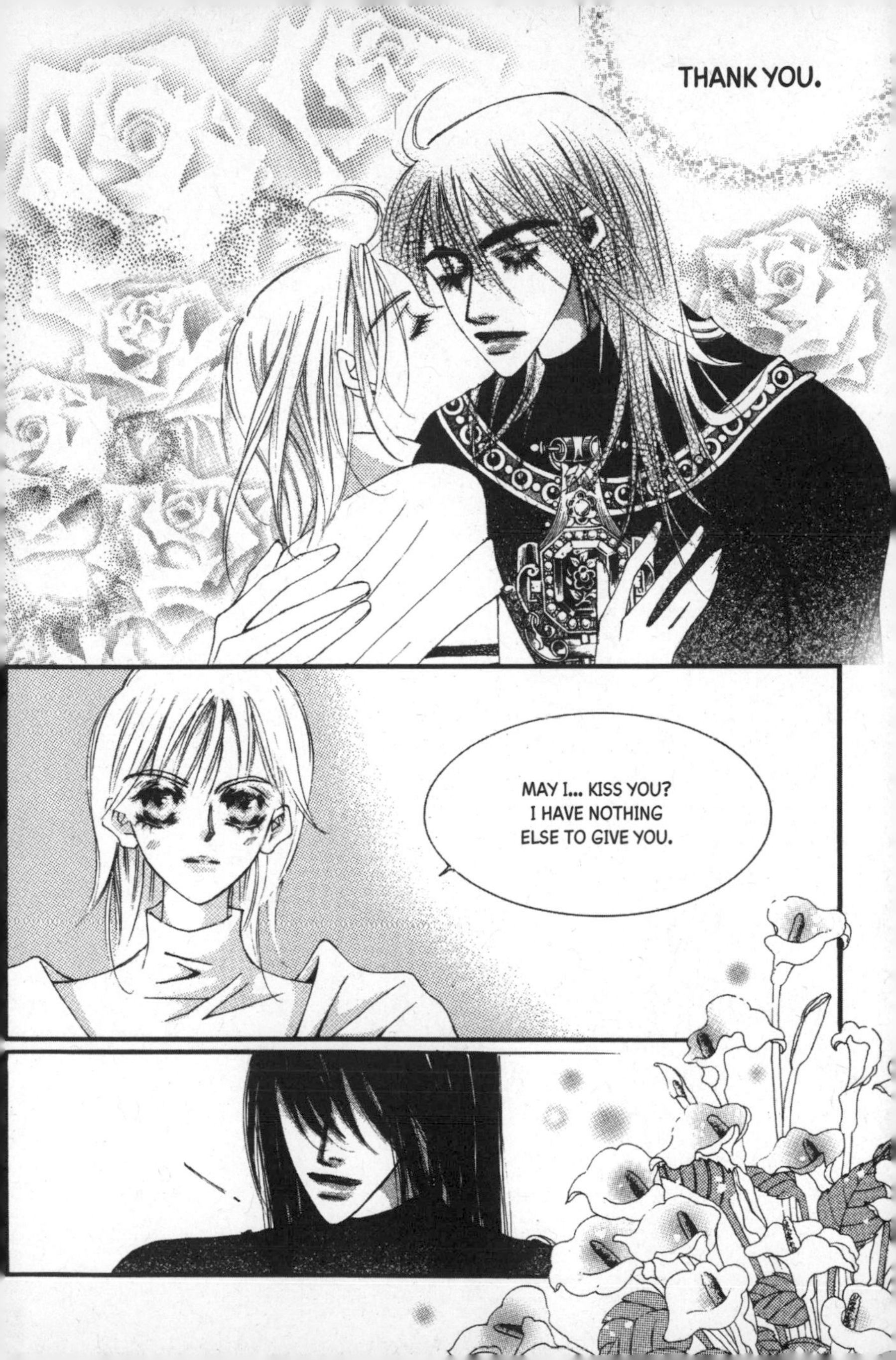
THANK YOU.
MAY I... KISS YOU? I HAVE NOTHING ELSE TO GIVE YOU.

NETCOMICS July 2006 Release

Youjung Lee

0/6
ZERO/SIX
VOL. 3

Unseen dangers creep ever closer to Moolchi. Jong-E suspects Kanghee is the threat, but can't tell Moolchi the truth about his situation or who he really is. She challenges Kanghee, but discovers that the parasitic presence inside Moolchi's girlfriend is much more than she bargained for. The mysterious creature inside of Kanghee manipulates Moolchi's love for her to deadly advantage in the lethal game between itself and Jong-E. Who sent the creature after Moolchi? More importantly, who will survive? The answer won't be known before the powerful student Narutbae makes his play. Meanwhile, seriously injured and restrained in a hospital far from Korea, a father dreams of returning home...

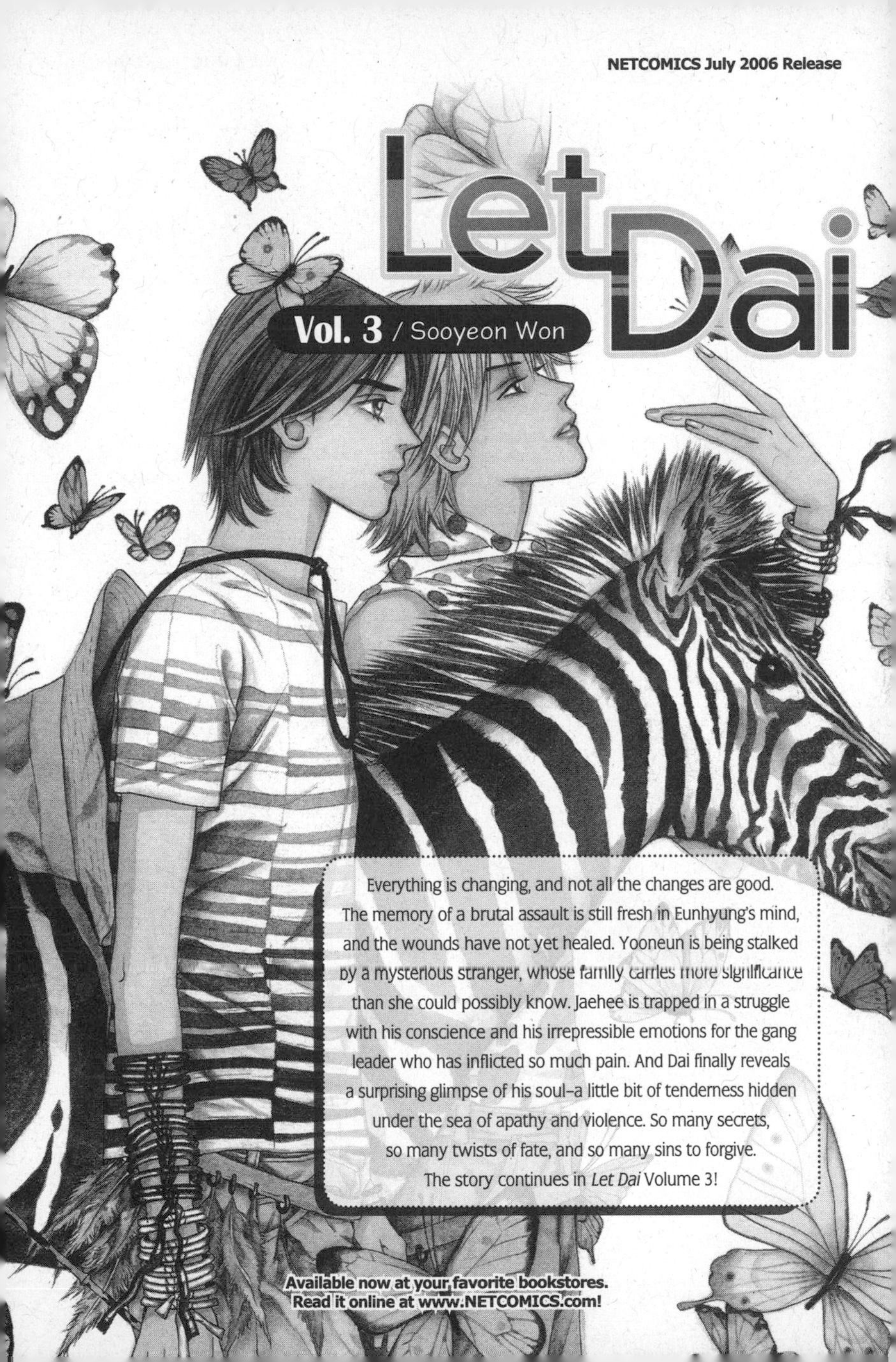
NETCOMICS July 2006 Release
Let Dai
Vol. 3 / Sooyeon Won
Everything is changing, and not all the changes are good. The memory of a brutal assault is still fresh in Eunhyung's mind, and the wounds have not yet healed. Yooneun is being stalked by a mysterious stranger, whose family carries more significance than she could possibly know. Jaehee is trapped in a struggle with his conscience and his irrepressible emotions for the gang leader who has inflicted so much pain. And Dai finally reveals a surprising glimpse of his soul–a little bit of tenderness hidden under the sea of apathy and violence. So many secrets, so many twists of fate, and so many sins to forgive. The story continues in Let Dai Volume 3!
Available now at your favorite bookstores.
Read it online at www.NETCOMICS.com!

Seyoung is an ordinary 17-year-old schoolgirl who plays mediocre roles in her school's drama productions. Her real-life drama develops as she finds herself falling for her childhood playmate Hyunwoo, who he is drifting away from her and toward a TV star schoolmate named Hyemi When Seyoung works up the nerve to profess her feelings to Hyunwoo, he thinks she is merely working on her acting! Seyoung lives out her youth as if the entire world is a stage, but as she basks in the bright lights of innocence she seeks someone in the audience to recognize the light within her. Written by Korea's eminent writer Kyungok Kang, *Narration of Love at 17* is a classic that will take you for a ride back to reliving your first love.

Kyungok Kang

NARRATION OF LOVE at 17

Vol. 1

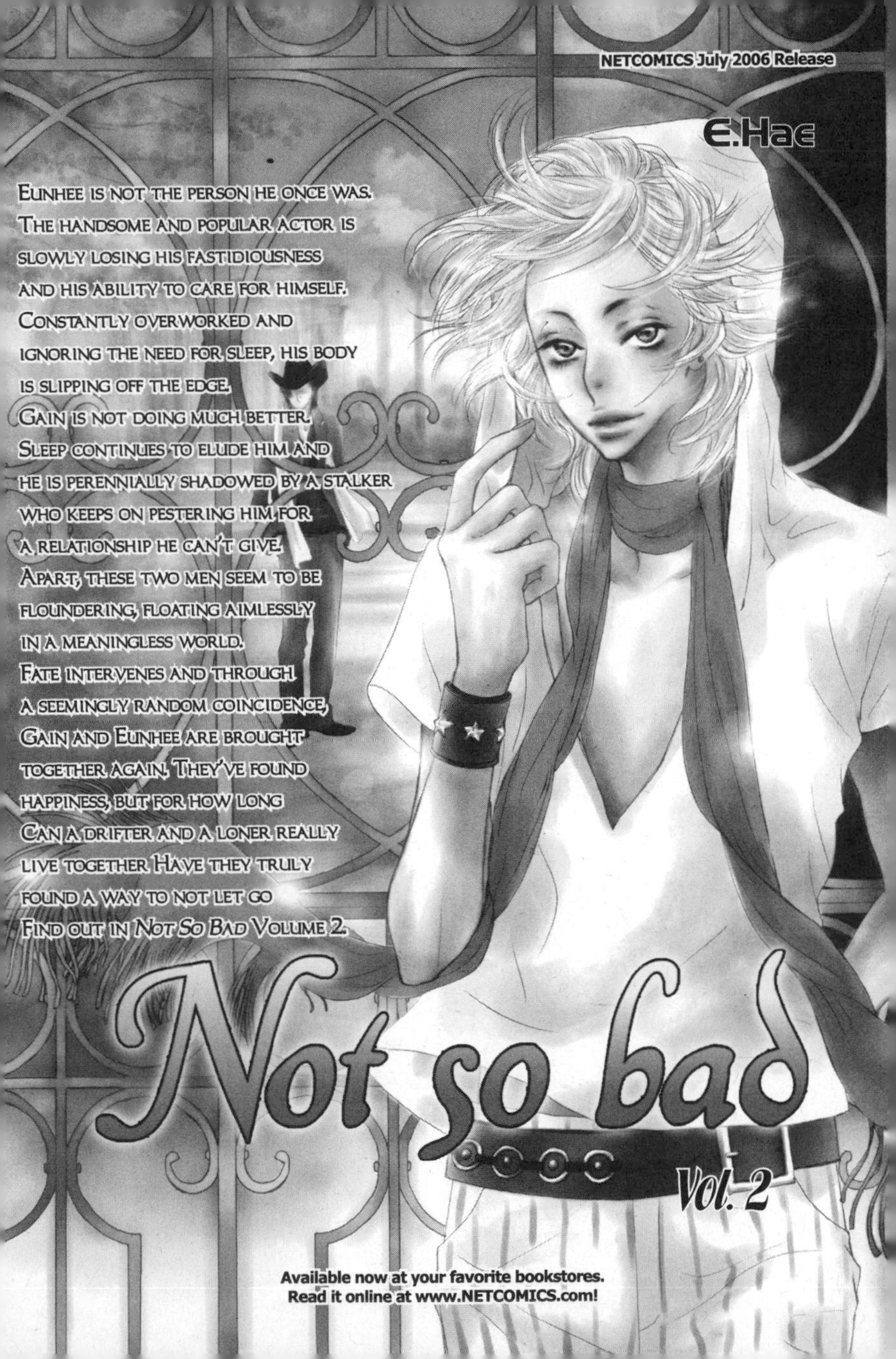
NETCOMICS July 2006 Release
E.Hae
Eunhee is not the person he once was.
The handsome and popular actor is
slowly losing his fastidiousness
and his ability to care for himself.
Constantly overworked and
ignoring the need for sleep, his body
is slipping off the edge.
Gain is not doing much better.
Sleep continues to elude him and
he is perennially shadowed by a stalker
who keeps on pestering him for
a relationship he can't give.
Apart, these two men seem to be
floundering, floating aimlessly
in a meaningless world.
Fate intervenes and through
a seemingly random coincidence,
Gain and Eunhee are brought
together again. They've found
happiness, but for how long
Can a drifter and a loner really
live together Have they truly
found a way to not let go
Find out in *Not So Bad* Volume 2.
Not so bad
Vol. 2
Available now at your favorite bookstores.
Read it online at www.NETCOMICS.com!

Hot gangster action, Emperor's Castle Vol. 1

by Sungmo Kim

Chunhoo Kang lives in a world of crime, sex and intrigue. He's the Nihon Saikono Warrior, Japan's greatest fighter in the yakuza underworld. However, he's also Korean. Haunted by past sins, Chunhoo abandons his crime life to search for the young woman and son he abandoned decades ago. But his yakuza bosses are unforgiving. They want his honor and title back. Who is the Emperor that Chunhoo seeks to become? Will he be for good or evil?

Sweetest love fantasy, Land of Silver Rain Vol. 3

by Mira Lee

Sirius' nanny is thunderstruck when she finds out that the young prince has made a contract with the 10th sea witch to stay in the human world, so he can be with his beloved Misty-Rain. Meanwhile, Misty-Rain recovers the memories of her past and Sirius risks his life to protect her from the dangers that are sure to come. Amid the confusion, the schemes, and all the magic twists, will their love ever have a chance to bloom? Let the story unravel in *Land of Silver Rain* V3.

Gut-busting black comedy, Madtown Hospital Vol. 3

by JTK

Madtown's staff must transplant someone else's head on to Dr. Woong-Dam's body to prevent the further spread of the dangerous Cuba Gooding Jr. disease. Madtown Hospital's Sex Education Class takes a wild ride when the doctors start discussing love motels and performing free vasectomies! Buckle up for another episode of hilarious chaos, crazy antics, and a lot of medical mayhem! The insanity continues in *Madtown Hospital* Volume 3!

First-ever, Manhwa Novella Collection Vol. 1

by Youngran Lee

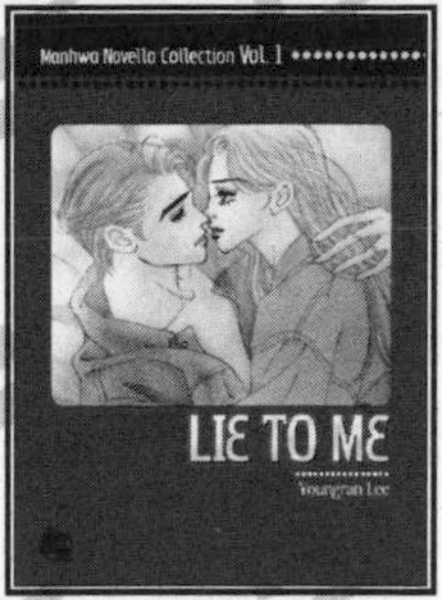
Manhwa Novella Collection Vol. 1
LIE TO ME
Youngran Lee

Lie to Me –Youngran Lee

Presenting the very first series of NETCOMICS' Manhwa Novella Collections—an anthology of the most prominent Korean authors and their works in which every page demonstrates their uniqueness and originality! Volume 1 of this sensational, groundbreaking new monthly series contains three of the most popular shorter works by one of the most famous shojo writers in Korea.

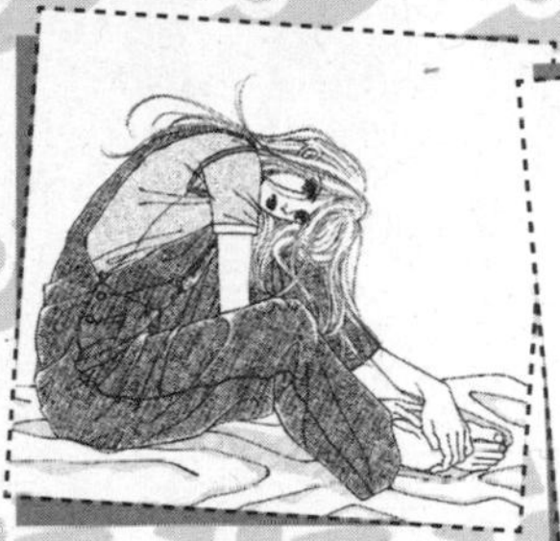

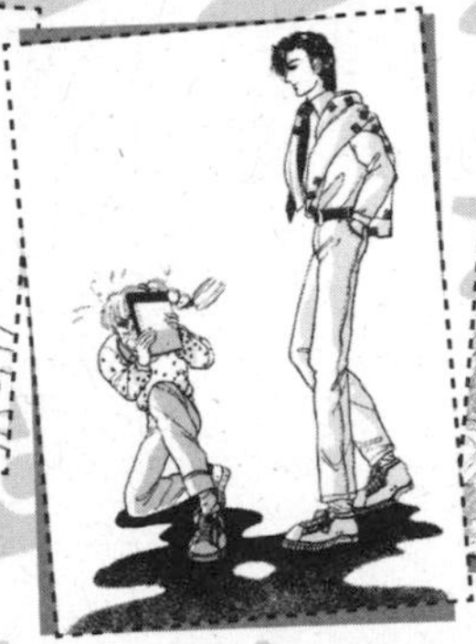

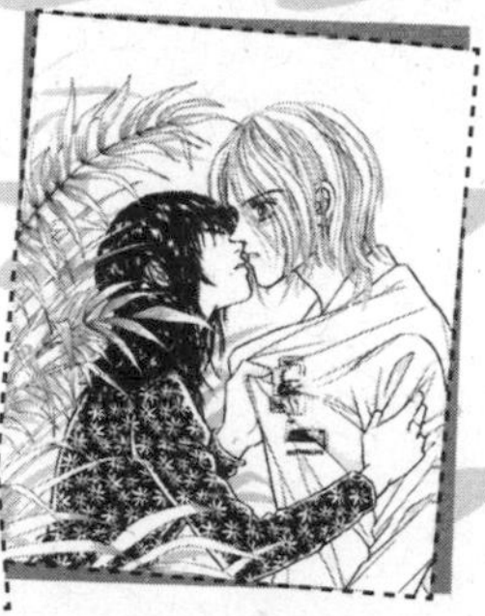

Contemporary high school drama, Pine Kiss Vol. 3

by Eunhye Lee

Dali and Sanghyung are in love with two different people, but they feel a strange chemistry between them. Meanwhile, Sebin's most vulnerable secret is revealed to the world. This revelation has Orion's co-worker urging him to leave the country. What is she afraid of? What is the connection between White Snake and Orion? And what other secrets are waiting to be cast into the light? Find out as the love search of young, wandering souls continues in *Pine Kiss* Volume 3.

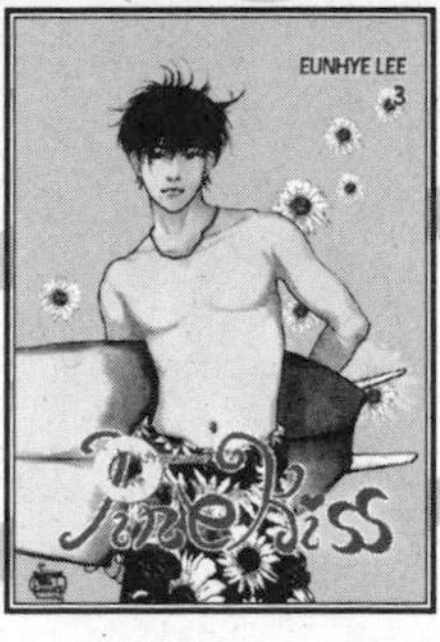
EUNHYE LEE
3
Pine Kiss

Read them ahead at www.NETCOMICS.com!

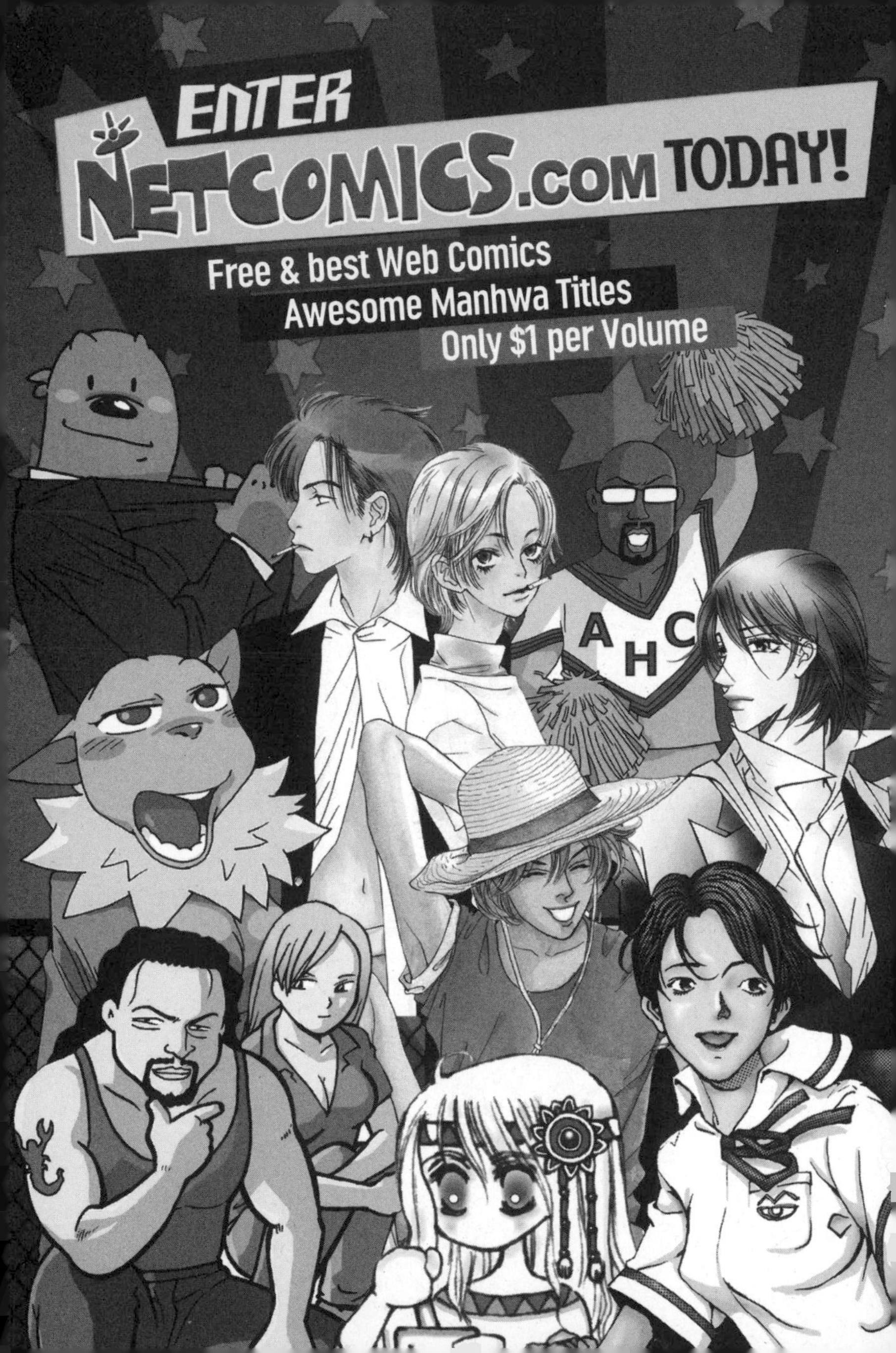
ENTER
NETCOMICS.com TODAY!
Free & best Web Comics
Awesome Manhwa Titles
Only $1 per Volume
AHC